D1616213

Wood
Reference
Handbook

Wood Reference Handbook

A guide to the
architectural use of
wood in building
construction

Canadian
Wood
Council

Conseil
canadien
du bois

ISBN 0-921628-10-2

Printed in Canada

Preface

The Canadian Wood Council (CWC) is the national federation of forest products associations. Its business is the development and promotion of technical product information to assist members of the specifying and regulatory community.

The *Wood Reference Handbook* has been produced to fill a need in the North American market for current information on the manufacturing, specification, and application of wood products.

The *Wood Reference Handbook* complements the *Wood Design Manual*, *Wood and Fire Safety*, and other CWC technical publications which, together, provide a comprehensive family of reference material for today's specifier.

The Handbook represents the efforts of many individuals including the Canadian Wood Council's professional staff, consultants, and a group of Canadian and United States architects who gave many hours to ensure its completeness. The CWC thanks them for their dedication.

The Canadian Wood Council also gratefully acknowledges the financial contribution of Industry, Science and Technology Canada (ISTC) toward the publishing of this book.

Special mention, however, is due to Mr. John Burrows, a member of CWC's professional team and, also, Mr. Glenn Fretz, Glenn Fretz Limited, who coordinated the Handbook's production.

The Board of Directors, staff, and members of the Canadian Wood Council trust that you will find this final result fully meets your needs.

James F. Shaw
President

June 21, 1991

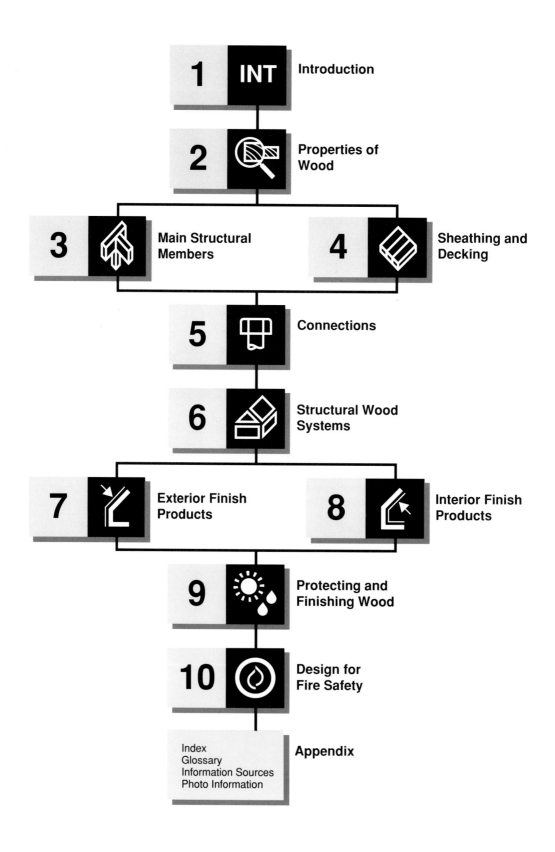

1 INT   Introduction

2   Properties of Wood

3   Main Structural Members

4   Sheathing and Decking

5   Connections

6   Structural Wood Systems

7   Exterior Finish Products

8   Interior Finish Products

9   Protecting and Finishing Wood

10   Design for Fire Safety

Index
Glossary
Information Sources
Photo Information   Appendix

How to Use this Book

The book has been organized, as much as possible, to approximate the sequence of building construction.

Section 1 begins with the basic information about wood products.

Section 2 gives a description of wood properties which, when understood, can assist the designer in using wood products to create effective, reliable, low maintenance designs.

Sections 3 and 4 describe the main structural members and sheathing products which are the basic structural elements for wood construction.

Section 5 demonstrates various means of connecting wood elements.

Section 6 is a reference to structural wood systems created by fastening together load bearing and sheathing products described in Sections 3 and 4.

The wood products used to complete building exteriors and interiors are described in **Sections 7 and 8**.

Section 9 explains how to ensure longevity of wood through good detailing, coating, preservative treatment, and fire-retardant treating.

Section 10 is a concise explanation of how wood products can be used in fire safe designs which meet the requirements of the four North American building codes.

The Wood Reference Handbook is completed with a detailed Index, Glossary of terms for wood construction, and Information Sources for products and technical assistance.

Table of Contents

Table of Contents continued

Introduction

1

INT

The beginning
of a new
generation, a
pine seedling
symbolizes
renewal and
regeneration.

Ever changing, a
mature forest
allows tunnels of
light to reach the
young growth
below.

Like the forest
itself, forest
management is
ever changing.
In Canada,
planting has
increased
significantly to
sustain forests
for all users.

Evidence of pioneer times, a dovetail corner, despite its age, demonstrates the craftsmanship of a bygone era.

A sense of
elegance,
tradition, and the
warm glow of
wood grace the
main lobby of
this log-
constructed
chateau.

Lacking an admiring custodian, this wood exterior awaits restoration to a state of good repair.

Balancing tenuously, a sculpture of wood dwarfs passers by.

Each different in response to the play of light, the undulations of this sculpture captivate and intrigue.

Brash and
modern, both
the interior and
exterior of this
contemporary
home show
creativity in the
use of wood.

Heavy members and a delicate trellis unite to soften the mid-day sun.

Traditional cedar shingles combine with glass to give a modern appearance to an ancient shape.

Wood products adorn these splendid reminders of an earlier era. Routinely maintained, wood lasts the test of time.

Intricate and
delicate in
appearance
(previous page
and above)
small members
create an
uplifting space
that nestles into
its surroundings

Let your
imagination run
free and wood is
a willing partner
in innovative
building design.

Fine, clean lines
and heavy
columns define
a spacious
verandah.

Juxtaposed with
stone (right),
wood siding and
lattice frame an
azure sky. The
courtyard entry
(below) catches
glimpses of
winter sun.

In North° America, wood is regaining favour for bridge construction as the non-permanence of other materials becomes evident. These more whimsical footbridges in Europe welcome pedestrians and cyclists.

A modern
building honours
architectural
tradition and
detail from
centuries past.

Like a giant big top, wood elements drape the roof of this industrial building. The chimney is the support giving a clearance at the centre of 67m (220') and a diameter of 170m (560').

Workers ponder their progress at the end of the day.

Often used for its beauty, wood is also functional (right). This potash storage facility uses wood because of its resistance to corrosion.

Reminiscent of the wood trestles which enabled railroads to span North America (opposite page), a roller coaster structure beckons thrill seekers.

Oak barrels and wood storage racks make a striking setting in this distillery-turned-museum.

Undulating like
the waters they
house, glulam
members arch
and turn high
above this
recreation
complex.

Attention to detail and craftsmanship is evident in both the structural elements and casework of this residence.

Working in combination with steel tension members, wood members support dramatic vaulted roofs.

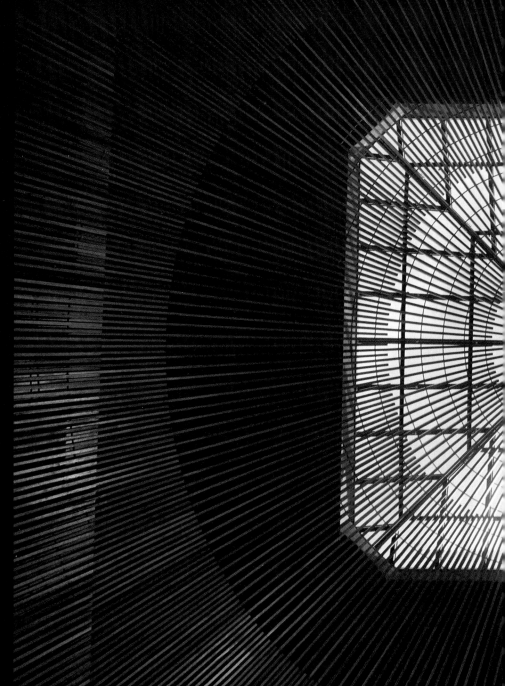

A skylight in a
courthouse
lobby highlights
the complex
intricacies of this
wood ceiling
lattice.

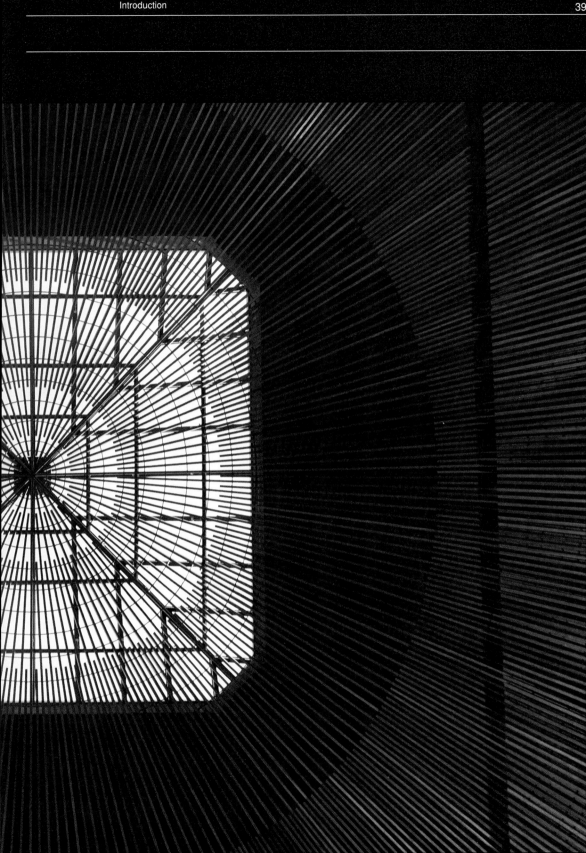

Like limbs of a

Intersecting
trusses above a
school courtyard
frame the sky.

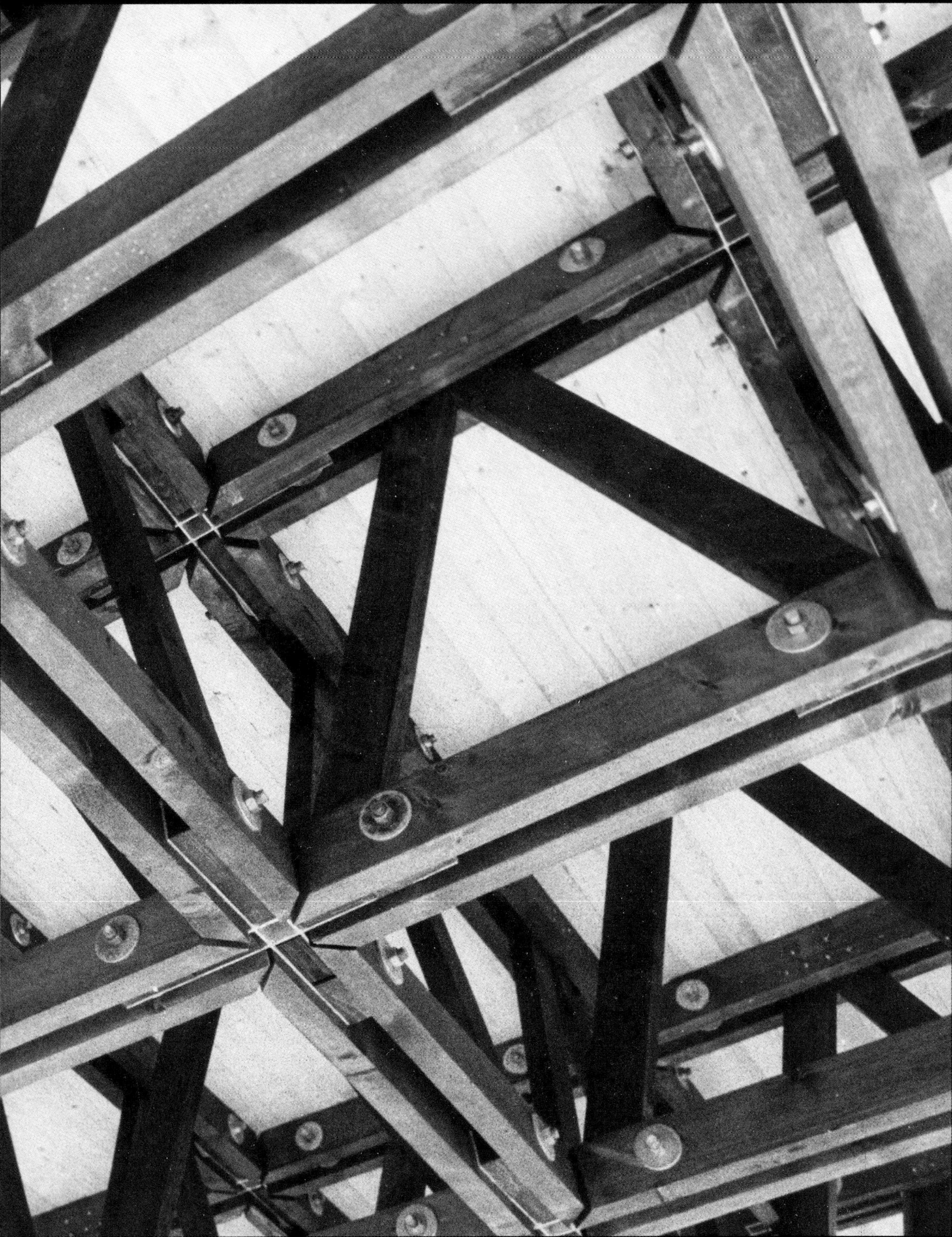

Parabolic arches
culminate at a
skylight in this
church.

Folded trusses
provide a
building diameter
of 31m (100')
without a hint of
metal fasteners.

The unmatched combination of wood and light graces this church sanctuary.

Glass and
precision-joined
timbers create a
bright, spacious
room.

Glulam-hinged
frames,
restrained by
steel tension

Like an
enormous rib
cage, a
parabolic roof
structure awaits
sheathing and
roofing.

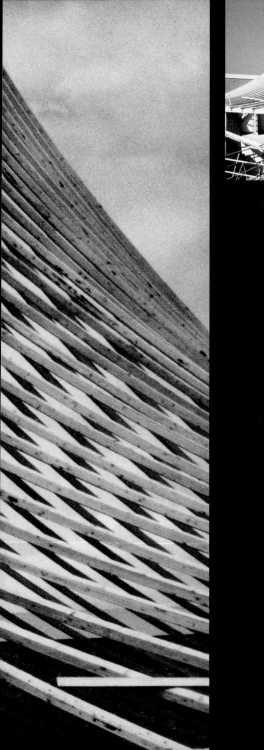

Conceived by means of a model (right), a salt storage dome (below) uses a unique arrangement of radial wood beams.

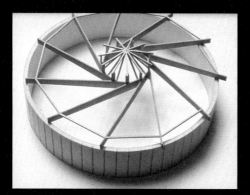

Member
orientation,
arrangement,
and connections
for innovative
timber designs
are often
developed by
modelling.

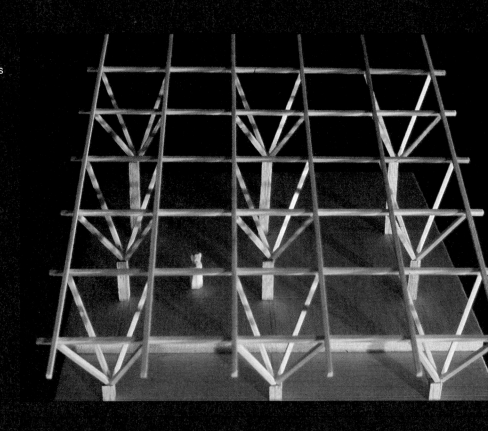

An airline
passenger
terminal
contrasts gently
curved glulam
roof arches and
western red
cedar against a
twilight sky.

Gusseted structural members and wood plank decking, accented by lighting, adorn this church ceiling.

In a bold, modern use of wood as a decorative building material, light coloured plywood sculpts a restaurant interior.

Awaiting the
application of
cedar shingles,
the symmetry
and form of the
underlying
support structure
is captivating in
itself.

For 159 years,
sunset has
illuminated the
stair and wall of
the lockmaster's
house.

Poles and shingles replicate, on a grand scale, a structure common to North America long before the arrival of European settlers.

Interesting to behold but demanding to construct, a multitude of curved shapes encompasses this residence.

A modern
example of a
traditional type
of North
American
construction, a
post and beam-
framed home
infilled with logs
progresses
toward
completion.

Exposed wood
structural
members, an
important aspect
of this type of
traditional
European
architecture,
have endured
for centuries.

In the dampness of the eastern seashore, wood shingles and siding, left to weather naturally, blend into the setting as their colour matures.

Proud against
the prairie sky, a
few of the
hundreds of
grain elevators
which serve the
wheat belts of
Canada and the
United States
attest to our
reliance on
wood as a
traditional,
versatile, and
enduring
construction
material.

1.1   General Information

Wood Construction:
A North American Tradition

Trees contribute greatly to the quality of life in Canada, the United States, and around the world.

Through the ages and still today, trees provide building materials for shelter from the elements, fuel for warmth and cooking, wood fibre for the production of paper, and the ingredients for many everyday consumer products. They perform an essential function in balancing oxygen and carbon dioxide in the earth's atmosphere.

Before the arrival of European settlers in North America, aboriginal peoples used poles and skins to build shelter and logs to build lodges. Early European settlers used logs to build all types of buildings. Initial construction of North America's transcontinental railways would not have been possible without the use of timbers to construct the bridges and trestles over which the rail lines passed.

Today, a wide range of high quality and innovative wood building materials are manufactured. Their performance and relative economy means that wood products are unrivaled as the principle structural materials for residential construction. They are also used extensively for the construction of commercial buildings.

In Canada, in 1989, the value of building construction was $22.4 billion, of which $5.0 billion was single-family and semi-detached residential construction.

The value of commercial, public, and apartment building was $17.4 billion. Of this amount, $8.1 billion (47 percent) fell within the height and area limitations for wood construction defined by the National Building Code of Canada.

Including residential construction, 58 percent of Canadian buildings are suited to wood construction based on current codes and standards. Similarly, more than half the building construction in the United States is suited to wood construction where 80 percent of modern commercial buildings are three storeys or less.

1

INT

Introduction

Figure 1.1
**Canada –
Productive
Forest Land**

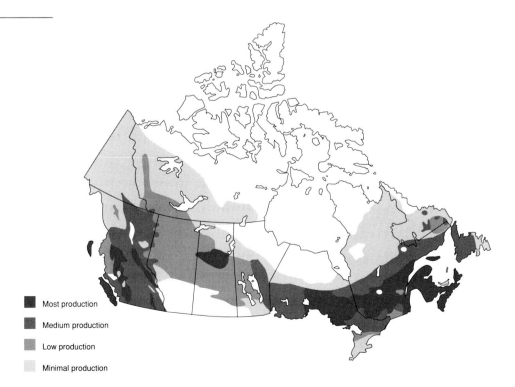

Most production

Medium production

Low production

Minimal production

The Canadian Forest Resource

Canada's forests contain 14 percent of the world's softwoods and are exceeded in area only by those of the USSR. Canada ranks third, after the USSR and the US, in softwood harvesting.

Canada has a productive forest area of 244 million Ha (942,000 sq. miles). Figure 1.1 (→ 67) illustrates the various levels of production geographically. Productive area refers to land having the capability of growing enough wood fibre for commercial purposes, as defined by today's criteria for economic viability. Of this area, 91 percent is public land (80 percent provincial, 11 percent federal) and 9 percent is private land, owned by some 430,000 woodlot owners.

Broken down another way, 85 percent of the productive forest area is used for commercial purposes, 11 percent is not used commercially, and 4 percent is reserved as provincial and federal park-land. The three provinces with the greatest productive forest area as a percent of the Canadian total are Québec (22 percent), British Columbia (21 percent), and Ontario (16 percent).

Under present silvicultural practices, 44 percent of Canada's productive forest land is ready for harvesting (mature or over-mature), 45 percent of productive forest land is too young for harvesting (immature and regenerating), 7 percent is nonstocked (recently harvested), and 4 percent is parkland.

Comparing Wood to Other Major Building Materials

Every material has properties which make it ideal for some applications, and unaccept-able for others. The purpose of the Wood Reference Handbook is to give the building design professional basic information needed to make best advantage of the many positive qualities of wood products, to explain the types of wood materials available, and to show how they can be used.

Like other major building materials such as steel and concrete, wood has both desir-able and undesirable features.

Steel is a strong, versatile material. On the other hand, it is prone to corrosion in some environments. Although termed noncom-bustible in the building codes, it begins to lose strength at temperatures as low as 375° to 550°C (700° to 1000°F). These temperatures are common in building fires and adversely affect the performance of exposed steel members.

Concrete is easily cast into a variety of shapes. It is strong in compression but must rely on reinforcing steel to develop acceptable tensile strength. Concrete is a high weight to strength ratio material, and the in situ properties of concrete are highly dependent on field conditions such as the correct placement of reinforcing steel, water content, curing techniques, and protection from freezing during curing. Concrete in itself is susceptible to break-down by some types of chemicals as is the steel used for reinforcement.

Wood is subject to decay under certain environmental conditions. However, just as steel can be coated or galvanized to resist corrosion, wood can be coated or pressure treated to resist decay. Both materials benefit from good detailing to keep them from destructive environments.

Like other materials, care must be taken to ensure that wood is installed in a fashion which allows it to meet fire performance criteria. For example, large timber sections have good fire endurance. Charring provides an insulating layer which retards the loss of cross section and therefore wood may perform better structurally than steel.

Since wood is an organic material, lumber exhibits a range of quality and properties dependent upon species, grade, and growing conditions. This variability ac-counts both for its aesthetic appeal as a building and finishing material, and for the need by the designer to have a basic knowledge of its nature and behaviour as an engineering material.

Environmental Considerations of Building with Wood

The manufacture of wood products is a major source of economic strength to both Canada and the United States.

In Canada, forest related industries account for 1 in 15 jobs, and in export value are almost equal to the aggregate of agriculture, fishing, mining, and energy.

As world population and the consequent need for housing and services grows, greater demand is placed on the forests of the world and in particular those of major producing countries such as Canada.

Timber is a naturally regenerating resource. Harvests are limited by the regeneration cycle.

In the Canadian climate, a hectare of good productive forest generates about 3.25m³ (115 ft³) of wood fibre per year. Each province calculates an annual allowable cut intended to ensure that harvest levels are in concert with the rate of replacement.

Urban growth in North America continues to impinge upon productive agricultural and forest land. Increasing populations increase the demand for wilderness and recreation areas.

For all these reasons, timber is becoming ever more valuable as a resource. Forest management and utilization techniques must and are adjusting to these new realities.

As with all resource-based industries, forest industry practices are facing intense public scrutiny. Practices which were accepted in the past are undergoing review and adaptation. We no longer rely solely on natural reforestation to restock the forests. Slash burning, wastage of undesirable species and the non-utilization of manufacturing residue such as bark and sawdust have given way to more enlightened resource management practices.

For example, sawmills were once characterized by waste piles of sawdust which served no useful purpose other than for insulating ice blocks used for refrigeration. As stockpiles increased and the volume of waste material became a problem, the incineration of sawing waste became commonplace. Now this waste has become a useful product.

The increasing value of wood fibre and wood products has brought about maximizing the use of wood fibre. Not only is waste being reduced, but new uses are being found for the remaining wastes. Thin kerf sawing technology has reduced the generation of sawing wastes, and sawdust is used for the manufacture of particleboard. Bark is increasingly used for the firing of clean burning cogenerating plants to provide energy for manufacturing processes thereby reducing demand for non-renewable fossil fuels. The slabs which are removed from the edges of logs are reduced to chips and sold to the paper manufacturing industry as an important source of wood fibre for that industry.

Reforestation and Species Utilization

Reforestation by seeding and planting is increasing at a rapid rate throughout Canada and the US. For example, in British Columbia, 20 million seedlings were planted in 1960, 60 million in 1980, and 330 million in 1990.

At one time, high-value species were extracted and other species were cut and left behind. Today, low-value species such as poplar command high value for the manufacture of waferboard. Products such as plywood and parallel strand lumber (PSL) can use technology to create high value and quality materials from below-average quality wood fibre.

Economics, public pressure, competition, and a desire to improve resource management practices has led the wood products manufacturing industry in Canada to utilize more completely the harvested resources. Now, more than ever before, more product per unit harvested is being produced. This means that less area need be harvested to meet demand.

Despite this more careful use of a valuable renewable resource, there are many issues facing the North American lumber industry.

The necessity of balancing employment, recreation, wildlife, native land claims, and forest regeneration issues are bringing rapid change to the forest industries of North America, and many more compromises and improvements will be made to ensure the viability of this important resource-based industry.

The Energy Impact of Wood Products

As a result of the energy shortages of the 1970s and more recent events, increased emphasis has been placed on the design of buildings which are more energy efficient in meeting heating and cooling demands.

Although wood is superior to steel and concrete as an insulating material, the insulating ability of wood is less than that of materials whose sole function is that of insulating. Wood construction techniques, however, provide for a compact building envelope which can be insulated to the most demanding requirements.

Energy costs go beyond the mere cost of operating a building. The amount of energy required initially to obtain products is an important consideration for the designer.

Consider the case of a small house of 100m^2 (1000 ft^2). The estimated energy required to process the building materials is 350,000,000 BTUs and the estimated annual energy requirement to heat in a northern climate is 325,000 BTUs per year. This means that the original energy sink for building materials is equivalent to about 11 years of annual energy heating requirements. This heavy initial outlay is greater for non-residential construction when the wood products common to residential construction are displaced by high-energy requirement materials such as concrete, steel, aluminum, and plastics.

Analyses of the energy required to manufacture building materials demonstrate that wood products have a low energy input for production. Materials such as steel, concrete, and plastics which require heat for production need high energy input.

Table 1.1 (→ 72) compares the energy embodied in steel and glulam beams for identical loading conditions and shows that structural steel requires approximately four times the energy for manufacture and delivery as does the wood beam. Published information shows a similar trend in entire roof and walls assemblies when comparing wood building materials to steel and masonry products.

The major difference between wood products and almost all other types of building materials is that trees, the origins of all lumber products, are renewable while most other materials are not. Seven years after harvest, a managed forest can easily exhibit a growth of head high conifers, and after 50 to 100 years, depending on the species and site conditions, be ready for reharvesting.

Forests and trees are indeed valuable resources serving a number of society's needs. When managed in a manner suiting the needs of society, forests yield a renewable source of beautiful, unique, and functional building materials which rival steel and masonry in application, and which match or exceed these other materials in energy requirements, energy conservation, regeneration and other very important environmental considerations.

The Potential of Wood Construction

Wood is a major building material. It is used in building construction to provide delicate detail in the form of trims and mouldings. It dominates the residential needs of North Americans. It provides functional framing for commercial buildings. And it is used to provide structure for striking buildings on a large scale.

The Tacoma Dome (1983) in Seattle, Washington, is of wood-frame construction and spans 160m (530') with a clear height of 34m (110') at centre field.

The Chateau Montebello (1920) in Montebello, Québec, is a splendid example of log and timber construction having a lobby area 60m (200') in diameter and 20m (65') high.

Huge blimp storage buildings built in Oregon in 1943 were built entirely of wood. The buildings have outlived their purpose but still stand today, spanning 90m (296') with a clear height in the centre of 47m (153') and an overall length of 305m (1000'), as testimony to the potential of using wood products to construct buildings of any type.

In addition to these outstanding examples are the many thousand buildings, old and modern, which are in use in North America.

The Wood Reference Handbook is intended to demonstrate the potential for using wood products in all types of North American buildings.

The book has been organized, as much as possible, to approximate the sequence of building construction. It begins with the basic information about wood products and then describes basic structural materials, means of connection, and resulting wood structural systems. Information about exterior- and interior-use wood products comes next, followed by supplemental information about protecting wood and designing to meet fire safety requirements.

Section 2 gives a description of wood properties which, when understood, can assist the designer in using wood products to create effective, reliable, low maintenance designs.

Sections 3 and 4 describe the main structural members and sheathing products which are the basic structural elements for wood construction. Section 5 explains the means of connecting wood elements.

Section 6 explains the structural wood systems created by fastening together the load bearing and sheathing products described in Sections 3 and 4. The wood products used to complete building exteriors and interiors are described in Sections 7 and 8.

Section 9 explains how to ensure longevity of wood through good detailing, coating, preservative treatment, and fire-retardant treating.

Section 10 is a concise explanation of how wood products can be used in fire safe designs which meet the requirements of the four North American building codes.

The Wood Reference Handbook is completed with a detailed Index, Glossary of terms for wood construction, and Information Sources for products and technical assistance.

References

Consistent Energy Accounting in Production of Wood Products and Competing Materials, A. Tenwolde and R.N. Stone, 1977

Energy Conservation through Building Design, Donald Watson, McGraw-Hill Book Company, 1979

Energy into Production – Delivery of Wood-Based and Other Housing Materials and Systems, Scanada Consultants, 1976

Forestry Facts, Forestry Canada, Minister of Supply and Services Canada, 1990

Renewable Resources for Building Design, National Academy of Sciences, 1976

1

INT

Introduction

Reference Table

Table 1.1
Energy Embodied in Wood and Steel Beams

	Total Load kPa psf		Beam Size mm	in.	Weight per Unit kg/m	lb/ft	Energy Embodied kJ/kg	BTU/lb	kJ/m	BTU/ft
Glulam Beam	3.6	75	130 x 798	5 x 31-1/2	55.5	37.2	2,835	5,912	157,000	220,000
WF Steel Beam	3.6	75	W410 x 60	W16 x 40	60	40	10,890	22,700	653,000	908,000
Glulam Beam	5.3	110	175 x 836	6-3/4 x 33	78.4	52.6	2,835	5,912	222,000	311,000
WF Steel Beam	5.3	110	W460 x 82	W18 x 55	82	55	10,890	22,700	893,000	1,249,000

Notes:
1. Energy units include mining or harvesting, manufacturing and transportation to the job site.
2. Based on a bay size of 7.5 x 7.5m (25' x 25').
3. Based on 20f-E Stress Grade glulam.

Properties of Wood

2

Easily shaped, worked, and fastened, wood is a principal building material for both structural and finish applications.

With minimal
processing from
tree to end use,
heavy wood
columns and
timbers exude
natural beauty.

Applying skill
and
craftsmanship,
wood responds
willingly to
precise details
and elegant
finishing.

Whether curved
or straight,
functional or
ornate, wood
endures and
amazes.

For both small, load-sharing members and large, structural members, wood dominates residential construction and offers an economical advantage for commercial buildings.

New uses for wood fibre promise continuing popularity and optimum use of forest resources.

With careful species selection and attention to detail, wood - such as this cedar siding - is an excellent material for use in humid conditions.

Small pieces of
high-quality
wood, formed
and glued
together into
specified
shapes, offer
remarkable
strength and
versatility.

Whether used decoratively or structurally, the colour, texture, and natural beauty of wood is clearly evident.

Careful handling and storage, as for any valuable material, ensures product performance and appearance.

2.1 General Information

This section includes general information on the design of wood structures together with basic information on the properties of wood. The basic information has been selected as pertinent to all wood products as well as solid wood products. It is intended to provide the information necessary for the designer to maximize the many advantageous qualities of wood construction materials.

As with any building material, the successful use of wood as a structural or decorative building material requires some knowledge of the behaviour and the properties of the material.

For example, an understanding of why wood fibre absorbs moisture gives an insight into how a wood joist reacts to water. To take another example, one would also understand how plywood, made up of veneers and glues, reacts to water, knowing that the glueline and orientation of the plies affects its performance.

As a naturally occurring material, wood fibre varies in physical properties, according to species and growing conditions.

Most Canadian trees require 65 to 120 years to reach maturity but they may live for several hundred years. Occasionally, mature trees of some species in Canada, such as Douglas fir, may attain heights of 100m (330') and diameters of 5m (16.5'). Silvicultural practices such as fertilization and pruning can significantly reduce the time required to reach maturity.

Canadian forestry companies and governments are co-operating in long-term programs which have significantly improved silvicultural practices not only in reducing the cycle of growth, but also in many other areas. For example, between 1980 and 1990, the number of seedlings planted per year increased fivefold. Further increases are anticipated in coming years.

Design Standards for Wood Structures

There are two fundamental methods of wood design in North America.

In the United States, wood design is based on Allowable Stress Design (ASD). This method was also used exclusively in Canada until 1984 when the Limit States Design (LSD) method was first introduced to parallel the design methods for steel and concrete.

For either method of design, the following relationship must exist:

$$\text{Strength of member} \geq \text{Effects of design load}$$

The Allowable Stress Design method requires that stresses induced in structural members by the specified design loads not exceed prescribed allowable stresses which have been determined by material testing. In addition, the deflections of structural members caused by the specified loads must not exceed prescribed guidelines.

With ASD, the strength of the member is conservatively established as a fraction of the ultimate strength and the factor of safety is present only in the strength value assigned to the member. If the design load is variable, as in the case of a live load in a region having heavy snowfall occurrences, the factor of safety is not consistent with that for a member carrying only a definable dead load.

With Limit States Design, the full ultimate strength of a member is used in the design equation. The design loads are factored to take into consideration the probability of the load being exceeded. In the foregoing example, the snow load of uncertain magnitude would have a factor different for that of dead load.

In the United States, the LSD approach is commonly referred to as Load and Resistance Factor Design (LRFD). An LRFD design specification for wood is currently under development in the US.

2

Properties of Wood

With both the ASD and LSD methods of design, product and design standards are established by means of testing and regulation. Although the agencies which maintain these standards are different in Canada and the United States, as shown in Table 2.1 (→ 95), the general approach is similar.

For Canadian building design, information and direction is provided by the *Wood Design Manual*, published by the Canadian Wood Council. Although based on Canadian standards, some of the general information is of interest to US designers.

Units of Measure
Canada has adopted metric (SI units) measure. In the United States, Imperial measure remains in effect.

Due to the large export market in the United States for Canadian lumber and panel products, Canadian products are still manufactured to Imperial standard sizes even though they have been assigned a metric size designation for domestic purposes. For example, a 38 x 89mm wood member is the same size as the former Canadian and present US 2" x 4". Similarly, a 1220 x 2440mm panel product measures 4 feet by 8 feet.

Under the Imperial system, the measurement of lumber is usually expressed in nominal sizes, which means the rough size after sawing but before final dressing (planing). The actual size of a nominal 2" x 4" is about 1-1/2" x 3-1/2", after a loss of 1/4" per face as a result of planing.

With the metric system of measurement, the stated size of 38 x 89mm is the actual size (to the nearest millimetre) after dressing and is therefore about 1-1/2" x 3-1/2" in dimension.

To suit users of both systems of measurement, this book provides both systems of measurement. The metric value and units are shown first, followed by the Imperial value and units. Wherever nominal size is shown, it will be indicated by the abbreviation, nom. (for example, 38 x 89mm (2" x 4" nom.)).

In general, dimensions for sawn lumber and timber are shown actual size for metric units and nominal size for Imperial units. All other wood products are shown actual size for both metric and Imperial units of measure.

Metric to Imperial and Imperial to metric conversion factors are provided in Tables 2.2 and 2.3 (→ 96, 97).

Trees and the Nature of Wood

Hardwoods and Softwoods
The terms hardwood and softwood are not a pure indication of hardness and softness. But generally, hardwoods do tend to be denser and therefore harder than softwoods.

Softwood is a commonly used term for coniferous trees which bear cones and have needle-like leaves. Except for the larches, the leaves stay green through winter and remain on the tree for two or more years resulting in the term evergreen.

The leaves of hardwood trees are generally broadleafed. They change colour and are shed at the completion of each growing season.

There are more than 30 species of softwoods and 100 species of hardwoods in Canada. Although there are more kinds of hardwoods, most of Canada's commercial lumber and wood products come from softwoods which are much more plentiful.

Trees grow by absorbing carbon dioxide from the air through leaves or needles and by taking in water and minerals from the soil through the roots. Sap, which is comprised of water and minerals, travels to the leaves to combine with the carbon dioxide, by photosynthesis, to form basic carbohydrate compounds.

These compounds travel to the cambium which is a thin layer under the bark where they provide food for growth of the tube-like cells or fibres that make up wood substance.

Figure 2.1
**Microscopic
Wood Structure**

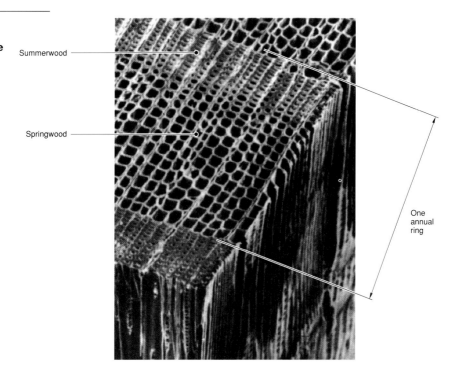

Summerwood

Springwood

One
annual
ring

Cells in softwoods are about 3 to 5mm (1/8" to 3/16") long and 0.030 to 0.045mm (0.001" to 0.002") thick. Although most cells (see Figure 2.1 above) are oriented vertically in the tree, ray cells run radially across the tree for the storage and horizontal transportation of food. A new layer of cells (growth ring) is added to the tree each growing season. The width of the rings varies with species, growing conditions, and tree age.

Growth Characteristics
Each tree, each log, and each piece of wood has unique growth characteristics such as grain, figure and colour. A knot is the base of a limb and may or may not be present in a piece of wood, depending on the location of the piece in the tree.

Sapwood and Heartwood
Each year, as a new layer forms in the cambium, cells in the past growing season's growth ring mature and die. The ray cells live longer, but when they ultimately die, residual substances form which often give distinct colour to the wood. Variations in wood colour usually allow the outer region of living wood, the sapwood, to be distinguished from the inner inactive region, the heartwood as shown in Figure 2.2 (→ 86).

Comparisons of sapwood and heartwood show that:

- Sapwood and heartwood, at equivalent moisture contents, are equally strong and have about the same weight.

- Sapwood has lower natural decay resistance than heartwood, but accepts preservatives more readily.

- Sapwood is usually lighter in colour than heartwood (this colour difference is less pronounced in the spruce, fir and hemlock species).

Figure 2.2
Tree Cross Section

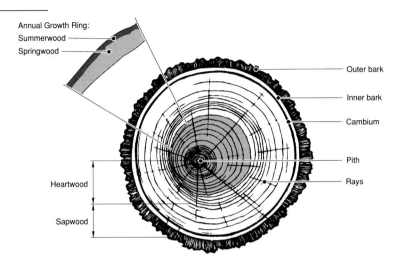

Annual Growth Ring:
Summerwood
Springwood

Outer bark

Inner bark

Cambium

Pith

Rays

Heartwood

Sapwood

Springwood and Summerwood

Springwood and summerwood together form one annual ring of growth and the total number of annual rings at the base of the tree is a measure of the age of a tree.

Each annual growth ring contains the larger cells produced in the spring when growing conditions are optimum, referred to as springwood, and the denser part of the ring comprised of smaller cells produced toward the decline of a growing season, called summerwood.

Usually, summerwood is denser and stronger than springwood, and the proportion of one to the other is a good indication of density and strength.

The overall growing conditions dictate the amount of wood fibre created in a growth ring and therefore the width of the ring. A slower growing tree has narrower rings and therefore a higher proportion of denser summerwood than a faster growing neighbour. Generally, the slower growing tree exhibits better strength characteristics because of this.

Chemical Composition

Wood substance is composed of 50 percent cellulose, 15 to 30 percent hemicellulose, 15 to 35 percent lignin and 5 to 30 percent ash and extractives. Lignin holds the cellulose and hemicellulose fibres together and if the lignin is dissolved away from the fibres as is done in a pulping process, the fibres can be reoriented and can be further manufactured into a variety of paper and paperboard products.

Moisture Content

Because living trees contain sap, newly felled timber usually has a high moisture content. Moisture content (MC) is the weight of water contained in the wood, expressed as a percentage of the weight of oven-dry wood. Oven-dry means there is no moisture in the cell fibre or in the cell cavity.

When the moisture content is between zero and about 28 percent, moisture is totally contained within the cell walls and the cell cavities are empty. In the range from 25 percent MC to 32 percent MC depending on the species, the cell walls become saturated and the wood is said to be at the fibre-saturation point.

Above the fibre-saturation point, additional moisture is held as free water in the cell cavities.

Figure 2.3 (opposite) shows typical moisture contents for wood and for a number of wood products for various conditions.

Figure 2.3
Moisture Content and Shrinkage of Lumber and Manufactured Wood Products

Moisture Content of Manufactured Wood Products

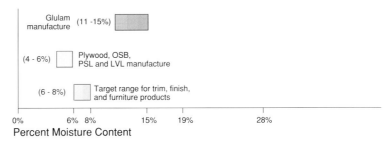

Moisture Content of Lumber

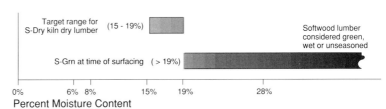

Moisture Content of Wood

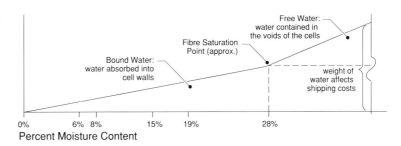

Wood Cell Moisture

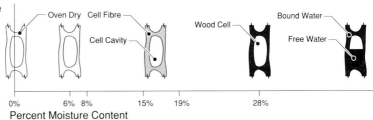

Relative Shrinkage

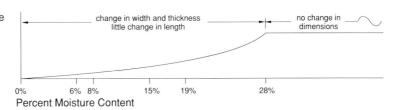

2

Properties of Wood

Wood gives off or takes on moisture until the moisture content of the wood has stabilized at its equilibrium moisture content (EMC). Assuming constant temperature, the ultimate moisture content that a given piece of wood will attain, expressed as a percentage of its oven-dry weight, depends entirely upon the relative humidity of the surrounding atmosphere. For exterior wood products, the EMC is dependant upon climate and exposure factors, and for interior wood products, is dependant upon building temperature, humidity, and ventilation. Table 2.4 (→ 98) shows summer and winter EMC values for exterior and interior uses for the major regions of North America.

Moisture content within living trees varies greatly. In many softwoods, sapwood contains more moisture than heartwood, but in the hardwoods, sapwood and heartwood may have nearly the same moisture content.

Moisture content may range from 30 percent in the heartwood of a living Douglas fir to 200 percent or more in the sapwood of some low density woods.

Seasoning
The behaviour of lumber and other wood products after manufacture is closely related to fluctuations of moisture content within the wood. Drying (seasoning) is usually necessary to bring the moisture content within specified limits.

Water can be removed from wood by kiln-drying, or, by natural or forced air-drying. During seasoning there is no volume change in wood until the fibre-saturation point is reached, but further drying below the fibre-saturation point results in shrinkage proportional to the amount of water removed.

Changes in dimension during shrinkage are not equal in all directions. In general:

• Dimensional change is greatest tangential to growth rings.

• Dimensional change radial to growth rings is about 60 percent of the amount of change tangential to growth rings.

• Dimensional change lengthwise (parallel to the axis of the tree) is very small. It is about 2 percent of radial change.

The terms S-Grn and S-Dry are shown on the grade stamp for dimension lumber. S-Grn is lumber having a moisture content greater than 19 percent at the time of surfacing. S-Dry is lumber having a moisture content of 19 percent or less at the time of surfacing. S-Dry lumber is almost always kiln dried. It may also be dried naturally, as long as the specified moisture content has been reached.

Table 2.5 (→ 98) shows specific shrinkage values for the major Canadian species. In a given bundle of lumber there will be some variance in the moisture contents of individual pieces because the pieces dry at different rates. For example, in a bundle of S-Dry product at 19 percent MC, the moisture content of some individual pieces may be considerably less than 19 percent.

Lumber is dried to ensure that shrinkage occurs before the material is used. Changes in dimension after installation can be minimized by seasoning lumber to or near the equilibrium moisture content it will attain in service.

Moisture content below fibre-saturation point can be measured instantaneously by electrical instruments.

Surface coatings such as paint, stain, and varnish help to minimize the effect of seasonal moisture fluctuations. However, no coating is entirely moisture proof and consequently tends only to retard the rate at which moisture is gained or lost.

Dimensional change in wood is a result of moisture gain or loss. The coefficient of expansion resulting from temperature change is insignificant for wood.

Heat Transfer

Wood is a natural thermal insulator due to the millions of tiny air pockets within its cellular structure. Since thermal conductivity increases with relative density, lightweight wood is a better insulator than dense wood. Thermal conductivity also varies slightly with moisture content, residual deposits in the wood, and natural characteristics, such as checks, knots and grain.

Softwood has about one half the thermal insulation ability of a comparable thickness of fibreglass batt insulation. Although wood is the best insulation of the prime construction products, a wood stud in frame construction is not as efficient as the abutting insulation. Therefore wood is not usually selected solely on the basis of low thermal conductivity. However, wood construction techniques are conducive to the inclusion of efficient insulating materials within a wall or roof structure.

In cases where large wood members penetrate into attic space, as in the case of post and beam construction, heat loss due to conduction will be much less for wood than for bare steel or concrete members.

Acoustical Properties

Wood, due to its air pocket composition, is an effective acoustical insulator. An important acoustical property of wood is its ability to dampen vibrations.

When used in wood frame construction, wood has less insulating effect than materials used specifically as insulators. However, wood products whose primary function is one of sheathing or cladding can add significantly to the assembly's resistance to sound transmission.

Strength Properties

Like other building materials, the design values of wood products used for structural members, are defined in terms of bending, shear, tension and compression stresses, as shown in Figure 2.4 (→ 90). Modulus of elasticity relates load to deflection for a member loaded in bending.

Single member design values are used where the strength of an individual piece, such as a beam, girder, or column is solely responsible for carrying a specific design load.

Where load sharing takes place due to the occurrence of repetitive parallel members as in the case of stud walls or floor joists, factors can be applied to augment the design values because the effect of a defect in a given piece is less critical. The load can be transferred from a weaker member in such a system to a stronger adjacent member.

To qualify as load sharing, members must be spaced no further apart than the spacing stipulated in wood engineering design standards, which is usually 600mm (24") or less.

Composite action occurs when two materials joined together are stronger than they would be individually. For example, secure fastening of floor sheathing to joists creates composite action with the sheathing acting like a beam flange and the joists acting like the web.

System action is said to take place when load sharing and composite action occur simultaneously, and when an allowance has been made for the probability of strength and stiffness parameters.

Like any other material, a wood member is weakened when the cross-sectional area is reduced by holes, notches or cuts, not only because of a loss of net area but also because of stress-concentrating effect, particularly if the hole or notch is not curvilinear in shape.

Bending (F_b)

Wood is much stronger parallel to grain than perpendicular to grain. Because of this, structural members are designed to take advantage of woods higher strength parallel to grain. Standing trees naturally take advantage of this property to resist gravity and external forces such as wind.

2

Properties of Wood

Figure 2.4
**Engineering
Properties of
Load Bearing
Members**

Bending

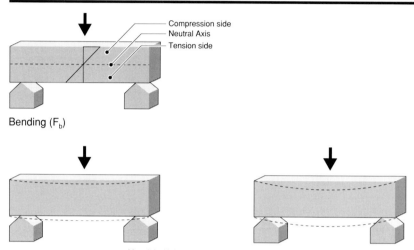

Bending (F_b)

Material with higher E value has less deflection

Modulus of Elasticity (E)

Shear

Shear (F_v)

Tension   Compression

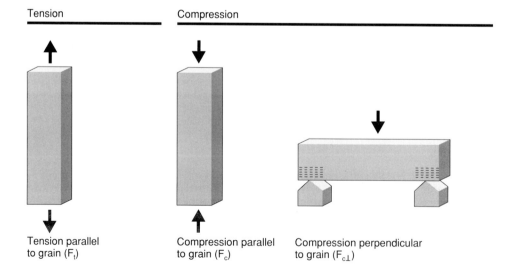

Tension parallel   Compression parallel   Compression perpendicular
to grain (F_t)   to grain (F_c)   to grain ($F_{c\perp}$)

When loads are applied perpendicular to grain, structural members bend and this produces tension in the fibres along the faces farthest from the applied load and compression in the fibres along the face nearest to the applied load. These induced stresses in the fibres are called bending or flexural action.

The Modulus of Elasticity (E) is a ratio of the amount a material will deflect in proportion to an applied load. It is an indication of stiffness, whereas F_b is an indication of strength.

Shear (F_v)

Longitudinal shear is introduced by bending loads, which create maximum stresses parallel to grain at the neutral axis. These stresses are checked using conventional engineering formulas. Holes, notches and cuts, which reduce the effective area resisting shear, must be considered in design.

In composite wood products, such as prefabricated wood I-joists, shear stresses can result in several different failure modes. Testing is necessary to properly evaluate the shear properties for these products.

Tension (F_t)

Wood is strong in tension parallel to grain. This property is important for members, such as in a truss tension chord. It is also important to the strength of bending members for the portion of a beam subjected to tensile forces.

Compression Parallel to Grain (F_c)

Wood columns, truss compression chords, and other applications require design for compression parallel to grain. Except for very short members, this design check includes consideration of lateral stability. The modulus of elasticity (E) influences the capacity of these members as much as the F_c value.

Compression Perpendicular to Grain ($F_{c\perp}$)

Wherever loaded beams or columns come in contact with a support, a design check must be made to ensure that the load is distributed over a large enough area of the wood to avoid deformation by crushing.

This is called bearing, or compression perpendicular to grain. If the bearing area is too small, it can sometimes be increased by using a metal bearing plate.

Fatigue Effect

Unlike crystalline structural materials, wood is very resistant to cyclic loading which occurs in structures subjected, for example, to high wind loads or the effects of vibrating machinery. This is one reason why wood structures exhibit good performance when subjected to extreme cyclic loadings, for example, as a result of an earthquake or hurricane.

Temperature Effect

Strength of wood is not affected to a large degree by temperature. At below freezing temperatures, strength values for bending and compression, and for resistance to shock, are slightly higher than for values at normal temperatures.

Wood subjected to very high temperatures can be weakened, but strength is unaffected in wood exposed to extended temperatures of up to 37°C (100°F). Above this temperature, strength (factored resistances) factors should be reduced. When used in normal construction applications, including roof truss and rafter applications, wood strength is considered to be the same for all naturally occurring temperatures.

Deterioration

As with other materials, wood is susceptible to certain types of deterioration. They include attack from decay, fire, insects and marine borers, weathering, and some chemicals. Section 9 covers in detail methods of protecting wood products from weathering and decay, and Section 10 covers the subject of fire safety.

Decay

Wood decay is caused by low forms of plant life known as fungi which feed on the wood substance (mostly cellulose) of the cell walls.

Under conditions favourable to such organisms, decay may spread from spores (seed-like bodies) produced by the fungi. For wood-destroying fungi to grow, moisture, oxygen, and warm temperature must prevail. If one of these ingredients is lacking, fungi growth will cease. There will be no further decay unless the suitable conditions are again allowed to occur.

At moisture contents below the fibre-saturation point, decay is greatly retarded, and below 20 percent, growth of fungi is completely inhibited. Therefore the use of seasoned lumber, adequate ventilation, and protection from direct exposure or ponding of water will provide protection from decay.

Dry rot is a term used to describe decay which has the appearance of occurring in dry conditions. As stated previously, all fungi require moisture. However, certain fungi can draw water by capillary action from a moist to a dry location thereby giving the impression that decay is in fact occurring without moisture.

The cell structure of all wood species contains entrapped air which supports the growth of fungi. But if air is excluded decay will not occur. For example, piling constantly submerged in fresh water or in uninfested salt water lasts indefinitely. Foundation piles under structures will not decay if the water table remains higher than the pile tops.

Decay organisms can grow and multiply throughout a wide range of temperatures, but usually develop best at around 27°C (80°F). At very low winter temperatures, they are dormant but quickly resume activity when the temperature becomes favourable. High temperatures, such as those used in kiln-drying, kill the fungi, but the wood can be quickly reinfected if exposed to conditions favourable for fungi.

Generally, sapwood has a low resistance to decay. Heartwood of some species, however, has some decay resistance because of natural preservatives contained in the residual deposits. When decay cannot be prevented by other means, wood may be treated, usually under pressure, with preservatives that penetrate the wood and render it poisonous to fungi (see Section 9.4).

Some species such as the cedars are particularly resistant to fungi as a result of naturally occurring chemicals in the wood.

Insect Attack
In the warm humid regions of the United States, wood buildings must be designed to take into account the destructive potential of insects. Protection includes separating wood members from the ground to discourage insect movement, detailing to discourage the entry of insects, and the use of chemically treated wood to make it unpalatable to insects.

Weathering
The appearance of unprotected wood is affected by exposure to sun and rain. Exposure to the elements results in a breakdown of wood at the surface. The resulting texture and colour may be desirable or undesirable, depending on the appearance specified.

In some cases, a weathered appearance is desired. Cladding will purposely be left unfinished to acquire a weathered appearance. Just as copper roofing acquires a pleasing green tint with age, cedar roofing or cladding will acquire a pleasing silver-grey colour. Species selection is important to insure that weathering can occur without risk of fungal attack.

Where weathering is not a desirable feature, some form of protection will be required (see Section 9).

Chemical Attack
Wood is resistant to some of the chemicals destructive to steel and concrete. For this reason, wood is often used for potash storage buildings and for highway salt storage domes.

Organic materials, hot or cold solutions of acids or neutral salts, dilute acids, industrial stack gases, sea air and high relative humidity are some of the solutions that wood resists.

Handling and Storage of Wood Products

Wood is a naturally occurring product which has an inherent ability to gain or lose moisture depending on ambient conditions. This characteristic is altered but not lost when wood fibre is manufactured into an engineered product such as plywood or laminated veneer lumber (LVL).

For this reason all wood products should be stored and handled in a fashion so that moisture damage to the product or additional moisture which will be released into the building after installation is completed is not permitted to occur, and to ensure that crushing damage does not take place prior to installation.

Figure 2.5 (→ 94) offers some general suggestions which apply to the handling and storage of all wood products.

References

Canadian Woods, Their Properties and Uses, E.J. Mullins and T.S. McKnight, University of Toronto Press, 1981

Limit States Design of Wood Structures, F.J. Keenan, Morrison Hershfield Limited, 1986

2

Properties of Wood

Figure 2.5
**Lumber
Product
Storage and
Handling**

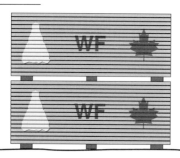

Provide adequate support by simulating the
methods used for rail and truck transport
of wood products.

Panels   Lumber   Glulam, PSL, LVL, Timber   Wood I-joists

For all S-Dry and dry manufactured panels
and members, use factory applied wrapping
or cover panel to protect from wetting.

For S-Green lumber in exposed locations, keep
bundle together to shed water and restrain
dimensional distortion. Cover to moderate
drying and wetting.

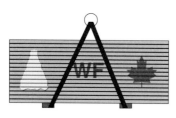
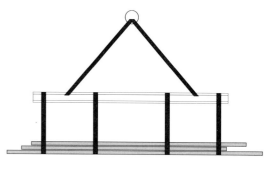

Provide protection against crushing from lifting by
using straps and blocking.

Use spreader bars for lifting long slender members.

Reference Tables

Table 2.1
North American Standards for Wood Products and Design

	Canada	United States
Sizes, Grading Requirements and Basis for Quality Control	CSA Standard O141 Softwood Lumber[1]	American Softwood Lumber Standard PS20-70
Grades and Commercial Species Groups, Quality Control	Standard Grading Rules for Canadian Lumber, NLGA[2]	NLMA[5] NHPMA[6] RIS[7] SPIB[8] WCLIB[9] WWPA[10]
Design Procedures and Design Data	CAN/CSA-O86.1-M89 [1] Engineering Design in Wood (Limit States Design)	NFPA National Design Specification for Wood Construction[11]
		AITC 117-87-Design
		APA Plywood Design Specification
Span Tables for Joists and Rafters	National Building Code of Canada[3]	Span Tables for Joists and Rafters[11]
Grade Marks, Inspection and Accreditation	Canadian Lumber Standards Accreditation Board[4]	American Lumber Standards[14]

Notes:
1. Published by Canadian Standards Association (CSA), 178 Rexdale Blvd., Rexdale, ON M9W 1R3.
2. National Lumber Grades Authority (NLGA), 260 - 1055 West Hastings St., Vancouver, BC V6E 2E9.
3. Division of Building Research, National Research Council (DBR/NRC), Montreal Road, Ottawa, ON K1A 0R6. (Refer to the Span Book published by the Canadian Wood Council).
4. Canadian Lumber Standards Accreditation Board (CLSAB), 260-1055 West Hastings St., Vancouver, BC V6E 2E9.
5. Northeastern Lumber Manufacturers Association (NLMA), 272 Tuttle Road, P.O. Box 87A, Cumberland Center, ME 04021.
6. Northern Hardwood and Pine Manufacturers Association (NHPMA), 272 Tuttle Road, P.O. Box 87A, Cumberland Center, ME 04021.
7. Redwood Inspection Service (RIS), 405 Enfrente Drive, Suite 200, Novato, CA 94949.
8. Southern Pine Inspection Bureau (SPIB), 4709 Scenic Highway, Pensacola, FL 32504-9094.
9. West Coast Lumber Inspection Bureau (WCLIB), 6980 S.W. Varns Street, P.O. Box 23145, Portland, OR 97223.
10. Western Wood Products Association (WWPA), 522 S.W. 5th Avenue, Yeon Building, Portland, OR 97204-2122.
11. National Forest Products Association (NFPA), 1250 Connecticut Avenue, Washington, DC 20036.
12. American Institute of Timber Construction (AITC), 11818 S.E. Mill Plain Boulevard, Suite 415, Vancouver, WA 98684.
13. American Plywood Association (APA), P.O. Box 11700, Tacoma, WA 98411.
14. American Lumber Standards Committee, P.O. Box 210, Germantown, MD 20875-0210.

Reference Tables continued

Table 2.2 **Metric Units Conversion Factors**	Metric Units		Imperial Equivalents
	Length		
	1 millimetre (mm)	=	0.0393701 inch
	1 metre (m)	=	39.3701 inches
		=	3.28084 feet
		=	1.09361 yards
	1 kilometre (km)	=	0.621371 mile
	Length / Time		
	1 metre per second (m/s)	=	3.28084 feet per second
	1 kilometre per hour (km/h)	=	0.621371 mile per hour
	Area		
	1 square millimetre (mm^2)	=	0.001550 square inch
	1 square metre (m^2)	=	10.7639 square feet
	1 hectare (ha)	=	2.47105 acres
	1 square kilometre (km^2)	=	0.386102 square mile
	Volume		
	1 cubic millimetre (mm^3)	=	0.0000610237 cubic inch
	1 cubic metre (m^3)	=	35.3147 cubic feet
		=	1.30795 cubic yards
	1 millilitre (mL)	=	0.0351951 fluid ounce
	1 litre (L)	=	0.219969 gallon
	Mass		
	1 gram (g)	=	0.0352740 ounce
	1 kilogram (kg)	=	2.20462 pounds
	1 tonne (t) (= 1,000 kg)	=	1.10231 tons (2,000 lbs.)
		=	2204.62 pounds
	Mass / Volume		
	1 kilogram per cubic metre (kg/m^3)	=	0.0622480 pound per cubic foot
	Force		
	1 newton (N)	=	0.224809 pound-force
	Stress		
	1 megapascal (MPa) (=1 N/mm^2)	=	145.038 pounds-force per sq. in.
	Loading		
	1 kilonewton per sq. metre (kN/m^2)	=	20.8854 pounds-force per sq. ft.
	1 kilonewton per metre (kN/m) (=1 N/mm)	=	68.5218 pounds-force per ft.
	Moment		
	1 kilonewtonmetre (kNm)	=	737.562 pound-force ft.
	Miscellaneous		
	1 joule (J)	=	0.00094781 Btu
	1 joule (J)	=	1 watt-second
	1 watt (W)	=	0.00134048 electric horsepower
	1 degree Celsius (°C)	=	32 + 1.8 (°C) degrees Fahrenheit

Notes:
1. 1.0 Newton = 1.0 kilogram x 9.80665 m/s^2 (International Standard Gravity Value)
2. 1.0 Pascal = 1.0 Newton per square metre

Reference Tables continued

Table 2.3
Imperial Units Conversion Factors

Imperial Units		Metric Equivalents
Length		
1 inch	=	25.4 mm
	=	0.0254 m
1 foot	=	0.3048 m
1 yard	=	0.9144 m
1 mile	=	1.60934 km
Length / Time		
1 foot per second	=	0.3048 m/s
1 mile per hour	=	1.60934 km/h
Area		
1 square inch	=	645.16 mm^2
1 square foot	=	0.0929030 m^2
1 acre	=	0.404686 ha
1 square mile	=	2.58999 km^2
Volume		
1 cubic inch	=	16387.1 mm^3
1 cubic foot	=	0.0283168 m^3
1 cubic yard	=	0.764555 m^3
1 fluid ounce	=	28.4131 mL
1 gallon	=	4.54609 L
Mass		
1 ounce	=	28.3495 g
1 pound	=	0.453592 kg
1 ton (2,000 lbs.)	=	0.907185 t
1 pound	=	0.0004539 t
Mass / Volume		
1 pcf	=	16.1085 kg/m^3
Force		
1 pound	=	4.44822 N
Stress		
1 psi	=	0.00689476 MPa
Loading		
1 psf	=	0.0478803 kN/m^2
1 plf	=	0.0145939 kN/m
Moment		
1 pound-force ft.	=	0.00135582 kNm
Miscellaneous		
1 Btu	=	1055.06 J
1 watt-second	=	1 J
1 horsepower	=	746 W
1 degree Fahrenheit	=	(°F − 32)/1.8 °C

Notes:
1. 1.0 Newton = 1.0 kilogram x 9.80665 m/s^2 (International Standard Gravity Value)
2. 1.0 Pascal = 1.0 Newton per square metre

Reference Tables continued

Table 2.4
Equilibrium Moisture Content (EMC) for Wood Products in North America

Location			Winter % EMC	Summer % EMC
Canada	West Coast	interior	8	12
		exterior	18	13
	Prairies	interior	5	8
		exterior	12	10
	Central	interior	5	10
		exterior	17	10
	East Coast	interior	7	10
		exterior	19	12
United States	North East	interior	7	11
		exterior	11	14
	South East	interior	10	12
		exterior	14	14
	Central	interior	7	10
		exterior	13	10
	North West	interior	8	11
		exterior	15	10
	South West	interior	8	9
		exterior	12	9

Table 2.5
Comparative Shrinkage (Percentage of Original Green Dimension)

Species	Direction of Shrinkage	Shrinkage (percent) of Green Wood to: 19%	15%	12%	6%
Red cedar (western)	Radial	0.9	1.2	1.4	1.9
	Tangential	1.8	2.5	3	4
Douglas fir (coast)	Radial	1.8	2.4	2.9	3.8
	Tangential	2.8	3.8	4.6	6.1
Douglas fir (interior)	Radial	1.4	1.9	2.3	3
	Tangential	2.5	3.4	4.1	5.5
Hemlock (western)	Radial	1.5	2.1	2.5	3.4
	Tangential	2.9	3.9	4.7	6.2
Larch (western)	Radial	1.7	2.2	2.7	3.6
	Tangential	3.3	4.6	5.5	7.3
Pine (eastern white)	Radial	0.8	1	1.3	1.7
	Tangential	2.2	3	3.7	4.9
Pine (red)	Radial	1.4	1.9	2.3	3.1
	Tangential	2.6	3.6	4.3	5.8
Pine (western white)	Radial	1.5	2	2.5	3.3
	Tangential	2.7	3.7	4.4	5.9
Spruce (eastern)	Radial	1.5	2	2.4	3.2
	Tangential	2.5	3.6	4.4	5.8
Spruce (Engelmann)	Radial	1.4	1.9	2.3	3.1
	Tangential	2.6	3.6	4.3	5.7

Notes:
1. Tangential shrinkage applies to the width of the flat-grain face. Radial shrinkage applies to the width of the edge-grain face.
2. To calculate expected shrinkage, determine the average equilibrium moisture content of wood for end use conditions.

Main Structural Members

3

Wood excels as a major structural building material for beams, joists, girders, and trusses.

During
construction,
many types of
wood structural
members are
exposed to view.

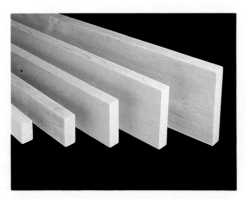

In the completed
building (right),
wood flooring ,
siding, doors,
windows, and
trim complement
the exposed
structural
members and
wood plank deck
roof.

Exposed
dimension
lumber joists,
supported by
heavy girder
trusses and
accentuated by
window light,
provide the focal
point for this
school assembly
room.

Round and sawn timbers provide the structural support for this building. Cantilevered timbers frame a skylight at the roof apex.

Parallel strand lumber (PSL), sanded and stained prior to erection, combines structural function with visual interest in supporting the roof of this library hall.

Sawn timber,
assembled into
heavy trusses
and colour-
matched to
decorative wood
finishes,
provides a
coordinated
appearance.

Prefabricated wood I-joists, available in many sizes and types, are used where high strength and long span structural members are required.

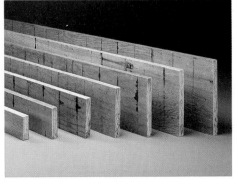

Laminated veneer lumber (LVL), available in many sizes, is a wood product used for beams, stringers, and lintels.

Glulam structural members, made from quality lumber and adhesives, are shown being placed into the roof structure of an arena.

Large dimension curved glulam members (opposite) provide a clear span of 45m (150'). Plank decking and PSL purlins complete the structure and the interior finish of the building.

Spaced, light
frame trusses,
highlighted by
lighting, provide
the structural
support and an
open ceiling
area for this
recreation hall.

Parallel strand
lumber (PSL)
supports a roof
of skylights over
this building
entrance.

Solid sawn
timber beams
and columns,
neatly joined and
stained, grace
this simple
structure.

Non-structural
built-up
members are
used effectively
to create a
sense of mass.

Detailing, complemented by fine workmanship, demonstrates the simple beauty of wood products.

3.1 General Information

Wood products are frequently used to provide the principal means of structural support for buildings. Economy and soundness of construction can be achieved in both residential and in commercial building construction by using wood products as members for structural applications such as joists, wall studs, rafters, beams, girders, and trusses.

The sheathing and decking wood products described in Section 4, in addition to performing a covering or enclosing function, also perform a structural role by transferring wind, snow, or occupant and content load to the main structural members which are described in this section.

Structural wood members, used in combination with wood sheathing and decking products, are capable of meeting engineering standard and building code requirements for durability, fire safety, energy efficiency and all other factors important to building performance.

While lumber remains the staple of wood building construction, a number of innovative manufactured wood products are readily available which add structural and appearance possibilities to those of lumber.

This section describes the characteristics, method of manufacture, sizes, quality control, and uses for the following types of main structural wood members:

3.2   Lumber:
      Dimension Lumber
      Timber

3.3   Glulam

3.4   Trusses:
      Light Frame Trusses
      Heavy Timber Trusses

3.5   Parallel Strand Lumber (PSL)

3.6   Laminated Veneer Lumber (LVL)

3.7   Prefabricated Wood I-Joists

The selection of the appropriate wood product to use for a building system will be affected to a large degree by availability and price for a given location. It will also be based on the spanning capability of the load bearing members under consideration. Table 3.1 (→ 118) is a simplified comparison of the spanning capabilities of the load bearing members described in this section for typical depths and widths.

3

Main Structural Members

Reference Table

Table 3.1
Comparison Table for Main Structural Members

Joists and Beams	Typical Maximum Spans Roof Applications m	ft.	Typical Thicknesses mm	in.	Typical Depths mm	in.
Dimension Lumber Joists	5.5	18	38	2	286	12
	5.5	18	64	3	286	12
	6	20	89	4	343	14
Prefabricated Wood I-Joists	9	30	44.5 - 102	1-3/4 - 4	228 - 508	9 - 20
	6	20	140	6	394	16
	7	24	191	8	445	18
	8	26	241	10	495	20
	8.5	28	292	12	495	20
PSL and LVL Beams	5	16	45	1-3/4	178 - 356	7 - 14
	7	24	89	3-1/2	178 - 457	7 - 18
	8	26	133	5-1/4	178 - 457	7 - 18
	9	30	178	7	178 - 457	7 - 18
Glulam Beams	13.5	45	80 - 130	3-1/8 - 5	up to 836	33
	21	70	175 - 215	6-3/4 - 8-1/2	608 - 1444	24 - 57
	26	85	265 - 315	10-1/2 - 12	1216 - 1824	48 - 72
	31	100	365	14 - 1/4	1520 - 1976	60 - 78

Trusses						
Light Frame	Flat	20	65		up to 1830	72
	Pitched	24	80		2:12 - 12:12 (Pitch)	
Sawn Timber	Pitched	26	85		up to 5180	204
	Flat	30	100		up to 3810	150
	Bowstring	36	120		up to 4900	193
Glulam	Pitched	30	100		up to 6100	240
	Flat	30	100		up to 3810	150
	Bowstring	50	160		up to 6705	264

Note:
These are general guidelines only. Exact design will depend on member configuration, spacing and deflection limits.

3.2   Lumber

Introduction

Lumber is a general term which includes boards, dimension lumber, and timber. The product is manufactured by sawing logs into rough size lumber or cants (square timbers) which are edged, resawn to final dimension and cut to length.

This section deals with lumber products used for structural framing. In the context of North American construction materials, it usually refers to wood originating from softwood species of trees. In the smaller sizes it is known as "dimension lumber," and in the larger sizes as "timbers."

The Table below shows the size classifications for Canadian lumber and the types of products which make up the three general groupings, including products which are not generally used as main structural members. Information on these other lumber products is located as follows:

- Decking – Section 4 Sheathing and Decking

- Boards – Section 7 Exterior Wood Products

Canadian lumber is manufactured according to *National Lumber Grades Authority Standard Grading Rules for Canadian Lumber*. This standard for the grading of Canadian lumber is approved by the Canadian Lumber Standards Accreditation Board and by the American Lumber Standards Board of Review.

Dimension lumber ranges in thickness from 38 to 89mm (2" to 4" nom.) and is used for framing applications such as joists, planks, rafters, studs, and small posts or beams.

Timber is lumber 140mm (5-1/2") or more in its smallest dimension. Beams and Stringers are timbers used as bending

members and are more than 51mm (2") wider than they are thick. Posts and Timbers are used as compression members and are no more than 51mm (2") in difference between width and thickness.

As defined for building construction, decking is lumber laid on its wide face to form a roof or wall surface (see Section 4.4).

Boards are used in building construction for sheathing, paneling, and siding (see Sections 7 and 8).

Canadian lumber is economical, easy to procure, easy to adjust in the field, and has a dependability based on North American applied grading rules.

Species

The four species groups from which Canadian lumber is manufactured and their characteristics are shown in the table on the next page.

The Spruce-Pine-Fir species group makes up by far the largest proportion of dimension lumber since the species in this group grow throughout most of Canada. The other major species groups for lumber are Douglas Fir-Larch and Hem-Fir. Several minor species round out the list of commercial species for Canadian lumber.

Grade Stamping

Canadian lumber which has been graded in accordance with requirements of North American building codes will carry a grade stamp, such as that shown in Figure 3.1 (→ 122). This stamp is applied to each individual piece of lumber about 600mm (2') from each end so that it is visible after a piece has been installed. The information on the stamp indicates the grading authority, the mill of manufacture, the grade, and the moisture content at the time of manufacture.

3

Main Structural Members

Terminology for Canadian Lumber	Boards (see Sections 7 and 8)	Dimension Lumber and Decking	Timber

	Sheathing and Form Lumber Specialties:
	   Paneling,
	   Siding, Flooring, Shaped
	   Mouldings etc.
		Light Framing
		Studs
		Structural Light Framing
		Structural Joists and Planks
		Plank Decking and Board Sheathing
		(see Section 4.4)
			Beams and Stringers
			Posts and Timbers

Commercial Species of Canadian Softwood Lumber	Species Combination	Abbr.	Species Included in Combination	Characteristics	Colour Ranges
	Douglas Fir-Larch	DF-L or D.Fir-L	Douglas fir, Western larch	• high degree of hardness • good resistance to decay	reddish brown to yellowish
	Hem-Fir	H-F or Hem-Fir	Pacific coast hemlock, Amabilis fir	• works easily • takes paint well • holds nails well • good gluing characteristics	yellow brown to white
	Spruce-Pine-Fir	S-P-F	Spruce (all species except coast sitka spruce), Jack pine, Lodgepole pine, Balsam fir, Alpine fir	• works easily • takes paint well • holds nails well	white to pale yellow
	Northern Species	Nor or North	Western red cedar	• exceptional resistance to decay • moderate strength • high in appearance qualities • works easily • takes fine finishes • lowest shrinkage	red cedar: reddish brown heartwood light sapwood
			Red pine	• works easily	reddish to pale brown heartwood
			Ponderosa pine	• takes finish well • holds nails well • holds screws well • seasons with little checking or cupping	pale yellow colour sapwood
			Western white pine, Eastern white pine	• softest of Canadian pines • works easily • finishes well • doesn't tend to split or splinter • holds nails well • low shrinkage • takes stains, paints, varnishes well	creamy white to light straw brown heartwood, almost white sapwood
			Trembling aspen, Largetooth aspen, Balsam poplar	• works easily • finishes well • holds nails well	almost white to greyish-white
			Any other Canadian species graded in accordance with the NLGA rules		

Surface Smoothness

There are three general levels of surface smoothness to which lumber is manufactured.

Rough lumber is lumber which has been sawn, trimmed, and edged. The saw blades used for mass manufacturing are coarse toothed for speed of production and, as a result, rough lumber is usually characterized by striations or saw lines.

Surfaced lumber is lumber which has been surfaced after sawing by passing through a planing machine for the purpose of adding smoothness and uniformity of size on one side (S1S), two sides (S2S), four sides (S4S), or a combination of sides and edges.

Worked lumber is surfaced lumber which has been further shaped by a jointer or moulder to be matched (tongue and groove), shiplapped, or patterned into a moulding shape (see Sections 7 and 8).

Uses

The two main types of lumber which are used for load bearing members, dimension lumber and timber, have specific uses in wood building construction.

Dimension lumber is generally used for light frame construction, and timber for post and beam construction (see Section 6).

Dimension Lumber

The predominant use of dimension lumber in building construction is in framing in combination structurally with sheathing (see Section 4) to create roofs, floors, shearwalls, diaphragms, and load bearing walls (see Section 6).

Machine stress-rated (MSR) lumber and fingerjoined lumber are specialty products falling within the size parameters of dimension lumber and are discussed later in this section.

Lumber may be used directly as framing materials or may be used to manufacture engineered structural products, such as light frame trusses (see Section 3.4) or prefabricated wood I-joists (see Section 3.7). Special grade dimension lumber called lamstock (laminating stock) is manufactured exclusively for glulam (see Section 3.3).

Dimension lumber is categorized into the following four groups: Structural Light Framing, Structural Joists and Planks, Light Framing, and Studs. Table 3.2 (→ 130) shows the grades and uses for these groups.

Timber

The term timber describes lumber which is 140mm (5-1/2") or more in its smallest dimension. There are two categories of timbers. Beams and Stringers (width more than 51mm (2") greater than thickness) are for bending members, and Posts and Timbers (width less than 51mm (2") greater than thickness) are used for columns.

Timbers, along with other materials, such as glulam and parallel strand lumber (PSL), are used in post and beam construction (see Section 6.3).

Manufacture

A schematic drawing of the lumber manufacturing process is shown in Figure 3.2 (→ 124). The sequence of the process is fairly consistent from mill to mill but large differences exist in the type of saw and other equipment depending on mill size, and the type of lumber being manufactured.

Dimension Lumber

Grading

Canadian dimension lumber is manufactured to conform to grading rules meeting Canadian and US requirements.

Each piece of lumber is inspected to determine its grade and a stamp is applied indicating the assigned grade, the mill of origin, a green or dry moisture content at time of manufacture, the species or species group, and the grading authority having jurisdiction over the mill of origin.

3

Main Structural Members

Figure 3.1
**Canadian
Lumber Grade
Stamps**

A.F.P.A.® 00 ————— Grading agency

——————— Mill designation

S — P — F. ————————— Species group

S-DRY ————————— Moisture content

No. 1 ————————— Assigned Grade

Alberta Forest Products Association
11710 Kingsway Avenue, Suite 104
Edmonton, AB T5G 0X5
403-452-2841
(Approved to supervise machine stress-rated lumber)

A.F.P.A.® 00
S — P — F
S-DRY
No. 1

Canadian Lumbermen's Association
27 Goulburn Avenue
Ottawa, ON K1N 8C7
613-233-6205

C L°A
S-P-F
100
No. 1
S-GRN.

Cariboo Lumber Manufacturers' Association
197 Second Avenue North, Suite 301
Williams Lake, BC V2G 1Z5
604-392-7778

LMA ¹₁   S-GRN ₁
           D FIR (N)

Central Forest Products Association, Inc.
P. O. Box 1169
Hudson Bay, SK S0E 0Y0
306-865-2595

CFPA® 38
S-P-F S-GRN
CONST

Council of Forest Industries of British Columbia
1200-555 Burrard Street
Vancouver, BC V7X 1S7
604-684-0211
(Approved to supervise fingerjoining and machine stress-rated lumber)

CФFI. S-P-F
             S-GRN
100   No 1

Northern Interior Lumber Sector
400-1488 Fourth Avenue
Prince Gearge, BC V2L 4Y2
604-564-5136
(Approved to supervise fingerjoining and machine stress-rated lumber)

Interior Lumber Manufacturers' Association
360, 1855 Kirschner Road
Kelowna, BC V1Y 4N7
604-860-9663
(Approved to supervise fingerjoining and machine stress-rated lumber)

ILMA S-DRY 1
00   S—P—F

Newfoundland Lumber Producers' Association
P. O. Box 8
Glovertown, NF A0G 2L0
709-533-2206
Note:
The Newfoundland Lumber Producers' Association is not an
American Lumber Standards approved agency.

NFLD LUMBER
NORTH
SPECIES
STUD
S-GRN
MILL 015

Figure 3.1
**Canadian
Lumber Grade
Stamps,
continued**

Macdonald Inspection
c/o Warnock Hersey Professional Services Ltd.
211 Schoolhouse Street
Coquitlam, BC V3K 4X9
604-520-3321
(Approved to supervise fingerjoining and machine stress-rated lumber)

Maritime Lumber Bureau
P. O. Box 459
Amherst, NS B4H 4A1
902-667-3889

Ontario Lumber Manufacturers' Association
55 University Avenue
Box 8, Suite. 325
Toronto, ON M5J 2H7
416-367-9717

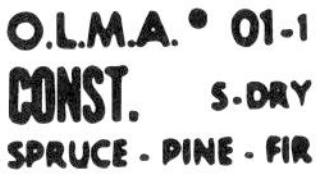

Pacific Lumber Inspection Bureau
P.O. Box 7235
3801-150th St S.E. - #202
Bellevue, WA 98008-1235
206-746-6542
B.C. Division:
1110-355 Burrard St.
Vancouver, BC V6C 2G8
604-689-1561

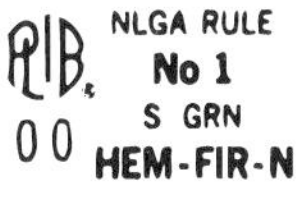

**Association des manufacturiers de bois de sciage du
Québec (Québec Lumber Manufacturers' Association)**
5055 boul. Hamel ouest, bureau 200
Québec, QC G2E 2G6
418-872-5610
(Approved to supervise fingerjoining and machine stress-rated lumber)

NWT Forest Industries Association
P.O. Box 979
Hay River, NT X0E 0R0
403-874-6814
Note:
The Northwest Territories Grade Stamping Agency is not an
American Lumber Standards approved agency.

3

Lumber has traditionally been graded by visual inspection. The grade of a given piece of lumber is based on visual observation of such characteristics as slope of grain and the location of knots.

Machine stress-rated (MSR) lumber is dimension lumber which is mechanically evaluated. In addition to mechanical evaluation, there are visual grade requirements for MSR lumber.

Dimension lumber is grade stamped about 600mm (2') from one end of each piece so that the stamp will be clearly visible during construction. (Specialty items such as lumber manufactured for millwork or for decorative purposes are seldom marked).

Figure 3.2
Manufacture of Sawn Lumber

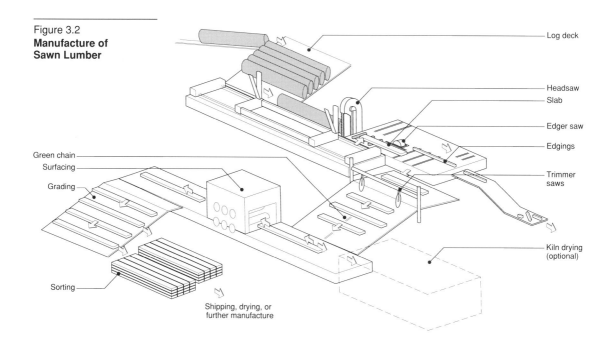

To keep sorting cost to a minimum, grades may be marketed by being grouped together. For example, there is an appearance difference between No.1 and No.2 Canadian dimension lumber but not a strength difference. Therefore the product mix No.2 and better is commonly used where the appearance of No.1 grade lumber is not required, as, for example, in the case of joists and rafters or trusses.

Unless regraded, graded lumber should not be ripped or resawn lengthwise for engineered applications. This changes the location of knots and grain slope relative to the areas of high stress concentration and therefore changes the grade.

Sizes Available
Standard dimension lumber sizes produced in North America are listed as surfaced dry sizes (19 percent moisture content or less) in Table 3.3 (→ 131). The availability of lumber sizes varies somewhat according to the area of the country from which the raw material originates.

Lengths up to 6.1m (20') are commonly available from western Canada and up to 4.9m (16') from eastern Canada. Longer lengths are available on special order. They are also available in the form of fingerjoined lumber.

Moisture Content
Moisture content (MC) is the weight of water contained in the wood compared to the wood's oven-dry weight. A change in the size of a piece of lumber is related to the amount of water it absorbs or loses. For moisture contents from 0 to about 28 percent, the moisture is held within the walls of the wood cells. At about 28 percent MC the cell walls reach their capacity or fibre saturation point (FSP) and any additional water must be held in the cell cavities (see Section 2.1 for a discussion on moisture). The manufactured moisture content of various products is shown in Figure 2.3 (→ 87).

Lumber stamped S-Grn (surfaced green) is lumber which had a moisture content exceeding 19 percent (unseasoned) at time of manufacture.

The designation S-Dry on the grade stamp stands for surfaced dry and means that the lumber was surfaced at a maximum moisture content of 19 percent (seasoned) or less. The grade stamp will not indicate whether seasoning resulted from air drying or kiln drying. Some mills apply a voluntary stamp indicating that the lumber was kiln dried but service performance is the same for kiln dried lumber as for lumber dried by seasoning.

Regardless of whether S-Grn or S-Dry at the time of manufacture, careless storage can lead to absorption of water which reverses the seasoning process and therefore increases the possibility that dimensional change will take place when the lumber has been placed into service which of course is not desirable.

Careful storage and handling of S-Dry lumber will ensure that it remains in seasoned condition when put into service. Careful storage of S-Grn lumber will allow further drying after service, thereby minimizing dimensional change which might occur after going into service. Refer to Section 2.1 for general information on the storage and handling of wood products.

S-Dry lumber is up to 15 percent more expensive than S-Grn lumber owing to packaging and drying costs.

Lumber Properties

For many years, the design values of Canadian dimension lumber were determined by testing small clear samples. Although this approach has worked well in the past, there were some indications that it did not always provide an accurate reflection of how a full sized member would behave in service.

Beginning in the 1970s, new data was gathered on full-size graded lumber. In the early 1980s, the wood industries in Canada and in the United States embarked on a joint comprehensive testing program which involved testing thousands of pieces of dimension lumber to destruction to determine their in-service characteristics. This is called in-grade testing.

The data which resulted from the in-grade testing programs has been used to update the design values which are applied in Canada and the United States.

Little data is available on full-size tests of timbers. Therefore the design values for timbers continue to be determined on the basis of small clear testing.

Specialty Products

Machine Stress-Rated Lumber (MSR lumber)

Lumber which is evaluated mechanically is called machine stress-rated (MSR) lumber. Canadian MSR lumber is manufactured in conformance with the National Lumber Grades Authority (NLGA) *Special Product Standard 2 (SPS-2)*.

Unlike visually graded lumber where the anticipated strength properties are determined from assessing a piece on the basis of appearance, the strength characteristics of MSR lumber are determined by applying forces to a member and actually measuring the stiffness of a particular piece. Because the stiffness of each piece is measured, and because strength is measured on some pieces through a quality control program, MSR lumber can be assigned higher design stresses than visually graded dimension lumber.

Figure 3.3 (→ 126) shows a schematic representation of the apparatus used to rate MSR lumber and some typical grade marks for Canadian MSR lumber. In addition to the information shown on a grade stamp for visually graded lumber, it indicates the grade, by reference to bending strength (F_b), and stiffness (E).

As lumber is fed continuously into the mechanical evaluating equipment, stiffness is measured and recorded by a small computer, and strength is assessed by correlation methods. MSR grading can be accomplished at speeds up to 365m (1000') per minute including the affixing of an MSR grade mark.

3

Main Structural Members

Figure 3.3
**Grading for
MSR Lumber**

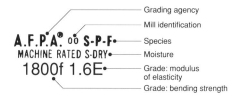

Sample MSR Grademarks

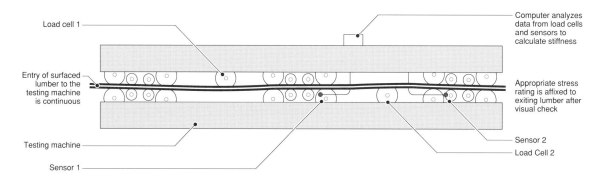

Schematic of Mechanical Evaluating Equipment
for MSR Lumber

MSR lumber is also visually checked for properties other than stiffness which might affect the suitability of a given piece.

The mechanical analysis of MSR lumber results in the affixing of an f-E stamp to a piece of lumber. The f-E classifications relate directly to allowable values: for example, an 1800f – 1.6E grade has been tested for an allowable stress in bending of 12.4 MPa (1800 psi) and a modulus of elasticity (E) of 11000 MPa (1.6 million psi) under normal duration of load.

MSR lumber is favoured particularly by specialized users such as truss manufacturers where higher strength per volume of lumber and reliability resulting from measured design values is required.

Fingerjoined Lumber
Fingerjoined lumber is dimension lumber into which finger profiles have been machined. The pieces which are then end-glued together (see Figure 3.4 opposite).

With fingerjoining, the length of a piece of lumber is not limited by tree size. In fact, the process may result in the production of joists and rafters in lengths of 12m (40') or more.

Although fingerjoining is used in several wood product manufacturing processes including the horizontal joints for glulam manufacture, the term fingerjoined lumber applies to dimension lumber.

Figure 3.4
**Fingerjoined
Lumber**

Typical Grade Stamps

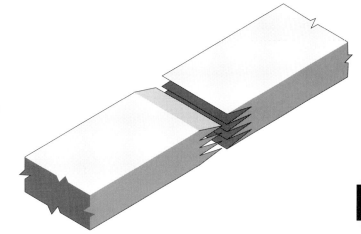

CQFI®   S-P-F
         S-DRY
000   **No.1**
NLGA   SPS   1
CERT   FGR   JNT

Vertical or Horizontal Use

CQFI®   S-P-F
         S-DRY
000   **STUD**
NLGA   SPS   3
CERT   FGR   JNT
VERTICAL USE ONLY

Vertical Use Only

3

Main Structural Members

Canadian fingerjoined lumber is manufactured in conformance with National Lumber Grades Authority (NLGA) *Special Product Standard 1 (SPS-1)* or *Special Product Standard 3 (SPS-3)*. Fingerjoined lumber produced to the requirements of SPS-1 is interchangeable with non-fingerjoined lumber of the same grade and length. For example, a No.2 fingerjoined joist may be assigned the same engineering properties as a No.2 joist made from one continuous length.

The fingerjoining process allows the removal of strength reducing defects to produce a product with higher engineering properties. The strength of the joints is controlled by stipulating the quality of wood which must be present in the area of the joint.

For example, Select Structural, No.1, and No.2 grade joints must be formed in sound, solid, pitch-free wood that meets the slope of grain and other general requirements of the grade.

For all other grades, joints are formed in wood that meets the visual requirements for No.2 or Standard grades, and the surface area of the joint having pitch or honeycomb must not exceed 10 percent of the area.

Each piece must be comprised of species from the same species group, and strict tolerances are established for the machining of the fingers, the quality, the mixing, and the curing of the adhesive. Depending on the type of fingerjoined lumber being manufactured, edge and flat bending tests and tension tests are performed on each piece to ensure the joint can meet the design value for the lumber.

Fingerjoined lumber is assessed for visual grade and for machine tested strength with the grade assigned being the lower of either the visual or the stress grade. As mentioned previously, there are two standards for Canadian fingerjoined lumber. One covers bending members (SPS-1) used in either the horizontal or vertical position, and the other covers members intended for use in a vertical position in stud walls (SPS-3).

All fingerjoined lumber manufactured to the Canadian NLGA standards carries a grade stamp indicating:

• the species or species combination identification

• the seasoning designation (S-Dry or S-Green)

• the registered symbol of the grading agency

• the grade

- the mill identification

- the NLGA standard number and the designation CERT FGR JNT. (certified finger joint) or Cert Fin Jnt Vertical Use Only (certified finger joint for vertical use only).

Timber

Grading of Timbers

Both categories of timbers, Beams and Stringers, and Posts and Timbers, contain three stress grades: Select Structural, No.1, and No.2, and two non-stress grades (Standard and Utility). These grades and their uses are shown in Table 3.4 (→ 131).

The stress grades are assigned design values for use as structural members. Non-stress grades have not been assigned design values.

No.1 or No.2 are the most common grades specified for structural purposes. No.1 may contain varying amounts of Select Structural, depending on the manufacturer. Unlike Canadian dimension lumber, there is a difference between design values for No.1 and No.2 grades for timbers.

Select Structural is specified when the highest quality appearance and strength are desired.

The Standard and Utility grades have not been assigned design values. Timbers of these grades are permitted for use in specific applications of building codes where high strength is not important, as in the case of deck uses, blocking or short bracing.

Timbers are generally not grade marked, since they are surfaced rough and may be used in exposed locations. If needed, a mill certificate may be obtained to certify the grade.

Cross cutting can affect the grade of timber in the Beams and Stringers category because the allowable size of knot varies along the length of the piece (a larger knot is allowed near the ends than in the middle). Therefore, for this grade category, the timber must be regraded if it is cross cut.

Sizes Available

Timbers are sometimes manufactured to large dimensions and resawn later to fill specific orders. Table 3.5 (→ 132) shows the most common sizes, which range from 140mm x 140mm (5-1/2" x 5-1/2") to 292 x 495mm (11-1/2" x 19-1/2") in lengths of 5m (16') to 9m (30') and longer, with longer lengths commanding a premium price.

Moisture Content

The large size of timbers makes kiln drying impractical due to the drying stresses which would result from differential moisture contents between the interior and exterior of the timber. For this reason, timbers are usually dressed green (moisture content above 19 percent), and the moisture content of timber upon delivery will depend on the amount of air drying which has taken place.

Like dimension lumber, timber begins to shrink when its moisture content falls below about 28 percent. The degree of shrinkage depends on the climatic conditions of the environment. For example, timbers exposed to the outdoors usually shrink from 1.8 to 2.6 percent in width and thickness, depending on the species. Timbers used indoors, where the air is often drier, experience greater shrinkage, in the range of 2.4 to 3.0 percent in width and thickness. Length change in either case is negligible.

When constructing with Posts and Timbers or Beams and Stringers, allowance should be made for anticipated shrinkage based on the moisture content at the time of assembly. Where the building envelope relies on caulked seals between timbers and other building components, the selection of caulks should take into account the amount of movement which must be accommodated as shrinkage occurs.

Minor checks on the surface of a timber are common in most service conditions and therefore an allowance has been made for them in the assignment of working stresses. Checks in columns are not of structural importance unless the check develops into a through split that will divide the column.

Fire Safety

Dimension Lumber

Dimension lumber is commonly used for Wood-Frame construction in floor, wall, and roof assemblies. Building codes provide guidance on how Wood-Frame construction can be used to meet fire safety requirements.

Dimension lumber can of course be used in assemblies which do not require a fire-resistance rating. Where a rating is required, the required level of performance can be met by sheathing the wood framing with materials such as gypsum wallboard to protect the wood and retard the spread of fire.

Section 10 outlines the potential for using dimension lumber for all types of buildings both for structural and decorative purposes while meeting fire safety requirements.

Timber

Timbers offer increased resistance to fire compared to unprotected dimension lumber. Because of this, timber is often used in Heavy Timber construction to meet minimum size and fire-resistance rating requirements of North American building codes.

Section 10 provides basic information on the minimum sizes and arrangement of timber members necessary to meet code requirements for Heavy Timber construction. Information is also provided on the means for calculating the fire resistance of timber beams and columns.

General Guidelines for Dimension Lumber and Timbers

- For economy, select a grade based on the strength and appearance requirements for each application.

- Specify lumber having moisture content suitable for the application. Whereas S-Green lumber might be economical for applications where shrinkage can be tolerated, S-Dry lumber is recommended for many applications where appearance of straight flat members is a requirement.

- Verify the availability and suitability of species, grades and sizes before indicating requirements on drawings and in the specifications.

- During construction, the inspection process must ensure that proper grades are placed where indicated on the drawings, and that wood products are stored and handled properly.

3

Main Structural Members

Reference Tables

Table 3.2
Canadian Dimension Lumber – Grades and Uses

Grade Category	Grades	Common Grade Mix	Principal Uses
Structural Light-Framing 38 to 89mm (2" to 4" nom.) thick 38 to 89mm (2" to 4" nom.) wide	Select Structural No.1 No.2 No.3	No.2 and Better	Used for engineering applications such as for trusses, lintels, rafters and joists in the smaller dimensions.
Structural Joists and Planks 38 to 89mm (2" to 4" nom.) thick 114mm (5" nom.) or more wide	Select Structural No.1 No.2 No.3	No.2 and Better	Used for engineering applications such as for trusses, lintels, rafters, and joists in the dimensions greater than 114mm (5" nom.).
Light Framing 38 to 89mm (2" to 4" nom.) thick 38 to 89mm (2" to 4" nom.) wide	Construction Standard Utility	Standard and Better (Std. & Btr.)	Used for general framing where high strength values are not required such as for plates, sills, and blocking.
Studs 38 to 89mm (2" to 4" nom.) thick 38 to 140mm (2" to 6" nom.) wide 3m (10') or less in length	Stud Economy Stud		Made principally for use in walls. Stud grade is suitable for bearing wall applications. Economy grade is suitable for temporary applications.

Notes:
1. Grades may be bundled individually or they may be individually stamped but they must be grouped together with the engineering properties dictated by the lowest strength grade in the bundle.
2. The common grade mix shown is the most economical blending of strength for most applications where appearance is not a factor and average strength is acceptable.
3. Except for economy grade, all grades are stress graded which means specified strengths have been assigned and span tables calculated. Economy and utility grades are suited for temporary construction or for applications where strength and appearance are not important.
4. Construction, Standard, Stud, and No.3 grades should be used in designs that are composed of 3 or more essentially parallel members (load sharing) spaced at 610mm (2') centres or less.
5. Strength properties and appearance are best in the premium grades such as Select Structural.

Reference Tables continued

Table 3.3
Sizes of Canadian Dimension Lumber

Surfaced Dry (S-Dry) Size mm	Surfaced Dry (S-Dry) Size in. (actual)	Rough Sawn Size in. (nom.)	Surfaced Green (S-Grn) Size in. (actual)
38 x 38	1-1/2 x 1-1/2	2 x 2	1-9/16 x 1-9/16
64	2-1/2	3	2-9/16
89	3-1/2	4	3-9/16
140	5-1/2	6	5-5/8
184	7-1/4	8	7-1/2
235	9-1/4	10	9-1/2
286	11-1/4	12	11-1/2
64 x 64	2-1/2 x 2-1/2	3 x 3	2-9/16 x 2-9/16
89	3-1/2	4	3-9/16
140	5-1/2	6	5-5/8
184	7-1/4	8	7-1/2
235	9-1/4	10	9-1/2
286	11-1/4	12	11-1/2
89 x 89	3-1/2 x 3-1/2	4 x 4	3-9/16 x 3-9/16
140	5-1/2	6	5-5/8
184	7-1/4	8	7-1/2
235	9-1/4	10	9-1/2
286	11-1/4	12	11-1/2

Notes:
1. 38mm (2" nominal) lumber is readily available as S-Dry.
2. S-Dry lumber is surfaced at a moisture content of 19 percent or less.
3. After drying, S-Green lumber sizes will be approximately the same as S-Dry lumber.
4. Tabulated metric sizes are equivalent to Imperial S-Dry sizes rounded to the nearest millimetre.
5. S-Dry is the final size for seasoned lumber in place and is the size used in design calculations.

Table 3.4
Canadian Timbers – Grades and Uses

Grade Category	Grades	Smaller dimension	Larger dimension	Principal Uses
Beam and Stringer	Select Structural No.1 No.2 Standard Utility	114mm (5") or more	Exceeds smaller dimension by more than 51mm (2")	Used for beams, stringers, and purlins where members are loaded in bending.
Post and Timber	Select Structural No.1 No.2 Standard Utility	114mm (5") or more	Exceeds smaller dimension by 51mm (2") or less	Used for columns, posts, and struts where members are loaded in compression.

Notes:
1. Strength and appearance are best in the premium grades such as Select Structural. The lower grades are more economical and are suitable where appearance and strength are less important.
2. Timbers are available rough sawn or custom surfaced.

Reference Tables continued

Table 3.5 **Sizes of Canadian Timber**	Surfaced Metric Sizes mm	Surfaced Imperial Sizes in. (actual)	Rough Sawn Imperial Sizes in. (nom.)
	140 x 140	5-1/2 x 5-1/2	6 x 6
	191	7-1/2	8
	241	9-1/2	10
	292	11-1/2	12
	343	13-1/2	14
	394	15-1/2	16
	445	17-1/2	18
	191 x 191	7-1/2 x 7-1/2	8 x 8
	241	9-1/2	10
	292	11-1/2	12
	343	13-1/2	14
	394	15-1/2	16
	445	17-1/2	18
	495	19-1/2	20
	241 x 241	9-1/2 x 9-1/2	10 x 10
	292	11-1/2	12
	343	13-1/2	14
	394	15-1/2	16
	445	17-1/2	18
	495	19-1/2	20
	292 x 292	11-1/2 x 11-1/2	12 x 12
	343	13-1/2	14
	394	15-1/2	16
	445	17-1/2	18
	495	19-1/2	20

Note:
Timbers are surfaced (dressed) and sold green.

3.3   Glulam

Introduction

Glulam (glued-laminated timber) is a structural timber product manufactured by gluing together individual pieces of dimension lumber under controlled conditions. The attributes of this wood product account for its frequent use as an attractive architectural and structural building material.

In the manufacture of glulam, the wood pieces are end jointed and arranged in horizontal layers or laminations.

Laminating is an effective way of using high strength lumber of limited dimension to manufacture large structural members in many shapes and sizes. Glulam is used for columns and for beams and frequently for

curved members loaded in combined bending and compression.

Vertically laminated beams, which are made by nailing or gluing together dimension lumber so that the narrow faces of the laminations are oriented perpendicular to the load, are considered to be load sharing systems (built-up beams) and are not to be confused with glulam (see Figure 3.5 below).

Glulam is manufactured at certified plants where standards governing lumber grading, end joining, gluing, and finishing are used to control quality. Qualified manufacturers can supply a certificate of conformance for their products upon request.

3

Main Structural Members

Figure 3.5
Comparing Glulam to Nail-Laminated Beam

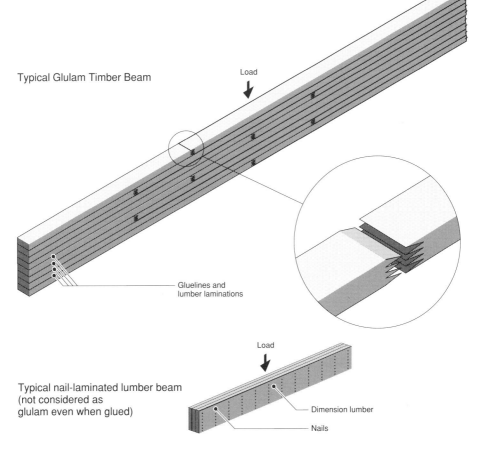

Typical Glulam Timber Beam

Load

Gluelines and lumber laminations

Load

Typical nail-laminated lumber beam (not considered as glulam even when glued)

Dimension lumber

Nails

The lumber used for the manufacture of glulam is a special grade (lamstock) which is purchased directly from lumber mills. It is dried to a maximum moisture content of 15 percent and it is planed to a closer tolerance than that required for dimension lumber.

Canadian glulam is manufactured in three species combinations: Douglas Fir-Larch; Hem-Fir and Spruce-Pine as shown in Table 3.6 (→ 141).

All Canadian glulam is manufactured using waterproof adhesives for end jointing and for face bonding and is therefore suitable for both exterior and interior applications. However, the specified strengths used in design will depend upon whether the service condition is wet or dry.

Figure 3.6
Common Glulam Shapes for Large Buildings

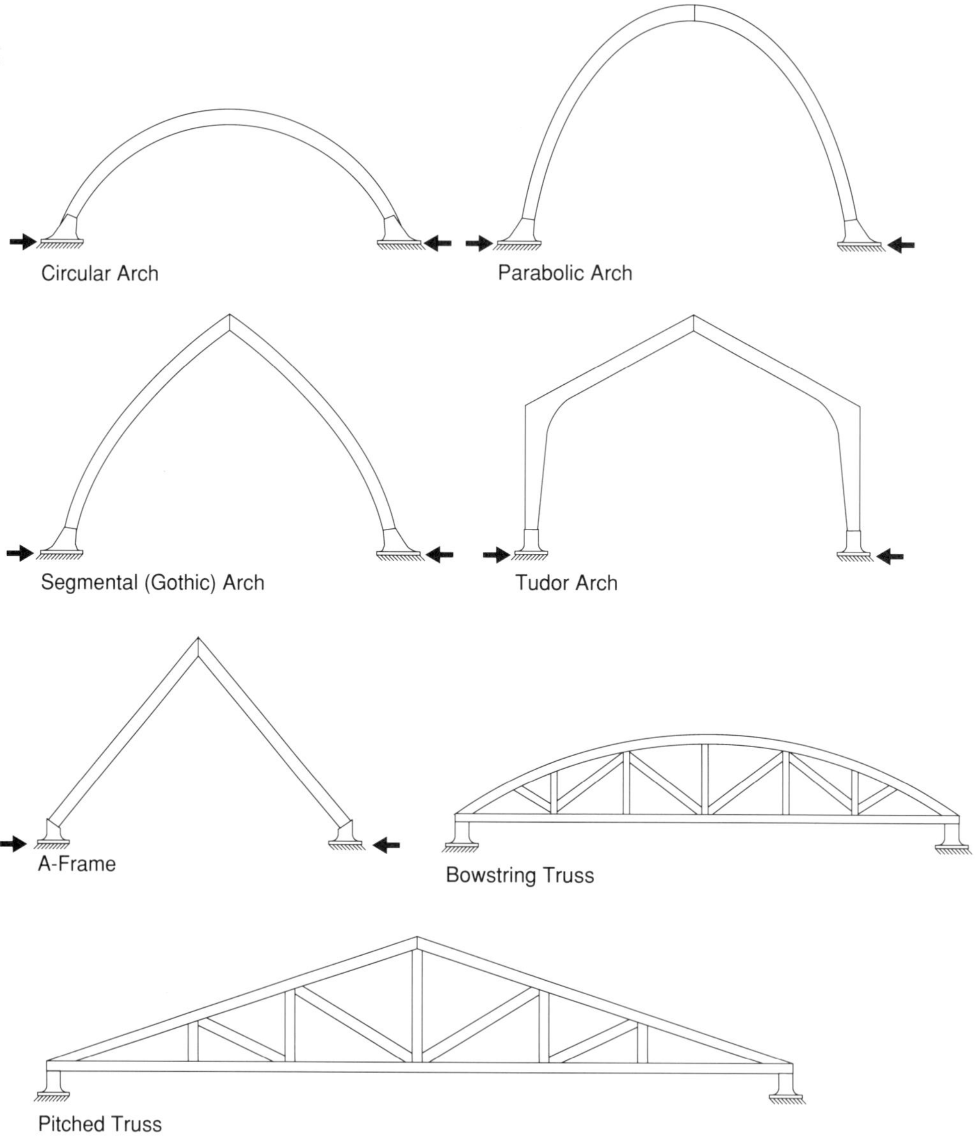

Circular Arch

Parabolic Arch

Segmental (Gothic) Arch

Tudor Arch

A-Frame

Bowstring Truss

Pitched Truss

Uses

Glulam is a structural product used for headers, beams, girders, columns, and for heavy trusses. It is often used where the structure of a building is left exposed as an architectural feature.

Glulam can be manufactured to an almost limitless variety of straight and curved configurations (see Figure 3.6 opposite). It offers the architect artistic freedom without sacrificing structural requirements.

Manufacture

The special grade of lumber used for glulam, lamstock, is received and stored at the laminating plant under controlled conditions (see Figure 3.7 below).

Prior to glulam fabrication, all lumber is visually graded for strength properties and mechanically evaluated to determine the modulus of elasticity (E). These two assessments of strength and stiffness are used to determine where a given piece will be situated in a beam or column.

For example, high strength pieces are placed in the outermost laminations of a beam where the bending stresses are the greatest. This blending of strength characteristics is known as grade combination and ensures consistent performance of the finished product.

Once graded, the individual pieces of lamstock are end joined into full length laminations of constant grade and each endjoint is proof tested. Then, the laminated lengths are arranged according to the required grade combination for the product being manufactured.

3

Main Structural Members

Figure 3.7
Manufacture of Glulam

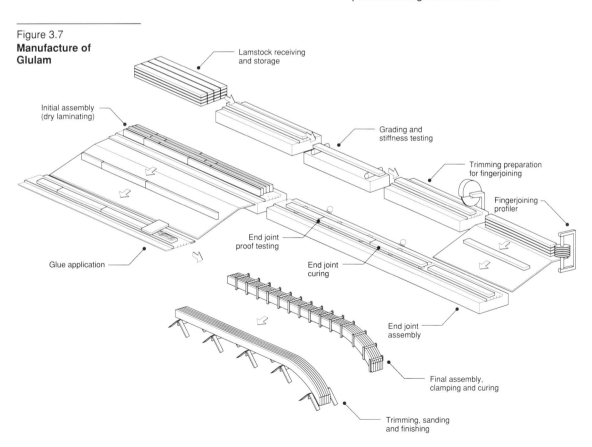

- Lamstock receiving and storage
- Initial assembly (dry laminating)
- Grading and stiffness testing
- Trimming preparation for fingerjoining
- Fingerjoining profiler
- Glue application
- End joint proof testing
- End joint curing
- End joint assembly
- Final assembly, clamping and curing
- Trimming, sanding and finishing

Each lamination then moves through a glue applicator and the pieces are reassembled into the desired configuration at the clamping area. Hydraulic or manually activated clamps are placed around the member, and are brought into contact with steel jigs which have been pre-anchored to the floor to provide the desired curvature or pattern.

As pressure is applied, the laminations are adjusted for proper alignment in a level plane to minimize the amount of stock which will be lost when the member is surface planed to a smooth finish. Once full clamping pressure is reached, the member is stored at a controlled temperature until the glue is fully cured.

When glue curing is complete, the members are moved to the finishing area where basic surface planing, patching, and end trimming is done. Depending on what the client has ordered, drilling and notching for connections, sanding, and staining and varnishing may also be done. Because of specialized equipment and mass production, these functions can usually be performed in the shop cheaper than at the building site.

As a final step, glulam members are wrapped in readiness for shipping.

Quality Control

Glulam is an engineered wood product requiring exacting quality control at all stages of manufacture.

Canadian manufacturers of glulam are required to be qualified under *CSA Standard O177*. This standard sets mandatory guidelines for equipment, manufacturing, testing and record keeping procedures.

As a mandatory manufacturing procedure, tests must be routinely performed on several critical manufacturing steps, and recording of test results must be done. For example, representative samples are tested for adequacy of glue bond and all end joints are stress tested to ensure that

each joint exceeds the design requirements. Each member fabricated has a quality assurance record indicating glue bond test results, lumber grading, end joint testing and laminating conditions for each member fabricated, including glue spread rate, assembly time, curing conditions and curing time.

In addition, mandatory quality audits are performed by independent certification agencies to ensure that in-plant procedures meet the requirements of the manufacturing standard.

A certificate of conformance to manufacturing standards for a given glulam order is available upon request.

Strength and Appearance

In specifying Canadian glulam products, it is necessary to indicate both the stress grade and the appearance grade required.

The specification of the appropriate stress grade depends on whether the intended end use of a member is for a beam, a column, or a tension member as shown in Table 3.7 (→ 141).

For the bending grades of 20f-E, 20f-EX, 24f-E and 24f-EX, the numbers 20 and 24 indicate allowable bending stress for bending in Imperial units (2000 and 2400 pounds per square inch). The f refers to flexure and E indicates that most laminations must be tested for stiffness by machine.

Stress grades with EX designation (20f-EX and 24f-EX) are specifically designed for cases where bending members are subjected to stress reversals. In these members the lamination requirements in the tension side are the mirror image of those in the compression side.

Similarly, the descriptions for compression grades, 16c-E and 12c-E, and tension grades, 18t-E and 14t-E indicate the allowable compression and tension stresses.

	Grade	Description
Glulam Appearance Grades	Industrial Grade	Intended for use where appearance is not primary concern such as in industrial buildings; laminating stock may contain natural characteristics allowed for specified stress grade; sides planed to specified dimensions but occasional misses and rough spots allowed; may have broken knots, knot holes, torn grain, checks, wane and other irregularities on surface.
	Commercial Grade	Intended for painted or flat-gloss varnished surfaces; laminating stock may contain natural characteristics allowed for specified stress grade; sides planed to specified dimensions and all squeezed-out glue removed from surface; knot holes, loose knots, voids, wane or pitch pockets are not replaced by wood inserts or filler on exposed surface.
	Quality Grade	Intended for high-gloss transparent or polished surfaces, displays natural beauty of wood for best aesthetic appeal; laminating stock may contain natural characteristics allowed for specified stress grade; sides planed to specified dimensions and all squeezed-out glue removed from surface; may have tight knots, firm heart stain and medium sap stain on sides; slightly broken or split knots, slivers, torn grain or checks on surface filled; loose knots, knot holes, wane and pitch pockets removed and replaced with non-shrinking filler or with wood inserts matching wood grain and colour; face laminations free of natural characteristics requiring replacement; faces and sides sanded smooth.

Note:
All Canadian glulam is made with glue suitable for exterior applications.

Glulam is manufactured in three appearance grades: Industrial, Commercial, and Quality (see Table above). Unlike visually graded sawn timbers where there is a correlation between appearance and strength, there is no relationship between the stress grades and the appearance grades of glulam since the exposed surface can be altered or repaired without affecting the strength characteristics.

The appearance of glulam is determined by the degree of finish work done after laminating and not by the appearance of the individual lamination pieces.

Sizes Available

Standard sizes have been developed for Canadian glued-laminated timber to allow optimum utilization of lumber which are multiples of the dimensions of the lamstock used for glulam manufacture. Suitable for most applications, standard sizes offer the designer economy and fast delivery. Other nonstandard dimensions may be specially ordered at additional cost because of the extra trimming required to produce non-standard sizes.

Standard finished widths of glulam members and common widths of the laminating stock they are made from are given in Table 3.8 (→ 141).

Size possibilities for glulam shapes are shown in Figure 3.8 (→ 138).

Single widths of stock are used for the complete width dimension for members less than 275mm (10-7/8") wide. However, members wider than 175mm (6-7/8") may consist of two boards laid side by side. All members wider than 275mm (10-7/8") are made from two pieces of lumber placed side by side, with edge joints staggered within the depth of the member.

Members wider than 365mm (14-1/4") are manufactured in 50mm (2") width increments, but will be more expensive than standard widths. Manufacturers should be consulted for advice.

3

Main Structural Members

Figure 3.8
Typical Glulam Shapes and Sizes

Straight Beams

Lengths up to 40m (130')
Depths up to 2128mm (7')
Standard widths as shown in Table 3.8 (→ 141)

Simple Straight Beam

Continuous Straight Beam

Cantilever Straight Beam

Single Tapered-Straight Beam

Double Tapered-Straight Beam

Curved Beams

Standard widths up to 315mm (12-1/2") and
depths up to 1482mm (4'-10")

Simple Curved Beam

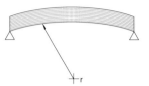

Double Tapered-Curved Beam

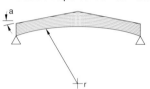

Pitched Beam

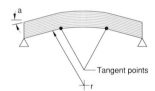

Double Tapered-Pitched Beam

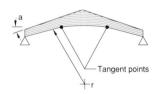

Columns

Lengths up
to 18m (60')

Camber Recommendations for Glulam Beams and Trusses

Type of Structure	Recommendation
Simple Glulam Roof Beams	Camber equal to deflection due to dead load plus half of live load or 30mm per 10m (1" per 30') of span; where ponding may occur, additional camber is usually provided for roof drainage.
Simple Glulam Floor Beams	Camber equal to dead load plus one quarter live load deflection or no camber.
Bowstring and Pitched Trusses	Only the bottom chord is cambered. For a continuous glulam bottom chord; camber in bottom chord equal to 20mm per 10m (3/4" in 30') of span.
Flat Roof Trusses (Howe and Pratt Roof Trusses (→ 146))	Camber in top and bottom glulam chords equal to 30mm per 10m (1" in 30') of span.

Standard depths for glulam members range from 114mm (4-1/2") to 2128mm (7') or more in increments of 38mm (1-1/2") and 19mm (3/4").

A member made from 38mm (1-1/2") laminations costs significantly less than an equivalent member made from 19mm (3/4") laminations. However, the 19mm (3/4") laminations allow for a greater amount of curvature than do the 38mm (1-1/2") laminations as shown in Table 3.9 (→ 142).

Laminating stock may be end jointed into lengths of up to 40m (130') but the practical limitation may depend on transportation clearance restrictions. Therefore shipping restrictions for a given region should be determined before specifying length, width or shipping height.

For long straight members, glulam is usually manufactured with a built in camber to ensure positive drainage by negating deflection. This ability to provide positive camber is a major advantage of glulam. Recommended cambers are shown in the Table on the opposite page.

Moisture Control

The checking of wood is due to differential shrinkage of the wood fibres in the inner and outer portions of a wood member. Glulam is manufactured from lamstock having a moisture content of 7 to 15 percent. Because this range approximates the moisture conditions for most end uses, checking is minimal in glulam members.

Proper transit, storage and construction methods help to avoid rapid changes in the moisture content of laminated members. Severe moisture content changes can result from the sudden application of heat to buildings under construction in cold weather, or from exposure of unprotected members to alternate wet and dry conditions as might occur during transit and storage.

Canadian glulam routinely receives a coat of protective sealer before shipping and is wrapped for protection during shipping and erection. The wrapping should be left in place as long as possible and ideally until permanent protection from the weather is in place.

During on-site storage, glulam should be stored off the ground with spacer blocks placed between members. If construction delays occur, the wrapping should be cut on the underside to prevent the accumulation of condensation.

Preservative Treatment

Preservative treatment is not often required but should be specified for any application where ground contact is likely. Advice on suitable preservative treatment should be sought from the manufacturer.

Untreated glulam can be used in humid environments such as swimming pools, curling rinks or in industrial buildings which use water in their manufacturing process.

Where the ends of glulam members will be subject to wetting, protective overhangs or flashings should be provided.

In applications where direct water contact is not a factor, a factory applied sealer will prevent large swings in moisture content.

Since wood is corrosion-resistant, glulam is used in many corrosive environments such as salt storage domes and potash warehousing.

Final Trimming and Finishing

With the large specialized equipment present in a glulam plant, it is possible to trim large members to close tolerances which would be difficult to attain under field conditions. Installation of connectors such as shear plates and split rings can be accomplished under factory conditions leaving only minor adjustments for the field.

3

Main Structural Members

Sanding and filling in accordance with the appearance grade specified, and additional staining and varnishing (when specified) can be done in the factory.

When properly designed, glulam members will be erected without the need for field trimming or cutting. If field adjustments are necessary, they should be permitted only with the approval of the designer.

Ordering

When designing large glued-laminated timber structures or members, it is advisable to consult a glulam manufacturer early in the design process. This will result in spacing and configuration recommendations which allow the product to be used to its maximum efficiency and ensure timely delivery. This is especially the case where unusual shapes or very large sizes are required.

Advice on connection design and detailing which may have a substantial effect on overall economy and in-service performance can also be obtained from the manufacturer.

Except for some common sizes held in stock, glulam is custom manufactured. Scheduling should make allowance for shop drawing preparation and review, product manufacture, and shipping.

Delivery should be co-ordinated by both contractor and manufacturer to ensure unloading equipment is available at the job site.

Fire Safety

Because glued-laminated timber is readily manufactured in large sizes, it is often used in Heavy Timber construction to meet minimum size and fire-resistance rating requirements of North American building codes.

Section 10 provides basic information on the minimum sizes and arrangement of glulam members necessary to meet code requirements for Heavy Timber construction. Information is also provided on the means for calculating the fire resistance of glulam beams and columns.

General Guidelines for Glulam

For the best economy and efficiency when ordering glulam members, specifiers should:

- Select the section with the smallest cross-sectional area or the least weight required for the job.

- Use 38mm (1-1/2") laminations and standard depths whenever possible. Use 38mm (1-1/2") laminations in straight members and in all curved members with radius of curvature of 8400mm (27') or more.

- Limit the size of glulam members to those which can be shipped economically and legally. This applies to both lengths and heights, since local overall shipping height limitations, usually about 4 to 6m (14' to 20'),may restrict arch sizes.

- Use the proper appearance grade for the project by matching the appearance and thus the cost premium to the requirements for appearance and visibility.

- In some instances, using larger than necessary members may simplify overall economy by simplifying connection details. Consult manufacturer.

- Minimize the number of concealed or semi-concealed connections which require costly shop fabrication.

- Outline protection measures to be taken during erection to protect the members from damage, including provision for temporary bracing.

- Steel connections should be painted to prevent rust from staining the wood. They should be galvanized for high humidity service conditions.

Reference Tables

Table 3.6 **Commercial Species for Canadian Glulam**	Commercial Species Group Designation	Species in Combination	Wood Characteristics
	Douglas Fir-Larch (D.Fir-L)	Douglas fir, western larch	Woods similar in strength and weight. High degree of hardness and good resistance to decay. Good nail holding, gluing and painting qualities. Colour ranges from reddish-brown to yellowish-white.
	Hem-Fir	Western hemlock, amabilis fir, Douglas fir	Lightwoods that work easily, take paint well and hold nails well. Good gluing characteristics. Colour range is yellow-brown to white.
	Spruce-Pine	Spruce (all species except coast sitka spruce) lodgepole pine, jack pine	Woods of similar characteristics, they work easily, take paint easily and hold nails well. Generally white to pale yellow in colour.

Table 3.7 **Glulam Stress Grades**	Stress Grade		Species	Description
	Bending Grades	20f-E and 20f-Ex	D.Fir-L or Spruce-Pine	Used for members stressed principally in bending (beams) or in combined bending and axial load.
		24f-E and 24f-Ex	D.Fir-L or Hem-Fir	Specify EX when members are subject to positive and negative moments or when members are subject to combined bending and axial load such as arches and truss top chords.
	Compression Grades	16c-E	D.Fir-L	Used for members stressed principally in axial compression, such as columns.
		12c-E	Spruce-Pine	
	Tension Grades	18t-E	D.Fir-L	Used for members stressed principally in axial tension, such as bottom chords of trusses.
		14t-E	Spruce-Pine	

Table 3.8 **Standard Glulam Widths**	Initial width of glulam stock		Finished width of glulam stock	
	mm	in.	mm	in.
	89	3-1/2	80	3
	140	5-1/2	130	5
	184	7-1/4	175	6-7/8
	235 (or 89 + 140)	9-1/4 (or 3-1/2 + 5-1/2)	225 (or 215)	8-7/8 (or 8-1/2)
	286 (or 89 + 184)	11-1/4 (or 3-1/2 + 7-1/4)	275 (or 265)	10-7/8 or 10-1/4
	140 + 184	5-1/2 + 7-1/4	315	12-1/4
	140 + 235	5-1/2 + 9-1/4	365	14-1/4

Notes:
1. Members wider than 365mm (14-1/4") are available in 50mm (2") increments but require a special order.
2. Members wider than 175mm (6-7/8") may consist of two boards laid side by side with longitudinal joints staggered in adjacent laminations.

Reference Tables continued

Table 3.9
Minimum Radius of Curvature for Laminations

Lamination Thickness			Minimum Radius of Curvature			
			Tangent Ends		Curved Ends	
mm	in.		m	ft.-in.	m	ft.-in.
38	1-1/2	Standard	8.4	27'-6"	10.8	35'-6"
19	3/4	Standard	2.8	9'-4"	3.8	12'-6"
35	1-3/8	Non Standard	7.4	24'-3"	9.6	31'-2"
32	1-1/4	Non Standard	6.3	20'-8"	8.5	27'-10"
29	1-1/8	Non Standard	5.6	18'-4"	7.3	24'-0"
25	1	Non Standard	4.6	15'-1"	6.2	20'-4"
16	5/8	Non Standard	2.3	7'-8"	3	9'-10"
13	1/2	Non Standard	1.8	6'-0"	2.2	7'-2"
10	3/8	Non Standard	1.2	4'-0"	1.4	4'-7"
6	1/4	Non Standard	0.8	2'-7"	0.8	2'-7

Notes:
1. For economy, curved members should be designed using standard lamination thicknesses. Members made from 38mm (1-1/2") laminations cost less than an equivalent member made from 19mm (3/4") laminations.
2. Non standard laminations less than 19mm (3/4") thick are made by resurfacing 19mm (3/4") stock which results in more waste material.

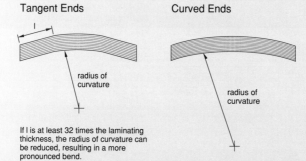

Tangent Ends

radius of curvature

If l is at least 32 times the laminating thickness, the radius of curvature can be reduced, resulting in a more pronounced bend.

Curved Ends

radius of curvature

3.4 Trusses

Introduction

A truss is a structural frame relying on a triangular arrangement of webs and chords to transfer loads to reaction points. The terminology used for trusses is shown in Figure 3.9 below.

Truss shape and size is restricted only by manufacturing capabilities, shipping limitations and handling considerations. Virtually any roof shape or area can be achieved using the unique flexibility of wood trusses. Since all trusses are custom designed, an almost unlimited variety of shapes or loading conditions can be accommodated.

Economy, ease of fabrication, fast delivery and simplified erection procedures make wood trusses competitive in many roof and floor applications. High strength to weight ratios permit long spans offering flexibility in floor layouts by often eliminating the need for interior load bearing walls.

Types of Trusses

Light Frame Trusses
Light frame trusses are made from dimension lumber of various sizes. The chords and webs are connected together by the use of toothed connector plates which transfer the tensile and shear forces. The connector plates are stamped from galva-

3

Main Structural Members

Figure 3.9
Truss Nomenclature

Pitched (triangular) Truss

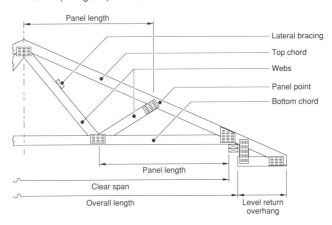

Parallel Chord (flat) Truss

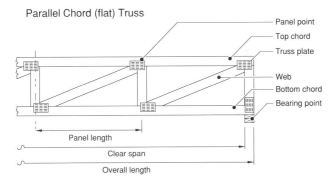

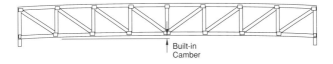

nized steel sheet metal of different grades and gauge thicknesses to provide different grip values. Design of these trusses is usually done by the truss manufacturers using computer software developed by the truss plate manufacturers. Other custom developed structural analysis software is also used.

Light frame trusses are used in a variety of residential and commercial applications. Spans up to 20m (60') are common although longer spans are also feasible. The shape and size of these trusses may be restricted by shipping and handling considerations.

Parallel chord trusses are widely used for floor systems and flat roof systems and are often more economical than open web steel joist systems.

Some types of parallel chord (flat) trusses utilize steel tension members. These composite wood/steel trusses, like most other wood trusses, are generally custom designed. Some examples of flat trusses including composite wood/steel trusses are shown in Figure 3.10 (below).

For estimating minimum depths required in conventional metal connector plated parallel chord trusses, allow a ratio of 1 to 12 for depth of truss to span.

Parallel chord trusses may be supported either at the top or the bottom chord and may be ordered with a built in camber to offset deflection and to provide positive drainage when used as a flat roof system.

Figure 3.10
Types of Parallel Chord Trusses

Wood Truss

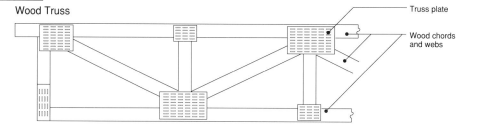

Tension Web Truss

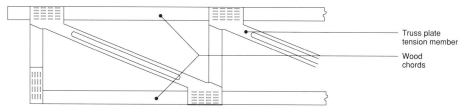

Open Web Truss

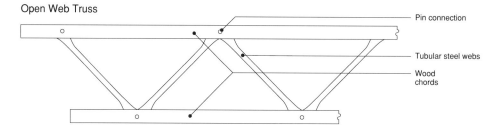

The long span capabilities of flat trusses permit large bay sizes. They reduce the need for intermediate support required for conventional floor joists using dimension lumber, beams or prefabricated wood I-joists.

Electrical, plumbing, heating and air conditioning services may be placed between the truss chords. These particular requirements must be specified for inclusion in the overall design of the truss system.

General information on span, slope and loading conditions is published by the truss fabricators. Due to the wide range in requirements of each construction project, the general information should be used as a guideline for reference purposes only. Specific loadings and other structural requirements must be clearly identified for proper design of any truss system. In designing the appropriate trusses, the truss manufacturer will incorporate these specifications with the architectural requirements.

Heavy Timber Trusses

Heavy timber trusses are made from timbers, or from manufactured wood products, such as glulam or parallel strand lumber (PSL), having the dimensions of timbers. Connections for members are made by using bolts and plates, split rings and special brackets and hangers. Heavy timber trusses provide long spans for applications where the space required for the depth of the trusses can be accommodated into a building plan.

Heavy timber trusses are often used to provide special architectural features such as open vaulted ceilings. They are usually custom designed by structural engineers to be used for roof and floor systems in residential and commercial buildings. They are usually field assembled rather than factory manufactured as in the case of light frame trusses.

Some types of heavy timber trusses, such as the bowstring trusses, use steel tension members for additional strength.

Shapes of Trusses

Trusses can be designed virtually to any shape, limited only to the load arrangement and the support locations.

Figures 3.11 (→ 146, 147) shows a number of standard shapes of light frame trusses which are commonly used in North America.

Heavy trusses can also be designed in a variety of shapes. As these trusses are custom designed, early consultation with a structural engineer is recommended in assessing the feasibility and cost of a proposed design.

Design

Light frame trusses, in almost all cases, are designed by the truss fabricator using specialized software, rather than by a structural engineer.

Computer software is well suited to the numerous, complex, and repetitive calculations required for each member with all the permutations of loads and shapes which are ordered.

Truss manufacturers may have structural engineering capability for ensuring design quality or may engage the services of an engineer to provide quality assurance or to stamp shop drawings when this is a requirement.

Allowable deflection of trusses is generally specified by the building designer or governed by the appropriate codes or building by-laws. Deflection characteristics of trusses are functions of truss type, chord panel length, span between supports, stiffness characteristics of the lumber used, and the size and grade of connector plates used.

Truss manufacturers are able to provide complex and intricate shapes specified by building designers.

3

Main Structural Members

Figure 3.11
**Common
Shapes for
Light Frame
Trusses**

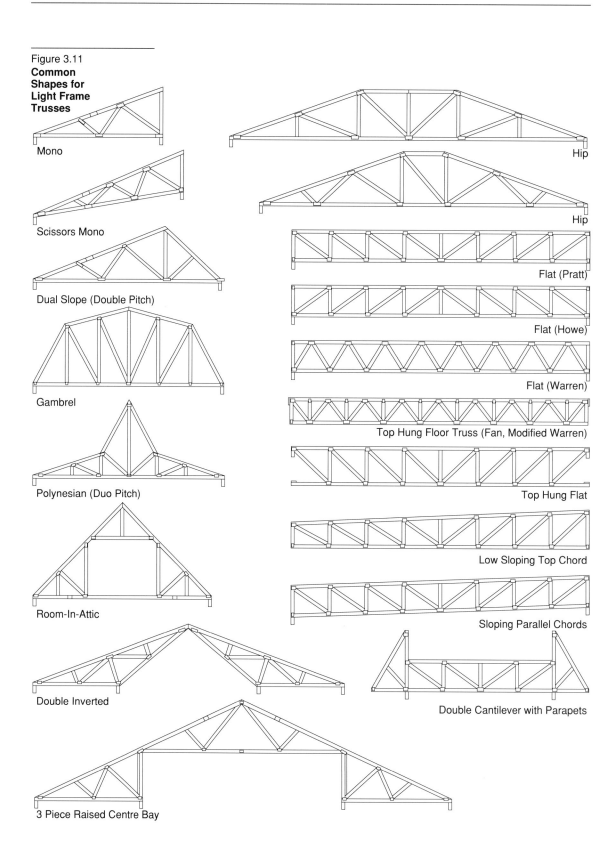

Mono

Scissors Mono

Dual Slope (Double Pitch)

Gambrel

Polynesian (Duo Pitch)

Room-In-Attic

Double Inverted

3 Piece Raised Centre Bay

Hip

Hip

Flat (Pratt)

Flat (Howe)

Flat (Warren)

Top Hung Floor Truss (Fan, Modified Warren)

Top Hung Flat

Low Sloping Top Chord

Sloping Parallel Chords

Double Cantilever with Parapets

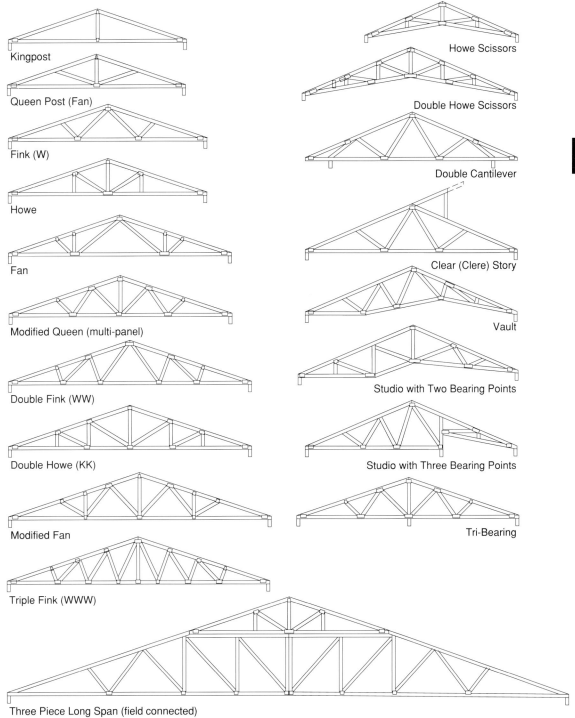

Kingpost

Queen Post (Fan)

Fink (W)

Howe

Fan

Modified Queen (multi-panel)

Double Fink (WW)

Double Howe (KK)

Modified Fan

Triple Fink (WWW)

Three Piece Long Span (field connected)

Howe Scissors

Double Howe Scissors

Double Cantilever

Clear (Clere) Story

Vault

Studio with Two Bearing Points

Studio with Three Bearing Points

Tri-Bearing

3

Main Structural Members

Figure 3.12
**Computer
Generated
Truss
Configuration**

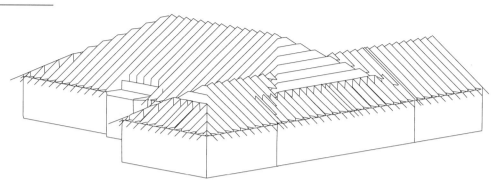

Once the roof shape has been modelled, the truss design software
calculates all member sizes and joint configurations.

The final design of individual trusses is the result of detailed analyses of the specific requirements. As a general rule, the maximum panel length for trusses supporting the dead load of a ceiling is about 3m (10') for 38 x 89mm (2" x 4" nom.) No.2 Spruce-Pine-Fir.

Heavy timber truss design is done by a structural engineer using structural analysis to determine member sizes and connection details.

Materials

The appropriate grade or grades of lumber having the strength qualities required for the design are determined for the truss chords and webs of light frame trusses. The grades used will include Select Structural, No.1, No.2, and MSR lumber of various species and sizes depending on the calculated stresses and truss configurations.

The minimum size of lumber used for residential and commercial building light frame trusses is 38 x 89mm (2" x 4" nom.) and the size of the members increases according to loading and truss spacing.

Prior to the widespread use of metal plates, nailed plywood gusset plates were used to make light frame truss connections and in fact are still acceptable for residential construction.

Today, almost all light frame trusses are connected by means of galvanized steel plates referred to commonly as truss plates or connector plates. The plates are manufactured by high speed stamping machines that punch out the plate teeth, and shear the plate to required size. Many sizes and gauges of connector plates are manufactured to suit a variety of joint geometries and loadings. The metal plates permit the plant fabrication of trusses having consistent and dependable engineering properties.

The metal connector plate transfers loads between adjoining members through the connector plate teeth. The connector plate strength is dependent on the grip of the teeth and the shear and tensile capacity of the steel plate. The plate is prevented from deforming during installation, and the minimum tooth penetration must be maintained, as monitored by the manufacturer's quality assurance personnel.

Truss plates are usually stamped from 16, 18 or 20 gauge (US Standard Gauge) sheet steel, in widths of 25mm (1") to 250mm (10") and lengths up to 600mm (2') or even longer. Stamping results in teeth with dimensions varying from about 6mm (1/4") to 25mm (1") or holes may be provided for nail-on application.

Nail-on plates are usually assembled by the builder on the site and are sometimes used to join separate halves of a split truss.

The material selection for heavy timber trusses will be based on engineering design requirements. Species and grades for sawn timber must be suitable for the design loads. Similar principles are also applicable where glulam or parallel strand lumber (PSL) members are used in a truss configuration.

Split ring or shear plate timber connectors and custom designed connectors and hangers may be used for heavy timber trusses. Currently, the feasibility of using pre-manufactured truss plates for heavy timber trusses is being examined.

Manufacture

The factory manufacture of light frame trusses is demonstrated in Figure 3.13 (below). Heavy timber trusses, due to their size, are usually site assembled from members which have been shop prepared for connection or which have been prepared on site.

The computer design of light frame trusses results in the generation of fabrication instructions which indicate the precise cutting patterns for each of the members and the type, size, and location of connector plates required.

A layout template is made for each configuration to ensure that like trusses are identical in dimension. The member pieces are cut to correct dimension and assembled in the template which is located on a floor or heavy table.

The pieces are cut and arranged using a template. Identical truss plates are placed directly opposite each other on opposing faces and are pressed into the wood members using hydraulic platen presses or rollers.

When the pressing of the plates has been completed, the trusses are checked for dimension and plate tooth penetration and moved to a storage area.

3

Main Structural Members

Figure 3.13
Manufacture of Light Frame Trusses

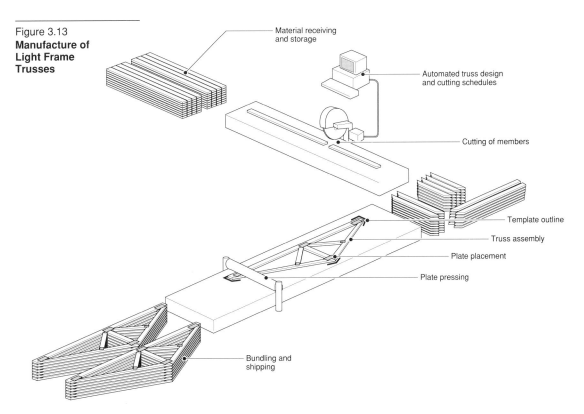

Material receiving and storage

Automated truss design and cutting schedules

Cutting of members

Template outline

Truss assembly

Plate placement

Plate pressing

Bundling and shipping

The completed trusses are then strapped together and placed in the storage yard in preparation for shipping.

Quality control

Criteria for design and use of light frame trusses is based on building code and engineering standard requirements. For example, in Canada, design is governed by the National Building Code of Canada and by *CSA O86 Engineering Design in Wood*. In the US, the model building codes, the *National Design Specification*, and the Truss Plate Institute's Standards govern design and quality control requirements.

In addition to the mandatory requirements for truss design and inspection established by code, many truss manufacturers belong to truss manufacturing associations which conduct on-site audits of design, manufacturing and handling procedures.

It is important that building designers review all truss drawings and installations to ensure that trusses are properly constructed and erected.

Design

The design of light frame trusses is usually based on structural analysis software developed by the truss plate manufacturers to reflect the engineering characteristics of the plates used by a given fabricator.

The approval and acceptance process of truss design drawings depends on the local requirements. In many jurisdictions, a professional engineer's stamp on the truss fabrication drawings may be compulsory. In some cases, the designer's certification may be acceptable. In either case, the truss manufacturer can arrange for these provisions.

Preliminary discussion of a design with a truss fabricator may result in suggestions leading to the most efficient and the most cost effective design. Input from this process will assist in the development of structural drawings by the building designer and the specification of loading, spacing, span, support, and spatial information. The truss fabricator's would then provide trusses in accordance with these specifications.

Truss design shop drawings showing member sizing and configuration, connector plate sizes, lumber species and grades, loads, lateral bracing requirements and all calculated values are generated for approval prior to manufacturing.

Demand for light frame trusses has fostered the development of a fabricating industry with sophisticated computerized design and manufacturing systems. However, trusses remain a building component which may require the direct participation of a structural engineer.

Span Capabilities

The span capability of light frame trusses is dependent upon the style of truss, the spacing of the truss members, the size and grade of the lumber used, and the properties of the plates used.

There are several truss plate manufacturers with whom a truss manufacturer can have a license agreement for the use of plates. Because the plate capacity varies from one manufacturer to another, truss capacities are not necessarily transferrable from one truss fabricator to another.

Tables 3.10 ($\rightarrow$ 158), 3.11 ($\rightarrow$ 159), 3.12 ($\rightarrow$ 160), and 3.13 ($\rightarrow$ 160) give some sample spans for parallel chord and pitched trusses. This information gives an indication of the types of spans possible but does not apply to all trusses or truss fabricators. For specific information, contact a local fabricator.

The span capabilities of heavy trusses should be discussed with a structural engineer.

Handling and Installing Trusses

Individual trusses, although very rigid in the vertical plane, have very little lateral strength or resistance to twisting, and do not develop their ultimate strength until bracing and sheathing installation is complete. They can be easily damaged or broken if they are stressed in the lateral direction.

Proper procedures must be followed in the handling, positioning and bracing of individual trusses. Some proper arrangements for lifting and handling of individual trusses are shown in Figure 3.14 (→ 152).

If trusses are to be stockpiled prior to erection, sufficient bearing points and/or bracing must be provided to prevent excessive lateral bending or overturning.

If truss plates are found to be separated from the wood member, or loose joints have resulted from improper teeth penetration, under no circumstances should the loose plate be hammered back into position. This is because the grip values of the truss plate and the integrity of the lumber are likely to be affected. If corrective repair measures are required, a structural engineer must be involved in identifying remedial measures.

Permanent and Temporary Truss Bracing

Although very strong in relation to their weight, light frame trusses are slender members subject to buckling until the combined action of permanent bracing, and diaphragm action from the installation of sheathing, come into effect. To allow the trusses to act together as a structural unit, during installation and as a completed system, temporary and permanent bracing is required.

Temporary Bracing

Temporary bracing is the support required during erection to enable the truss assembly to withstand the gravity forces of its own weight, to resist wind loads to which it might be exposed to during construction, and to support temporary construction dead loads such as the weight of sheathing and roofing materials.

Permanent bracing is required for the structure to withstand design live and dead loads, to maintain the proper spacing, to distribute loading to adjacent trusses and to spread lateral forces to diaphragms, shearwalls, or other structural supports.

Proper inspection is required to ensure that all temporary and permanent bracing is installed as specified.

Most truss system failures occur during or immediately after erection. In the case of roof trusses, the cause of almost all failures is due to inadequate temporary bracing, required to stabilize the trusses until all permanent bracing, roof purlins and roof sheathing is installed and adequately fastened in place.

When such a failure occurs, it usually takes place in one of two ways:

- The trusses fall over because they have not been adequately tied to the supporting structure or to each other. This type is called a domino or toppling failure.

- Before bracing or sheathing has been installed, the top chords of the trusses are subject to compressive loads from their own weight and buckle sideways.

It is crucial that the first truss erected be braced in such a manner that it can be used as an anchor for supporting subsequent trusses until bracing can be installed. This may be accomplished by erecting a single truss against one or more bracing frames, as shown in Figure 3.15a (→ 153), or, if lifting equipment permits, by preassembling several trusses complete with bracing and lifting the structural unit into place, to act as a brace to which other trusses can be affixed.

3

Main Structural Members

Figure 3.14
**Handling and
Installing
Trusses**

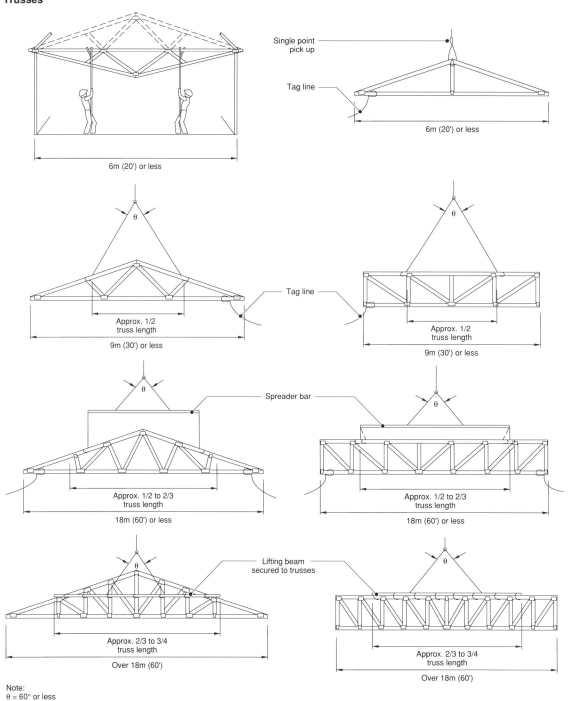

Single point
pick up

Tag line

6m (20') or less

6m (20') or less

θ

Tag line

Approx. 1/2
truss length

9m (30') or less

θ

Approx. 1/2
truss length

9m (30') or less

θ

Spreader bar

Approx. 1/2 to 2/3
truss length

18m (60') or less

θ

Approx. 1/2 to 2/3
truss length

18m (60') or less

θ

Lifting beam
secured to trusses

Approx. 2/3 to 3/4
truss length

Over 18m (60')

θ

Approx. 2/3 to 3/4
truss length

Over 18m (60')

Note:
θ = 60° or less

The trusses become a temporary structural unit when lateral bracing is in place in the planes of the top and bottom chords to prevent chord buckling, and when cross bracing is installed in the vertical plane between trusses (see Figure 3.15a below and 3.15b → 154) to prevent toppling. Without bracing in all these locations, temporary bracing is incomplete, and either of the failures outlined previously could occur.

The spacing of lateral braces (temporary purlins) should be from 1.8m (6') to 3m (10') with the smaller spacing used on longer spans.

Temporary vertical cross bracing should be no less than 38 x 89mm (2" x 4" nom.)

nailed at each intersection with no less than two 75mm (3") nails. Lateral bracing can be 19 x 89mm (1" x 4" nom.) members fastened with two 65mm (2-1/2") nails at each intersection where trusses are spaced at 600mm (2') or less. Wider spacing requires the use of 38 x 89mm (2" x 4" nom.) lateral braces.

The loads resulting from temporary storage of building materials can be substantial for an incomplete structure and could far exceed the design capacity of the finished structure. For example a 600mm (2') high stack of sheathing panels weighs in the order of 1000kg (2,200 lbs.). For this reason, the quantity of material stored on an incomplete light frame truss structure should be carefully monitored.

3

Main Structural Members

Figure 3.15a
Temporary and Permanent Bracing

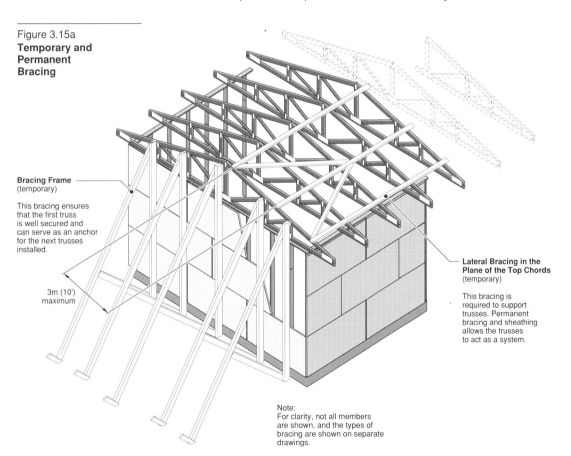

Bracing Frame (temporary)

This bracing ensures that the first truss is well secured and can serve as an anchor for the next trusses installed.

3m (10') maximum

Lateral Bracing in the Plane of the Top Chords (temporary)

This bracing is required to support trusses. Permanent bracing and sheathing allows the trusses to act as a system.

Note:
For clarity, not all members are shown, and the types of bracing are shown on separate drawings.

Figure 3.15b
**Temporary and
Permanent
Bracing**

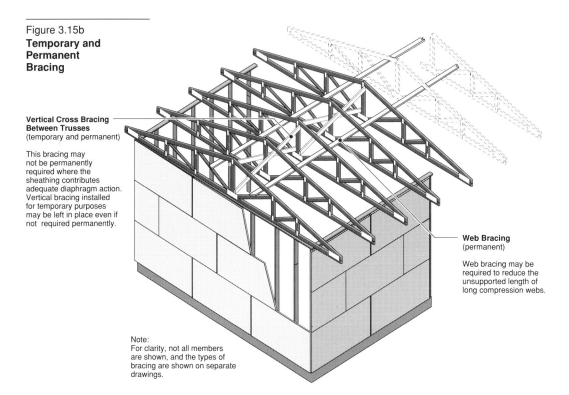

**Vertical Cross Bracing
Between Trusses**
(temporary and permanent)

This bracing may
not be permanently
required where the
sheathing contributes
adequate diaphragm action.
Vertical bracing installed
for temporary purposes
may be left in place even if
not required permanently.

Web Bracing
(permanent)

Web bracing may be
required to reduce the
unsupported length of
long compression webs.

Note:
For clarity, not all members
are shown, and the types of
bracing are shown on separate
drawings.

Figure 3.15c
**Temporary and
Permanent
Bracing**

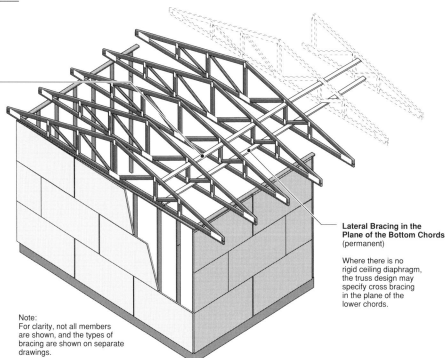

**Lateral Bracing in the
Plane of the Top Chords**
(permanent)

Top chord permanent bracing
may not be required if
sheathing provides adequate
diaphragm action.
Where it is required, the
temporary bracing should
be installed on the underside
of the top chords and left
permanently to forgo the need
of removing temorary bracing
from the top of the chords,
only to have to relocate to
the underside.

**Lateral Bracing in the
Plane of the Bottom Chords**
(permanent)

Where there is no
rigid ceiling diaphragm,
the truss design may
specify cross bracing
in the plane of the
lower chords.

Note:
For clarity, not all members
are shown, and the types of
bracing are shown on separate
drawings.

Permanent Bracing

Permanent bracing is specified by the truss fabricator and indicated on the shop drawings based on the assumptions that:

- Trusses are vertical
- Truss chords are straight
- Chords are laterally supported by sheathing, purlins and bracing.
- Trusses are properly spaced.
- Compression webs are braced as required on the drawing.

If the trusses are installed in such a manner that one or more of these conditions are not met, the truss system will not have the designed structural capability.

It is the responsibility of the contractor to ensure that all permanent bracing specified on the truss design drawing is properly installed.

Permanent bracing can be divided into four main types:

1. Vertical Cross Bracing between Trusses

   This type of bracing as shown in Figure 3.15b (→ 154) is required at the ends of bottom chord bearing flat trusses to maintain truss alignment and to transfer shear loads between the roof diaphragm and the side walls of the building.
   Pitched trusses up to 12m (40') in length may not require permanent bracing in the vertical plane between trusses if adequate roof and ceiling diaphragm action exists.

2. Web Bracing

   Provision of lateral restraint for long compression webs as shown in Figure 3.15b (→ 154) allows these members to carry much more load than they could otherwise carry before buckling.
   Because a uniform load on the roof will initiate some tendency for long compression webs to buckle, forces can be developed in the lateral brace which will cause all of the webs tied together to tend to buckle in the same direction, carrying the lateral brace with them. Thus, the lateral brace must be stabilized by bracing it to the roof or ceiling

diaphragm by means of vertical cross bracing located at intervals along the length of the building.

3. Lateral Bracing in the Planes of the Top Chords

   Bracing in the plane of the top chord as shown in Figure 3.15c (→ 154) is used to prevent lateral movement of the top chord. Where adequate diaphragm action is developed, permanent top chord bracing may not be required. This issue requires engineering design and inspection.

4. Lateral Bracing in the Plane of the Bottom Chords

   This bracing as shown in Figure 3.15c (→ 154) is required where there is no rigid ceiling diaphragm for open ended buildings and any other buildings where there is no bearing support on the end walls to carry wind loads to the roof and foundation. This bracing allows the roof assembly to resist lateral forces.
   It is also used to provide lateral support for the bottom chord to resist buckling in the event of a reversal of stress due to wind uplift or unequal floor loading. The spacing of lateral braces must be specified by the truss designer where the bottom chord is not held in alignment by a rigid ceiling diaphragm.

Truss Uplift

Trusses installed in situations where the bottom chord is isolated from moisture changes by insulation may be susceptible to truss uplift. The bottom chords of trusses are buried in insulation and remain warm and dry whereas the top chords are exposed to moisture fluctuations.

This phenomenon is called roof truss uplift and may cause separation cracks between a ceiling and partition.

In situations where differential moisture conditions between the top and bottom chords are expected, a slip joint detail can be used to allow for movement without damage to interior finish as shown in Figure 3.16 (→ 156).

3

Main Structural Members

Fire Safety

Light Frame Trusses

Similar to dimension lumber, light frame trusses are used in floor and roof assemblies. The North American building codes permit the use of these trusses in many types of multi-storey buildings while providing the required degree of fire safety. In most cases, the codes require that the assemblies which incorporate these light frame members be protected from fire by affixing gypsum wallboard to the underside of the assembly.

Section 10 outlines the code requirements for fire safety and height and area potential for buildings making use of light frame trusses. As well, details are provided on how to calculate the fire-resistance rating of floor and roof assemblies made of plate-connected wood trusses.

Heavy Timber Trusses

Heavy timber trusses, provided their members meet the minimum size requirements, qualify under the codes as Heavy Timber construction.

Like glulam and timber members, when of adequate cross section, heavy timber trusses often exhibit superior fire resistance relative to lighter wood-frame systems. The codes acknowledge this by either equating Heavy Timber construction to protected Wood-Frame construction or by assigning additional building height and area allowances.

Section 10 provides basic information on the minimum sizes and arrangement of heavy timber truss members necessary to meet code requirements for Heavy Timber construction.

Figure 3.16
Truss Uplift

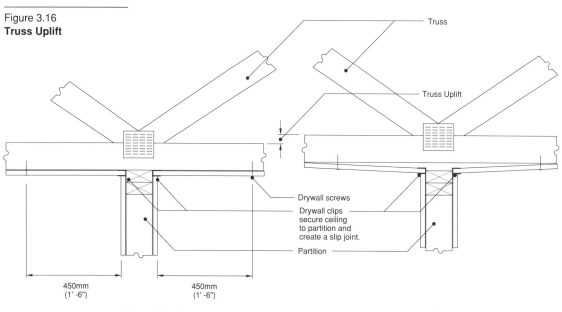

Truss in Normal Position

Truss in Uplifted Position
(exaggerated)

General Guidelines for Trusses

Light Frame Trusses

- Discuss unusual truss configurations with a fabricator.

- Provide the truss fabricator with the following information:

  - The length of the bottom chord (nominal span).

  - The horizontal distance from the end of the bottom chord to the bottom edge of the top chord (overhang length).

  - Number of trusses required. (Trusses are most often spaced at 400 or 600mm (16" or 24") centres).

  - Top and bottom chord live and dead loads.

- Type of cut for the end of the top chord.

- Type of gable end if applicable.

- Roof Slope.

- Soffit framing detail.

- Type of truss required.

- Special requirements such as cantilevers and girders.

- Request and review shop drawings.

Heavy Timber Trusses

- Review heavy timber truss requirements with a structural engineer early in the project.

- Select fastener type and arrangement which satisfies the appearance for trusses exposed to view (see Section 5).

3

Main Structural Members

Floor Trusses

Reference Tables

Table 3.10 **Sample Spans for Parallel-Chord Floor Trusses**	Chord Size		Total Load		Depth		Sample Spans	
	mm	in. (nom.)	kN/m²	psf	mm	in.	m	ft.
	64 x 38, 89 x 38	3 x 2, 4 x 2	2.6	55	250	10	4.0 - 5.5	13 - 18
	38 x 89	2 x 4	3.6	75	400	16	5.5 - 6.5	18 - 21
					600	24	6.5 - 9.0	21 - 30
					800	32	7.0 - 10.5	23 - 35
			5.7	120	400	16	4.5 - 5.5	15 - 18
					600	24	5.0 -7.5	16 - 25
					800	32	4.5 - 8.0	15 - 26
	38 x 140	2 x 6	3.6	75	600	24	8.0 - 9.5	26 - 31
					800	32	9.5 - 12.0	31 - 40
					1400	56	12.5 - 15.0	41 - 50
			5.7	120	600	24	6.5 - 8.0	21 - 26
					800	32	7.5 - 10.0	25 - 33
					1400	56	10.0 - 14.0	33 - 46
	38 x 184	2 x 8	3.6	75	700	28	9.5 - 11.5	31 - 38
					900	36	11.0 - 14.0	36 - 46
					1600	64	15+	50.0+
			5.7	120	700	28	7.5 - 9.5	25 - 31
					900	36	9.0 - 11.5	30 - 38
					1600	64	12.0 - 15.0	40 - 50

Notes:
1. Deflection: L/360 under total specified load.
2. Based on a spacing of 400mm (16") and typical lumber values.
3. Light frame truss spans and capacities vary. Refer to a local manufacturer for specific values.

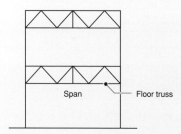

Span — Floor truss

Roof Trusses

Reference Tables continued

Table 3.11	Chord Size		Total Load		Depth		Sample Spans	
Sample Spans for Parallel-Chord Roof Trusses	mm	in. (nom.)	kN/m²	psf	mm	in.	m	ft.
	38 x 89	2 x 4	1.8	38	400	16	6.5 - 7.5	21 - 25
					800	32	8.5 - 12.5	28 - 41
			2.4	50	400	16	6.0 - 7.5	20 - 25
					800	32	7.5 - 10.5	25 - 35
			3.3	69	400	16	5.0 - 6.5	16 - 21
					800	32	6.5 - 9.5	21 - 31
			4.4	92	400	16	4.5 - 5.5	15 - 18
					800	32	4.5 - 8.0	15 - 26
	38 x 140	2 x 6	1.8	38	600	24	10.0 - 12.5	33 - 41
					1400	56	16.5 - 20.0	54 - 60
			2.4	50	600	24	8.5 - 11.0	28 - 36
					1400	56	14.0 - 17.5	46 - 57
			3.3	69	600	24	7.5 - 9.5	25 - 31
					1400	56	11.5 - 15.0	38 - 50
			4.4	92	600	24	6.0 - 8.5	20 - 28
					1400	56	9.0 - 13.0	30 - 43
	38 x 184	2 x 8	1.8	38	700	28	12.0 - 14.5	40 - 48
					1600	64	20.0+	60+
			2.4	50	700	28	10.5 - 13.0	35 - 43
					1600	64	20.0+	60+
			3.3	69	700	28	9.0 - 11.0	30 - 36
					1600	64	14.5 - 18.0	48 - 59
			4.4	92	700	28	7.5 - 10.0	25 - 33
					1600	64	11.5 - 15.5	38 - 51

Notes:
1. Deflection: L/360 under total specified load.
2. Based on a spacing of 600mm (24") and typical lumber properties.
3. Light frame truss spans and capacities vary. Refer to a local manufacturer for specific values.

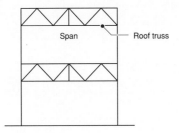

Span   Roof truss

Roof Trusses

Reference Tables continued

Table 3.12 **Sample Spans for Mono Sloped Trusses**	Chord Size mm	in. (nom.)	Total Load kN/m²	psf	Sample Spans m	ft.
	38 x 89	2 x 4	1.8	38	8.5 - 10.0	28 - 33
			2	42	8.0 - 9.5	26 - 31
			2.3	48	7.5 - 9.0	25 - 30
			2.7	56	6.5 - 8.5	21 - 28
			3.1	65	6.0 - 8.0	20 - 26
			3.8	79	5.5 - 7.0	18 - 23

Notes:
1. Deflection: L/360 under total specified load.
2. Top chord slope 4/12.
3. Based on spacing of 600mm (24") and typical lumber properties.
4. Light frame truss spans and capacities vary. Refer to a local manufacturer for specific values and for values for larger chord sizes.

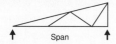

Span

Table 3.13 **Sample Spans for Common Sloped Trusses**	Chord Size mm	in. (nom.)	Total Load kN/m²	psf	Sample Spans m	ft.
	38 x 89	2 x 4	1.8	38.0	12.5 - 16.5	41 - 54
			2	42.0	11.0 - 15.5	36 - 51
			2.3	48.0	10.0 - 14.5	33 - 48
			2.7	56.0	9.0 - 13.0	30 - 43
			3.1	65.0	8.0 - 12.0	26 - 40
			3.8	79.0	7.0 - 10.5	23 - 35

Notes:
1. Deflection: L/360 under total specified load.
2. Top chord slope 4/12.
3. Based on spacing of 600mm (24") and typical lumber properties.
4. Light frame truss spans and capacities vary. Refer to a local manufacturer for specific values and for values for larger chord sizes.

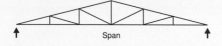

Span

3.5   Parallel Strand Lumber (PSL)

Introduction

Parallel strand lumber (PSL) is a high strength structural composite lumber product manufactured by gluing strands of wood together under pressure. It is a proprietary product marketed under the trade name Parallam®.

Because it is a glued-manufactured product, PSL can be made in long lengths but it is usually limited to 20m (66 ft.) by transportation constraints.

Manufactured at a moisture content of 11 percent, which is approximately the equilibrium moisture content of wood in most service conditions, PSL is less prone to shrinking, warping , cupping, bowing or splitting.

It is manufactured in Canada from Douglas fir and in the United States from southern pine from wood strands from which the growth imperfections have been removed. This results in product having consistent properties and high load carrying ability. As smaller plantation and second growth timber finds its way into the market place to a greater extent, PSL provides a means of ensuring the availability of a large dimension and high quality wood product.

The manufacturing process for PSL results in a strong, consistent material that is resistant to seasoning stresses.

Engineering standards in Canada and the US refer to PSL and laminated veneer lumber (LVL) together as structural composite lumber (SCL).

Uses

PSL is well suited for use as beams and columns, for post and beam construction, and for beams, headers, and lintels for light framing construction.

It is used for large members in residential construction and as intermediate and large members in commercial building construction.

Visually, PSL is an attractive material which is suited to applications where finished appearance is important. It is also suited to concealed structural applications where appearance is not a factor.

Sizes Available

The stock sizes available for PSL are intended to be compatible with established wood framing materials and standard dimensions. Stock PSL sizes for beams and columns are shown in Table 3.14 (→ 164).

PSL beams are sold in thicknesses of 45mm (1-3/4"), 68mm (2-11/16"), 89mm (3-1/2"), 133mm (5-1/4"), and 178mm (7"). The smaller thicknesses can be used individually as single plies or can be combined for multi-ply applications.

PSL can be ordered in lengths up to 20m (66 ft.). Although it can be sawn to any dimension, its economy is maximized in uses where light to medium steel sections are practical.

High design values, a multitude of cross sections, and long lengths permit flexibility in building design.

Manufacture

The initial steps of PSL manufacture as shown in Figure 3.17 (→ 162) are similar to those used in the manufacture of plywood as shown in Figure 4.2 (→ 192). Logs are turned on a lathe to create veneer and the veneer sheets are oven dried.

The veneer sheets are clipped into long narrow strands of wood up to 2.4m (8') in length and about 13mm (1/2") in width. Major strength reducing defects are removed from the sheets.

The strands are coated completely with an exterior-type adhesive (phenol-formalde-hyde), laid-up with the strands oriented to the length of the member, and formed into a continuous billet which is fed into a belt press. Under pressure and microwave generated heat, the glue is cured to produce a finished continuous billet 280 x 406mm (11" x 16") in cross-section.

3

Main Structural Members

Figure 3.17
**Manufacture of
Parallel Strand
Lumber**

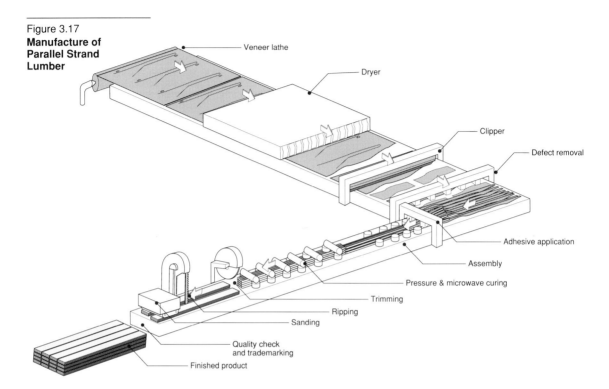

Veneer lathe

Dryer

Clipper

Defect removal

Adhesive application

Assembly

Pressure & microwave curing

Trimming

Ripping

Sanding

Quality check
and trademarking

Finished product

The billet is cross cut to desired lengths, rip sawn to produce rough stock dimensions or custom sizes, and sanded down to finish dimensions. Larger dimensions are produced by edge gluing billets together using techniques common to those used for the manufacture of glulam.

Quality Control

The PSL manufacturing process includes tight controls on the raw material inputs, product assembly, and finished product properties to ensure a consistent , high quality, reliable product. Because the process involves the removal of strength reducing defects from the wood strands, the main quality control procedure is the checking for consistent density in the finished product.

Process control is monitored by resident quality control testing and quality assurance inspections are made by the American Plywood Association (APA). APA monitoring includes random checks of process parameters and testing procedures, and review of test results.

Testing of the glue bond quality and the mechanical properties is done daily and complemented by more stringent tests of each day's production at the APA laboratory.

PSL is a proprietary product which has been evaluated and accepted for use by the Canadian Construction Materials Centre (CCMC) and by the Council of American Building Officials (CABO).

A standard for the manufacture of PSL (and other structural composite materials such as laminated veneer lumber (LVL)) is under development by ASTM. This standard will outline procedures for establishing, monitoring and re-evaluating structural capacities of structural composite lumber and will also detail minimum requirements for establishment of quality control, assurance and audit.

Strength and Appearance

Parallel strand lumber exhibits the dark glue line of glue-laminated timber except that the glue lines are much more numerous.

PSL can be machined, stained, and finished using the techniques applicable to sawn lumber.

Differing slightly from the finished appearance of sawn lumber or glulam, PSL retains the rich textures displayed by wood products used for exposed structure, as in post and beam construction.

The appearance of PSL allows for the structural members to be designed to view so that both functional and aesthetic design needs can be met. PSL members readily accept stain to enhance the warmth and texture of wood.

All PSL is sanded at the tail end of the production process to ensure precise dimensions and to provide a high quality surface for appearance.

PSL readily accepts preservative treatment and a very high degree of penetration and therefore protection is possible. Treated PSL should be specified for members which will be directly exposed to high humidity conditions.

Connections

Common wood connectors appropriate to the size of the members are used for PSL. These range from nails and joist hangers for the smallest sections to bolts, split rings, and shear plates for larger sized members (see Section 5).

As for all wood materials and in fact all major building materials, galvanized connections should be used for high humidity applications.

Fire Safety

Research conducted to measure the performance of PSL when exposed to fire demonstrates that it is appropriate for use in all applications for which solid sawn lumber and timbers are suited.

As a result of evaluations done in Canada by the Canadian Construction Materials Center (CCMC) and in the US by the Council of American Building Officials (CABO), PSL has been accepted for use in Heavy Timber construction when of appropriate cross section. Like timbers and glulam members, PSL of large cross section has proven to be resistant to fire because the low thermal conductivity of wood retards heat penetration, and slow charring rates allow these large members to maintain a high percentage of their original section.

Section 10 provides further information on building code requirements relating to fire safety and details the minimum size requirements for Heavy Timber construction.

General Guidelines for PSL

- Determine the load capacity required.

- Select size of PSL member which will meet the required load capacity.

- Ask the local distributor for technical literature and contact the manufacturer if engineering assistance is required.

- Determine if PSL members will be directly exposed to weathering or high temperature and high humidity for significant periods during the life of the structure. If so, consult with the manufacturer for information about preservative treatment.

- Check local availability for sizes and lengths.

- PSL is a patented product manufactured in both Canada and the US. For additional product information or technical information, contact MacMillan Bloedel Limited.

3

Main Structural Members

Reference Table

Table 3.14	Beams	Size (b x d)	
Typical Dimensions of Parallel Strand Lumber (PSL)		mm	in.
		45 x 241	1-3/4 x 9-1/2
		45 x 292	1-3/4 x 11-1/2
		45 x 318	1-3/4 x 12-1/2
		45 x 356	1-3/4 x 14
		89 x 241	3-1/2 x 9-1/2
		89 x 292	3-1/2 x 11-1/2
		89 x 318	3-1/2 x 12-1/2
		89 x 356	3-1/2 x 14
		89 x 406	3-1/2 x 16
		89 x 457	3-1/2 x 18
		133 x 241	5-1/4 x 9-1/2
		133 x 292	5-1/4 x 11-1/2
		133 x 318	5-1/4 x 12-1/2
		133 x 356	5-1/4 x 14
		133 x 406	5-1/4 x 16
		133 x 457	5-1/4 x 18
		178 x 241	7 x 9-1/2
		178 x 292	7 x 11-1/2
		178 x 318	7 x 12-1/2
		178 x 356	7 x 14
		178 x 406	7 x 16
		178 x 457	7 x 18
	Columns		
		89 x 89	3-1/2 x 3-1/2
		89 x 133	3-1/2 x 5-1/4
		89 x 178	3-1/2 x 7
		133 x 133	5-1/4 x 5-1/4
		133 x 178	5-1/4 x 7
		178 x 178	7 x 7

3.6   Laminated Veneer Lumber (LVL)

Introduction

Laminated veneer lumber (LVL) is a layered composite of wood veneers and adhesive. Once it is fabricated into billets of various thicknesses and widths, it can be cut at the factory into stock for headers and beams, flanges for prefabricated wood I-joists, or for other specific uses. Veneer thicknesses range from 2.5mm (0.10") to 4.8mm (3/16") and common species are Douglas fir, larch and southern yellow pine.

The distinguishing difference between LVL and plywood is in the orientation of the plies as shown in Figure 3.18 (→ 166). Plywood is cross-laminated, meaning that the grain of each veneer layer runs at 90 degrees to adjacent layers. This enables the panel to be relatively strong in both the wide and narrow directions when loaded on the sheathing face. However, when loaded on the edge as a beam, plywood is not as strong as the same cross section of LVL because not all of the plies are longitudinal to the beam.

In LVL, the grain of each layer of veneer runs in the same (long) direction with the result that it is strong when edge loaded as a beam or face loaded as a plank. This kind of lamination is called parallel-lamination, and it produces a material with greater uniformity and predictability than the same dimension material made by cross-lamination.

LVL is a solid, highly predictable, uniform lumber product because natural defects such as knots, slope of grain and splits have been dispersed throughout the material or have been removed altogether. It is made of dried and graded veneer which is coated with waterproof adhesives, assembled in an arranged pattern, and formed into billets by curing in a heated press.

One leading manufacturer grades the veneers with advanced ultrasonic grading technology in addition to visual grading. Dependent on the end use of the LVL product the ultrasonically graded veneers are specifically located in the material to utilize efficiently the strength characteristics of the veneer grades. For example, if the end use of the LVL product is scaffold plank, the higher grade veneers will be placed at the outer faces of the plank.

LVL was first used during World War II to make airplane propellers, and since the mid-1970s, has been available as a construction product for beams and headers where high strength, dimensional stability, and reliability are required.

Like other products made by laminating pieces of wood together to create a structural element such as plywood, glulam, parallel strand lumber (PSL), or OSB/waferboard, LVL offers the advantages of higher reliability and lower variability through defect removal and dispersal.

The veneering and gluing process of LVL enables large members to be made from relatively small trees thereby providing for efficient utilization of wood fibre.

Engineering standards in Canada and the US refer to LVL and parallel strand lumber (PSL) together as structural composite lumber (SCL).

Uses

LVL is used primarily as structural framing for residential and commercial construction and is well suited to applications where open web steel joists and light steel beams might be considered.

Other uses include scaffold planking and as flange members for some proprietary prefabricated wood I-joists.

LVL has also been used as distribution and transmission cross arms in utility structures, box shaped roadway sign posts, and as truckbed decking with hardwood face veneers.

LVL can easily be cut to length at the jobsite. The fastening and connection details and requirements are similar to those of solid sawn lumber. However, all special cutting, notching or drilling should be done in accordance with manufacturer's recommendations.

3

Main Structural Members

Figure 3.18
**Ply Orientation
of LVL**

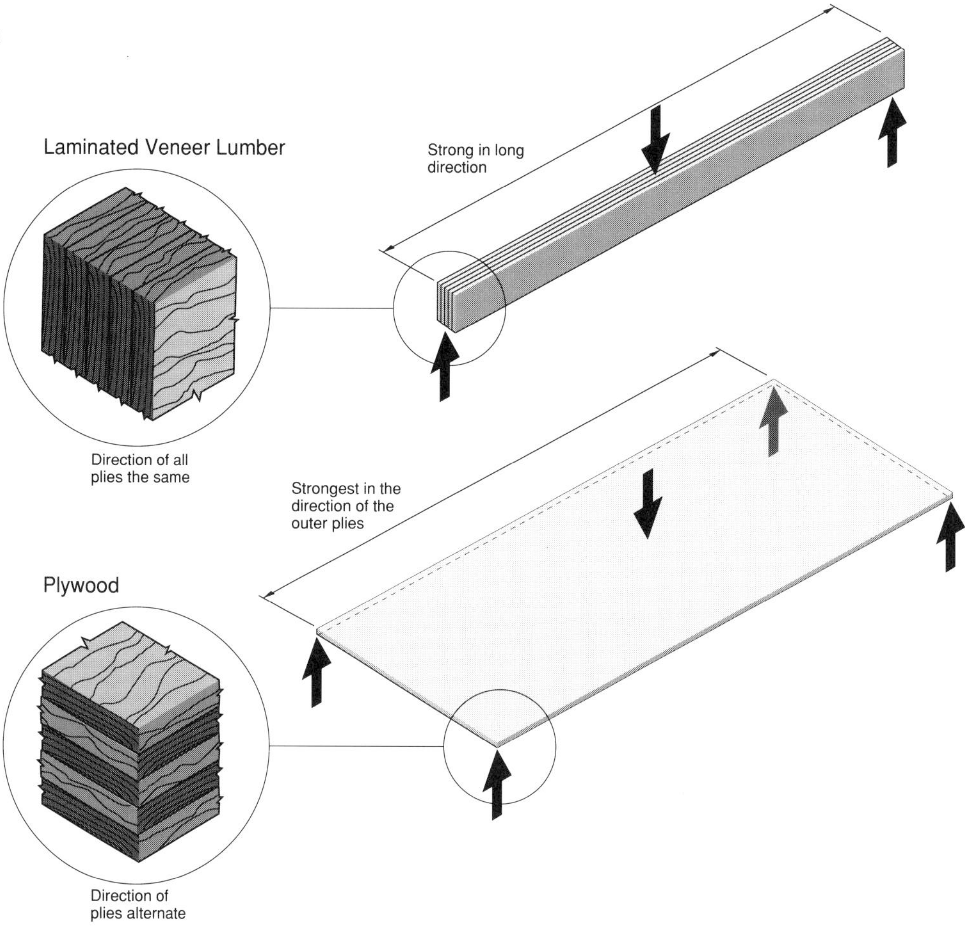

Laminated Veneer Lumber

Strong in long
direction

Direction of all
plies the same

Strongest in the
direction of the
outer plies

Plywood

Direction of
plies alternate

Manufacture

A schematic diagram of the manufacture of LVL is shown in Figure 3.19 (opposite).

The initial steps of manufacture of LVL are similar to those used in the manufacture of plywood. Typically, logs are rotary peeled on a lathe to create veneer sheets from 2.5mm (1/10") up to 4.8mm (3/16") in thickness. Veneer sheets are generally about 2640mm (104") long by either 1320mm (52") or 660mm (26") wide.

The veneer sheets are dried, clipped to remove major strength reducing defects, and graded. The sheets are cut to the required width for the billet to be produced.

The individual veneers are then assembled with the grain of all veneers running in the long direction of the billet. End joints between individual pieces of veneer are staggered along the length of the billet to disperse any remaining strength reducing defects. The joints may be scarf jointed or overlapped for some distance to provide load transfer.

Figure 3.19
**Manufacture of
LVL**

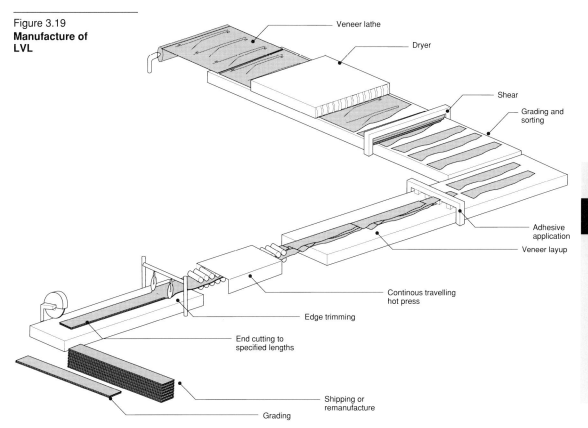

The veneer lengths are coated with a waterproof phenol-formaldehyde resin adhesive. The assembled billets are subjected simultaneously to pressure to consolidate the veneers, and to heat to accelerate curing of the adhesive. Once again, this aspect of the process is similar to that for plywood except that rather than being in a thin flat panel shape, the LVL material is formed into long billets up to 25m (80') in length.

Once cured, the billets are sawn to custom lengths and widths as desired for the product end use.

Sizes Available

LVL is available in lengths up to 24.4m (80'), while more common lengths are 14.6m (48'), 17m (56'), 18.3m (60') and 20.1m (66').

LVL is manufactured in thicknesses from 19mm (3/4") to 64mm (2-1/2"). One manufacturer also offers an 89mm (3-1/2") thickness.

The most common thickness used in construction is 45mm (1-3/4"), from which wider beams can be easily constructed by gun-nailing the plies together on site.

LVL is manufactured in billet widths of 610mm (24") or 1220mm (48"). The desired LVL beam depth may be cut from these billet widths. Commonly used LVL beam depths, as shown in Table 3.15 (→ 170), are 241mm (9-1/2"), 302mm (11-7/8"), 356mm (14"), 406mm (16") and 476mm (18-3/4"). Depths of 140mm (5-1/2"), 184mm (7-1/4") and 610mm (24") are also available.

Quality Control

The manufacture of LVL requires an in-house quality assurance organization. Regular independent third party quality audits by a certification organization are a required part of the manufacturers' quality assurance program.

LVL products are tested and approved for use by the major code and product evaluation agencies in the United States and Canada. All manufactured LVL products which have been tested and approved in this way should bear the seal of the certification agency, the manufacturer, date of manufacture, grade of LVL and reference to any applicable code or evaluation agency approval numbers.

LVL is a proprietary product having engineering properties that are dependent on the materials used in the manufacture and on the product assembly and manufacturing processes. As such, it does not meet a common standard of production. Therefore, designers and installers follow the design, use and installation guidelines of the individual manufacturers.

The Canadian Construction Materials Centre (CCMC) has issued product evaluations for many of the LVL products marketed in Canada.

In the United States, most manufacturers have obtained product evaluation reports from the Council of American Building Officials (CABO).

Currently, a standard for the specification for evaluation of structural composite lumber products (such as LVL and PSL) is under development by ASTM. This standard will outline procedures for establishing, monitoring and re-evaluating structural capacities of structural composite lumber and will also detail minimum requirements for establishment of quality control, assurance and audit.

Strength and Appearance

LVL is mainly a structural material, most often used in applications where the material is concealed and therefore where appearance is not important. Finished or architectural grade appearance is available from some manufacturers, usually at an additional cost.

However, when it is desired to use LVL in applications where appearance is important, common wood finishing techniques can be used to accent grain and to protect the wood surface. In finished appearance, LVL resembles plywood or lumber on the beam face.

Fire Safety

LVL is a wood-based product and will react to fire much the same as a comparable size of solid sawn lumber or a glued-laminated beam.

The phenol-formaldehyde resin adhesives used in manufacture are inert once cured. Therefore they do not contribute to the fire load and the strength of the bond is not adversely affected by heat. When used in fire-rated floor or roof assemblies, the performance of LVL is similar to solid sawn lumber or glued-laminated timber. For more detailed information regarding the fire ratings of LVL products, contact a manufacturer.

Section 10 provides information on where wood frame and Heavy Timber construction can be used to meet the fire safety requirements of the North American building codes.

General Guidelines for LVL

- LVL products are available from most major lumber dealers in Canada and the United States. LVL products may also be ordered directly from the manufacturer.

- Manufacturers' catalogues and evaluation reports are the primary sources of information for design, typical installation details, and performance characteristics.

- Typical considerations for product specification should include: product availability, product sizes available (i.e. widths, depths & lengths), availability of connectors, engineering and technical support provided by the manufacturer, product quality, product warranty, product acceptance and code approvals and installed cost effectiveness.

- As with any other wood product, LVL should be protected from the weather, during jobsite storage and after installation. Wrapping of the product for shipment to the job site is important in providing moisture protection. End and edge sealing of the product will enhance its resistance to moisture penetration.

Main Structural Members

Reference Table

Table 3.15	Depth	
Typical Depths of Laminated Veneer Lumber (LVL)	mm	in.
	241	9-1/2
	302	11-7/8
	356	14
	406	16
	476	18-3/4

Notes:
1. Available in thickness of 45mm (1-3/4") for laminating wider members.
2. Refer to manufacturer's literature for specific load bearing capacity.

3.7 Prefabricated Wood I-Joists

Introduction

Prefabricated wood I-joists are made by gluing solid sawn lumber or laminated veneer lumber (LVL) flanges to a plywood or oriented strandboard (OSB) panel web to produce a dimensionally stable light-weight member with known engineering properties.

The uniform stiffness, strength, and light weight of these prefabricated structural products makes them well suited for longer span joist and rafter applications for both residential and commercial construction.

The "I" shape of these products gives a high strength to weight ratio. For example, wood I-joists 241mm (9-1/2") deep and 8m (26'-3") long weigh between 23kg (50 lbs.) and 32kg (70 lbs.), depending on the flange size. This means that they can be installed manually, giving advantages in labour and economy.

Factory-prepunched knock-out holes in the webs facilitate the installation of electrical services. The knockout holes also provide ventilation when the joists are used in a cathedral type ceiling with no attic above. Some manufacturers specifically offer I-joists with ventilation holes predrilled through the web for use in cathedral ceilings.

Holes for plumbing and mechanical ductwork may be drilled easily through the web, but must be located according to the manufacturer's recommendations.

The wide flanges allow for a good fastening surface for sheathing, and the product can be cut and worked using common wood working tools. However, the flanges should never be notched or drilled and all special cuts, such as bird's mouth bearing cuts, must follow the manufacturer's recommendations.

In some areas there may be difficulty in obtaining large dimensions of solid sawn framing lumber. The availability of wood I-joists used as floor joists and as deep, insulated roof joists has made them a popular product for lightweight structural members for rafter and joist applications. They are an economical alternative to open web steel joists.

Several different types of prefabricated wood I-joists are commercially available. Each type features a different combination of flange and web materials, and a different connection between the web and the flanges.

The joint between the flange and the web is a critical element of member strength and is typically protected by patent by each manufacturer (see Figure 3.20 below).

3

Main Structural Members

Figure 3.20
Flange to Web Joints for Wood I-Joists

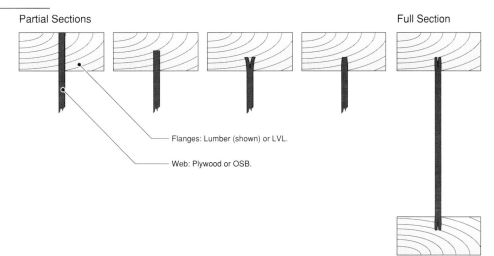

Partial Sections

Full Section

Flanges: Lumber (shown) or LVL.

Web: Plywood or OSB.

Flanges are commonly made of laminated veneer lumber, (LVL) visually graded lumber, or MSR lumber.

The webs are made of either oriented strandboard (OSB) or plywood.

Web panel joints are glued and mated by several methods such as butting of square panel ends, scarfing of the panel ends, and shaping of either a toothed or tongue and groove type joint. The use of longer OSB panels is gaining acceptance as a means of lowering the number of end-to-end panel joints in the web.

Exterior rated phenol-formaldehyde and phenol-resorcinol are the principle adhesives used for the web to web and web to flange joints.

Manufacture

Wood I-joists are proprietary products and the method of manufacture varies somewhat from one manufacturer to another. A general representation of the manufacturing process is shown in Figure 3.21 (opposite).

As in the manufacture of other engineered wood products, moisture control of the flange and web material is important to ensure optimum gluing conditions, and dimensional stability of the finished product. All material must be dry, with an equilibrium moisture content (EMC) in the range of at least 8 percent and no more than 18 percent. It must also be conditioned to room temperature of at least 10°C (50°F).

Prior to assembly, the solid sawn flange material is fingerjoined into long lengths (no butt joints are allowed in the flanges of prefabricated wood I-joists). A groove for acceptance of the web is routed into one face of the flange material.

The web material is cut to the size required to give the appropriate depth to the assembled wood I-joist. The web ends that form the web joints are cut or machined as required and the web edges that mate with the flanges are machined, shaped or crimped as required.

Adhesive is spread on the web ends to form glued web joints and adhesive is placed into the flange routs to form a glued flange to web connection. The top and bottom flanges are of equal specified lengths and are end aligned with one another, prior to joist assembly. The flanges are pressed onto the long edges of the webs just after the web joints are mated to complete assembly of the joist.

Prior to curing, the assembled joists are cut to specified lengths. The joists are generally placed in a low temperature oven or curing environment (21 to 65°C (70 to 150°F)) for a specified period to insure proper cure of the adhesive.

After curing, the product is inspected and then bundled and wrapped for temporary storage or shipment.

Sizes Available

Prefabricated wood I-joists are manufactured in a range of sizes. Long lengths use fingerjoining to splice flanges and butt jointing or toothed, tongue and groove or scarf configurations to splice the webs. The actual length is limited only by transportation restrictions to about 20m (66').

The depths of prefabricated wood I-joists range from 241mm (9-1/2") to 508mm (20") as shown in Table 3.16 (→ 176) although special orders in depths up to 762mm (30") can be made.

Flange depths are commonly 38mm (1-1/2") and common flange widths vary from 45mm (1-3/4") to 89mm (3-1/2"). Web thickness varies from 9.5mm (3/8") to 12.7mm (1/2").

Prefabricated wood I-joists generally weigh from about 3kg per metre (2 lbs. per foot) to 9kg per metre (6 lbs. per foot) for the deepest sections.

Figure 3.21
**Manufacture of
Prefabricated
Wood I-Joists**

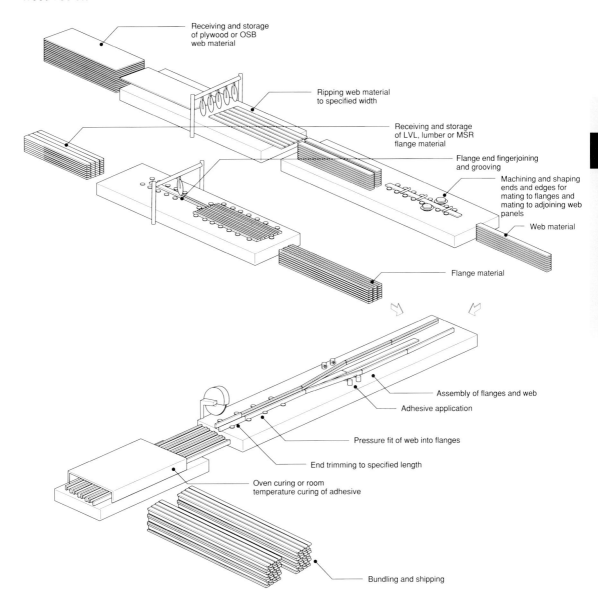

Receiving and storage
of plywood or OSB
web material

Ripping web material
to specified width

Receiving and storage
of LVL, lumber or MSR
flange material

Flange end fingerjoining
and grooving

Machining and shaping
ends and edges for
mating to flanges and
mating to adjoining web
panels

Web material

Flange material

Assembly of flanges and web

Adhesive application

Pressure fit of web into flanges

End trimming to specified length

Oven curing or room
temperature curing of adhesive

Bundling and shipping

Quality Control

The expected performance of a prefabricated wood I-joist is dependent upon the quality of the material used in its production and the quality of the production process.

Because each manufacturer is likely to use a different material source and a different production process, custom production procedures must be established.

Moreover, the quality of material purchased for the manufacture of wood I-joists varies and therefore a quality assurance program that monitors daily production, and independent third party quality audits conducted by an accredited certifying agency on a regular basis are necessary.

Before commercial production begins, each manufacturer's product must be extensively tested to determine the engineering properties. Once production is started, a random sample of product is frequently selected for testing to ensure the manufacturing materials and processes meet prescribed strength values.

Prefabricated wood I-joists are proprietary products having engineering qualities dependent on the materials and flange joints used and production process variables. Therefore designers and installers follow the design guidelines as well as the installation guidelines of the individual manufacturers.

The Canadian Construction Materials Centre (CCMC) has issued product evaluations for many of the prefabricated wood I-joists marketed in Canada.

In the United States, the International Conference of Building Officials (ICBO) has published a document titled *Acceptance Criteria for Prefabricated Wood I-Joists*, for evaluation of these products. The Council of American Building Officials (BOCA) has issued product evaluations for I-joists.

The recent ASTM Standard D5055, *Standard Specification for Establishing and Monitoring Structural Capacities of Prefabricated Wood I-Joists*, outlines procedures for establishing strength values and controlling the quality of prefabricated wood I-joists.

Installation

Openings can be cut through the webs of prefabricated wood I-joists for the passage of utilities such as heat ducts and plumbing. Manufacturers provide clear, definite guidelines in their product catalogues for the shape (round and rectangular), size, and location of holes in the web.

The permissible placement and size of holes is different for each manufacturer and therefore the specific manufacturers' recommendations for a product should be followed.

While limited size holes can be made for ductwork and mechanical services, the location and size must be specifically approved by the manufacturer.

Manufacturers are also specific about the use of web reinforcement or blocking at beam supports and points of concentrated loads. Reinforcement is intended to prevent local buckling of the web material, to minimize bearing distance at supports, and to transfer shear loads into reaction.

Vertical transfer of loads from above at the bearing locations may require the addition of cripples or blocking. This may be accomplished with pieces of lumber, plywood, OSB or short sections of the I-joist itself. All blocking should be installed according to the manufacturers recommendations.

As with all structural elements, prefabricated wood I-joists must be adequately braced during installation. The manufacturer's recommendations must be followed and include required bracing to end walls or existing deck at the ends of building bays.

Most recommendations require that all hangers, blocking, rim joists, and temporary bracing be installed before workers are allowed on the I-joists. Lateral bracing of the top flanges with 19 x 89mm (1" x 4" nom.) wood strapping, spaced at 2.4m (8') to 3.05m (10') before sheathing is permanently attached, is typical.

Where it is necessary to suspend mechanical services from a prefabricated wood I-joist floor or roof, precautions should be taken to ensure that concentrated loads are not passed directly to the lower flanges (refer to Section 5.6 for suggested details for concentrated loads). In all cases, the manufacturers' recommendations should be followed.

Connections

The cross section shape of prefabricated wood I-joists makes specialized hangers and hardware essential in many applications. Several metal fastener manufacturers make special products for use with prefabricated wood I-joists. This is done by modifying existing products for solid sawn lumber to accommodate the range of product sizes available, and also to meet performance requirements.

Information about attachment hardware and joist hangers is found in the prefabricated wood I-joist and metal fastener manufacturers' catalogues. Some common connections are shown in Section 5.6.

Fire Safety

Prefabricated wood I-joists are used in light wood-frame floor and roof assemblies for many residential and commercial buildings. Most of the leading manufacturers have conducted fire tests and evaluations for common floor and roof assemblies to determine the fire performance of their wood I-joist products.

These evaluations are usually done by accredited certifying agencies and are applicable only to the specific proprietary prefabricated wood I-joist product and other assembly components being evaluated.

Information regarding the fire performance of assemblies incorporating specific prefabricated wood I-joists is available from the manufacturers. Such information is also available in listings books of the accredited certifying agencies such as Underwriters' Laboratories of Canada (ULC) or Warnock Hersey Professional Services Ltd. in Canada or Underwriters' Laboratories Inc. (ULI) in the US.

Section 10 provides details on the types of buildings which can be constructed using prefabricated wood I-joists in light frame construction while meeting fire safety requirements.

General Guidelines for Prefabricated Wood I-Joists

- Manufacturers' catalogues and evaluation reports are the primary sources of information for design, typical installation details, and performance characteristics.

- Typical considerations needed for product specification include: product availability, product sizes available (i.e. depths and lengths) availability of approved connectors, certified fire and sound assembly information, engineering and technical support provided by the manufacturer, product quality, product warranty, product acceptance and code approvals, and installed cost effectiveness.

- It is particularly important that prefabricated wood I-joists should be protected from the weather during job site storage and installation. Wrapping of the product for shipment to the job site is important in providing moisture protection.

3

Main Structural Members

Reference Table

Table 3.16 **Typical Depths of Prefabricated Wood I-Joists**	Depth mm	in.
	241	9-1/2
	292	11-1/2
	302	11-7/8
	318	12-1/2
	356	14
	406	16
	457	18
	508	20

Note:
Refer to manufacturer's literature for widths and specific load bearing capacity.

Sheathing and Decking

4

Plank decking, supported by curved glulam members and bowstring trusses, serves structurally and as an interior ceiling finish.

Plank decking, trusses, and heavy timber beams combine to create a passageway.

Set against a
backdrop of
concrete, a
canopy of plank
decking provides
shelter and
visual interest to
strollers.

OSB/waferboard is a versatile and economical sheathing product which encloses and contributes to structural rigidity.

Plywood and OSB/waferboard are wood panel products that install quickly and are easily cut to sheath surfaces of all shapes.

Prefinished, groove-patterned plywood serves as exterior cladding and as sheathing which provides lateral resistance to ocean storms.

Approved preservative-treated plywood is the sheathing material used for dry, comfortable permanent wood foundations (PWF).

Plywood and OSB/waferboard have strength and weight advantages for resisting lateral forces such as earthquakes.

With imagination, ordinary building materials can be used to create extraordinary living spaces. A waferboard floor and a plywood ceiling demonstrate the striking results.

Plywood

Douglas Fir Plywood (DFP) and Canadian
Softwood Plywood (CSP) vary in appearance
according to grade.

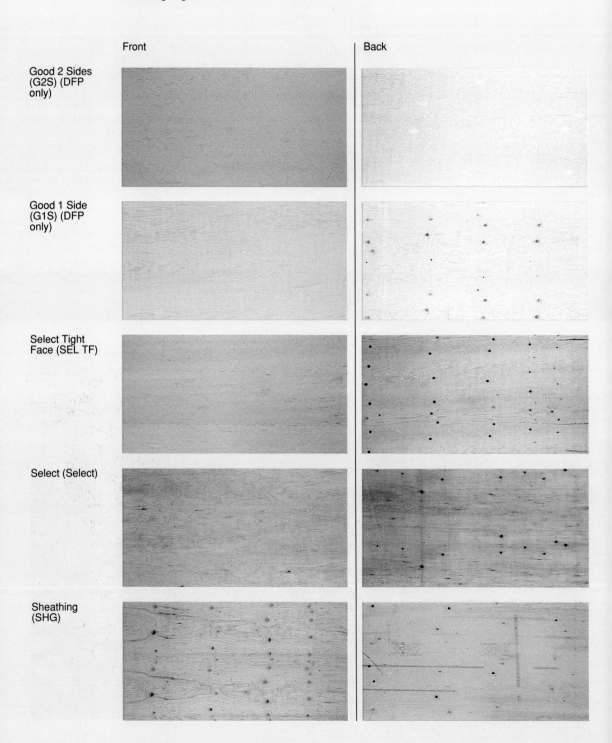

Front

Back

Good 2 Sides
(G2S) (DFP
only)

Good 1 Side
(G1S) (DFP
only)

Select Tight
Face (SEL TF)

Select (Select)

Sheathing
(SHG)

4.1   General Information

Wood sheathing and decking materials are used to form building envelopes and surfaces. Sheathing and decking play a structural role by carrying wind and earthquake, as well as gravity loads, to the main structural members which were described in Section 3.

Sheathing forms the structural envelope used for floors, walls and roofs. Siding is a finish product placed over the wall sheathing on the exterior of the building.

Sheathing and decking can contribute to structural integrity by stiffening buildings from racking forces through the provision of shearwall and diaphragm action (see Section 6.4).

This section describes the characteristics, methods of manufacture, quality control and uses for the following wood sheathing and decking products:

4.2   Plywood

4.3   Oriented Strandboard (OSB) and Waferboard

4.4   Plank Decking and Board Sheathing

Panels such as plywood, oriented strandboard (OSB) and waferboard are well suited for use as sheathing. Before the manufacture of panel products, wood buildings were sheathed with boards. While more labour intensive to install, board sheathing is still used extensively in some areas of North America.

Tongue and groove plank decking is most often used in conjunction with Heavy Timber construction because the thickness of the material accommodates spacing between main members, and meets fire-resistance requirements of building codes.

4

Sheathing and Decking

4.2   Plywood

Introduction

Plywood is a panel product consisting of thin veneers (plies) glued together so that the grain direction of each ply is perpendicular to that of the adjacent ply and symmetrical about the central ply or panel centreline (except for modified plywood).

This cross-lamination provides two-way strength and stiffness properties, and good dimensional stability.

Many kinds of plywood are manufactured in Canada. Two kinds (which are supplied in several grades) are assigned specified engineering strength values under Canadian standards. These are unsanded Douglas Fir Plywood (DFP) and unsanded Canadian Softwood Plywood (CSP). The sanded grades of these products are used primarily in formwork or non-structural applications.

DFP and CSP plywoods are made with a waterproof phenol-formaldehyde resin glue and are therefore certified for exterior use.

Panels are manufactured in standard and modified constructions. Modified construction varies from standard in the grain direction of the plies, the number of plies, or the thickness of the panel.

Standard plywood, symmetrical about the centre ply, is used for most structural sheathing applications. Modified plywood is used for most formwork and for non-engineered sheathing applications.

A discussion of non-structural plywood products such as hardwood and specialty plywoods is found in Section 7.

Grades of Plywood

Two types of standard Canadian plywoods are commonly used in sheathing and other applications.

The two types are named for the species of wood used for the front and back faces (the outer layers). Douglas fir plywood is manufactured to *CSA O121-M1989 Douglas Fir Plywood*, and plywoods containing other Canadian softwood species are manufactured to *CSA O151-M1989 Canadian Softwood Plywood*. These standards are for material and manufacturing tolerances.

Typical face and edge stamps for Canadian plywood meeting the above standards are shown in Figure 4.1 (→ 190). Canadian plywood meets or exceeds the standards of most countries.

Both Douglas Fir and Canadian Softwood Plywoods are manufactured in several grades. The grades are dependent upon the appearance and the quality of the veneers used for the outer plies. The three qualities of veneer are designated by the letter A (the highest grade), B, and C (the lowest grade). The manufacturer, using these veneer grades in various combinations, can produce panels suitable for a variety of uses as shown in Table 4.1 (→ 196).

Sheathing grades which are not specified for appearance usually carry the grade stamp on one of the faces, and the grades such as Good Two Sides carry the stamp on the edge so that it does not mar appearance.

The appearance of both sides of various grades of plywood is shown in the colour photographs at the beginning of this section.

Species of Wood

Douglas Fir Plywood (DFP) is manufactured with face veneers of Douglas fir. The inner plies may be of Douglas fir or other selected western softwood species.

Most Canadian eastern and western softwood species are permitted for use as face, back, or core veneers for Canadian Softwood Plywood (CSP) plywood. CSP is manufactured in western and eastern Canada. Both western and eastern products must meet the requirements of the Canadian Standards Association.

4

Sheathing and Decking

Figure 4.1
**Sample Panel
Marks for
Canadian
Plywood**

Depending on appearance requirement, either a face stamp or edge stamp is used. Where a face stamp is used, the grade designation is shown separately on the edge stamp.

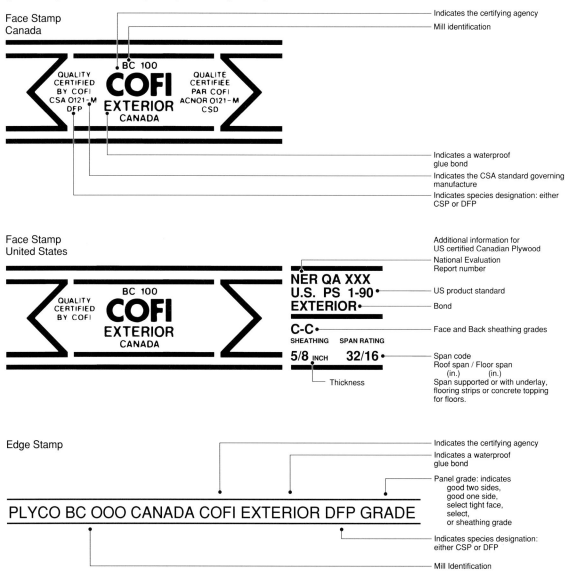

Face Stamp
Canada

Indicates the certifying agency
Mill identification

BC 100
QUALITY CERTIFIED BY COFI CSA O121-M DFP
COFI EXTERIOR CANADA
QUALITE CERTIFIEE PAR COFI ACNOR O121-M CSD

Indicates a waterproof glue bond
Indicates the CSA standard governing manufacture
Indicates species designation: either CSP or DFP

Face Stamp
United States

Additional information for US certified Canadian Plywood
National Evaluation Report number

BC 100
QUALITY CERTIFIED BY COFI
COFI EXTERIOR CANADA

**NER QA XXX
U.S. PS 1-90
EXTERIOR**

US product standard
Bond

C-C
Face and Back sheathing grades

SHEATHING   SPAN RATING

5/8 INCH   **32/16**

Span code
Roof span / Floor span
(in.)   (in.)
Span supported or with underlay, flooring strips or concrete topping for floors.

Thickness

Edge Stamp

Indicates the certifying agency
Indicates a waterproof glue bond
Panel grade: indicates good two sides, good one side, select tight face, select, or sheathing grade

PLYCO BC OOO CANADA COFI EXTERIOR DFP GRADE

Indicates species designation: either CSP or DFP
Mill Identification

Sizes

Canadian plywood is manufactured in several sizes and thicknesses as shown in Table 4.2 (→ 197). It is most commonly available in sheets 1220mm (4') wide by 2440mm (8') long. It is also available in a metric size of 1200 x 2400mm. Other sizes are manufactured to fill custom orders.

Thicknesses of sheathing panels, although now stated in metric terms, remain similar to those Imperial thicknesses established through experience and traditional usage. The thicknesses for sanded (Good Two Sides and Good One Side grades) and unsanded (Select Tight Face, Select, and Sheathing) grades for DFP and CSP plywoods are given in Table 4.2 (→ 197).

The new metric thicknesses used in conjunction with the new metric support spacings will provide equivalent performance to Imperial thicknesses used with Imperial spans. Metric spans are fractionally less than Imperial spans and hence are more conservative. Metric panel thicknesses have been selected so that straight substitutions can safely be made for standard sheathing applications.

Manufacture

Each peeler log is conveyed to a barker where it is rotated against a steel claw that strips the bark from the log. The debarked block is moved to the veneering lathe and centred in the chucks as shown in Figure 4.2 (→ 192). As the log is rotated, a steel blade peels a continuous sheet of veneer. A large diameter log may yield more than a kilometre (half mile) of veneer.

As veneer is produced, it is directed to semi-automatic clippers that cut it into desired widths. The clipper blade can also be actuated manually to remove defective pieces of veneer. Next, the veneer moves to the sorting area where it is graded and separated into stacks of veneer originating from either the heartwood or sapwood sectors of the tree. This segregation is necessary because the heartwood and sapwood contain very different moisture contents and therefore require different drying times.

Steam or gas-heated ovens are used to dry the veneer to a moisture content of about 5 percent. The speed of passage of veneer through the drying chamber depends on the thickness of the veneer and whether it is of heartwood or sapwood origin.

After drying, electronic moisture detectors are used to verify the moisture content of all pieces. Pieces not meeting dryness requirements are returned for further drying.

Next, the veneer is graded. In some types of plywood, narrow strips are then edge trimmed and edge glued to form a continuous sheet. In other types, only the face plies are made from full sheets, and the interior plies are comprised of loose lain strips placed edge to edge.

Substandard face veneer with oversize imperfections is channelled to patching machines where the imperfections are neatly replaced with sound wooden patches.

Sound face and interior veneer moves to the glue spreader or automatic layup line. There the veneers are uniformly coated with phenol-formaldehyde resin glue and laid at right angles to the adjacent face and back veneers.

After layup, the veneer sandwiches go to the hot press, the key operation in the manufacturing process. Here, depending upon the thickness of the plywood panel, one or more sandwiches are loaded into each press opening. The press is then hydraulically closed and the panels subjected to a temperature of 150°C (300°F) and a pressure of 1.38 MPa (200 psi) which cures the glue.

After removal from the hot press, trim saws cut the plywood panels to the required dimensions, usually 1220mm x 2440mm (4' x 8'). Panel edges and ends are trimmed in consecutive operations.

Panels are then graded as sheathing or selected for further finishing. Panels to be produced as sanded grades pass to a sander where faces and backs are sanded smooth simultaneously.

4

Sheathing and Decking

Figure 4.2
Manufacture of Plywood

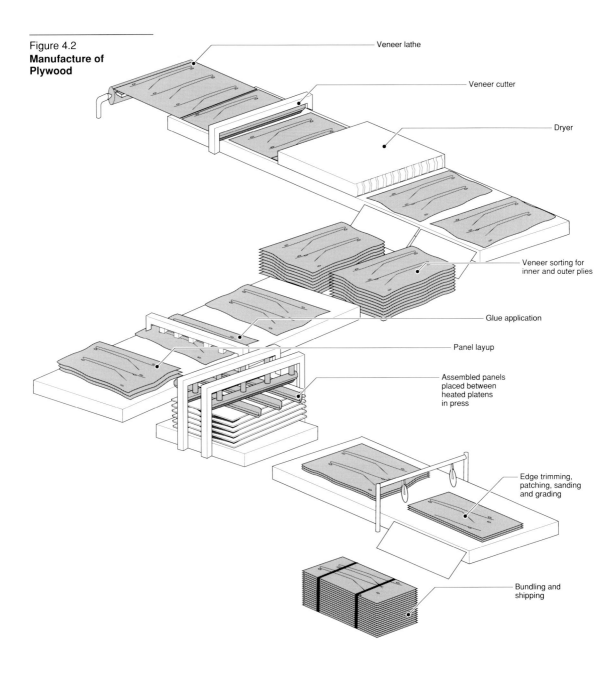

Veneer lathe

Veneer cutter

Dryer

Veneer sorting for inner and outer plies

Glue application

Panel layup

Assembled panels placed between heated platens in press

Edge trimming, patching, sanding and grading

Bundling and shipping

Any minor imperfections remaining in the face and back veneers are repaired with wood inlays or synthetic filler before the panels are finally graded.

Overlaid Plywood

Plywood is also manufactured with overlays which improve the appearance and durability of the panel. Refer to Section 7 for information on these non-engineering types of plywood products and other specialty plywoods.

Quality Control

Each plywood plant has resident quality control to ensure that the product will meet standards at completion. Veneer thickness, moisture control for veneer drying, and glue bonding are examples of stages of manufacture which are particularly important in quality control.

In western Canada, many plywood plants manufacture structural plywoods under the supervision of Council of Forest Industries of British Colombia (COFI) which continually monitors glue bond strength and other properties to ensure that the products meet the requirements of the CSA standards.

Other western plywoods may carry a WPMA stamp (Western Plywood Manufacturers Association). For eastern Canadian plywood plants, it is required that quality audits be performed by independent certification agencies to ensure conformance to CSA standards.

Tongue and Groove Plywood

Tongue and groove (T&G) plywood is usually a Sheathing or Select grade panel with a factory-machined tongue along one of the long edges and a groove along the other. Where diaphragm action is not an overriding concern, T&G profiles can be used to dispense with the need for blocking by maintaining abutting panels in the same plane, thus ensuring the effective transmission of loads across joints.

Plywood T&G panels are usually manufactured in thicknesses of 12.5mm (1/2") or more. Some T&G profiles are designed to butt at the tip of the tongue to leave a 0.8mm (1/32") gap on the face and underside of the joint between panels to allow for swelling caused by exposure to wet conditions before a building's weather membrane has been applied. Some common T&G profiles and an H clip profile are shown in Figure 4.3 (→ 194).

COFI has developed a patented edge profile for roof sheathing panels, available in 11.0 (7/16") and 12.5mm (1/2") thicknesses in Select and Sheathing grades of DFP and CSP.

Typical Applications

Floor Sheathing and Underlayment
Plywood provides a good floor beneath resilient flooring and carpeting because it is dimensionally stable. It remains flat to give a smooth, uniform surface that does not crack, cup or twist. T&G plywood panels reduce labour and material costs by eliminating the need for blocking at panel edges.

Select Tight Face grade is particularly suitable for use under resilient finish flooring. If Select Sheathing grade is used, the splits and other minor defects permitted in the grade and the small gaps between panels should be filled with a material which, on setting, will provide a hard, firm surface.

Sheathing grade is suitable for concrete topped plywood floors and may be used as an underlayment, provided open defects are suitably filled.

Wall Sheathing
Plywood panels used as wall sheathing provide shearwall action when framing and nail spacing is in accordance with engineering standards. Refer to Section 6.4 for information on the importance of shearwall action.

The use of panel sheathing also contributes to the over-all thermal performance of the wall because the large panels have fewer joints through which heat can escape.

4

Sheathing and Decking

Figure 4.3
**Plywood Joint
Profiles**

Standard T&G Profile

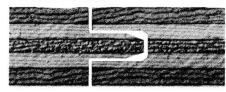

COFI T&G Profile (Patented)

H-Clip Profile

One plywood layer may be used as both a structural sheathing and a finish cladding or one layer may be used as sheathing, separate from the cladding panel. In either case, specialty textured plywoods are manufactured to provide a good appearance for the exterior.

Available in a broad range of patterns and textures, plywood siding panels combine the natural characteristics of wood with the superior strength and stiffness imparted by cross-laminated construction. See Section 7 for information on textured and other specialty plywoods.

Roof Sheathing
Plywood is a often used for roof sheathing. The panel size combines speed of erection with portability, and the stiffness of the panels constitutes diaphragm action (see Section 6.4) when prescribed framing and nailing patterns are used.

Panels should be applied with the face grain at right angles to the supports to provide maximum strength. A small gap should be left between panels to allow for expansion.

H-clips, used only for roof sheathing, are an alternative to solid blocking in conjunction with 9.5mm (3/8") plywood roof sheathing, spanning rafters placed 600mm (2') apart, subject to the following conditions:

• One H-clip (see Figure 4.3 above) shall be placed midway in the joint of abutting sheets between each pair of rafters or joists. Rafter or joist spacing shall not exceed 600mm (2').

• H-clips must fit snugly.

• Abutting plywood sheets shall be fitted as closely as clips permit. Occasional misfit of abutting sheets may be tolerated providing gaps at maximum opening do not exceed 6mm (1/4").

**Exterior Finishes for
Plywood**

Plywood can be painted, stained, or ordered with factory applied stains or finishes. Refer to Section 9 for details.

Preservative Treatment

Plywood is commonly used for permanent wood foundations (PWF, see Section 6.7) and has preservative penetration especially specified for this purpose.

It is also desirable to use treated plywood for applications where there is ground contact, or anywhere where it may be subject to insect or fungal attack.

Storage and Handling

Plywood, like any other panel product, requires careful handling and storage. Despite its sturdy cross-laminated construction, face veneers, panel edges and panel corners are particularly vulnerable to damage and should always be protected.

Plywood is manufactured at a low moisture content and while small changes in moisture content will not appreciably affect its dimensions, large changes should be avoided since they may encourage checking of the face veneer with consequent impairment in its qualities as a paint base. It is good practice to store plywood, which is to be used for interior finish, under conditions that approximate those expected in service.

When handling or storing plywood, practice the following:

- Store plywood panels flat and level.

- Keep finish faced inward and cover stacks to protect from bumping and abrasion.

- Protect panel edges and corners. This is especially important with tongue and groove plywood.

- Carry panels on edge (always being careful not to damage faces, edges and corners).

- Protect panels from water.

Fire Safety

Plywood products are used structurally in fire rated floor, wall, and roof assemblies. Plywood panels may also be used for fire stops in concealed spaces such as attics.

Section 10 provides information on the uses of plywood in fire-rated assemblies for all types of buildings.

General Guidelines for Plywood

- Indicate the type of plywood required. The specifications covering manufacture are: *CSA O121-M1989 Douglas Fir Plywood* and *CSA O151-M1989 Canadian Softwood Plywood.*

- Indicate the grade or grades acceptable, and the minimum thickness.

- Indicate the support spacing and direction of face grain orientation with relation to supports.

- Indicate the type, size and spacing of fasteners.

- Check the product for a quality certification grade mark as an assurance that the plywood meets the industry's standards and conforms to a CSA specification.

- Plywood panels should be protected from rain and snow before and after installation to prevent an increase in moisture content.

4

Sheathing and Decking

Reference Tables

Table 4.1
Standard Grades of Canadian Exterior Plywood

Grade	Governing Canadian Standard	Individual Veneer Grades			Characteristics	Typical Applications
		Face	Inner Plies	Back		
Good Two Sides (G2S)	CSA O121 (DFP)	A	C	A	Sanded. Best appearance both faces. May contain neat wood patches, inlays or synthetic patching material.	Used where appearance of both sides is important. Furniture, cabinet doors, partitions, shelving, and concrete formwork.
Good One Side (G1S)	CSA O121 (DFP)	A	C	C	Sanded. Best appearance one side only. May contain neat wood patches, inlays or synthetic patching material.	Used where appearance on one side is important. Furniture, cabinet doors, partitions, shelving, and concrete formwork.
Select-Tight Face (SEL TF)	CSA O121 (DFP) or CSA O151 (CSP)	B	C	C	Unsanded. Permissible face openings filled. May be light sanded to clean and size patches.	Used where appearance on one side is important. Furniture, cabinet doors, partitions, shelving, and concrete formwork.
Select (SELECT)	CSA O121 (DFP) or CSA O151 (CSP)	B	C	C	Unsanded. Uniform surface with minor open splits. May be cleaned and sized.	Underlayment, combined subfloor and underlayment, and sheathing.
Sheathing (SHG)	CSA O121 (DFP) or CSA O151 (CSP)	C	C	C	Unsanded. Face may contain limited size knots and other defects.	Roof, wall, and floor sheathing.

Notes:
1. Permissible openings filled with wood patches or putty.
2. For information on specialty plywoods, refer to Section 7.
3. All grades are bonded with waterproof phenolic glue.
4. Veneer grades: A: highest grade; B: medium grade; and C: low grade.

Reproduced in part with the permission of COFI.

Reference Tables continued

Table 4.2

Thicknesses and Panel Sizes of Canadian Plywood

Thicknesses

Unsanded		Sanded	
Select Tight Face, Select and Sheathing		Good Two Sides and Good One Side	
mm	in. nom.	mm	in. nom.
7.5	9/32	6	1/4
9.5	3/8	8	11/32
12.5	1/2	11	7/16
15.5	5/8	14	9/16
18.5	23/32	17	2-1/32
20.5	25/32	19	3/4
22.5	7/8	21	13/16
25.5	1	24	15/16
28.5	1-3/32	27	1-1/16
31.5	1-7/32	30	1-3/16

Panel sizes

mm	in.	ft.
1220 x 2440	48 x 96	4 x 8
1220 x 2740	48 x 108	4 x 9
1220 x 3050	48 x 120	4 x 10
1200 x 2400	47.2 x 94.5	
1250 x 2500	49.2 x 98.4	

Notes:
1. Canadian plywood is made in metric thicknesses. Some, but not all thicknesses approximate Imperial sizes: 6mm (1/4"), 9.5mm (3/8"), 12.5mm (1/2"),15.5mm (5/8"), 19mm (3/4"), and 25.5mm (1").
2. Tongue and groove plywood is usually available in Sheathing and Select Grades in thicknesses of 12.5mm and greater.
3. Other thicknesses may be obtained by special order.

4.3 Oriented Strandboard (OSB) and Waferboard

Introduction

Oriented strandboard (OSB) and wafer-board are panel products which illustrate the trend toward more efficient use of forest resources, while employing less valuable, fast-growing species. At the same time, they provide economy of construction and substantial insulation and structural advantages.

OSB and waferboard are panel products made of aspen or poplar (as well as southern yellow pine in the US) wafers or strands which are bonded together under heat and pressure using a waterproof phenolic resin adhesive or equivalent waterproof binder.

Oriented strandboard (OSB) has been developed in recent years. Like wafer-board, OSB is made of aspen-poplar strands or southern yellow pine. However, the strands in the outer faces of OSB are oriented along the long axis of the panel thereby, like plywood, making it stronger along the long axis as compared to the narrow axis.

The strands used in the manufacture of OSB are generally 80mm (3-1/8") long in the grain direction and less than 1mm (1/32") in thickness. The wafers used in the manufacture of waferboard are generally 30mm long (1-1/4") along the grain direction, and about 1mm (1/32") in thickness.

Waferboard has been used in North American construction for over twenty years, for interior and exterior and for structural and non-structural applications.

In Canada, OSB and waferboard are manufactured to meet the requirements of Canadian Standards Association (CSA) standard *CAN3-O437.0-M85, Waferboard and Strandboard*. In the US, the requirements of American National Standards Institute (ANSI) A208.1 must be met.

OSB and waferboard are used in construction as roof sheathing, wall sheathing, siding, soffits, floor underlayment, subfloors and combination subfloor-underlayment. They are also suitable for shearwall and diaphragm applications (see Section 6.4).

OSB and waferboard are efficient additions to the family of wood building materials because:

- They are made from abundant, fast growing, small diameter poplar and aspen species to produce an economical structural panel.

- The manufacturing process can make use of crooked, deformed trees which would not otherwise have commercial value, thereby maximizing forest utilization.

- During manufacturing many strength reducing defects are removed, and any remaining defects are evenly dispersed throughout the panel, resulting in consistent strength properties.

- The random orientation of strands and wafers gives consistent strength properties throughout a panel.

- Specific strength properties can be produced by adjusting the orientation of strand or wafer layers.

Differentiating Oriented Strandboard (OSB) and Waferboard

In regular waferboard, the wafers are placed so that their flat planes are parallel to the plane of the board, but their grain directions are random. As a result, strength and stiffness properties are roughly equal in all directions in the plane of the board.

If the wafers or strands are oriented in a particular direction, the properties in that direction will increase and those in the perpendicular direction will decrease. Products in which some or all of the wafers or strands have been oriented are called oriented waferboard or oriented strand-board (OSB).

4

Sheathing and Decking

Figure 4.4
**Composition of
OSB and
Waferboard**

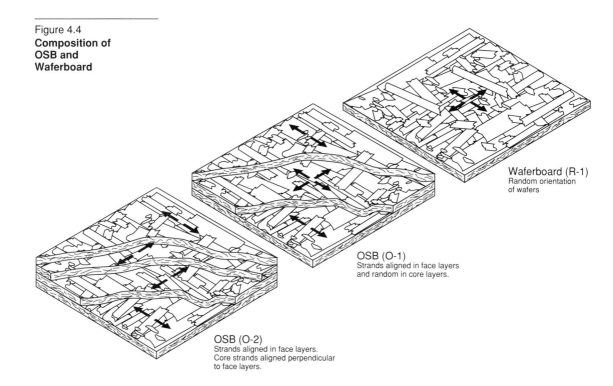

Waferboard (R-1)
Random orientation
of wafers

OSB (O-1)
Strands aligned in face layers
and random in core layers.

OSB (O-2)
Strands aligned in face layers.
Core strands aligned perpendicular
to face layers.

Figure 4.4 (above) shows the wafer or strand orientation for the three main categories of structural board products.

Waferboard (R-1) has a random orientation of all wafers. OSB surface strands are aligned parallel to the long axis of the board with random core strands (OSB O-1), or successive layers of strands are aligned at 90° to one another (OSB O-2). The two latter constructions increase the strength and stiffness of OSB in the long axis at the expense of reduced strength across the board.

For most engineering uses, the greater strength and stiffness in the long direction of an OSB panel when compared to the short dimension is an advantage. An example of this is when roof sheathing spans the top chords of roof trusses and supports snow loads. Here the sheathing panel is stressed in bending in the direction perpendicular to the direction of the trusses.

Panel Marks for OSB and Waferboard

It has become increasingly common to grade panels in accordance with performance based standards.

OSB and waferboard conforming to the Canadian CSA Standard, or the US APA Standard may be used for subfloors, roofs, and wall sheathing in accordance with end uses and spans shown on the panel mark.

These performance based standards evaluate panels installed on framing for their ability to carry loads and to resist deflection under loads and conditions similar to or exceeding those experienced in construction or service.

The ability of a panel to meet performance requirements of a given end use is shown on the panel by a panel mark. This panel mark consists of:

• End use mark - 1F, 2F, 1R, 2R, and W

• Span mark - 16, 20, 24, 32, 40, 48.

In the end use mark, the "F", "R" and "W" indicate, respectively, floor, roof and wall sheathing, while the "1" indicates the panel may be used alone to meet structural requirements. The "2" means that the panel must have an additional support element such as underlay for floors or H clips or blocking for roofs.

The two digit span mark indicates the span between support in inches. For example, 16 indicates a maximum span of 16 inches.

The panel mark 1R24/2F16/W24 means that the panel may be used without blocking on a roof with trusses at 600mm (24") on centre, on a floor with underlay on joists with centres at 400mm (16"), or on a wall with studs at 600mm (24") on centre.

Canadian OSB and waferboard suitable for building construction is identified by a stamp containing the manufacturer's name or logo; the CSA reference standard, "CSA-O437.0-M"; the words "EXTERIOR BOND" or "EXT.BOND"; the grade, R-1, O-1, or O-2; the nominal thickness; on T & G panels, the words "THIS SIDE DOWN"; and on O-1 and O-2 panels, an arrow showing the direction of face orientation. A sample of this information is shown in Figures 4.5 (→ 202) and 4.6 (→ 203).

Other information including the Structural Board Association logo, Canada Mortgage and Housing Corporation (CMHC) Building Materials Evaluation Report numbers, other reference standards and installation advice may appear.

Mills may apply the reference standard stamps and the Structural Board Association logo only when the panels meet the requirements of the standards.

Species used for OSB and Waferboard

Self propagating, fast growing aspen-poplar is used for OSB and waferboard in the northern part of North America, while southern yellow pine from plantation stands is used in the south. Other species, such as birch, maple or sweetgum are used in limited quantities to supplement the aspen or southern yellow pine resource.

Although some crooked, knotty wood can be used for OSB and waferboard, logs with excessive decay in the heartwood are avoided.

OSB and waferboard may include fine particles incidentally generated from making strands and wafers, but manufacturers limit the amount of fine material which can be used. It is not acceptable to use as a filler wood residue from other process such as sawmilling or planing.

Sizes

OSB and waferboard are available in a variety of thicknesses and sizes as shown in Table 4.3 (→ 207).

The most common panel size is 1220 x 2440mm (4' x 8'). Panels can also be made to a metric size of 1200 x 2400mm. Panels may be specially ordered up to 2440 x 7320mm (4' x 24'). Larger panel sizes are desired by the manufacturers of wood I-joists because the long lengths reduce the need for web splicing.

Sizes smaller than the standard size can also be specially ordered.

Thicknesses are available from 6mm (1/4") to 28.5mm (1-1/8").

Panels may be sanded on one or both faces on special order.

Manufacture

The process described here is general and may vary in detail from one manufacturer to another but it is always comprised of log conditioning, waferizing, drying, blending, forming, pressing, and final processing.

A schematic representation of a typical manufacturing process is shown in Figure 4.7 (→ 204).

Freshly cut logs are taken from the log storage yard and placed in hot water ponds. The soaking softens the wood to facilitate debarking and making of strands and wafers, thereby reducing the amount of fines and slivers generated. To maintain effectiveness, hot pond temperatures are increased in cold weather conditions.

After conditioning, the logs are debarked and are fed into a machine with sharp knives which cuts the log pieces into strands or wafers along the grain.

The strands or wafers are conveyed to wet storage bins and are screened after drying to remove fine particles. Most mills process core and surface strands and wafers separately and then deposit them together in layers to form the mat.

The strands or wafers are placed in large cylindrical dryers where they are dried to a moisture content of three to seven percent. While in the dryer, the strands or wafers are shifted in a manner which minimizes breakage of the wafers while ensuring consistent moisture content.

When dry, the strands or wafers proceed to the blender where they are mixed with resin and wax. The small quantity of hot wax (about 1.5 percent of the weight of wafers) sprayed on the wafers helps to distribute evenly the powdered phenol-formaldehyde resin (2 percent to 2.75 percent by weight).

Figure 4.5
Panel Marks for OSB and Waferboard (Canada)

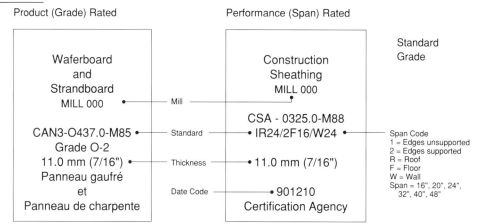

The strands or wafers are continuously weight metered to ensure the proper quantities enter the blenders so that the correct resin coverage is achieved.

The forming machine arranges the strands or wafers in several layers to form a mat on stainless steel press sheets or on a continuous belt. For waferboard, the wafers are randomly deposited. For OSB, the strands for the faces are oriented parallel with the long direction of the panel and the core layers are either oriented or random.

The size of the mats varies but generally, one mat will be large enough to produce several standard sized finished panels.

The mats are placed in a press accommodating up to 24 sheets at a time. Each mat sits between a pair of heated platens. When all the mats have been inserted, the press is closed under heavy pressure.

The layup of the mat and the press operation are important in ensuring proper panel thickness. The duration of the press cycle varies from plant to plant and with the desired thickness of the board. For example, a press cycle of 3-1/2 minutes might be required for 6.35mm (1/4") thick panels, and eight minutes for 15.5mm (5/8") panels. The heat and pressure polymerize the resin which binds the strands or wafers together strongly into a rigid panel.

4

Sheathing and Decking

Figure 4.6
Panel Marks for OSB and Waferboard (United States)

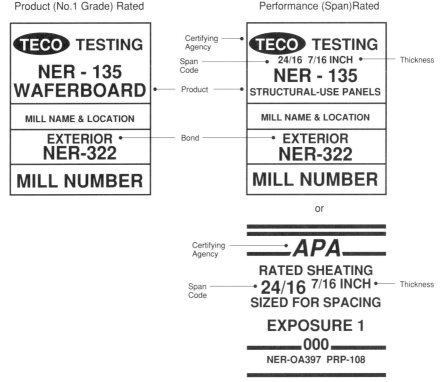

SPAN CODE

ROOF SPAN (in.) / FLOOR SPAN (in.)

Span supported or with underlay, flooring strips or concrete topping for floors.

Figure 4.7
**Manufacture of
OSB/
Waferboard**

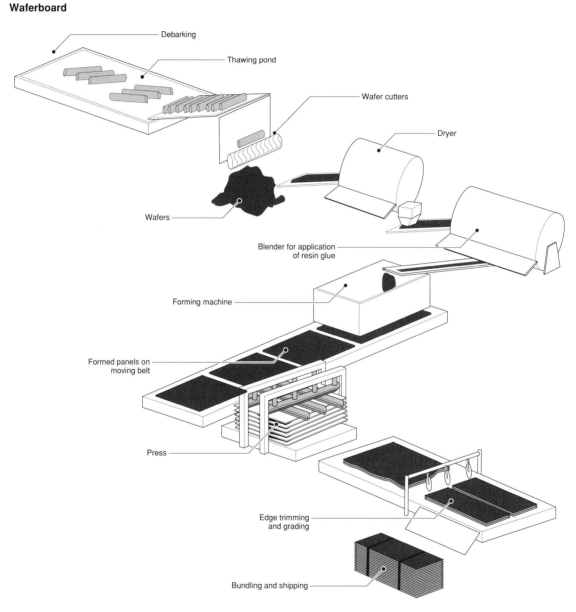

Debarking

Thawing pond

Wafer cutters

Dryer

Wafers

Blender for application
of resin glue

Forming machine

Formed panels on
moving belt

Press

Edge trimming
and grading

Bundling and shipping

After pressing, the panels are conveyed to trim saws where they are edge-trimmed into 1220 x 2440mm (4' x 8') panels or to special order sizes.

Last, the panels are inspected, graded, and sorted. Final curing of the resin occurs during the time the panels are in heated storage.

Further processing such as tongue and grooving may also be done at this stage. In some cases, panels may be sanded to attain required thickness.

Quality Control

The quality of OSB and waferboard is the responsibility of the individual manufacturer. Each mill must establish its own program of in-plant quality control to ensure the finished product meets or exceeds the requirements for the grade specified in the applicable standard. Panel quality is affected by every process in the plant and by the quality and consistency of the raw materials used to manufacture the panels.

Process control is uniquely designed for each mill and reflects the particular combination of machinery, control devices, materials and product mix. Continuous monitoring of all process variables by the plant quality control staff maintains the product as required by the applicable standards.

Among the factors most carefully monitored and controlled are the sorting of logs by species, size, and moisture content, strand or wafer size and thickness, moisture content following drying, the consistent blending of strands or wafers, resin and wax, the uniformity of the mat leaving the forming machine, the press temperature, pressures, closing speed, thickness control and pressure release control, quality of panel faces and edges, panel dimensions and the appearance of the finished panel.

Physical testing of the panels according to standard test procedures is necessary to verify that production conforms to the applicable standard. In addition, mills monitor panel quality on a continuing basis by carrying out such tests on hot panels right off the production line to ensure process control is maintained. These hot tests are correlated to the standard conformance tests.

All OSB and waferboard manufactured in Canada must be certified as to quality by independent quality assurance organizations who monitor manufacturing performance and mill quality control programs. All construction grade panels show the stamp of the quality assurance agency on the panel face or edge.

Special Features of OSB and Waferboard Panels

Panels 15.5mm (5/8") and thicker are manufactured either with a square-edge or tongue and groove on the long edges.

Panels may be sanded smooth on one or both sides for particular end uses such as floor underlayment or interior finish, or they may be spot sanded to meet the required thickness tolerances.

Manufacturers may alter the surface of some of their OSB and waferboard panels to make them more suitable for a particular end-use.

For example, to improve worker safety, manufacturers may impart various skid resistant surfaces to OSB and waferboard roof sheathing by skip sanding to give a rough surface, or by imprinting with a screen mesh pattern during the press cycle.

Typical Applications

OSB and waferboard are used in construction mainly as roof, wall and floor sheathing, and are accepted for structural purposes in diaphragm and shearwall applications (see Section 6.4). Some specialty products are made for siding and for concrete formwork.

4

Sheathing and Decking

OSB is also used as the web material for some types of prefabricated wood I-joists (see Section 3.7).

The panels are cut and machined using regular carpentry tools. Carbide tipped blades are recommended.

OSB and waferboard have many inter-leaved layers which provide a panel with good nail and screw holding properties. Fasteners can be driven as close as 6mm (1/4") from the panel edge without risk of splitting or breaking out.

Storage and Handling

All wood products are hygroscopic in nature and therefore gain and lose mois-ture in accordance with climatic conditions. OSB and waferboard change in dimension, as do other wood products, as humidity fluctuations change the moisture content.

Panels should be protected from excessive wetting during storage and construction. Manufacturers protect the panel edges with paint or a special sealer, and recommend a 2mm (1/8") gap be left between panels during installation to accommodate linear expansion.

Panel products are susceptible to corner and edge damage from handling and must be handled carefully to avoid wastage.

In summary, points to watch for when storing and handling OSB and waferboard are:

- Store bundles indoors or under cover with enough support to keep panels flat.

- On the job site, schedule delivery as close as possible to time of use and close in the structure as quickly as practical.

- Protect panel edges and corners. This is especially true for tongue and groove panels.

Fire Safety

OSB/waferboard products are used in wood-frame floor, wall, and roof assemblies having a fire-resistance rating and for fire stops in concealed spaces. For more information on the fire performance characteristics of these panels, contact the Structural Board Association (see Informa-tion Sources).

Section 10 provides information on how fire-rated Wood-Frame construction which incorporates OSB/waferboard can be used in all types of buildings.

General Guidelines for Oriented Strandboard (OSB) and Waferboard

- Require that panels carry a CSA, TECO, or APA panel marks and quality assur-ance stamp.

- Specify the appropriate grade or the performance based standard required.

- Specify the panel size, and the panel thickness or panel mark and support spacing in accordance with the building code having jurisdiction.

- Indicate special requirements such as tongue and groove.

- Indicate fastening type, length, and spacing.

Reference Table

Table 4.3
Thicknesses and Weights of OSB and Waferboard

OSB (O-1) and Waferboard (R-1)

Thickness		1220 x 2440mm (4' x 8') Panel Weight	
mm	in.	kg	lb.
6.35	1/4	12	27
7.9	5/16	15	33
9.5	3/8	18	40
11.1	7/16	21	47
12.7	1/2	24	53
15.9	5/8	30	67
19	3/4	36	80

OSB (O-2)

Thickness		1220 x 2440mm (4' x 8') Panel Weight	
mm	in.	kg	lb.
6	1/4	12	26
7.5	5/16	15	32
9.5	3/8	18	39
11	7/16	21	46
12.5	1/2	24	52
15.5	5/8	30	66
18.5	3/4	36	78
28.5	1-1/8	54	120

Notes:
1. Panel weight calculated on the basis of 640 kg/m^2 (40 lbs/cu.ft.) density and nominal thickness.
2. Panels in thicknesses of 15.5, 15.9, 18.5 and 19mm (5/8" and 3/4") are available in either square-edge or tongue and groove on the long edges.
3. Other thicknesses are available on special order.

4.4   Plank Decking and Board Sheathing

Introduction

As in the case of Lumber (see Section 3), the products in this section are graded according to the *National Standard Grading Rules for Canadian Lumber*. Plank decking and board sheathing graded to this standard are approved for use in Canada and the United States.

Plank Decking

Plank decking is tongue and groove lumber at least 38mm (1-1/2") thick, with the flat face laid over supports such as beams or purlins to provide a structural deck for floors and roofs. It is used where the appearance of the decking is desired as an architectural feature, or where the mass of decking is required to add to the fire safety of Heavy Timber construction (see Section 10).

Individual planks can span simply between supports, but are generally random lengths spanning several supports for economy, and to take advantage of increased stiffness.

Wood species commonly used for plank decking include western red cedar, Douglas fir, western hemlock, and various species of the Spruce-Pine-Fir group. Cedar is often selected for exposed applications where its natural durability is an added advantage to its attractiveness.

The general term decking is used to describe both tongue and groove lumber laid flat (plank decking), and lumber laid on edge (laminated decking).

Laminated decking is dimension lumber placed on edge so that each member acts like a joist, and adjoining pieces are usually nailed to each other to create a nail-laminated load sharing unit.

Laminated decking was once a popular method of building construction where a heavy floor was required and may in fact have some building applications where an industrial type floor is required.

Sizes and Shapes

Plank decking is produced in three thicknesses; 38mm (1-1/2"), 64mm (2-1/2"), and 89mm (3-1/2"). The 38mm (1-1/2") decking has a single tongue and groove and is available in 127mm (5") or 178mm (7") widths.

The two thicker sizes are double tongue and groove and usually available only in 133mm (5-1/4") face width. These sizes may be ordered with pre-drilled 6mm (1/4") holes at 760mm (30") spacings so that each piece may be nailed to the adjacent piece with 200mm (8") No.3 gauge decking spikes.

All decking is V-grooved on the face which is the best in appearance.

The sizes, face patterns, and suggested fastening details are shown in Figure 4.8 (→ 210).

Grades

Plank decking is available in two grades, Select and Commercial, based on the appearance of the best face as shown in Table 4.4 (→ 214).

Select grade is used for high quality construction where high strength and fine appearance for exposed locations are desired.

Commercial grade contains more growth characteristics and more manufacturing defects than Select grade. Commercial grade is chosen when appearance and strength are less critical such as in industrial buildings.

The permitted characteristics for Select and Commercial grades are shown in Tables 4.5 and 4.6 (→ 214).

Manufacture

Plank decking is a solid sawn lumber product manufactured as shown in Figure 3.2 (→ 124), except that unlike dimension lumber and timbers, additional manufacturing is necessary to provide the tongue and groove profile, V-jointing, and any other special surface machining.

4

Sheathing and Decking

Figure 4.8
**Faces, Sizes
and Nailing for
Plank Decking**

38mm (1-1/2") Decking

Faces

Exposed face
(V-joint)

64 and 89mm (2-1/2" and 3-1/2") Decking

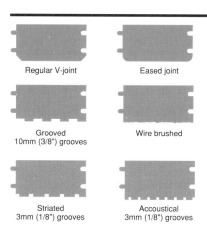

Regular V-joint

Eased joint

Grooved
10mm (3/8") grooves

Wire brushed

Striated
3mm (1/8") grooves

Accoustical
3mm (1/8") grooves

Sizes

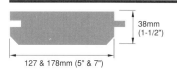

38mm
(1-1/2")

127 & 178mm (5" & 7")

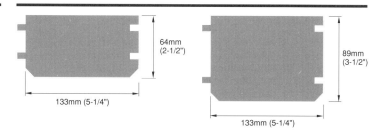

64mm
(2-1/2")

89mm
(3-1/2")

133mm (5-1/4")

133mm (5-1/4")

Nail Patterns

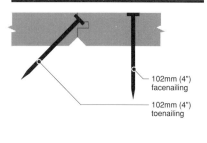

102mm (4")
facenailing

102mm (4")
toenailing

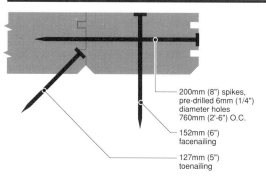

200mm (8") spikes,
pre-drilled 6mm (1/4")
diameter holes
760mm (2'-6") O.C.

152mm (6")
facenailing

127mm (5")
toenailing

Moisture Content

Plank decking is generally specified, dressed, and supplied S-Dry (moisture content 19 percent or less at time of surfacing). It is generally kiln dried to an average moisture content of 15 percent to minimize on site shrinkage or warping.

Ordering

Plank decking is usually purchased in random lengths ranging from 1.83m (7') to 6.10m (20'). Longer lengths may be specially ordered. While decking may be ordered in specific lengths, designers should expect limited availability and extra costs. A typical specification for random lengths is as follows:

- 90 percent of planks 3.0m (10') and longer

- 40 percent to 50 percent of planks 4.9m (16') and longer

For both 64 and 89mm (2-1/2" and 3-1/2") decking, designers should check that decking lengths are adequate for spans. A rule of thumb is that spans should not be more than about 600mm (2') longer than the length which 40 percent of the decking shipment exceeds. Long lengths may only be available in certain species such as Douglas fir and western red cedar.

For simple-span or two-span continuous decking, uniform lengths should be specified even though unit material costs will be higher.

Installation

There are three methods of installing plank decking.

The first method, called controlled random, is the most economical because random length material is used. The controlled random pattern is shown in Figure 4.9 (below) and consists of the following:

4

Sheathing and Decking

Figure 4.9
Controlled Random Pattern for Plank Decking

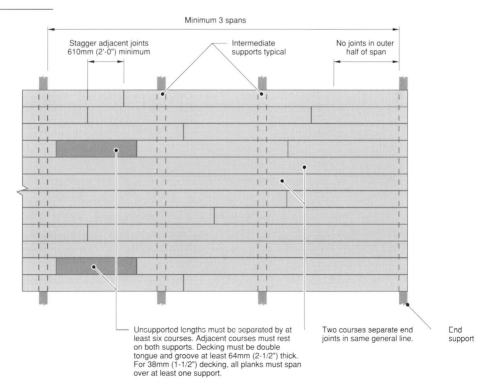

Minimum 3 spans

Stagger adjacent joints 610mm (2'-0") minimum

Intermediate supports typical

No joints in outer half of span

Unsupported lengths must be separated by at least six courses. Adjacent courses must rest on both supports. Decking must be double tongue and groove at least 64mm (2-1/2") thick. For 38mm (1-1/2") decking, all planks must span over at least one support.

Two courses separate end joints in same general line.

End support

Notes:
1. Random pattern is not permitted for bridges.
2. The other methods, Simple Span and Two Span Continous installation patterns, require that all butt joints occur over a support.

- Each deck must consist of at least three spans.

- End joints are not permitted in the outer half of end spans.

- End joints in adjacent courses must be staggered at least 600mm (2').

- Where end joints occur in the same general line, they must be separated by at least two intervening courses.

- In floors and roofs, planks which do not span more than one support must be flanked by courses resting on both supports of that span. They must be separated from the next unsupported plank by at least six courses extending over at least one support (this is only permitted for double tongue and groove planks at least 64mm (2-1/2") thick).

The second method is called Simple Span. All pieces rest on two supports and are the same length. The third method is Two Span Continuous. All pieces rest on three supports and are the same length. Both the latter methods require planks of predetermined length and a consequent cost premium.

Fire Safety

The thickness of plank decking makes it a more fire-resistant material compared to panel and board sheathing. For this reason, it is often used in large commercial buildings where fire performance must meet Heavy Timber construction requirements for fire safety and where the superior appearance characteristics of this material are desired.

Section 10 provides further information on building code requirements relating to fire safety and details the minimum size requirements for Heavy Timber construction including minimum thicknesses for decks.

Board Sheathing

A board is a piece of lumber less than 38mm (2" nom.) thick and at least 50mm (2") wide.

Boards used for sheathing purposes may be flat edge or tongue and groove. There are many other uses for boards in building construction other than for sheathing. Information on boards used for cladding, mouldings, and other finish purposes are presented in Section 7.

Board sheathing was once the most common method of sheathing for frame construction, and in some parts of North America it is still used, particularly for the construction of residential walls, floors, and roofs.

The larger loadings of commercial buildings usually favour panel sheathing products, where the higher material costs can be offset by lower labour costs for installation and increased rigidity for shearwall and diaphragm action is facilitated.

Sizes
The most common size for board sheathing is 19 x 140mm (1" x 6" nom.) and it may be either flat or tongue and groove finished on the edges. Other common widths are 89 and 184mm (4" and 8" nom.).

Grades
Boards are available in five grades listed in order of decreasing strength and appearance properties: Select Merchantable, Construction, Standard, Utility, and Economy.

Manufacture
Board sheathing is a solid sawn lumber product manufactured as shown in Figure 3.2 (→ 124). Boards may be S-Dry or S-Green and may or may not have a tongue and groove profile.

Uses
Board sheathing is used as wall, floor and roof sheathing.

Shearwall action (see Section 6.4) is provided by the boards when they are installed diagonally to the wall framing and when specified nailing patterns are met.

Board sheathing used as sub-flooring is best covered with a panel overlay when resilient flooring is used so that differential deflection does not occur between adjoining boards.

General Guidelines for Plank Decking and Board Sheathing

Plank Decking

- Select the species and grade which best combines strength, appearance , and economy for the application.

- Select the layout pattern and the lengths required.

- Allow at least 5 percent for waste.

- Take measures to protect the decking from excessive wetting during installation.

Board Sheathing

- Standard grade or better is recommended for most board sheathing applications.

References

Wood Design Manual, Canadian Wood Council, 1990.

Standard Grading Rules for Canadian Lumber, National Lumber Grades Authority, 1989.

4

Sheathing and Decking

Reference Tables

Table 4.4 **Plank Decking Grades**	Grade	Principal Uses	Size metric	Imperial (actual)
	Select	For roof and floor decking where strength and fine appearance are required.	38, 64 and 89mm thick 127mm and wider	1-1/2", 2-1/2", and 3-1/2" thick 5" and wider
	Commercial	For roof and floor decking where strength is required but appearance is not so important. Grade contains pieces that do not meet Select Grade requirements.	38, 64 and 89mm thick 127mm and wider	1-1/2", 2-1/2", and 3-1/2" thick 5" and wider

Table 4.5 **Permitted Characteristics for Select Grade Plank Decking**	Category	Permitted Characteristics	
	Growth	• medium stained wood • small holes, equivalent to chipped knots • slope of grain not to exceed 1 in 10 • medium bark pockets • sound and tight knots on exposed face • knots well spaced, not larger than approximately 60mm (2-3/8") in diameter permitted both wide faces for 38 x 127mm (2" x 6" nom.) and 83mm (3-1/4") for 38 x 178 mm (2" x 8" nom.) • in occasional pieces, unsound knots, if tight and not exceeding 38mm (1-1/2") in diameter, are permitted if medium checks not through the piece and do not exceed 2 in a 4m (13') length or equivalent smaller.	• spike and narrow face knots are permitted if judged to have no more effect on strength than other knots. • chipped and/or broken-out knots not larger than approximately 19mm (3/4") in diameter are permitted if not through the piece and do not exceed 2 in a 4m (13') length • on unexposed face and edges, hit and miss skips or wane approximately 1/3 of the face width, pecky spots in narrow streaks, skips 10 percent of exposed face in occasional pieces and other characteristics not interfering with the intended use are permitted
	Seasoning	• medium checks • occasional short splits	• occasional light crook
	Manufacturing	• tongue 2mm (1/8") narrow on occasional pieces • medium torn grain	• hit and miss skips

Table 4.6 **Permitted Characteristics for Commercial Grade Plank Decking**	Category	Permitted Characteristics	
	Growth	• stained wood • holes, 25mm (1") • slope of grain not to exceed 1 in 8, full length • bark or pitch pockets • unsound wood and/or peck not exceeding approximately 1/3 of any face • shake not serious • occasional crook medium • knots well spaced not larger than approximately 73mm (3") permitted on both wide faces for 38 x 127mm (2" x 6" nom.) and 95mm (3") for 38 x 178mm (2" x 8" nom.)	• spike and narrow knots are permitted if judged to have no more effect on strength than other knots • chipped and/or broken-out knots or portions of knots not larger than approximately 38mm (2" nom.) in diameter are permitted if not through the piece • on unexposed face and edges wane approximately 1/3 of the face and other characteristics not interfering with intended use.
	Seasoning	• checks • splits approximately 1/6 of the length	• wane approximately 1/6 of the face width
	Manufacturing	• tongue 2mm (1/16") narrow • torn grain • hit and miss skips	

Connections

5

Connections, as
essential
structural
elements, can
be used
effectively to add
interest and
texture.

Metal fasteners figure prominently in the appearance of the roof structure for this commuter train station.

A compact custom metal fastener and precision fitting of adjoining members combine to make a strong, tidy connection.

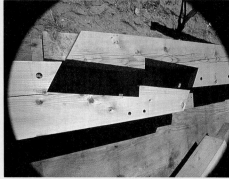

A versatile structural material, wood is easily fastened to itself and to other materials.

Many types of
light frame
connectors,
such as truss
plates and
skewed truss
hangers, are
available as
stock items.

Custom
fasteners (left
and above),
fabricated for
specialized
applications, are
used where
there is a unique
arrangement of
wood structural
members.

A special dapping tool is used for seating shear plates which are used with steel side plates.

Another dapping tool is used for seating split rings which are used with wood side plates.

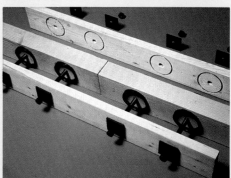

Split rings, bolts, and wood side plates give a neat, uncluttered appearance to this spaced truss.

Well-proportioned, tight-fitting joints and good quality timber are essential to timber joinery.

Traditional in origin and regaining popularity, timber joinery construction continues to fascinate.

Painting can be used to distinguish or accentuate metal fasteners.

A wide variety of top mounted (right) and side mounted (far right) light connectors are manufactured for standard member sizes and orientations.

In Canada, glulam rivets are popular fasteners which give compact, unobtrusive connections.

Automatic nailing guns are fast and effective tools for attaching sheathing and framing elements.

Whether ornamental or structural, wood members (opposite) are easily fastened. Here, painting makes the fasteners indistinguishable.

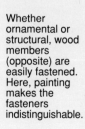

Attention to detail results in the total concealment of metal fasteners within the large members of this waffle roof.

Excellent craftsmanship brings together an intricate arrangement of members with no visual evidence of metal fasteners.

5.1   General Information

As for all other building materials, a critical aspect of wood structures is the manner by which members are connected. Wood products are building materials which are easily drilled, chiselled, or otherwise shaped to facilitate the connection of members, and a number of methods and a wide range of products are available for connecting wood.

The installation of metal fasteners is the most common method of connecting wood products and a wide range of hardware is available. These range from the nails and light connectors used for light framing construction to the bolts, side plates and other hardware used for heavy member connections. Each type of fastener is designed to be used with a particular type of construction. When used appropriately, metal fasteners provide means of connection which are easy to install and which offer trouble free performance.

Nailing for example, which is a basic means of connection with which everyone has some degree of familiarity, is an effective means of connection which, when applied according to specified layouts, results in strong structural systems which perform well under the most adverse loading conditions such as the effects of earthquake.

The performance of metal fastener connections is based upon the fasteners being large enough to carry and transfer loads over a large enough area of the wood so that the wood fibre in contact with the fastener is not deformed. Spacing and load arrangement considerations for metal fasteners are shown in Figure 5.1 ($\rightarrow$ 230).

Timber joinery is a traditional method of connecting wood members without the use of metal fasteners. Although the use of metal fasteners for connections is almost universal, timber joinery still offers a unique visual appearance exhibiting a high degree of craftsmanship.

The cellular structure of wood and modern chemistry combine to produce glue bonds between wood members which are at least as strong as the wood fibre itself. For this reason, adhesives play a crucial role in the manufacture of wood products such as plywood and parallel strand lumber (PSL). They are also used structurally, for example, in improving the performance of floor assemblies.

For many applications, such as nailing for frame wall construction, metal fasteners serve only a structural purpose, and will be hidden from view by interior and exterior finishes. In other cases where wood members serve a structural purpose and are left exposed to add visual interest to a design, as much thought must be given to the appearance of connections as to the selection and finishing of the wood products themselves.

Where metal fasteners are exposed to view, the designer will in some cases want them to be as inconspicuous as possible. This can be done by selecting fasteners such as split rings and bolts (which are effective means of transferring loads), by reducing the visual impact of hardware such as steel side plates by recessing them into the wood members, or by using painting to reduce prominence. In other cases, it may be desired to highlight the hardware to give a robust appearance to a structure.

Most attention in this section is given to metal fasteners because of their prominence in modern wood building construction. Information on timber joinery and adhesives are also provided, and for each connection method, information is provided on the appearance aspects of wood connections. For structural applications, a number of connection details are listed. The section is arranged as follows:

5.2   Metal Fasteners

5.3   Timber Joinery

5.4   Adhesives

5.5   Appearance of Connections

5.6   Connection Details

5

Connections

Figure 5.1
**Terminology
for Metal
Fasteners**

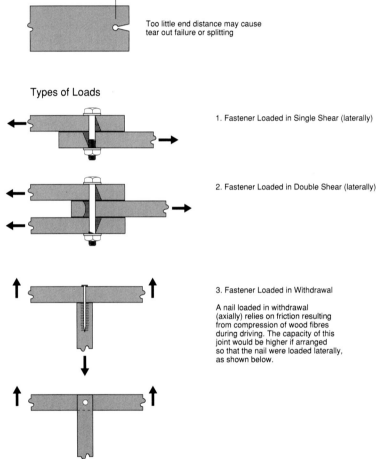

Spacing

Too little end distance may cause
tear out failure or splitting

Types of Loads

1. Fastener Loaded in Single Shear (laterally)

2. Fastener Loaded in Double Shear (laterally)

3. Fastener Loaded in Withdrawal

A nail loaded in withdrawal
(axially) relies on friction resulting
from compression of wood fibres
during driving. The capacity of this
joint would be higher if arranged
so that the nail were loaded laterally,
as shown below.

5.2   Metal Fasteners

Light Connections

Nails

Nailing is the most basic and most commonly used means of attaching members in wood frame construction. Usually, nailing is used as a structural connection and appearance is not a factor. Exceptions to this are nails used for cladding, decking and finish work, where care in the selection of the type of nail can lead to enhanced appearance.

Screws rely on their threads to develop resistance to withdrawal. Nails are faster to install but rely mainly on friction to resist withdrawal. For this reason, designs should ensure that nails are loaded laterally and that withdrawal loads are kept to a minimum as shown in Figure 5.1 (→ 230).

Nails are made in lengths from 13mm (1/2") to 150mm (6"). Spikes are made in lengths from 100mm (4") to 350mm (14") and are of sturdier proportion than nails.

Types of Nails
Nails are manufactured in many types as shown in Figure 5.2 (→ 232, 233), and shapes as shown in Figure 5.3 (→ 234) to suit specific applications.

In Canada, nails are specified by the type and length and are still manufactured to Imperial dimensions. Diameter is specified by gauge number (British Imperial standard) and is the same as the wire diameter used in manufacture.

In the US, the length of nails is designated by "penny" abbreviated "d". For example a twenty-penny nail (20d) has a length of four inches.

Pneumatic or mechanical nailing guns have found wide-spread acceptance in North America due to the speed with which nails can be driven. They are especially cost effective in repetitive applications such as in shearwall construction where nail spacing may be as close as 75mm (3") to distribute load.

The nails for power nailers are lightly attached to each other or joined with plastic, allowing quick loading nail clips, similar to joined paper staples. Fasteners for these tools are available for every application from heavy framing nails up to 89mm (3-1/2") down to upholstery staples 4.8mm (3/16") in length. These fasteners are also available in galvanized form for corrosive applications.

Shanks
Nail shanks are made smooth or deformed. The deformed shank is usually spiral (or helical) or ringed.

Spiral nails provide greater withdrawal resistance than smooth shank nails and are particularly effective in resisting shock loads. Some typical applications are for: flooring underlay, panelling, gusset plates, soffits, siding, and roofing.

Ring-threaded nails also have high withdrawal resistance created by the keying action of displaced wood fibres against the nail grooves. Applications include fastening for gypsum wallboard, plywood underlay for flooring, and sheathing.

Points
The shape of the point affects the tendency of the wood to split when a nail is used close to an end or edge because the shape dictates whether the nail acts like a wedge or like a punch. The sharper the point, the higher the holding power due to wedging of wood fibres against the fastener, the easier it is to drive the nail, but the greater the tendency of the nail to split the wood.

The most widely used nail point is the diamond which is a good compromise between ease of driving, minimization of splitting, and holding power.

Materials
The types of materials used for nails are shown in the Table on page 235. The most common nails are made of low or medium carbon steels or aluminum. Medium-carbon steels are sometimes hardened by heat treating and quenching to increase toughness. Nails of copper, brass, bronze, stainless steel, monel and other special metals are available if specially ordered.

5

Connections

Figure 5.2 **Nail Types**	Type of Nail	Head	Shank	Point	Material	Finishes and Coatings	Common Lengths mm	in.
	Common (Spike) 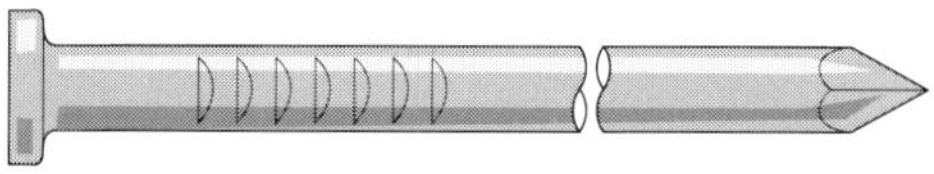	F	C, S	D	S, E	B	100 - 350	4 - 14
	Eavestrough (Spike) 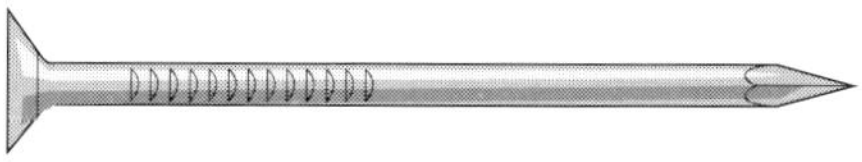	Cs, F	C, S	D, N	S	B, Ghd	125 - 250	5 - 10
	Standard or Common 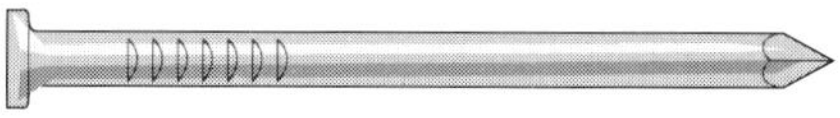	F	C, R, S	D	A, S, E	B, Ge	25 - 150	1 - 6
	Box 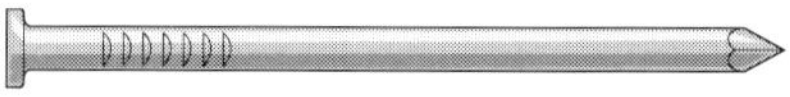	F, Lf	C, R, S	D	S	B, Pt, Ghd	19 - 125	3/4 - 5
	Finishing 	Bd	C, S	D	S	B, Bl	25 - 100	1 - 4
	Flooring and Casing 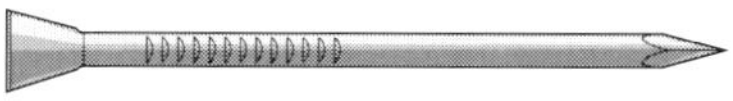	Cs	C, S	Bt, D	S	B, Bl, Ht	28 - 80	1-1/8 - 3-1/4
	Concrete 	Cs	S	Con, Bt, D	Sc	Ht	13 - 75	1/2 - 3
	Cladding and Decking 	F, O	C, S	D	A, S	B, Ghd	50 - 63	2 - 2-1/2

Notes:
1. Refer to Figure 5.3 (→ 234) for Head, Shank and Point abbreviations.
2. Refer to Table (→ 235) for Materials, Finishes and Coatings abbreviations.

Type of Nail	Head	Shank	Point	Material	Finishes and Coatings	Common Lengths mm	in.
Clinch	F, Lf	C, S	Db	S 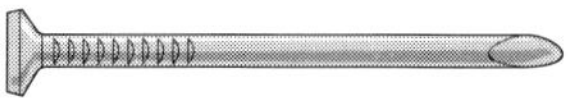	B	19 - 63	3/4 - 2-1/2
Hardwood Flooring	Cs	S	Bt	S 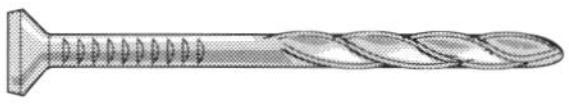	B, Ht	14 - 63	1-1/2 - 2-1/2
Gypsum Wallboard	Dw, F	C, R, S	D, N	S 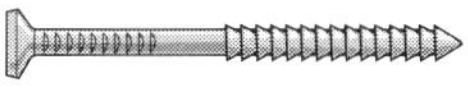	B, Bl, Ge	28 - 50	1-1/8 - 2
Underlay and Underlay Subfloor	F, Cs	C, R	D	S 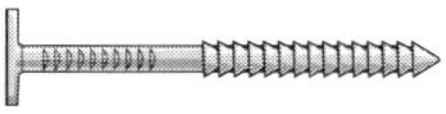	B, Ht	19 - 50	3/4 - 2
Roundwire Sash Pins	-	C	D	S 	B	19 - 50	3/4 - 2
Roofing	Lf, F	C	D	A, S 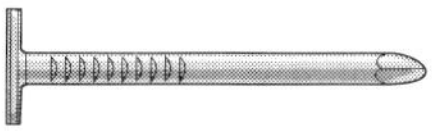	B, Ghd	19 - 50	3/4 - 2
Wood Shingle	F	C, R, S	D	A, S 	B, Ghd	31 - 44	1-1/4 - 1-3/4
Gypsum Lath	F	C, S	D, N	S 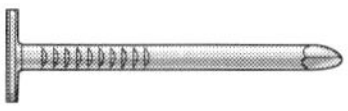	B, Bl, Ge	31	1-1/4
Wood Lath	F	C, S	D	S 	Bl	25 - 28	1 - 1-1/8

Notes:
1. Refer to Figure 5.3 (→ 234) for Head, Shank and Point abbreviations.
2. Refer to Table (→ 235) for Materials, Finishes and Coatings abbreviations.

5

Connections

Figure 5.3	Part	Type	Abbr.	Remarks	
Nail Heads, Shanks and Points	Heads	Flat Counter-Sink	Cs	For nail concealment; light construction, flooring, and interior trim	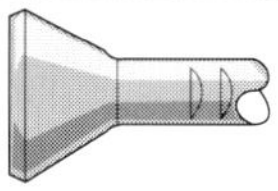
		Gypsum Wallboard	Dw	For gypsum wallboard	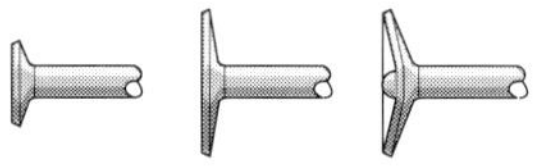
		Finishing	Bd	For nail concealment; cabinet-work, furniture	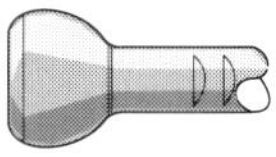
		Flat	F	For general construction	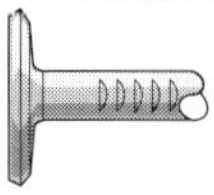
		Large flat	Lf	For tear resistance; roofing paper	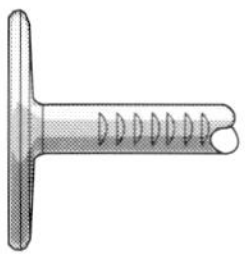
		Oval	O	For special effects; cladding and decking	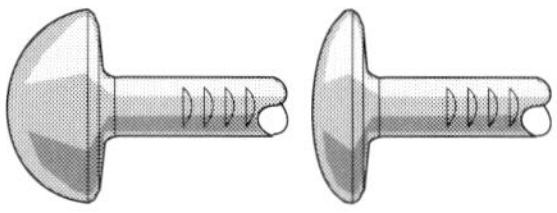
	Shanks	Smooth	C	For normal holding power; temporary fastening 	
		Spiral or Helical	S	For greater holding power; permanent fastening 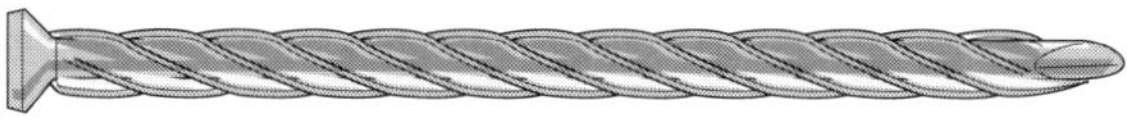	
		Ringed	R	For highest holding power; permanent fastening 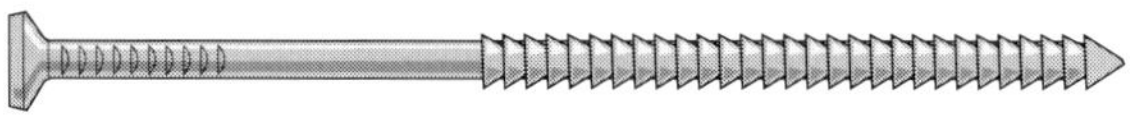	
	Points	Diamond	D	For general use, 35° angle; length about 1.5 x diameter	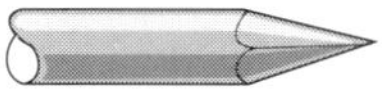
		Blunt Diamond	Bt	For harder wood species to reduce splitting, 45° angle	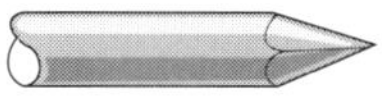
		Long Diamond	N	For fast driving, 25° angle; may tend to split harder species	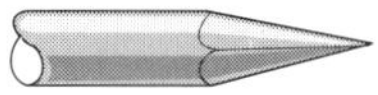
		Duckbill	Db	For ease of clinching	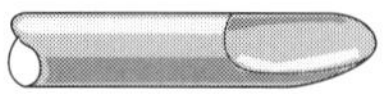
		Conical	Con	For use in masonry; penetrates better than diamond	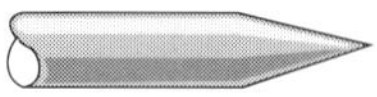

Nail Materials, Finishes and Coatings	Material	Abbr.	Application
	Aluminum	A	For improved appearance and long life: increased strain and corrosion resistance
	Steel – mild	S	For general construction
	Steel – high carbon	Sc	For special driving conditions: improved impact resistance
	Stainless steel, copper and silicon bronze	E	For superior corrosion resistance; more expensive than hot-dip galvanizing

	Finishes and Coatings		
	Bright	B	For general construction, normal finish, not recommended for exposure to weather
	Blued	Bl	For increased holding power in hardwood, thin oxide finish produced by heat treatment
	Heat treated	Ht	For increased stiffness and holding power: black oxide finish
	Phoscoated	Pt	For increased holding power; not corrosion resistant
	Electro galvanized	Ge	For limited corrosion resistance; thin zinc plating; smooth surface; for interior use
	Hot-dip galvanized	Ghd	For improved corrosion resistance; thick zinc coating; rough surface; for exterior use

Uncoated steel nails used in areas subject to wetting will corrode and result in staining of the wood surface. In addition, the naturally occurring extractives in the cedars react with unprotected steel and with copper and blued or electro-galvanized fasteners. In such cases, hot-dip galvanized nails or stainless steel or copper nails should be used.

Sheathing Nailing
Nail popping may occur if a sheathing material is applied to lumber with a high moisture content. As the lumber shrinks, the depth of the hole in which the nail sits reduces and the nail head is pushed above the surface of the plywood. This tendency can be reduced by:

• Using dry lumber whenever possible. If unseasoned lumber is used, allow time for on site drying and reseat nails which project from the sheathing.

• Using ringed nails and driving nails at a slight angle or using screws. Set all nail heads prior to laying resilient flooring.

• Using a length of fastener which gives the minimum acceptable depth of penetration in the framing member.

Screws
Wood screws are usually used for millwork and finishing rather than for structural framing. They are used in fastening millwork where resistance to withdrawal is a requirement.

Screws find some applications in structural framing as in the case of floor sheathing which is glued and screwed to the joists or the positive attachment of gypsum wallboard to support members. They are higher in cost than nails because of the machining required to make the thread and head.

Screws are designed to be much better at resisting withdrawal than nails. However, when used for structural purposes, it is better that screws not be loaded in withdrawal as shown in Figure 5.1 (→ 230) but rather use the withdrawal resistance property to produce and maintain close contact between the elements being joined.

The types of wood screws commonly used are shown in Figure 5.4 (→ 236).

5

Connections

Figure 5.4 **Types of Screws**	Part	Type	Use	
	Head Shapes	Flat	For countersinking flush with or below the surface	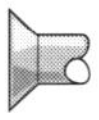
		Oval	For partial countersinking	
		Pan	Recommended to replace round headed screws; for use with washers or thin side pieces	
	Head Drive Shapes	Slot Recess	Common use	 Slot
		Cross Recess	To minimize screwdriver slipout	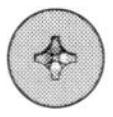 Phillips  Pozidriv
		Square Recess	To minimize screwdriver slipout	 Socket (Robertson)
	Shanks	Double Lead	For faster turning; requires greater torque	
		Single Lead	For shorter screws (less than 25mm (1"))	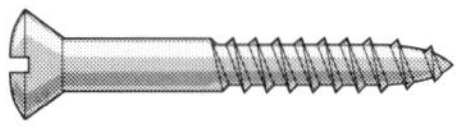
		Tapping	For better penetration; higher strength; designed for sheet metal but can be used with wood	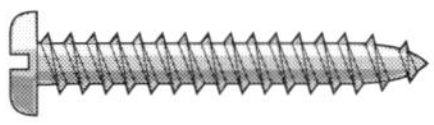
	Points	Gimlet	For wood and some tapping screws	
		Blunt	For some tapping screws	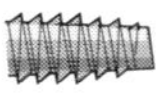

Figure 5.5 **Screw Lead Holes**	Lead Hole	Wood Screws Diameter	Depth
	Countersunk Head	Same diameter as head	Same depth as head
	Shank	Slightly smaller than shank diameter; 7/8 of shank diameter for withdrawal loading	For softwoods, about 1/2 of screw length for shank and thread lead holes combined (may be same diameter); for hardwoods or soft screws, lead holes nearly as deep as screw
	Thread	About 70 percent if loaded in withdrawal; about 90 percent of diameter for hardwoods	

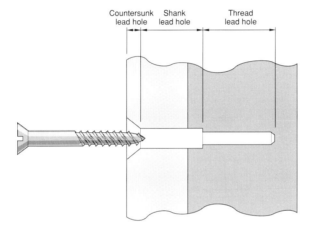

Countersunk lead hole   Shank lead hole   Thread lead hole

5

Connections

Framing Connectors

Framing connectors are made of sheet metal and are manufactured with prepunched holes to accept nails as shown in Figure 5.6(→ 238).

They are used to provide a more positive connection between wood members by allowing the nails securing the framing connector to be loaded laterally rather than in partial withdrawal as would be the case if the members were toenailed together. They are also used in frame construction where additional protection is required against uplift from seismic or wind induced forces.

Framing connectors are suitable for most joints in wood framing of 38mm (2" nom.) and thicker lumber. These include connections between: joists and headers; rafters and plates or ridges; purlins and trusses; and studs and sill plates.

The load transfer capacity of framing connectors is affected by the thickness of steel used. Standard duty framing connectors are commonly made of 18-gauge zinc-coated sheet steel.

Medium and heavy-duty anchors are made from heavier zinc-coated steel usually 12 gauge and 7 gauge respectively. They are suitable for similar connections between larger members where the loads to be carried exceed those permissible for the light anchors such as: header or beam to post; purlin to beam; and purlin to truss.

Special nails are provided with framing anchors, and the required number must be used with each anchor to provide the load-carrying capacity of the anchor. Anchors are typically used in pairs to avoid eccentricity.

Figure 5.6
Framing Connectors

All-purpose framing anchor

Tie-down framing anchor

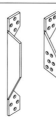 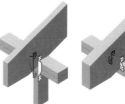 

Triple grip framing anchor

Framing angle

 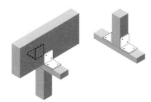

Joist and purlin hangers

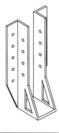 

Truss plates

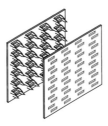 

Joist and Purlin Hangers

Framing connectors are manufactured to connect joists and purlins to supporting wood members. They are generally available for member sizes from 38 x 89mm (2" x 4") joists to 89 x 377mm (4" x 14") purlins or double joists.

Joist and purlin hangers are made from light gauge galvanized sheet metal and are affixed to wood members with special nails. As with framing anchors, the required number of nails must be used to provide the load-carrying capacity.

Hangers can reduce the overall depth of a floor or roof assembly or increase clearance below the framing where joists abut headers rather than rest on top of them (see Figure 5.7 below).

Load capacities for hangers are determined by testing and manufacturers' data for a particular hanger should be used for design.

Truss Plates

Truss plates are light gauge metal plates used to connect prefabricated light frame wood trusses. Truss plates are produced by punching light gauge galvanized steel (usually 16, 18, or 20 gauge) so that teeth protrude from one side.

Since most truss plate designs are proprietary, North American engineering design standards do not provide design values but rather require that plates be tested and accredited to establish design values. There are a number of truss plate manufacturers and each has its own tooth pattern for which design values have been determined through testing and accreditation by independent testing agencies.

Light frame trusses connected with truss plates should not be used in corrosive conditions or with fire-retardant treated lumber in wet service conditions due to the potential for loss of strength if deterioration of the teeth takes place.

Truss plates are installed by first orienting the members to be connected and then pressing the plate into the members using a hydraulic press, roller, or ram.

Good practise dictates that: identical truss plates placed on opposing faces are directly opposite each other; the plates are not deformed during installation; the teeth are normal to the surface of the lumber; the teeth are fully embedded in the wood so that the plate is tight to the wood surface (the plate must not be embedded into the lumber deeper than half the plate thickness); and the lumber where the plates are situated must not contain wane, loose knots, or knot holes.

Miscellaneous

Some other types of light metal connections are shown in Figure 5.8 (→ 240, 241), and many other types are available or can be specially ordered to suit a specific need.

5

Connections

Figure 5.7
Space Advantage of Joist Hangers

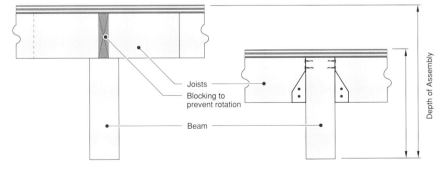

Joists

Blocking to prevent rotation

Beam

Depth of Assembly

Joist Resting
on top of Beam

Joists and Joist Hangers
Abutting Beam

Figure 5.8
Miscellaneous Connectors

Post caps

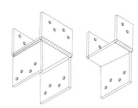
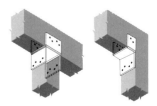

Post anchor

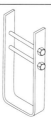

Sill plate anchor

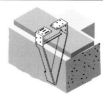

Straps

Nail-on Plates

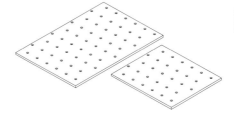

H-clip

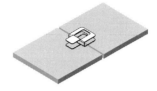

Back-up gypsum
wallboard clip

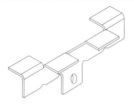

Heavy Connections

Bolts

Bolts are used with plates, washers, or, more efficiently, in conjunction with split rings or shear plates to connect wood members. They are often used in purlin to beam, beam to column, or column to base connections of wood structures. When bolts are used alone with washers or side plates as shown in Figure 5.9 (→ 242), the load transfer area of the wood is the surface area of the bolt.

Timber connectors such as split rings and shear plates are a means of distributing loads over a larger area of wood and are discussed later in this section (→ 246).

Several types of bolts as shown in Figure 5.10 (→ 243) are used for wood construction with the hexagon head type being the most common. Countersunk heads are used where a flush surface is desired. Carriage bolts can be tightened by turning the nut without holding the bolt since the shoulders under the head grip the wood.

Depending on diameter, bolts are available in lengths from 75mm (3") up to 400mm (16") with other lengths available on special order. Where long length is required, threaded rods may be used in lieu of bolts, either alone or with shear connectors.

Spacing
Placement of bolts is important in design since it can affect load carrying capacity. Minimum end distance is based on bolt diameter and wood species, while minimum edge distance and spacing requirements are based on bolt diameters.

The net section of wood members (area of wood remaining after drilling of holes) in a bolted joint must also be checked by referring to wood engineering codes.

Washers
As a minimum, standard cut washers should be used with bolts to keep a bolt head or nut from causing crushing when tightening is taking place. Where a steel plate is used, the head or nut bears directly on steel, and washers are not required.

Common types of washers are shown in Figure 5.11 (→ 243).

If square or round steel plate washers are used, they must be of adequate thickness to prevent cupping and overstressing of the steel. Round plate washers may be used instead of square plate washers for appearance reasons such as for exposed trusses. Bevelled washers are necessary where the bolts are not perpendicular to the bearing surface.

Figure 5.9
**Loading
Arrangements
for Bolts**

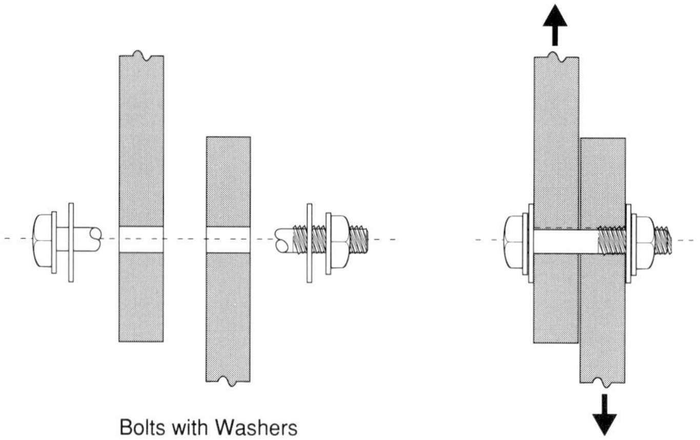

Bolts with Washers

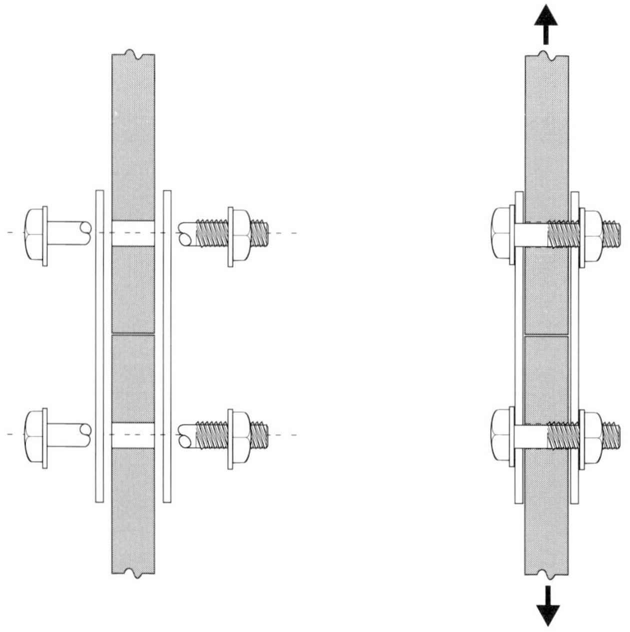

Bolts with Side Plates

Figure 5.10
Types of Bolts for Wood Construction

Bolt Type	Usual Range of Diameters mm	in.	Uses	
Finished Hexagon Bolt	6.4 to 38	1/4 to 1-1/2	For countersinking flush or below the surface	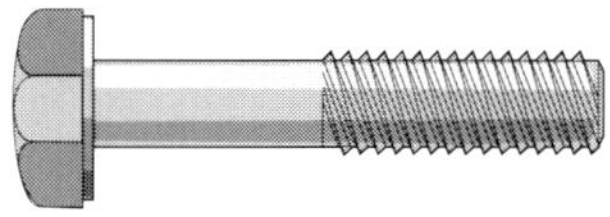
Square Headed Machine Bolt	6.4 to 51	1/4 to 2	Same as finished hexagon bolt but gradually being replaced by them	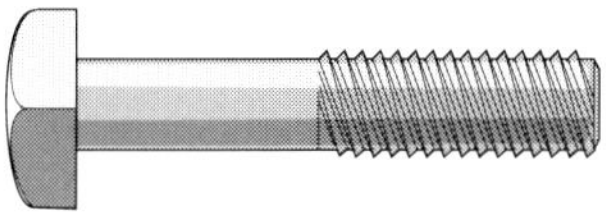
Machine Bolt with Countersunk Head	12.7 to 32	1/2 to 1-1/4	Used where flush surface is required (may have to be used with countersunk washer	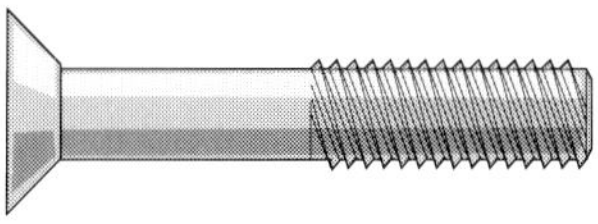
Carriage Bolt	4.8 to 19	0.19 (No.10) to 3/4	Used where head may be inaccessible during tightening	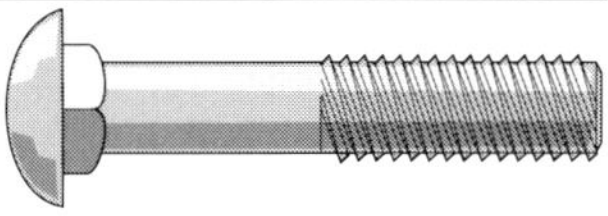

Figure 5.11
Washers for Bolts and Lag Screws

Washer Type	Uses	
Standard cut washer	Used for screws and bolts where the loading is lateral. Should not be used with split rings or shear plates.	
Square plate washer	Used for bolts and with split rings and shear plates. Suitable for tensile loads.	
Round plate washer	Used for bolts and with split rings and shear plates. Suitable for tensile loads.	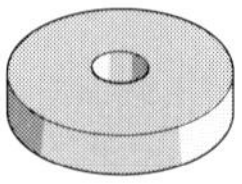
Ogee (cast iron) washer	Used for bolts and with split rings and shear plates. Suitable for tensile loads.	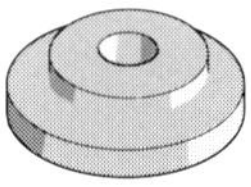
Malleable iron washer	Used for bolts and with split rings and shear plates. Suitable for tensile loads.	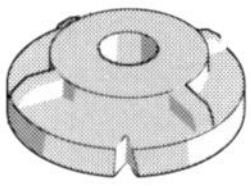
Bevel washer	Used where the bolt to member alignment is not perpendicular.	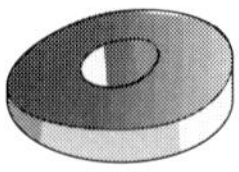

5

Connections

Minimum dimensions for washers used in timber connector joints depend on the type of washer and size of the bolt and connector (split rings and shear plates), and are specified in engineering design standards (CAN/CSA-O86.1-M89 and AITC 117-87).

If bolts carry a tensile load, the washers must provide enough bearing area so that resistance in compression perpendicular to the grain of the wood is not exceeded.

Side Plates
Side plates are frequently used to transfer load from one wood member to another by allowing a butt joint rather than an overlapping joint.

Installation
Bolts are installed in holes drilled slightly (1.0 to 2.0mm (1/32" to 1/16") larger than the bolt diameter to prevent any splitting and stress development that could be caused by installation or subsequent wood shrinkage.

Wood shrinkage requires special consideration in the design of bolted connections for sawn timber because of the potential high moisture content of the members. It is less important in designing connections for glulam, PSL, or other wood products manufactured at low moisture content.

As shrinkage across the grain takes place in timber, movement may be restrained by the steel side plates leading to splitting of the wood. If steel side plates hold bolts further than 125mm (5") apart across the width in a splice joint, separate side plates should be used (see Figure 5.12 below).

Wood may not be completely seasoned when connections are assembled and therefore, bolts should be checked for tightness about one year after installation.

Lag Screws
Lag screws are bolts with sharp points and coarse threads designed to penetrate and grip wood fibre (see Figure 5.13 opposite). They are used to anchor metal, or wood, to wood in areas inaccessible to the placement of a nut for a throughbolt, or where an especially long bolt would be needed to penetrate a joint fully.

Although lag screws do have some unique applications, throughbolts are considered to be a more positive means of connection since they are less dependent on workmanship for reliable installation.

Figure 5.12
Types of Bolted Splices

Joint Spliced with Wood Side Members

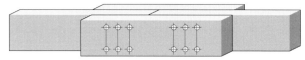

Joint Spliced with Steel Side Plates

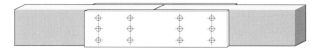

Joint Spliced with Multiple Steel Side Plates

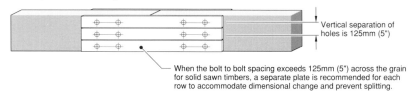

Vertical separation of holes is 125mm (5")

When the bolt to bolt spacing exceeds 125mm (5") across the grain for solid sawn timbers, a separate plate is recommended for each row to accommodate dimensional change and prevent splitting.

Figure 5.13
Lag Screws for Wood Construction

Bolt Type	Usual Range of Diameters mm	in.	Uses
Lag Screw (Bolt)	6.4 to 25	1/4 to 1	In lieu of bolts where nut location would be inaccessible; sometimes used for split ring and shear plate joints

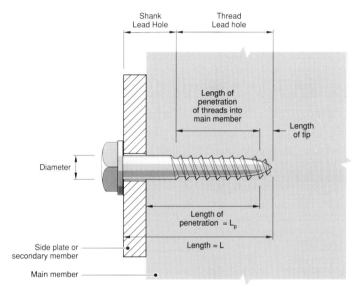

The resistance of a lag screw generally increases with the length of the embedded threaded portion. However, it is also affected by other considerations such as side plate thickness.

As with other types of metal fasteners, sufficient end and edge distance must be provided to prevent splitting and to provide sufficient area for shear and bearing resistance in accordance with engineering design codes.

Stock sizes of lag screws range from 25 to 400mm (1" to 16") in length and 6 to 25mm (1/4" to 1") in diameter.

Washers
The same requirements for washers apply to those used with lag screws as to those used with bolts.

Installation
Two hole diameters are used to prepare a member to accept a lag screw, drill bits of two dimensions must be used. The smaller diameter hole is drilled to accept the threaded portion of the lag screw, and a larger diameter hole is drilled to accommodate the shank portion.

Glulam Rivets
A glulam rivet as shown in Figure 5.14 ($\rightarrow$ 247) is a high strength fastener which resembles a nail but has a flattened oval shank with a wedge shaped head. The rivet is driven through pre-drilled holes in a steel side plate until the tapered head is wedged into the hole.

In Canada, glulam rivets have become the fastener of choice for glulam members because performance is proven, and machining for acceptance of bolts or split rings is eliminated. US design codes do not yet provide information on the glulam rivet.

5

Connections

The development of the glulam rivet is the outcome of a long search for a new type of fastener particularly suited to laminated timber products. More than 40,000 rivets were tested either individually or in groups to determine capacities.

Glulam rivets are used with Douglas Fir-Larch and Spruce-Pine glulam species categories in Canada but are not yet approved for use with solid timber.

Glulam rivets (see Figure 5.14 opposite) are manufactured of heat-treated steel in lengths from 40mm to 90mm (1-1/2" to 3-1/2").

Steel plates used in conjunction with rivets must have a minimum thickness of 4.8mm (3/16") and meet specific requirements for strength and ductility.

Glulam rivets have numerous advantages over other fasteners such as bolts and shear plates. They permit a greater load transfer per unit contact area than any other fastener, resulting in substantial saving in the size of steel side plates. Reductions in glued-laminated member sizes are possible in some instances since member design can be based on the entire cross-sectional area rather than the net area remaining after removal of wood material for the installation of fasteners such as bolts and split rings. Field assembly is simplified and the chance of alignment error is reduced in comparison to other types of fasteners.

Split Rings and Shear Plates
Split rings and shear plates are load transferring devices which rely on bolts or lag screws to restrain the joint assembly. They are more efficient structurally than bolts or lag screws used alone because they enlarge the wood area over which a load is distributed as shown in Figure 5.15 (→ 248).

Split rings and shear plates are used mainly to transfer loads in heavy timber or glulam members such as in roof trusses. These connector units transfer shear either between the faces of two timber members or between a timber member and a metal sideplate. They are not usually protectively coated and need be galvanized only if used with preservative treated wood or in wet service conditions.

It is important that the proper size of bolt be used with a connector since it is an integral part of the assembly. The bolt clamps the joint together so that the connector acts effectively.

Split ring and shear plate joints are fabricated using the special tools as shown in the photographs at the beginning of this section (→ 222). Care must be taken to ensure a good fit.

Split Rings
Split rings are manufactured in Imperial sizes in diameters of 63mm (2-1/2") and 100mm (4") from hot-rolled carbon steel for use with 13mm (1/2") and 19mm (3/4") diameter bolts respectively.

A single split ring insets into both the pre-cut grooves in the wood surfaces being joined as shown in Figure 5.16 (→ 249). A tongue and groove split in the ring permits the ring to deform slightly under load so that all contact areas distribute load, and the special wedge shape on both sides of the ring eases insertion and ensures a tight fitting joint when the ring is fully seated in the grooves.

Shear Plates
Shear plates are manufactured in Imperial sizes in a diameter of 67mm (2-5/8") in pressed steel for use with 19mm (3/4") bolts or lagscrews, and in a diameter of 100mm (4") in malleable iron for use with 19mm (3/4") or 22mm (7/8") bolts or lagscrews.

Grooves for shear plates must also be precision machined by special tools which recess the wood so that the shear plates sit flush with the surface.

Figure 5.14
Glulam Rivets

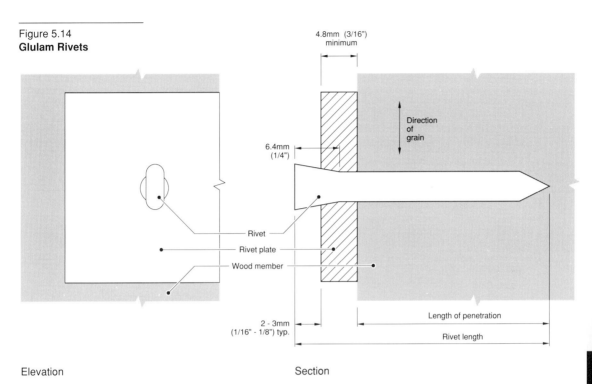

4.8mm (3/16")
minimum

Direction
of
grain

6.4mm
(1/4")

Rivet

Rivet plate

Wood member

Length of penetration

2 - 3mm
(1/16" - 1/8") typ.

Rivet length

Elevation   Section

Stress Distribution for Rivet Joint

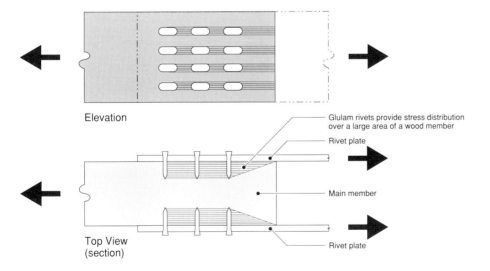

Elevation

Glulam rivets provide stress distribution
over a large area of a wood member

Rivet plate

Main member

Top View
(section)

Rivet plate

5

Connections

Shear plates can be used singly to connect wood to steel, or be paired back to back to connect wood to wood as shown in Figure 5.17 (→ 250).

Typical wood-to-metal applications occur at purlin to beam, column to foundation, arch peak, and steel gusset connections.

Steel side plates used in conjunction with bolts must be sized according to wood engineering standards to resist tensile and compressive forces as well as buckling at critical sections.

Figure 5.15
Stress Distribution for Bolted Joints with and without Split Rings and Shear Plates

Bolted Joint

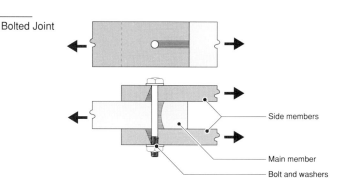

Side members

Main member

Bolt and washers

Split Ring Connector Joint

Split ring and Shear plate connectors distribute compressive loads over a larger wood area than bolts and are therefore capable of carrying greater loads

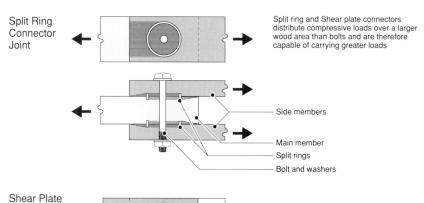

Side members

Main member

Split rings

Bolt and washers

Shear Plate Connector Joint

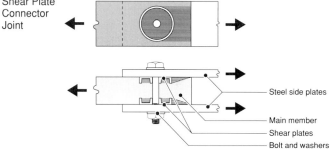

Steel side plates

Main member

Shear plates

Bolt and washers

Figure 5.16
**Split Ring
Loading
Arrangements**

Split Ring Connector
(Available in 63mm (2-1/2") and 100mm (4") diameters)

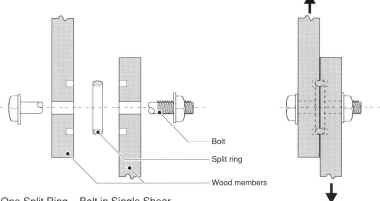

Bolt

Split ring

Wood members

One Split Ring – Bolt in Single Shear

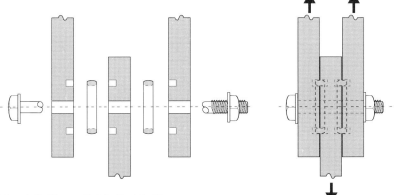

Two Split Rings – Bolt in Double Shear

5

Connections

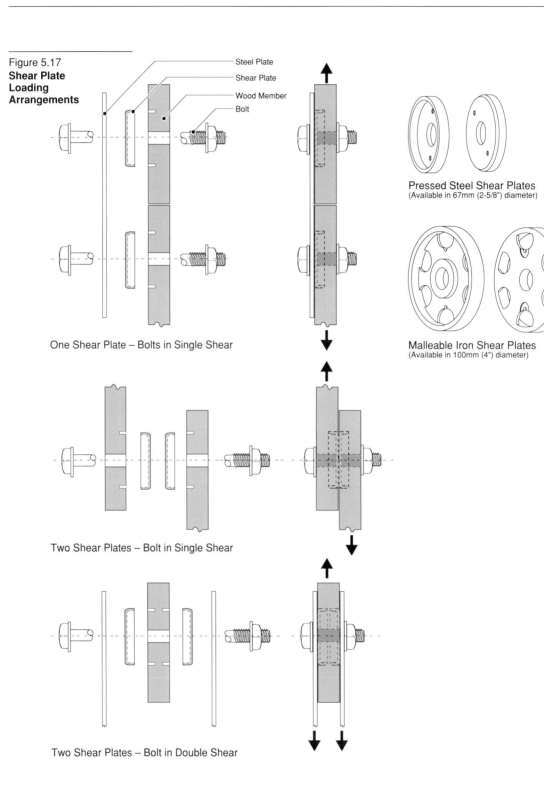

Figure 5.17
**Shear Plate
Loading
Arrangements**

Steel Plate
Shear Plate
Wood Member
Bolt

One Shear Plate – Bolts in Single Shear

Two Shear Plates – Bolt in Single Shear

Two Shear Plates – Bolt in Double Shear

Pressed Steel Shear Plates
(Available in 67mm (2-5/8") diameter)

Malleable Iron Shear Plates
(Available in 100mm (4") diameter)

5.3   Timber Joinery

Timber joinery is a post and beam wood construction technique which does not make use of metal fasteners. For connection, it relies upon the precision interlocking of members for load transfer.

Many historic structures in North America were built at a time when metal fasteners were not readily available. Instead, wood members were joined by shaping the adjoining wood members to interlock using mortise and tenon joinery as shown in Figure 5.18 (→ 252) similar to that which is still used in the making of strong inconspicuous joints for furniture. The mated joints were restrained by inserting wooden pegs into holes bored through the interlocked members.

Timber joinery is presently undergoing a resurgence in popularity. It is being used where the exhibition of the craftsmanship required to precisely shape and interlock large wood members is a desired building feature. Although used mainly for upscale residential construction, timber joinery is also being used for commercial construction in some instances.

Metal fasteners are efficient means of transferring loads. They permit the use of moderate sized members to carry and transfer loads because the installation of metal fasteners requires only minimal removal of wood fibre in the area of the fasteners. Timber joinery, on the contrary, requires the removal of significant wood fibre where joints occur. For this reason, the adequacy of timber joinery is usually governed by the connections. Increased member size in relation to what would be required for construction employing metal fasters is often required.

In addition, wood engineering codes do not provide specific load transfer information for timber joinery due to sensitivity to quality of workmanship and material quality. As a result, engineering design must be conservative.

The amount of skill and time required for measuring, fitting, cutting, and trial assembly is far greater for timber joinery than for other types of wood construction. Therefore it is not the most economical means of connecting the members of wood buildings. Timber joinery is not used where economy is the overriding concern. Instead, it is used to provide a unique structural appearance which portrays the natural beauty of wood without distraction.

5

Connections

Figure 5.18
**Basic Joints for
Timber Joinery
Construction**

Basic Mortise and Tenon Joint

Dovetail Joint

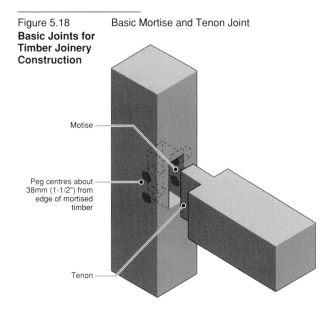

Motise

Peg centres about
38mm (1-1/2") from
edge of mortised
timber

Tenon

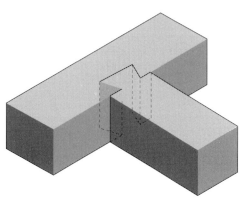

Timber in tension must be bound with
joint that can prevent withdrawl.

Bevelled Shoulder Joint

Housed Mortise and Tenon Joint

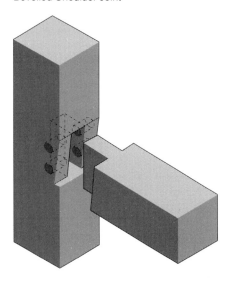

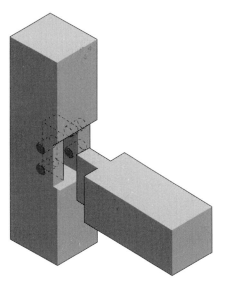

5.4   Adhesives

Adhesives play a prominent role in wood construction. They are used for:

- The manufacture of laminated products

- As a means of increasing the structural rigidity of sheathing/joist combinations in floors and of affixing non-structural panel products

- End joining dimension lumber

- Repair

Adhesives Used for Laminated Products

Structural composites such as plywood, oriented strandboard (OSB) and wafer-board, prefabricated wood I-joists, laminated parallel strand lumber (PSL), laminated veneer lumber (LVL) and glulam are dependent upon adhesives to transfer the stresses between adjoining wood fibre.

Interior use wood products such as particleboard, which is used for furniture and for some structural applications such as flooring underlay, and hardwood plywood, which is used for furniture and decorative panelling, also rely on adhesives for laminating wood material.

The selection, application rate, and curing conditions for adhesives for these products is controlled at the point of manufacture. A brief discussion of the principal adhesives used in these products is presented to address questions which some times arise about permanence of bond, reliability, resistance to environmental factors, and emission of volatile chemicals into buildings.

There are two principle types of adhesive used for the manufacture of Canadian wood products. These are urea-formaldehyde (UF) which is suitable only for interior use products and phenol-formaldehyde (PF) which is used for exterior applications.

Interior Wood Products
Urea-formaldehyde adhesive is a thick creamy syrup which cures to a colourless solid.

UF adhesives are very economical and fast curing but are not suitable for damp conditions. For this reason, UF glues are used for panels intended for nonstructural use such as particleboard and hardwood plywood.

UF adhesives are non-staining and therefore have the further advantage of not blemishing the high quality expensive face veneers used for hardwood panels for interior finish applications.

The raw materials for UF adhesives are derived from natural gas through the intermediates of ammonia for urea and methanol for formaldehyde.

Exterior Wood Products
Phenol-formaldehyde (PF) adhesives are a dark purple-brown colour and give the dark glue lines associated with products such as plywood and OSB.

Known as the phenolics, they are a derivative of crude oil and the principle resins approved for the manufacture of wood products intended for exterior applications.

PF adhesives are used for the manufacture of glulam, PSL, LVL, plywood, OSB/waferboard and for fingerjoining stress graded lumber.

PF adhesives are somewhat more expensive than UF adhesives and exhibit lower levels of formaldehyde emissions.

Various types of extenders such as walnut shell flour, Douglas fir bark flour, alder bark flour, and wood flour are used to moderate the cost of PF glues, control penetration into the wood fibre, and moderate strength properties to suit the materials being bonded.

5

Connections

Resorcinol-formaldehyde (RF) adhesive is a phenolic substance which is more reactive than the PF adhesives. Being more reactive means that curing is faster and takes place at room temperature and below. Otherwise these glues have the same basic properties as the PF adhesives. However, high cost of the resorcinols means in practice that they are often blended with the PF adhesives to moderate the cost.

Emissions from Wood Product Adhesives

Formaldehyde is a chemical used in the manufacture of many contemporary products including, for example, upholstery, permanent press clothing, and carpet. It is also a component of the adhesives used to manufacture most wood panel and composite products. Formaldehyde is an allergic irritant to some people when the time and level of exposure is high. Effects are compounded when a building has air change rates below accepted standards.

The level of formaldehyde emission from any new product is time dependant. Emission level is highest when the product is new, and decreases steadily as the time in service increases.

Housing and Urban Development (HUD) in the United States has set limits on the amount of allowable formaldehyde which may be emitted for building materials and contents. These levels are recognized in Canada and in the US.

Wood products made with PF adhesive wood products are substantially below the HUD limit for formaldehyde emissions. Emission standards for products made from UF adhesive products are also below the limits established.

Wood products made with PF adhesives have a low level of formaldehyde emission because the phenol resins chemically fix the formaldehyde.

Since the formaldehyde component of UF adhesives is not completely chemically fixed by the urea, some is free to dissipate. Adhesive manufacturers have met HUD standards by reducing the formaldehyde content and consequently increasing the amount of adhesive and the curing time.

Wood products containing formaldehyde meet or surpass present HUD standards. With standards for formaldehyde emissions expected to become increasingly stringent, chemists will be challenged to formulate acceptable low cost adhesives for the wood and other products which house and furnish modern living and work spaces.

Sheathing and Panel Application

There are many adhesives available to improve the structural performance of building elements or to apply non-structural panels in a way that does not leave surface blemish on the panel, as would nailing.

These field applied tube type adhesives are available in many types suitable for both interior and exterior use. The recommended application temperature can range between −10 and 40°C (15 and 105°F). These fast setting adhesives can be used to bond wood and panels to metal, gypsum wallboard, concrete, and foam insulation.

Where floor sheathing is affixed to joists with a field applied elastomeric adhesive in addition to nails or screws, improved vibration and deflection can be gained. In this situation, the joists and sheathing act as a single composite section and increases in spans of 5 to 10 percent when compared to nailed or screwed floors are possible.

Repairs to Wood Members

As with all building materials, wood is subject to damage if exposed for a long period of time to adverse conditions, if original design was faulty, or if overstressed due to loadings beyond design specifications.

Damage assessment requires the analysis of a structural engineer. In some cases, on site repair rather than replacement may be possible.

Where a repair is recommended by a structural engineer qualified in designing and supervising repairs, it may require the use of epoxy adhesives. The procedure for such repair will usually mean sealing the area to be repaired using a high viscosity epoxy with putty-like properties which is trowelled over cracks and holes to contain the epoxy repair material. The putty is also used to embed injection and vent port hoses to accept pressure injection equipment.

A low viscosity two-part epoxy is then pumped into the injection port until all areas of the crack or defect are filled as evidenced by escape of epoxy through the vent port.

Once the epoxy repair has cured, the excess epoxy can be chipped and sanded away to restore the appearance of the member.

5

Connections

5.5 Appearance of Connections

Metal Wood Fasteners

Light Connections
Nails
Nails are often used structurally in light frame construction which is hidden from view at completion. In this application, the role of the nails is strictly functional, and appearance is not important.

Depending on the siding type, some nails used for exterior siding may not be hidden from view. Nails used for securing decking for porches and verandas are also usually visible.

The aesthetics are improved if visible nails have unobtrusive heads and are evenly spaced. Corrosion-resistant nails should be used in conditions where rust may occur to prevent wood staining.

Framing Connectors
Like nails, framing connectors are typically used for structural applications where connections will be concealed from view by interior finish and exterior cladding. One exception is the occasional use of light frame trusses in an open ceiling.

Truss plates are designed to be as compact as possible and are therefore relatively unobtrusive. Manufacturing procedures call for the careful placement of plates to ensure appropriate strength. This requirement should result in a symmetrical appearance.

Wood trusses are commonly made from No.1/No.2 visual grades or MSR lumber to provide superior strength and reliability. The specification of high quality lumber which gives truss lumber greater strength also improves appearance.

The truss plates are made usually from galvanized sheet steel. Light frame trusses, when left exposed, are often painted to eliminate contrast between the plates and the lumber.

Heavy Timber Connections
The visible portion of a heavy timber connection is comprised of bolt heads and side plates.

Bolts and lag screws may be used with or without side plates as dictated by the application.

Split rings and shear plate connectors are not visible in the finished joint assembly. Only the bolt head, nut and side plate, if required, are exposed to view.

However, using split rings and shear plates may affect the appearance of connections by reducing the number of bolts and the size of side plates required.

Heavy timber connectors by their nature transfer significant forces, and are often arranged in groups.

Such connectors can cover a large wood surface and often incorporate steel side plates.

The size of the side plates and the number and arrangement of bolts will affect the appearance of the connection. Painting can be used effectively to either de-emphasize or accentuate the appearance of bolts and plates used to connect wood members.

Side plates of standard steel plate dimensions will reduce the amount of fabrication, and result in a more economical connection.

Except where the connector group is exposed either to the elements or a corrosive environment, prime painted steel side plates and metal fasteners are usually adequate. Otherwise, steel hardware should be hot-dip galvanized.

Accurate machining of the grooves by special dappers must be specified when using shear plates and split rings.

When a group of large numbers of connectors is used in a group, consideration should be given to using a common template to lay out the holes in both the steel and the wood. This will minimize on-site enlarging of holes to provide for alignment.

5

Connections

Details calling for field welding of steel components adjacent to wood surfaces should be avoided so that damage to the wood surfaces does not occur.

For some applications, the prominence of side plates may be desired to accent exposed structural members. Where this is not desired, the visual impact of connections can be reduced by concealing steel hardware in kerfs machined into the wood members. Such concealment is more complex and costly than standard connection detailing.

Glulam rivet connections tend to be compact and therefore relatively unobtrusive. Side plates may be galvanized for humid locations and be painted to contrast or blend relative to the wood members.

Timber Joinery

Timber joinery is the use of interlocking members held in place by wood pegs to make structural connections. Compared to construction techniques employing mechanical fasteners, timber joinery requires additional skill and time. The resulting traditional uncluttered appearance of timber joinery connections may outweigh the additional labour required for some applications.

Adhesives

Wood members such as glulam, laminated veneer lumber (LVL) and parallel strand lumber (PSL) contain phenol-formaldehyde adhesives which give deep brown gluelines. This appearance can add visual appeal. As for any wood staining, test samples should be prepared and assessed in lighting conditions simulating actual conditions to ensure that the appearance is suitable.

Adhesives used to apply panels, as in the case of interior finish work, are hidden. However, if glue accidentally contacts finish faces, the ability of the wood to accept stains and fine finishes may be impaired.

Finishes and Coatings for Fasteners

Special coatings and treatments for metal fasteners provide corrosion resistance thereby guaranteeing structural integrity, and ensuring that good appearance is maintained.

For interior applications at normal comfort levels of humidity, fasteners exposed to view are usually painted.

For exterior applications, corrosive environments, and interior applications which have a high humidity level, as in the case of a swimming pool enclosure, protective coatings or corrosion-resistant materials for fasteners must be specified.

Small fasteners such as nails are available in aluminum or stainless steel, or plated with brass, bronze, copper, chrome or nickel to improve appearance and corrosion resistance.

Galvanizing is the most economical means of protecting both large and small steel fasteners.

Galvanizing is a process whereby zinc coatings are applied to steel either by hot processing (dipping or tumbling) or by electrolytic action. The protective zinc coating is gradually oxidized. Therefore the degree of protection provided is dependent on the thickness of zinc applied, with the most robust coatings specified for extreme environments such as continual exposure to salt water.

After application the galvanized coating is a bright metallic silver. After oxidation begins, the colour changes to dull grey which is usually an acceptable colour finish. Where a painted finish is required, a galvanizing primer should be used over galvanized metal, prior to applying an alkyd finish coat.

5.6   Connection Details

Wood is a versatile structural material capable of forming the entire structure and envelope of a building. It is also well suited to being used in conjunction with other building materials, where so desired by the designer.

This section illustrates many common details for wood to wood connections and for connecting wood members to other major building materials.

This section is organized as follows:

*   Wood to Wood
    Details 5.1 to 5.39

*   Wood to Masonry/Concrete
    Details 5.40 to 5.72

*   Wood to Steel
    Details 5.73 to 5.76

*   Suspended Loads
    Details 5.77 to 5.82

5

Connections

Connection Details

Wood to Wood

Light Connections

Light connections are those made using metal fasteners to connect dimension lumber and engineered wood products such as prefabricated wood I-joists and trusses, and the smaller dimensions of

laminated veneer lumber (LVL) and parallel strand lumber (PSL) in light framing applications (see Section 6.2).

Refer to manufacturers' literature for specific installation procedures and load capacities.

Truss-to-Stud Wall

Detail 5.1   Bottom chord bears on top of load bearing wall.

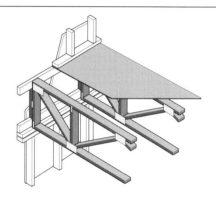

Detail 5.2   Top chord bears on top of load bearing wall. Bearing block increases ceiling height below truss, and can be prefabricated as part of the truss or be installed on site.

Bearing block —

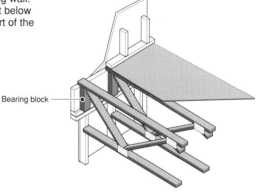

Detail 5.3   Bottom chord bears on top of interior loadbearing stud wall. Intermediate panel or cross bracing is required to provide lateral stability.

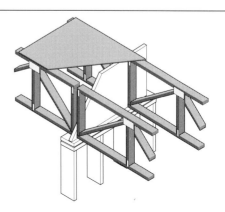

Connection Details

Wood to Wood

Truss-to-Beam

Detail 5.4

Top chord bears on top of beam or header. Alternatively, bottom chord bearing arrangement may be used.

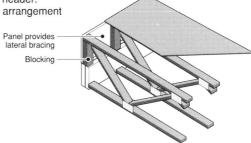

Panel provides lateral bracing

Blocking

Detail 5.5

Top chord bears on top of glulam beam. Rotation of truss bottom chord is restricted by blocking. A good fit between the top chord bearing trusses and the beam provides lateral support for the beam.

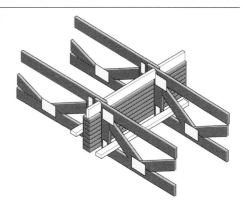

Detail 5.6

In this detail, clips are used to provide lateral support for the trusses. When it is desired for the beam to extend below the trusses, bearing blocks or top chord bearing trusses are used to elevate the trusses.

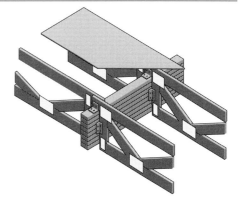

5

Connections

Connection Details

Wood to Wood

Cantilevered Truss

Detail 5.7

Bottom chord bearing truss supports wall above.
For clarity, truss cross bracing is not shown.

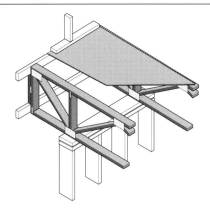

Detail 5.8

Cantilevered sections can be prefabricated in
many different shapes to provide many soffit
forms, such as this drop soffit.

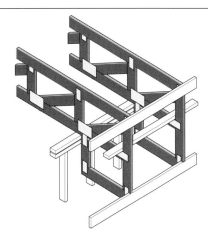

Detail 5.9

A variation of Detail 5.8 with sloped soffit.

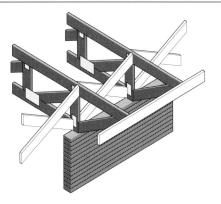

Connection Details

Wood to Wood

Wood I-Joists

Detail 5.10

Joist hangers sized specifically for prefabricated wood I-joists provide good load transfer. Blocking is used at intersection points of wood I-joists to reinforce the webs.

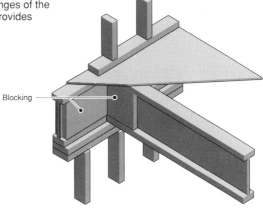

Blocking

Detail 5.11

Prefabricated wood I-joist floor supports a load bearing wall. Blocking between the flanges of the wood I-joists reinforces the web and provides lateral stability.

Blocking

5

Connections

Detail 5.12

Specialized joist hangers are available for dimension lumber and prefabricated wood I-joists for angled and skewed connections such as this sloped joist.

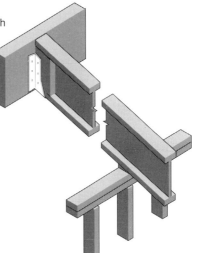

Connection Details

Wood to Wood

Heavy Connections

Heavy connections are used to connect timber and timber sized members of glulam, laminated veneer lumber (LVL) and parallel strand lumber (PSL).

Included in this category of wood-to-wood connections are hangers, angles, bolts, lag screws, glulam rivets, split rings and shear plates.

A wide variety of stock hardware is available but custom fabrication is frequently required for special loadings or member configurations.

Beam to Column

Detail 5.13

The simplest connection for a beam which continues over a column is a steel dowel driven through a hole drilled partially or fully through the beam. This connection is not visible but resistance to uplift is minimal. Rotation of the column is to be prevented at the base, or by means of other infill framing.

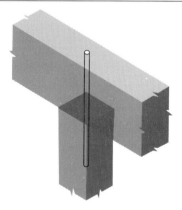

Detail 5.14

This standard beam-to-column connection provides resistance to uplift and to rotation of the beam.

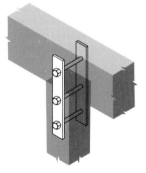

Detail 5.15

This detail may be used where beams abut over a column. This type of narrow side plate can be shaped to provide a degree of ornamentation as shown at the bottom.

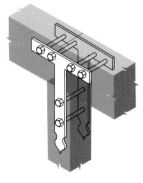

Connection Details

Wood to Wood

Detail 5.16

Uplift is resisted by this standard beam-to-column connection. The shear plates and dowel are only included when lateral forces are to be resisted.

A separate bearing plate may be included when the cross section of the column does not provide adequate bearing for the beam.

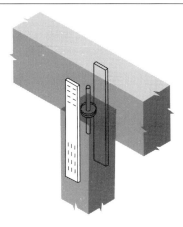

Detail 5.17

A steel pipe in the column and beam receives pins driven through the beam to resist uplift and rotation in this concealed connection. A bearing plate may be required to satisfy bearing requirements.

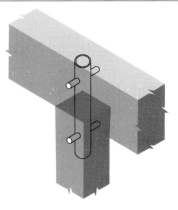

5

Connections

Detail 5.18

This concealed connection utilizes a steel plate in the sawn kerf. Machine bolt heads and nuts may be countersunk and plugged, resulting in a concealed connection.

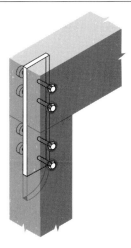

Connection Details

Wood to Wood

Detail 5.19   When the beam and column are of different widths, a welded assembly as shown may be used to transfer loads effectively using bolts.

For multi-storey buildings with beams continuous through the columns, these weldments may be used on both the top and bottom of the beam.

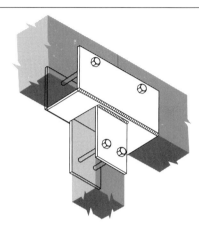

Detail 5.20   A welded assembly may also be secured by means of glulam rivets.

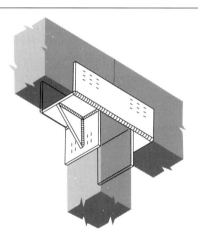

Detail 5.21   This connection is another method for connecting beams that splice over columns. If the cross section of the column is insufficient for beam bearing, a steel bearing plate may be used to distribute the load.

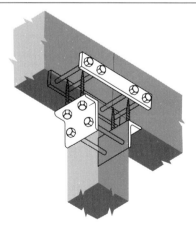

Connection Details

Wood to Wood

Detail 5.22

This detail may be used where a continuous beam is supported by a column and supports another column for the floor above. Lateral stability for the beam must be ensured by purlin framing for the floor.

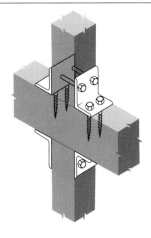

Detail 5.23

For use in multi-storey buildings with continuous beams, this detail uses clip angles and bearing plates to distribute the load over the required bearing area. Bolts or lag screws may be used in lieu of glulam rivets for timber members.

5

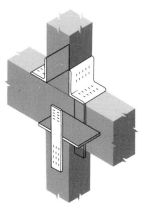

Connections

Detail 5.24

Where beams must be affixed to a continuous column, this bolted connection may be used.

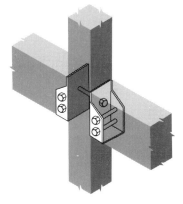

Connection Details

Wood to Wood

Detail 5.25

Beam loads are transferred to continuous column by shear-plate- or glulam-rivet-connected hangers in multi-storey applications with continuous columns. If bolts are used, beams must be slotted to allow for nuts and bolt heads.

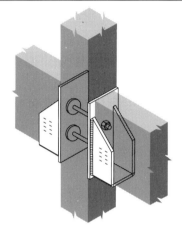

Purlin to Beam

Detail 5.26

This connection is recommended for purlins of moderate depth where support for two members is required.

The longer angle leg faces the purlin, providing maximum end distance for the purlin fasteners, and facilitating transfer of longitudinal forces through the beam.

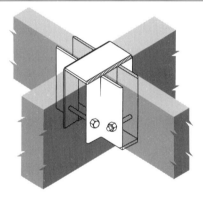

Detail 5.27

Purlins or beams of greater depth may be connected by hangers as shown. The clip angles at the top prevent rotation of the end of the suspended beam but do not restrain shrinkage in either member.

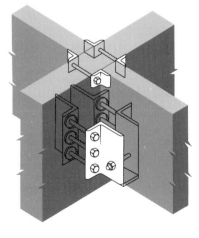

Connection Details

Wood to Wood

Detail 5.28   This welded and bent plate hanger is suitable for supporting moderate loads. The purlins should be raised above the top of the beam for hanger clearance. The purlins provide lateral stability to the beam.

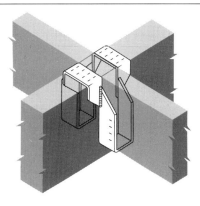

Detail 5.29   One-sided connections are well served by this arrangement, which uses glulam rivets.

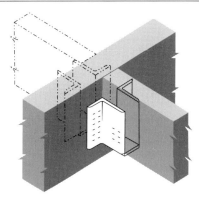

5

Detail 5.30   The rectangular shape of the centre gusset provides anchorage for, and prevents rotation of, the purlin in this semi-concealed connection. The bearing plate may be recessed into the bottom of the purlin to provide a flush detail.

The pin is shorter than the width of the purlin and the holes are plugged after installation of the pin.

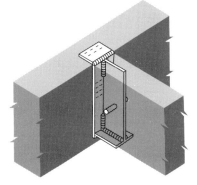

Connection Details

Wood to Wood

Ridge Purlin to Beam

Detail 5.31

Clips are used to fasten purlins supported or spliced on top of a beam or arch. Appropriate end and edge distances for the fasteners must be provided.

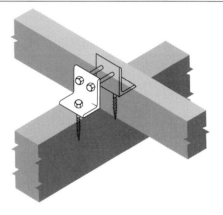

A variation of the above detail using glulam rivets.

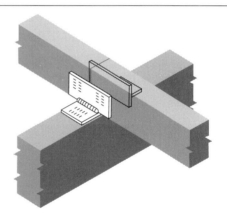

Connection Details

Wood to Wood

Detail 5.32

For ridge purlins supported on the top of an arch, bent plates are used in lieu of the clip angles shown in the foregoing details. The arch peak is bevelled to provide a horizontal bearing surface for the ridge purlin.

Arch peak connection must also be provided as shown in Details 5.37 to 5.39 (→ 273, 274).

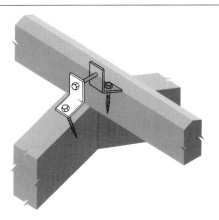

A variation of the above detail using glulam rivets.

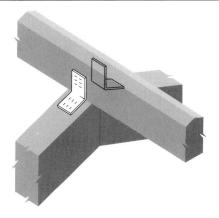

5

Connections

Connection Details

Wood to Wood

Detail 5.33

For ridge purlins set between arches, the purlin hanger may be combined with the peak connection. The wide plates on each arch face are fastened to the arch and transmit shear and axial forces between the arch halves.

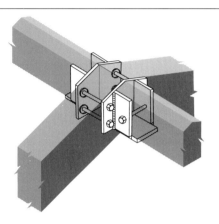

A variation of the above detail using glulam rivets.

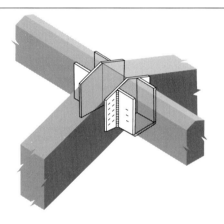

Cantilevered-Suspended Beam

Detail 5.34

This cantilevered-suspended beam support is arranged so that the rod or bolt is in tension, with plate washers providing the necessary bearing area. This arrangement avoids concentrated shear stresses by using a sloped cut.

Sloped cuts should be within lines drawn at 60° from the ends of the plate washers. The horizontal cut is made at mid-depth.

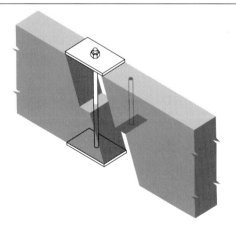

Connection Details

Wood to Wood

Detail 5.35

A cantilevered-suspended beam may be supported by this hanger detail where the vertical reaction of the supported member is transferred to the upper bearing plate by side plates.

Rotation of the hanger is resisted by bearing on the edges of the top plates, which are recessed into the members.

The bolts through the extended side plates resist both the separation force developed by eccentricity, and any axial tension to be transferred between the beams.

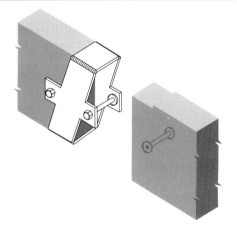

Detail 5.36

In this simple cantilevered-suspended beam support, the beam ends are cut at an angle. Rotation is resisted by bolts through the side plates. No recessing of the plate into the member is required.

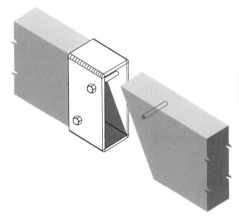

Arch Peaks

Detail 5.37

For steep arches with rafter slopes of 20° or more, this connection transfers both horizontal and vertical loads.

Two shear plates back to back are drawn together with a machine bolt or threaded rod with washers counter-bored into the arch. Bevelling the arch peak tips prevents splitting and crushing at the apex.

5

Connections

Connection Details

Wood to Wood

Detail 5.38

When vertical shear is too great for one pair of shear plates, or where the depth of section requires restraint for alignment, additional shear plates with a 19mm (3/4") diameter by 225mm (10") long dowel may be used.

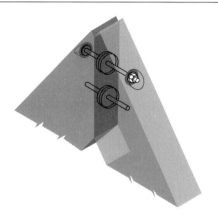

Detail 5.39

For arches with a low rafter slope, the rod lengths for the connections shown in Details 5.37 and 5.38 become excessive. Here, shear plates with a 19mm (3/4") diameter by 225mm (10") long dowel in conjunction with steel side plates and through bolts provide a suitable detail.

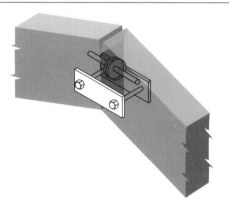

Connection Details

Wood to Masonry/ Concrete

Wood is frequently used in conjunction with masonry and concrete foundations, walls, and firewalls.

Bearing plates are often used between wood and masonry/concrete to provide adequate bearing area, reduce moisture migration, and to provide a level base.

Wall Connections

Detail 5.40   Masonry block wall supports prefabricated wood I-joist or solid-sawn lumber floor.

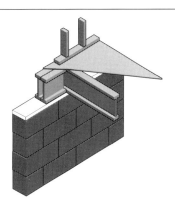

Detail 5.41   Masonry block wall supports top chord bearing parallel chord trusses.

Blocking

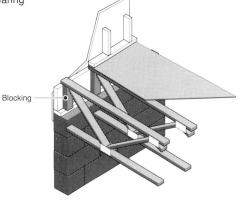

Detail 5.42   Masonry wall extends above the wood floor or roof. Wood members are supported by a continuous ledge in the masonry wall.

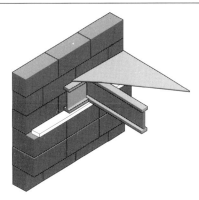

5

Connections

Connection Details

Wood to Masonry/ Concrete

Detail 5.43   Masonry block pilaster supports beam. Parallel chord trusses rest on beam and bracing between trusses provides lateral stability.

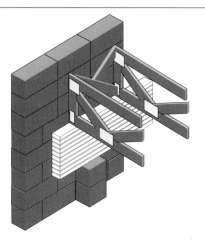

Detail 5.44   Truss is supported on wood ledgers that are bolted to masonry wall.

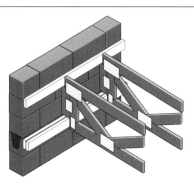

Detail 5.45   Roof support members run parallel to masonry wall. Truss bracing is anchored to masonry wall.

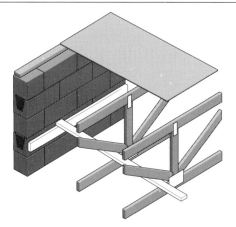

Connection Details

Wood to Masonry/ Concrete

Detail 5.46

Truss is tied to top of masonry wall using embedded anchor strap to provide resistance to uplift. When wood trusses or other wood members are supported by wood stud walls, tie-down framing anchors as shown in Figure 5.7 (→ 238) are used to provide the resistance to uplift.

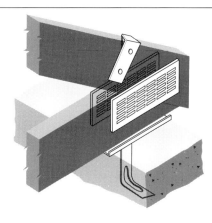

Column to Foundation

Detail 5.47

This simple base connection, which typically uses a 19mm (3/4") diameter dowel, is effective when uplift and lateral forces are negligible. A base plate of at least 3mm (1/8") thickness prevents moisture transfer from the concrete support.

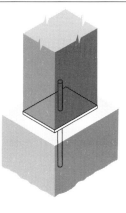

5

Connections

Detail 5.48

These connections resist both uplift and lateral loading. The vertical leg of the angle may be increased as necessary for greater end distance or multiple bolting.

Where bearing requires the base plate to be larger than the column, the base plate thickness will depend on the area over which the load is distributed, but should not be less than 6mm (1/4").

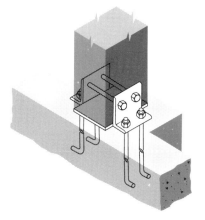

Connection Details

Wood to Masonry/ Concrete

A variation of Detail 5.48 using glulam rivets.

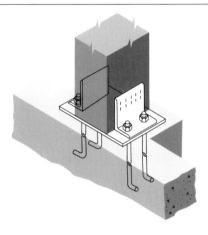

Detail 5.49

If concrete pedestal dimensions are limited, and the cross section of the column is adequate for bearing on the concrete, this connection is suggested.

Some uplift and horizontal forces may be resisted. The end of the column must be countersunk to receive the anchor bolt and nut.

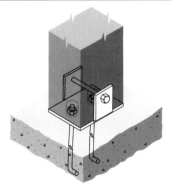

Detail 5.50

A U-shaped anchorage to a concrete support will resist both uplift and lateral loads. A 3mm (1/8") bearing plate should be used.

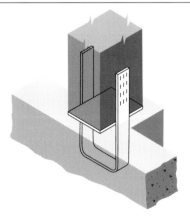

Connection Details

Wood to Masonry/ Concrete

Detail 5.51   To conceal a column base connection, the base is shown set below the floor slab. This detail will allow moisture to migrate into the wood, and may lead to decay.

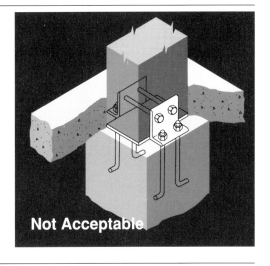

Not Acceptable

Detail 5.52   Alternative arrangements provide for the column base to be raised to the slab level, and a steel plate used as a moisture barrier. In this case, a base trim may be used if it is necessary to conceal the hardware.

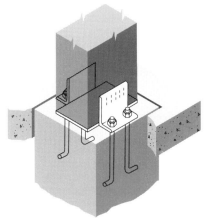

5

Connections

Detail 5.53   A steel shoe using glulam rivets encases the wood below the level of the slab and protects the wood against moisture as long as the top of the shoe projects slightly above the slab.

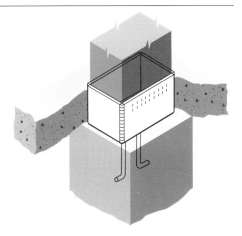

Connection Details

Wood to Masonry/ Concrete

Arch Base to Foundation

Detail 5.54

Arch to foundation connections result in outward thrust at the foundation which must be resisted by the foundation or by a tension device spanning between the opposite arch supports.

This is the most common connection between an arch base and foundation. The tension rod is embedded in the concrete floor.

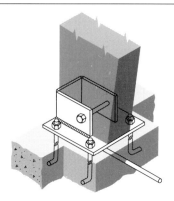

Detail 5.55

This detail has the tie rod extending through the arch, and anchored by a nut and washer on the threaded part of the rod at the back face of the shoe. Again, the arch base is counter-bored to receive the anchor bolts.

This detail may be used when the floor construction can accommodate the tie rod, as in the case of standard joist framing.

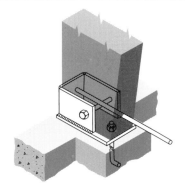

Detail 5.56

In this arrangement, the anchor bolts hold the base plate in place but do not transfer the horizontal thrust. The short rod stub is threaded to receive a turnbuckle and tension rod, and the arch base is counter-bored to receive the anchor bolts and nuts.

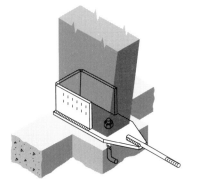

Connection Details

Wood to Masonry/ Concrete

Detail 5.57

For arches which are based outside the building envelope, a foundation support is required for the arches.

A true hinge connection should be provided for long span or deep section arches to permit rotation at the base.

The fasteners to the arch may be required to resist uplift as well as shear. Drainage at the lower inside face plate must be provided to permit the escape of water.

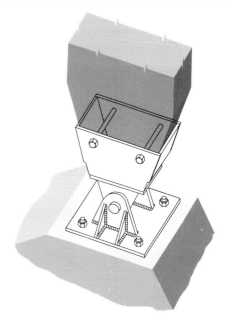

5

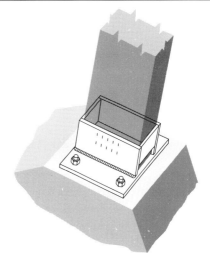

Connections

Detail 5.58

A smaller foundation arch may not require a true hinge at the base. This detail may be used with or without an elastomeric bearing pad as required by the degree of anticipated rotation.

Weep holes or a slot should be provided at the lower (inside) faceplate to allow the escape of precipitation.

Connection Details

Wood to Masonry/ Concrete

Beam to Foundation

Detail 5.59

This simple anchorage for beams up to 600mm (24") deep resists both uplift and minor lateral forces. Top of beam may be counterbored to provide a flush surface.

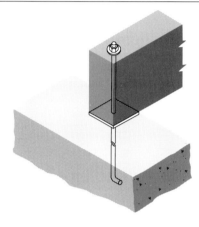

Detail 5.60

The slotted holes in the steel side plates allow for the slight horizontal movement that accompanies vertical deflection under live load in curved and tapered beams. The length of the slot required varies with the span and rise of the beam.

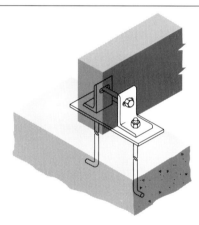

Detail 5.61

This U-shaped anchorage is suitable where adequate masonry bearing is provided under the beam and the pilaster is not wide enough to receive outside anchor bolts.

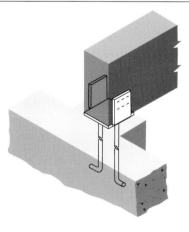

Connection Details

Wood to Masonry/ Concrete

Detail 5.62   Should loading on the masonry not require the
bearing plate to extend beyond the edge of the
beam, this connection may be used. The bearing
plate prevents the migration of moisture from the
wall to the beam and should be at least 3mm
(1/8") thick.

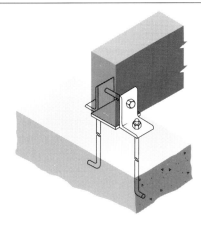

Detail 5.63   Glulam rivets are used for this detail. The side
plates may be extended out to allow easy
installation of glulam rivets if the wall continues
up above the beam.

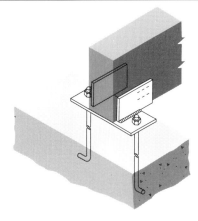

5

Connections

Detail 5.64   This standard anchorage of a beam to a
masonry wall resists both uplift and lateral
forces. The bearing plate should be a minimum
of 6mm (1/4") thick when required to distribute
the load over a larger area of masonry.

Clearance should be maintained between the
wall and end of the beam to allow for ventilation.

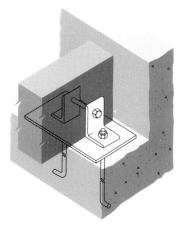

Connection Details

Wood to Masonry/ Concrete

Detail 5.65

Clearance considerations sometimes limit the depth of beam which may project above the bearing level. Stress concentrations at the notch may lead to splitting at this location.

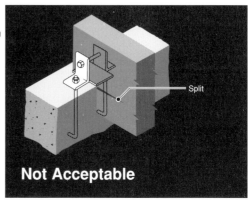

Not Acceptable

Detail 5.66

This is an acceptable method for limiting the projection of the beam above the foundation.

The beam hanger provides support for the beam at the lower face. A 6mm (1/4") clearance should be maintained between the horizontal notched face of the beam and the plate bearing on the masonry to ensure the beam is fully supported by the hanger.

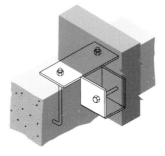

Detail 5.67

It may be possible to lower the bearing elevation of the masonry support either along the full length of the wall, or at least at the bearing point as a pocket. In this case, the notch in the wood member is eliminated altogether.

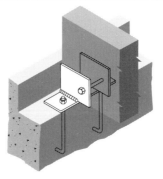

Connection Details

Wood to Masonry/ Concrete

Detail 5.68

It is necessary that inclined beams be supported in a manner which does not promote splitting. In this detail, support is inadequate.

Methods for preventing the tendency for the member to split are shown in the next details.

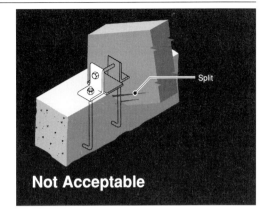

Not Acceptable

Detail 5.69

The trimmed portion of the beam is fully supported on the bearing pad and there is no tendency for the beam to split.

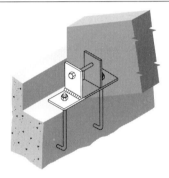

Detail 5.70

The beam hanger provides support for the beam at the lower face. A 6mm (1/4") clearance should be maintained between the horizontal notched face of the beam and the plate bearing on the masonry.

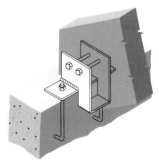

5

Connections

Connection Details

Wood to Masonry/ Concrete

Detail 5.71 Beam is restrained from lateral rotation by clip angles. The bearing plate provides an even bearing surface for the wood member.

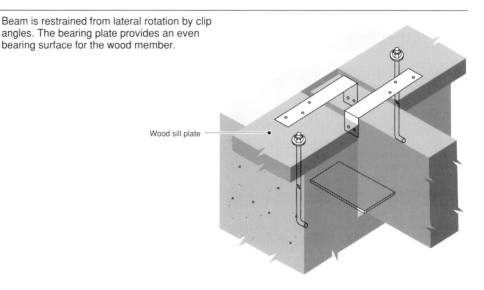

Wood sill plate

Detail 5.72 Beam is restrained from lateral rotation by wedged blocking. The beam is shaped so that if it fails under fire conditions, its failure does not compromise the masonry wall.

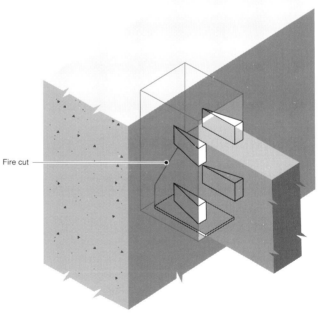

Fire cut

Connection Details

Wood to Steel

Wood in the form of timber, glulam, laminated veneer lumber (LVL), parallel strand lumber (PSL) and trusses is used frequently for primary structural members.

Where the designer chooses to substitute steel for wood primary members, the secondary wood framing can be connected effectively to the steel.

Joist or Truss to Beam

Detail 5.73

Wood blocking is bolted to steel beam flange and trusses are attached to the blocking using nails or tie-down framing anchors, depending on the degree of resistance to uplift required. Blocking and bracing is used to provide lateral stability.

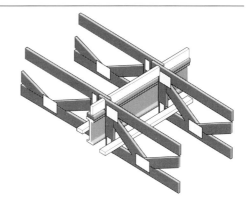

Detail 5.74

Trusses or joists bear on wood blocking bolted to the top flange of the steel beam. Continuous panel or bracing is used to provide lateral stability.

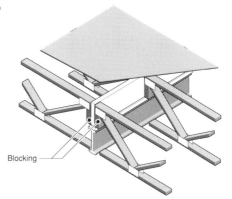

Blocking

Beam to Column

Detail 5.75

Continuous or spliced beams are connected to the U-shaped column cap by bolts or glulam rivets through the side plates. The cap is welded to the steel column. A continuous beam may be anchored by bolts or lag screws through the bottom plate.

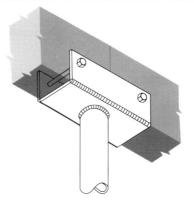

5

Connections

Connection Details

Wood to Steel

Arch Base to Support

Detail 5.76   The steel beam serves as a beam for floor
support and as a tension tie between arch
bases.

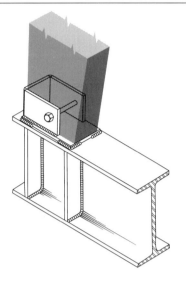

Connection Details

Suspended Loads

Where concentrated loads are suspended from wood members, care must be taken to ensure that the capacity of the member is not compromised by the location or configuration of the fasteners.

Detail 5.77

Whenever point loads are suspended from wood members, it is good practice to connect the load toward the top of the member rather than at the bottom.

This arrangement places undue stress on the flange to web bond of the prefabricated wood I-joist.

Not Acceptable

Detail 5.78

The bolts are placed high on the joist web and the blocking distributes the load throughout the joist.

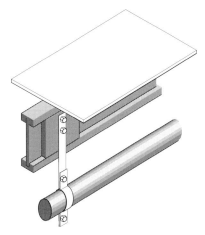

5

Connection Details

Suspended Loads

Detail 5.79

This detail can be used where a concrete floor topping has been specified. The concrete covers the protruding hanger rod and nut.

The load is taken to the top of the joist by bolting hangers through the floor sheathing. The hanger must be adjacent to the joist so that the sheathing is not overloaded.

Concrete topping —

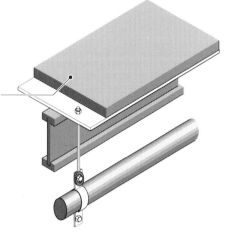

Detail 5.80

Additional members and hangers may be necessary when the magnitude of suspended loads exceeds the capacity of a member spaced to support normal uniform floor loads.

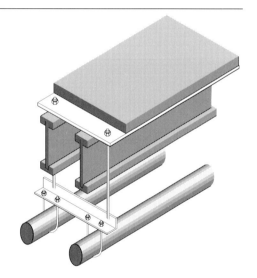

Connection Details

Suspended Loads

Detail 5.81

Hangers or straps that support significant loads and are connected near the bottom of the supporting beam may lead to splitting at the connector group.

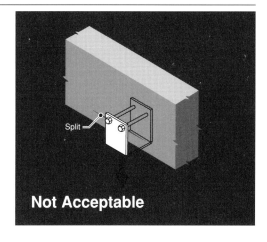

Not Acceptable

Detail 5.82

Such hangers should be connected into the upper half of the supporting member, or replaced by a saddle type hanger that would transfer all the load to the top surface of the beam.

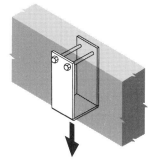

5

Connections

General Guidelines for Connections

- Standardize fasteners on a project to speed installation and to reduce the chances of error.

- Select a fastener material or finish which suits the moisture conditions.

- Design connection details to accommodate seasoning effect as moisture level in the wood product adjusts to the building environment.

- Specify a finished appearance which suits visual prominence of the fasteners.

- Connection design must respect wood end and edge distance setbacks to ensure adequacy.

- Connection design must provide stipulated distances between connectors. Ensure that adequate wood material remains after boring for connectors to transfer forces.

- Fastener capacity varies with the in-service moisture content of wood. Most building applications will be for dry service conditions which give good fastener capacity values.

References

TTS Wood Trusses, Jaeger Industries Inc., Calgary, AB, 1989

Wood Design Manual, Canadian Wood Council, 1990

Wood Engineering and Construction Handbook, Keith E. Flaherty and Thomas G. Williamson, McGraw Hill Publishing, 1989

Wood Handbook: Wood as an Engineering Material, United States Department of Agriculture, Agriculture Handbook 72, 1987

Structural Wood Systems

6

Traditional timber joinery relies on the interlocking of wood members and results in clean connections made without metal fasteners.

Delicate in skeletal form, light frame buildings become robust and durable when the nailed sheathing is applied.

Parallel chord trusses are economical, light weight framing members for large span, commercial applications.

Light frame roof systems, when used with prescribed, close-spaced sheathing nailing patterns, result in effective diaphragm action.

Plywood
stressed-skin
panels, pre-
manufactured
and insulated,
are strong
structural units
for floors, walls
and roofs.

Permanent wood foundations (PWF) provide comfortable and durable basement living areas by utilizing superior drainage methods and high-quality pressure-treated plywood and lumber.

Pre-manufactured on-site, a shearwall module is lifted into position.

A close-spaced nailing pattern results in a light-weight building system that is effective in resisting high wind and seismic effects.

Light frame construction easily accommodates varying roof shapes and mating with other structural materials.

This high, light frame acts as a bearing wall by transmitting gravity loads and as a shearwall by resisting lateral loads.

The preassembled roof for this post and beam building is lifted into place and then supported by modular columns.

6.1 General Information

This section explains how the main structural members of Section 3, and the sheathing products of Section 4, connected using one or more of the techniques in Section 5, combine to make the structural systems used to construct buildings of many types and sizes. It covers:

6.2   Light Framing

6.3   Post and Beam

6.4   Shearwalls and Diaphragms

6.5   Bearing Stud Walls

6.6   Composite Panels

6.7   Permanent Wood Foundations

The two basic methods of wood construction are light framing and post and beam. The major differences between the two are shown in Figure 6.1 (→ 304). Each method is discussed in detail in the appropriate section.

Many buildings combine light frame and post and beam construction techniques, and most light frame buildings gain their basic structural support from shearwall and diaphragm action and bearing stud walls.

The last two sections, covering composite panels and permanent wood foundations (see Sections 6.6 and 6.7) describe specialized wood construction techniques which offer the designer additional opportunity for innovative design.

6

Structural Wood Systems

Figure 6.1
Two Principal Wood Construction Techniques

Light Frame Construction

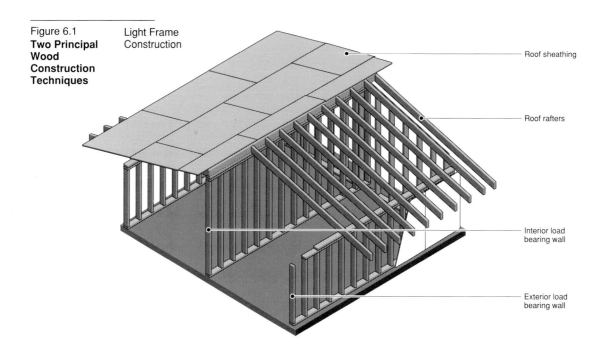

Roof sheathing

Roof rafters

Interior load bearing wall

Exterior load bearing wall

Post and Beam Construction

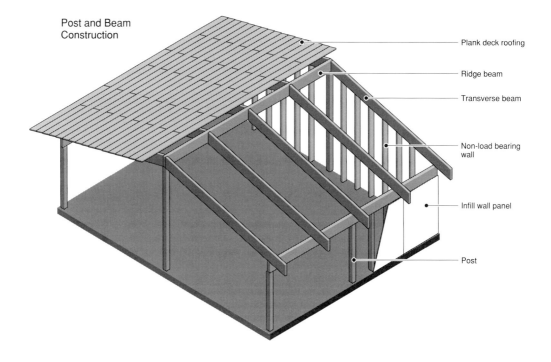

Plank deck roofing

Ridge beam

Transverse beam

Non-load bearing wall

Infill wall panel

Post

6.2 Light Framing

Introduction

Light framing is the use of closely spaced members of dimension lumber size combined with sheathing to form structural elements of a building. The structural elements provide rigidity, support for interior finish and exterior cladding, and a cavity for the installation of insulation.

Light framing is the most common method of residential construction in North America. It is also a form of construction which can be used on a larger scale for commercial and public buildings. For example, the Forintek Canada Corp. forest products research facility in Vancouver, Canada, a 9300m² (100,000 sq. ft.) building, uses light frame construction on a large scale to house offices and laboratories.

Where a typical wall in a residence might be a 38 x 89mm (2" x 4" nom.) extending 2.4m (8'), the walls in the Forintek building are built of 38 x 235mm (2" x 10" nom.) studs which extend 5m (16') from floor to ceiling. The result is a solid building meeting the exacting requirements for a research facility.

Light framing makes use of dimension lumber (generally sawn lumber 38mm (2" nom.) wide and up to 286mm (12" nom.) deep) and manufactured wood products of comparable size to build structural frameworks. These main structural members are used in concert with sheathing elements to provide rigidity for walls, floors, and roofs. Typically, light frame members are spaced no further apart than 600mm (2').

For some loading configurations, engineered wood products such as light frame trusses, prefabricated wood I-joists, or other structural products such as laminated veneer lumber (LVL), parallel strand lumber (PSL) and glulam may be used as framing elements. Where large or clear spans are a requirement, light framing members may be used in combination with heavy beams or columns to transfer loads directly to foundations.

Figure 6.2 (→ 306) demonstrates a typical arrangement of framed members.

Frame construction, by using small repetitive members and fasteners, develops a redundancy of design. This means that alternate paths of load transmittal become available when the primary path fails. For this reason, frame construction is not prone to sudden failure and is recognized as a good construction technique for resisting, for example, seismic and wind forces.

Features of Light Framing

Multiple Function
Light framing is a method of construction which is functional and versatile. Light frame construction may be thought of as roof, floor and wall planes which serve the following functions:

- Structure: walls can be designed to be load bearing (see Section 6.5) so that the wall transmits vertical loads to the foundation. They can also be designed to act as shearwalls to resist lateral forces from wind and seismic loads both perpendicular to and parallel to the direction of the wall.
  Roofs and floors are designed to accept building design loads and in addition can be designed to provide diaphragm (see Section 6.4) action thereby providing resistance to racking.

- Strength: the good structural performance of light framing is due to two primary factors: load sharing and composite action. Load sharing means that alternate paths of load transfer become available when the assembly is stressed. Composite action is the contribution that sheathing and fasteners make to the strength of lumber members. As a result, light framing has reserve strength and stiffness.

- Envelope: the sheathing materials used to provide rigidity also serve as the building envelope to which exterior finishes are attached.

- Insulation and finishes: the space between the framing is used for insulation, and the framing is used for affixing vapour barrier and interior finish.

6

Structural Wood Systems

Figure 6.2
**Terms Used in
Light Framing**

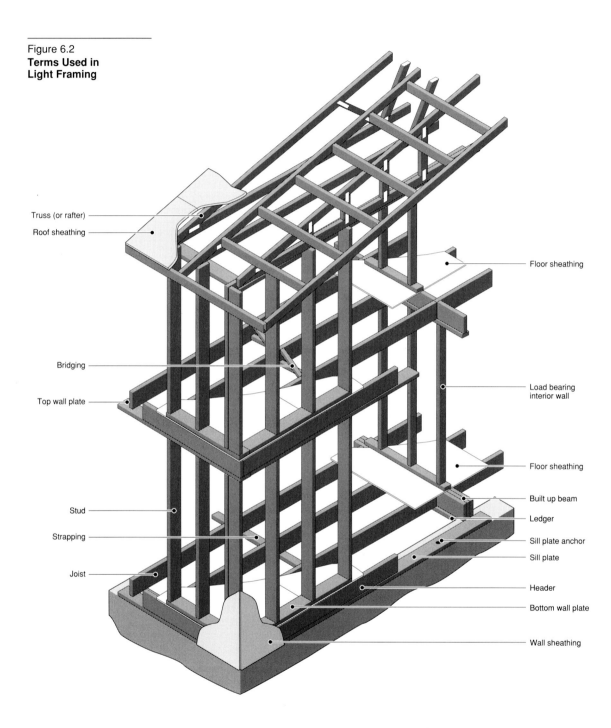

Truss (or rafter)

Roof sheathing

Floor sheathing

Bridging

Load bearing
interior wall

Top wall plate

Floor sheathing

Built up beam

Stud

Ledger

Strapping

Sill plate anchor

Sill plate

Joist

Header

Bottom wall plate

Wall sheathing

Prefabrication

Frame construction lends itself to prefabrication. Modules can easily be prefabricated using indoor working conditions and perhaps automated nailing systems to speed assembly. Alternately, prefabrication can be performed on site with panel units being raised into place manually or, where necessary, hoisted into place by crane.

Feasible Sizes

Frame construction can be applied to larger buildings using small building techniques. Larger members are used to ensure the larger forces developed are adequately transferred. In this way, light frame construction can be applied to many commercial applications.

The use of light frame trusses for roof and floors permits spans greater than 20m (60'). Long spans can be achieved by using prefabricated wood I-joists, laminated veneer lumber (LVL), parallel strand lumber (PSL) or glulam.

Stud walls, using readily available dimension lumber and platform construction, can easily be made up to 5m (16') high, and, by special order, up to 7m (23') high. Substituting wood I-joists for dimension lumber studs increases further the wall heights possible, or adds strength where high wind loading is a design parameter. In addition, frame construction can be combined with post and beam construction (see Section 6.3) where there is a special need for clear areas. Figure 6.3 below shows one method of bolstering a frame wall to accept a concentrated beam load.

Availability of Materials

Light framing employs materials which are readily available. For materials which must be custom manufactured, such as light frame trusses, the time required for shop drawing approval and manufacture, about three weeks, can be significantly less than for other materials such as fabricated steel.

Site Adjustment

Wood construction in general and light frame construction in particular is easy to adjust to account for changes or errors, and to accommodate future additions.

The materials, fasteners, and skills required for light framing construction are readily available in all areas of North America, and wood is easy to cut, splice, and fasten.

6

Structural Wood Systems

Figure 6.3
Combining Post and Beam and Light Framing

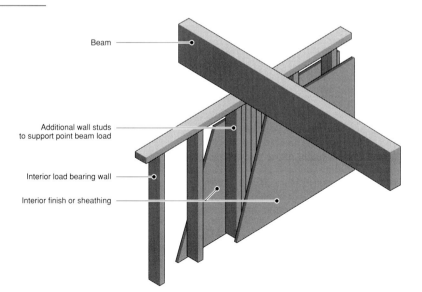

Beam

Additional wall studs to support point beam load

Interior load bearing wall

Interior finish or sheathing

Cost

While definitive information is not presented due to regional differences for material and labour, light frame construction has been shown to be economical in comparison to alternate building methods.

This economy is a principle reason for the predominant use of wood in residential construction in North America, and also a good part of the reason for selecting wood as the structural material for many commercial buildings.

Even when sprinklers or requirements for firewalls are specified, wood construction remains cost competitive with other types of construction while still providing a high degree of fire safety (see Section 10).

Types of Framing

There are two basic methods of light framing construction. The most common method is platform construction, which is discussed in detail in this section. The less common type is balloon framing.

Figure 6.4 (opposite) shows the difference between the two methods. The platform method constructs a floor platform upon which the walls are built. The second storey floor is built on top of the walls.

The chief advantage of platform construction is that the floor system, assembled independently from the walls, provides a platform or working system upon which the walls and partitions for the next storey can be fabricated.

Since the studs are one storey in height, walls can be easily fabricated one storey at a time, and for all but the highest walls, can be lifted into place manually.

The top and bottom wall plates are required for nailing support for wall sheathing and interior finish. They also serve as fire stops between floors.

In balloon construction, the wall members continue past the floors. The joists are then suspended from the completed wall frames. Since the connections between the floor joists and the studs in balloon framing are not easily prefabricated, this method of framing is not commonly used at the present time. However, some aspects of balloon framing may be incorporated into platform construction as, for example, where it is required to provide convenient passage between floors of heating ducts and pipes.

Framing Materials

Light frame construction consists of joining load bearing framing members with sheathing to create building components such as floors, walls, and roofs, and specialized building systems such as shearwalls, diaphragms, load bearing walls, and permanent wood foundations.

Load Bearing Framing Members

Framing members, in the form of studs, joists, and rafters, provide reinforcing and support for vertical and horizontal sheathing, and are the main load bearing members conducting forces to the supports. The members also derive strength from the sheathing fastened to it through composite action.

Framing entails the placement of light members at spacings of between 300 and 600mm (12" and 24") and in so doing creating a load sharing action whereby a below average member, through the rigidity of the sheathing, transfers excess load to an adjoining above average member. In this way, the overall strength is not governed by the weakest member but by the combined strength of all the members.

There are several types of main structural members used in light framing construction:

• Dimension lumber

• Light frame trusses

• Laminated veneer lumber(LVL)

• Prefabricated wood I-joists

• Parallel strand lumber (PSL)

• Glulam

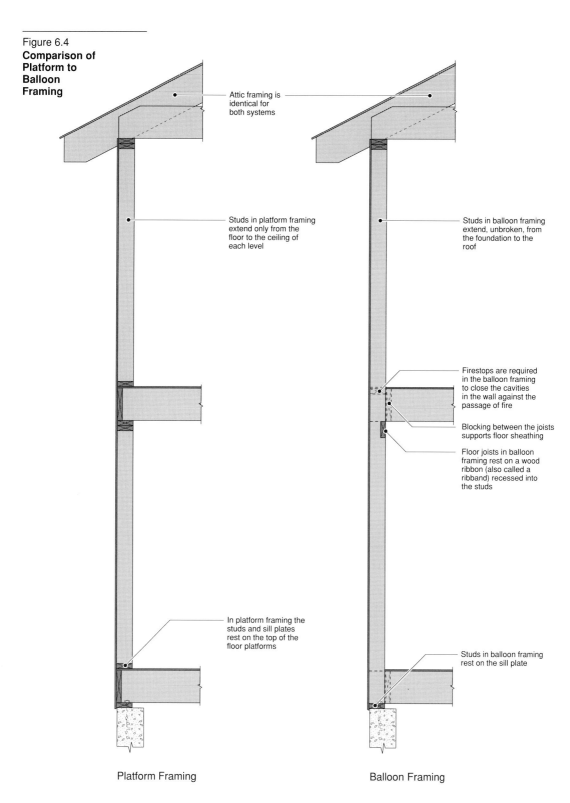

Figure 6.4
**Comparison of
Platform to
Balloon
Framing**

Attic framing is
identical for
both systems

Studs in platform framing
extend only from the
floor to the ceiling of
each level

Studs in balloon framing
extend, unbroken, from
the foundation to the
roof

Firestops are required
in the balloon framing
to close the cavities
in the wall against the
passage of fire

Blocking between the joists
supports floor sheathing

Floor joists in balloon
framing rest on a wood
ribbon (also called a
ribband) recessed into
the studs

In platform framing the
studs and sill plates
rest on the top of the
floor platforms

Studs in balloon framing
rest on the sill plate

Platform Framing   Balloon Framing

LVL, PSL and glulam, while usually used in the larger sizes required for post and beam construction, are often used with frame construction where a beam or header is required.

For residential applications, most North American building codes provide span tables which allow the selection of floor and roof members having suitable strength and deflection characteristics.

For larger buildings, members must be designed based on the design values of the wood products.

Typically, Stud grade lumber is used for wall studs (up to 140mm (6" nom.) deep) and No.2 grade for roof and floor members. For trusses, the lumber grades are selected by the truss manufacturer. A higher grade may be specified where additional strength is required or where members will be exposed to view and require a better appearance.

Lumber, whether kiln dried or air dried, should have a moisture content not exceeding 19 percent at the time of installation to minimize dimensional change as the building adjusts to its equilibrium humidity level. One way to accomplish this is to specify kiln dried lumber which carries a slight cost premium of about 10 to 15 percent, or to ensure that after manufacture, S-Green lumber has had time to season to the moisture content equivalent of S-Dry lumber. In either case, lumber should be protected from wetting during construction.

Sheathing

Sheathing, in light frame construction, performs the roles of strengthening and stiffening the framing load bearing members acting as columns and beams, and forming the building envelope to which cladding, flooring, and roofing materials are affixed.

Sheathing also plays the crucial role of providing stiffness for the resistance of lateral loads through shearwall and diaphragm action (see Section 6.4).

Plywood, oriented strandboard (OSB)/waferboard, and boards (see Section 4) are the common materials used for the structural sheathing of frame construction. Thicker wood decking (plank decking) is most often used for post and beam construction where the spans are greater than the spans in frame construction.

Plywood and OSB/waferboard sheathing, usually manufactured in 1200 x 2400mm (4' x 8') sheets, is applied to the wall frame horizontally or vertically. Gaps of 2mm (3/32") should be left between sheets to allow for expansion and to prevent buckling of the sheets.

If applied horizontally, vertical joints should be staggered for additional wall stiffness.

Lumber sheathing which may have shiplap, tongue and groove or square edges may be applied horizontally, vertically over blocking, or diagonally with all ends supported and end joints staggered for additional stiffness. Lumber is usually laid horizontally to reduce installation time and minimize waste material and because angled cuts are not required.

Fasteners

Light framing makes uses of many small fasteners in the form of nails, spikes, or staples to attach framing members to each other and to attach the sheathing to the framing members (see Section 5).

A variety of metal fasteners, such as joist hangers, are available which can reduce installation time and improve connection strength. Most light framing connectors rely on nails for attachment.

Truss plates, once affixed by nailing, are now almost entirely made from light gauge metal toothed plates which are forced by pressure into the wood surfaces to be joined.

Nailing requirements for light framing are established by the North American building codes. For larger buildings, nailing patterns must be designed to ensure adequate transfer of horizontal and vertical loads. Care must be taken to ensure that such nailing patterns are clearly indicated in bid documents to ensure that proper installation follows.

Mechanical and pneumatic nail and staple guns reduce the labour time required for dense nailing patterns.

Floor Design

A platform floor is started by attaching a sill plate to the foundation for the first floor.

Sill plates are 38 x 89mm (2" x 4" nom.), or larger lumber laid flat on the foundation with full, even bearing. They form a base for the frame, and provide a tie between foundation and superstructure. For residential construction, the fasteners are usually 12.7mm (1/2") diameter steel anchor bolts cast into the foundation at 2.4m (8') centres, or less, which secure the sill plate.

For larger buildings, the hold-down devices should be engineered to resist uplift and shear forces resulting from wind or earthquake loads. The anchors should be cast in the concrete foundation, or be the cinch anchor type installed after the concrete has cured. The anchors can be restrained during concrete placement by temporary supports or the sill plate can be drilled to act as a template during concrete placement.

Inserting anchors into concrete after initial set has begun results in uncertain holding power for the anchor and is not recommended.

If placed after concrete curing, sill plates can be levelled on a bed of mortar. If the foundation is level, no mortar is required, providing the junction between foundation and sill plate is sealed with caulking around the building perimeter to prevent passage of air and moisture. Otherwise, a gasket material is placed between the sill and the concrete. In some North American locations, the sill plate may have to be treated for protection against termite attack.

Beams
Beams provide intermediate support for floor and roof joists, where joists do not span fully between walls. Beams may be solid timbers, built-up members, glulam members, parallel strand lumber, (PSL), laminated veneer lumber (LVL), or any other type of building material which gives the required engineering performance.

Wood beams framed into concrete or masonry at or below ground level should have at least a 12mm (1/2") air space around all vertical surfaces for air circulation. To keep wood dry from below, framing should be separated from concrete by polyethylene, gaskets, or similar materials if there is minimum clearance between wood and ground.

Maximum allowable spans for various combinations of built-up wood beams for basements, cellars and crawl spaces of one- and two-storey houses are given in North American building codes. Sizes and spans for other combinations, or solid or glued-laminated beams, can be calculated using standard engineering design formulas.

Joists
Products most commonly used for joists are dimension lumber, and prefabricated wood I-joists. Parallel chord light frame trusses, LVL, PSL and glulam may also be used. They are particularly effective where extra strength is required as, for example, around openings.

Maximum allowable spans for light service conditions for various loads and spacings of wood joists are given in North American building codes. Custom design of the joists is required for heavier loads.

Deflection is a critical design criterion for joists. Deflection relates to user acceptability and is considered in the calculation of span tables for joists. The following methods are used for improving load sharing amongst joists and thus decreasing deflection:

* Strapping the bottom edge of the joists, or blocking or cross bracing between the joists to provide lateral support. These are usually installed at mid span or at the one third span points

- Adhesive in combination with fasteners affixing the floor sheathing to the joists, thereby increasing the composite action between sheathing and joists.

Joist spacing and sheathing thicknesses for medium duty applications are shown in Table 6.1 (→ 317) as a rough guideline for preliminary layout.

Joists may rest on top of beams, or frame into their sides to save headroom by using joist hangers or ledger strips (see Section 5.2 for connection details).

Band (header) joists frame between the top of foundation or sill plate and the bottom of subflooring around the building perimeter. They provide lateral restraint to joists, and help transfer vertical loads between walls.

Other Materials
For some occupancies a layer of concrete or gypcrete may be placed over a wood floor to enhance acoustical performance.

A thickness of 38mm (1-1/2") is often used, and all members below the topping must be designed to accept the additional concrete dead load (see Figure 6.5 below).

No special preparation of the plywood or OSB/waferboard subfloor is necessary, and reinforcement is not usually placed in the concrete.

In addition to constituting a solid heavy duty floor, the concrete topping will improve

acoustical isolation between floors and minimize vibration.

Holes and Notches
It may be necessary to drill holes or cut notches in joists to pass electrical wiring, plumbing pipes or other services.

Designers should refer to their appropriate building codes for the sizes of holes allowed. As a general guide, diameters of drilled holes in lumber joists should not exceed one quarter of the member's depth, and should be located at least 50mm (2") from edges.

The removed material will not affect the strength of the member if the size of hole is limited and placed near the centre of the joist depth, where bending stresses are least.

For all openings in prefabricated wood I-joists, refer to manufacturers' information, which gives clear direction on the permissable sizes and locations of holes.

Overhangs
Floor joists can be cantilevered past the foundation wall to provide support for bay windows or additional floor space.

Cantilevered portions must not support floor loads from other storeys unless calculations are provided to show that the allowable design stress of the cantilevered joists is not exceeded.

Figure 6.5
**Concrete
Topped Wood
Frame Floor**

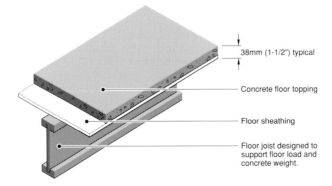

38mm (1-1/2") typical

Concrete floor topping

Floor sheathing

Floor joist designed to support floor load and concrete weight.

Wall Design

Light frame walls consist of the vertical members, called studs, affixed at the top and bottom to horizontal plates, and a sheathing material attached to this framework.

Walls may be non-load bearing (partition walls) or load bearing (exterior walls and interior load bearing walls). Bearing stud walls, which transfer vertical loads to the foundation, are discussed in more detail in Section 6.5.

When a framed wall is designed to resist lateral loads, it is said to be a shearwall. Shearwalls are used to resist wind and earthquake loading on a building and are covered in detail in Section 6.4.

Wood joists are commonly used for residential construction and for commercial buildings for spans up to the length limitations of dimension lumber. When span and load requirements dictate the use of prefabricated wood I-joists or trusses for floors or roofs, the wall to floor and wall to roof connection remains basically the same as it would be with dimension lumber joists. Some examples of such configurations are shown in Figure 6.6 (→ 314).

Interior load-bearing walls should be placed directly above beams or walls, but may be located anywhere provided the joists and other supports are specifically designed to support the loads.

Non-load-bearing walls perpendicular to floor joists may be placed anywhere, but if placed parallel to floor joists, the wall must be supported by joists beneath it, or by blocking between the joists.

Sheathing is usually started below the bottom of the sill plate to provide an additional tie between wall framing and foundation.

Where uplift due to wind or earthquake is a concern, a mechanical tension connection penetrating the joist area may be necessary because of the limited effectiveness of toe nailing when subjected to withdrawal forces.

Wall Plates

Wall plates are used at the top and bottom of studs to provide a large bearing area for distributing vertical loads to and from the studs. They are usually the same width as the studs and are normally 38mm (2" nom.) thick.

Because walls studs are not continued between floors for platform construction, mechanical hold-down devices may be required for larger buildings to provide hold down protection from uplift induced by lateral loads.

There are three alternatives for securing walls to floors:

- Plywood or OSB/waferboard sheathing extending over floor framing and attached to floor framing by nails or staples. In this instance, dry lumber should be used for joists and headers to avoid significant lumber shrinkage which may cause the sheathing to buckle.

- Galvanized-metal strips, sized in accordance with code requirements, can be nailed to the vertical members above and below a floor to provide tie-down.

- Bolts and brackets can be used where large forces are developed (see Section 5.2).

The sizing and number of wood plates required varies amongst the North American building codes. The following is a general guideline:

- Top wall plates must be at least 38mm (2" nom.) thick. They may be single in non-load-bearing partitions and in load-bearing walls if the supported concentrated loads occur within 50mm (2") of supporting studs. In all other cases, top plates should be doubled. Intersecting walls should be tied together by overlapping the plates or by use of metal splice plates. Doubled plates should be nailed together with joints staggered at least one stud spacing.

6

Structural Wood Systems

Figure 6.6
**Prefabricated
Wood I-Joist
and Truss Light
Framing Details**

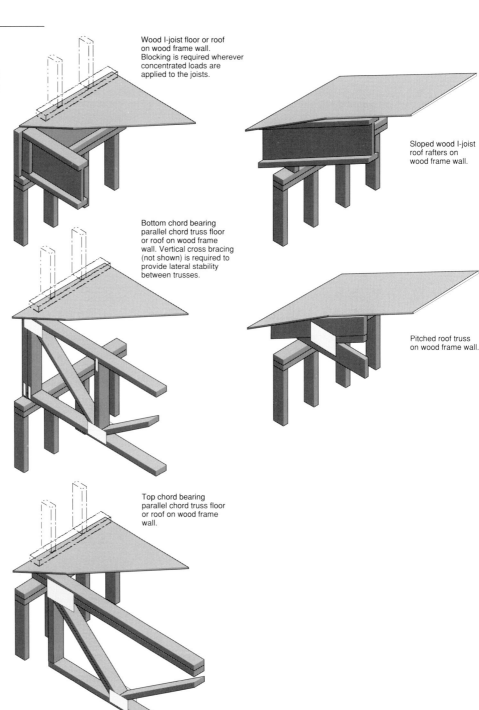

Wood I-joist floor or roof
on wood frame wall.
Blocking is required wherever
concentrated loads are
applied to the joists.

Sloped wood I-joist
roof rafters on
wood frame wall.

Bottom chord bearing
parallel chord truss floor
or roof on wood frame
wall. Vertical cross bracing
(not shown) is required to
provide lateral stability
between trusses.

Pitched roof truss
on wood frame wall.

Top chord bearing
parallel chord truss floor
or roof on wood frame
wall.

Studs

A stud is a load bearing member used in a vertical position to frame a wall (Stud is also a particular grade category and grade of lumber specially suited for walls). Dimension lumber is the wood product used almost exclusively for studs. Fingerjoined dimension lumber studs are available and are equivalent to solid wood studs of like grade.

For residential construction, there is a growing trend toward 38 x 140mm (2" x 6" nom.) as a minimum stud size due to the additional insulation space provided as compared to 38 x 89 (2" x 4" nom.) studs.

For heavier construction, studs must be designed to accommodate axial and bending forces. Depending on length and load, studs for commercial building walls may be 38 x 184, 235, or 286mm (2" x 8", 10", or 12" nom.). Vertical members of this size are not available in Stud grade. No.2 grade should be specified.

For high walls, prefabricated wood I-joists are sometimes used vertically as wall studs.

Except at openings, studs should be continuous to the full storey height for full strength development.

Stud spacing and sheathing thicknesses for medium duty applications are shown in Table 6.2 (→ 317) as a rough guideline for preliminary layout.

Lintels

Lintels are beams placed horizontally over windows, doors or other openings to transfer vertical loads from above openings to adjacent studs.

In load-bearing walls, lintels may be solid lumber of the same width as the studs, or two or more pieces of 38mm (2" nom.) lumber laid on edge and separated with spacers to make the lintels the same width as the studs.

For larger openings and loads, parallel strand lumber (PSL), laminated veneer lumber (LVL) or glulam may be desirable because of the high strength to size ratio.

Roof Design

Light frame roofs most often employ dimension lumber rafters and ceiling joists for moderate loads and spans, and prefabricated wood I-joists or trusses for long spans or heavy loads. Fingerjoined joists and rafters are manufactured in lengths up to 12m (40').

In combination with these load bearing members, sheathing, in addition to supporting the gravity loads acting on the roof, increases the resistance of the load bearing members.

As discussed in detail in Section 6.4, light frame roofs can be designed to provide diaphragm action for resisting the racking effect of lateral loads from wind and earthquake.

As with other materials, light frame roofs may be pitched or flat. Trusses for flat roofs can be fabricated to provide the desired degree of slope for drainage.

Rafters and Joists

For light duty (typically residential) applications, the allowable spans for roof rafters and joists are given in tabular form in the North American building codes. For applications which fall outside the limits of the tables, the size and spacing requirements must be calculated.

Rafters and joists should be continuous, except where spliced over vertical supports, and should be doubled for extra strength on both sides of openings wider than two rafter or joist spacings.

Roof Trusses

Roof trusses must be designed to limit deflection. This is especially crucial on flat roofs where deflection will result in ponding and a consequent increase in load.

For residential construction, some of the North American building codes list spans and sizes of members of some wood species for some of the more common truss types. Generally, these tables apply only to roof trusses of up to 12m (40') span spaced up to 600mm (2') on centre. For longer spans or heavy loads, engineering analysis is required.

6

Structural Wood Systems

Roof Sheathing

Roof sheathing provides rigidity and support for the roof covering and may be lumber, plywood or OSB/waferboard. The thicknesses required for various support spacings are shown in Table 6.3 (→ 318) as a rough guideline for preliminary layout. Actual sizing must be adjusted to suit the snow load where applicable.

Lumber sheathing should be laid perpendicular to joists or rafters with all ends supported and end joints staggered. It should be laid continuously for asphalt shingles or built-up roofing, but may be spaced at a distance equal to the shingle exposure for wood shingle roofs (see Section 7). Spaced sheathing allows free movement of air under the sheathing, preventing build-up of moisture.

Panel sheathing (plywood and OSB/waferboard) should be installed with surface grain perpendicular to joists, rafters or trusses with 6mm (1/4") gaps left between adjacent panels to allow for expansion. If panel edges are supported between rafters with metal H-clips, tongue and groove edges or at least 38 x 38mm (2" x 2" nom.) blocking securely nailed to framing, the minimum thicknesses of panels can be decreased.

Refer to Section 4 for more detailed information on sheathing and decking products.

Roofing Materials over Roof Sheathing

Many types of roofing materials have proven satisfactory under various service conditions when applied over light frame roofs. The most common types of roofing materials for use on sloping roofs are western red cedar shingles and shakes, asphalt shingles, and tiles. For flat or flat-pitched roofs, built-up roofing is generally used.

General Guidelines for Light Framing

- Light framing construction relies almost exclusively on nailed connections. Ensure that the prescribed nailing patterns are installed particularly where shearwall and diaphragm action has been specified and that anchor bolt hold down protection is adequate.

- Select framing materials which are best suited to a given project location to provide economy and performance.

- Ensure that the materials specified are readily available to meet schedule requirements.

- Using S-Dry lumber will minimize dimensional change as framing adjusts to the humidity level of a building.

References

Wood Frame House Construction, Canada Mortgage and Housing Corporation, 1988

Wood Frame House Construction, United States Department of Agriculture, Forest Service, US Government Printing Office, 1989

Wood Design Manual, Canadian Wood Council, 1990.

Reference Tables

Table 6.1
Typical Joist Spacing and Sheathing Thickness for Floors

Floor Sheathing Material	Joist Spacing		Minimum Material Thickness	
	mm	in.	mm	in.
Lumber	400	16	17	11/16
	500	19.2	19	3/4
	600	24	19	3/4
Plywood	400	16	15.5	5/8
	500	19.2	15.5	5/8
	600	24	19.0	3/4
OSB/waferboard	400	16	15.9	5/8
	500	19.2	15.9	5/8
	600	24	19.0	3/4

Note:
Sheathing thickness and support spacing varies according to the building code in effect. This information is presented as a general guideline. Refer to the building code in effect for specific information.

Table 6.2
Typical Stud Spacing and Sheathing Thickness for Walls

Wall Sheathing Material	Stud Spacing		Minimum Material Thickness	
	mm	in.	mm	in.
Lumber	400	16	17.0	11/16
	600	24	17.0	11/16
Plywood	400	16	6.0	1/4
	600	24	7.5	9/32
OSB/waferboard	400	16	6.35	1/4
	600	24	7.9	5/16

Note:
Sheathing thickness and support spacing varies according to the building code in effect. This information is presented as a general guideline. Refer to the building code in effect for specific information.

Reference Tables continued

Table 6.3
Typical Rafter or Truss Spacing and Sheathing Thickness for Roofs

Roof Sheathing Material			Rafter or Truss Spacing		Minimum Material Thickness	
			mm	in.	mm	in.
Lumber			300	12	17.5	11/16
			400	16	17.5	11/16
			500	19.2	19	3/4
			600	24	19	3/4
Plywood	edges supported		300	12	7.5	9/32
			400	16	7.5	9/32
			500	19.2	9.5	3/8
			600	24	9.5	3/8
	edges unsupported		300	12	7.5	9/32
			400	16	7.5	9/32
			500	19.2	9.5	3/8
			600	24	9.5	3/8
OSB/waferboard	edges supported		300	12	9.5	3/8
			400	16	9.5	3/8
			500	19.2	11.1	7/16
			600	24	11.1	7/16
	edges unsupported		300	12	9.5	3/8
			400	16	11.1	7/16
			500	19.2	12.7	1/2
			600	24	12.7	1/2

Note:
Sheathing thickness and support spacing varies according to the building code in effect. This information is presented as a general guideline. Refer to the building code in effect for specific information.

6.3   Post and Beam

Introduction

Post and beam construction is a method of construction which uses large, widely spaced members to provide structural support. It is a principal method of wood construction which offers the designer the possibility of combining function with the unique beauty of wood.

In light framing construction, the framing serves as structure, as exterior sheathing and interior finish support, and as the insulation cavity. The sheathing and framing together resist lateral loads or racking (see Section 6.4).

With post and beam construction, the columns and beams support vertical loads, intermediate framing is required to support exterior sheathing and interior finish and provide space for insulation, and diagonal bracing or other support is required to resist lateral loads.

Post and beam construction uses timber, glulam, and parallel strand lumber (PSL) for beams, columns, girders, and purlins for structure, and decking for floor and roof sheathing. Using these large members, post and beam construction can be used to create dramatic and appealing appearances inside and outside a building while providing the degree of fire safety for Heavy Timber construction allowed by North American building codes (see Section 10).

Most contemporary post and beam construction makes extensive use of metal fasteners for connecting members. Many historic post and beam buildings, built in North America before metal fasteners were readily available, were assembled using joinery techniques. Members were shaped to mate to each other and to be held together with wood dowels, or were shaped to be held together without the use of any type of fastener.

Timber joinery has seen a resurgence in popularity in the last decade especially for exclusive residences and for some commercial buildings where the joinery craftsmanship is used as an architectural feature.

Modern materials for members and connections result in a form of post and beam construction which has cost advantages over timber joinery because of strength and speed of installation.

Whether modern materials and connections are used to create wood post and beam construction or whether the historic and traditional timber joinery is used to join members, the resulting product can be functional and striking.

Features of Post and Beam Construction

Preparation of Members
Post and beam construction entails fewer but larger-sized pieces than conventional framing. It is usually cost effective to undertake joint preparation prior to delivery to the site but this practice is more common for manufactured wood products like glulam than it is for sawn timber.

When off site preparation is done, drilling, cutting, and milling can be done with only erection and fastening left to be done in the field. Although some site adjustments will usually be required, wood is a building product which is easily cut and shaped with hand and power tools quickly and easily.

The advance preparation of members for erection and the speed with which wood panels and particularly wood plank decking can be installed, means a building can quickly be covered from above to provide protection to ongoing work inside.

Appearance
In general, the wood structure of light framing buildings does not remain exposed when a building is completed. Interior and exterior finishes are added to the structure which conceal the wood framework.

Post and beam buildings, on the other hand, are most often constructed with the main structural members left exposed. The exposed wood colour and texture can result in dramatic and pleasing appearance to both the exterior and the interior.

6

Structural Wood Systems

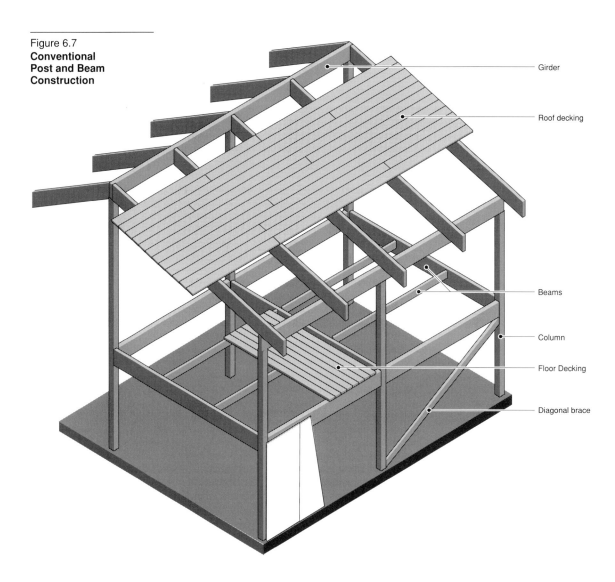

Figure 6.7
**Conventional
Post and Beam
Construction**

Girder

Roof decking

Beams

Column

Floor Decking

Diagonal brace

Because appearance is often of primary importance, appropriate care must be taken to avoid damage from impact and weather by protecting materials during storage, handling, erection, fitting and connecting.

Once erection commences, building closure should follow as quickly as possible to avoid dimensional change from moisture absorption, discolouration from sun, moisture, or staining resulting from the oxidation of metal connectors.

Flexibility
Partitions in post and beam construction do not normally carry vertical loads. Therefore the location of interior walls can be situated based on function rather than on the need for load bearing support. This allows freedom in layout of interior floor plans.

However, post and beam methods can be combined with conventional framing load bearing walls where a partition is required and a column is not suitable. In such cases, the load bearing wall must be designed to accept concentrated beam loads.

Fire Safety

Post and beam construction qualifies as Heavy Timber construction for the purpose of fire safety when the members are of certain dimensions (see Section 10). This allows roof and floor members to remain exposed rather than be covered with a protective layer of gypsum wallboard.

Materials

Lumber

Sawn timber was once the only wood product available for heavy members and is still commonly used. In North America, lengths are readily available to about 6m (20') and longer members can be ordered. Sawn timber is used rough or dressed depending on the texture and appearance desired. Large posts and beams are not commonly stocked at retail lumber yards but may be ordered.

It is not practical to kiln dry timber members because accelerated drying causes differential drying between the surface and the interior which leads to checking and splitting. For this reason, timbers are surfaced green and care should be taken to foresee dimensional changes resulting from continuing drying after installation. To prevent twisting and checking in large members it is best to acquire timbers which are at least partly seasoned, and additional seasoning should be allowed to occur slowly.

For solid sawn timber post and beam construction, typical lumber grade specifications are as follows (see Section 3.2):

- Posts: No.2 grade from the Structural Light Framing category, and No.1 or No.2 grade from the Posts and Timbers category depending on the size required.

- Floor and roof beams: No.2 grade from the Structural Joists and Planks category, and No.1 and No.2 grade from the Beams and Stringers category, depending on the size required.

- Floor and roof planks: Select or Commercial grades from the Decking category depending on the appearance desired.

Timber joinery, being a traditional method of construction predating the advent of composite wood products, continues to employ sawn timber as the principal building product. In addition to the softwoods which predominate as building materials in North America, timber joinery also uses common hardwoods where economy is not an overriding consideration.

Glulam, PSL and LVL

The manufactured products, glulam, parallel strand lumber (PSL) and laminated veneer lumber (LVL) are used extensively for post and beam construction. All these manufactured products have the advantage of being available in lengths up to 25m (80'). In some cases, where special transportation arrangements can be made, they can be manufactured to longer lengths.

Glulam was, for many years, the only product, other than timber, available for post and beam construction. It remains the only large scale wood product whose manufacturing process can accommodate curved and shaped members (see Section 3.3).

Parallel strand lumber (PSL) is a relatively new product finding rapid acceptance as a large scale building material for post and beam construction. Although manufactured in straight sections of prescribed dimensions, PSL can be further laminated and sawn to produce larger members and some shapes. It offers a pleasing appearance distinctive from solid wood members.

Laminated veneer lumber (LVL) may also be laminated into larger members to be used for post and beam applications.

All these manufactured products are dependent on raw materials and manufacturing processes having low moisture content. Therefore they are building products which are dimensionally stable and do not change substantially because of moisture loss or gain. It is important to protect the products during shipping and construction, to maintain this level of quality.

6

Structural Wood Systems

Design

The arrangement, span, and loadings on post and beam structures vary from building to building. Because post and beam construction involves fewer members than the load sharing arrangements of convention framing, loads in structural members tend to be considerable. For these reasons, proper engineering analysis of members and connections is essential.

The ends of overhanging beams, exposed to weather, are subject to rapid and extreme fluctuations in moisture content as moisture leaves or enters end grain of the wood. These ends should be coated to reduce moisture absorption and prevent splitting and decay.

Foundations

Either pier foundations or continuous foundation walls may be used for post and beam construction. Connections between the foundation and superstructure should be protected from collection or pooling of water.

Walls and Partitions

The beams and columns used in post and beam construction provide the structural support for a building. Regular spacing of posts and beams form natural frames for infill panels to enclose the building.

These spaces between posts can be infilled by means of conventional framing and sheathing, by windows, or by composite panels made especially for this purpose (see Section 6.6) which combine interior and exterior wall finishes, insulation, and resistance to racking without the need for scribing panels to fit between posts.

Where glazing is used to infill the space between structural members, care must be taken to ensure a sufficient framed and caulked space is left to allow for settlement or movement without damaging the glazing.

It is often desired by the designer that the structural members contribute to the appearance of a building rather than be concealed within wall and roof cavities. In some cases, it may be desired to have columns visible from both the interior and the exterior of the building in which case infill panels must abut the columns and employ caulking to complete a weather seal between column and panel.

In other cases, the structure may be a visible feature on only the inside or the outside in which case a continuous building envelope can be erected on either the inside or the outside of the exterior walls (see Figure 6.8 opposite).

Deck Flooring and Roofing

The horizontal spaces between beams are normally spanned by plank decking, but conventional joist construction may also be used.

Roof and floor decks may consist of exposed planking or conventional joist construction. The use of plank decking may offer the possibility of using the appearance of the wood decking as a building feature.

Appearance, as well as structural requirements, must be considered when a plank floor or roof serves as a finished ceiling. Lumber of the proper grade must be specified, and its appearance should be protected by careful storage and handling. Because decking is graded based on the appearance of the best face, the pieces should be arranged prior to nailing so that the more attractive face is displayed.

The appearance of exposed decking can be affected by its moisture content at the time of installation. For best results, decking should be supplied and installed at a moisture content not exceeding 15 percent. If decking with a higher moisture content is used, unsightly gaps may develop between planks as the wood dries.

Figure 6.8
**Building
Envelope for
Post & Beam
Construction**

6

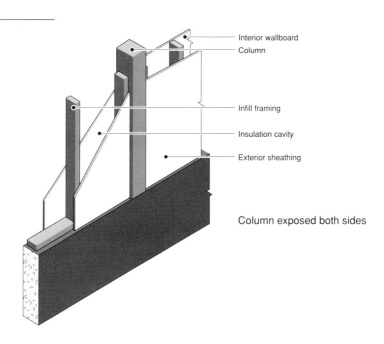

Interior wallboard
Column

Infill framing

Insulation cavity

Exterior sheathing

Column exposed both sides

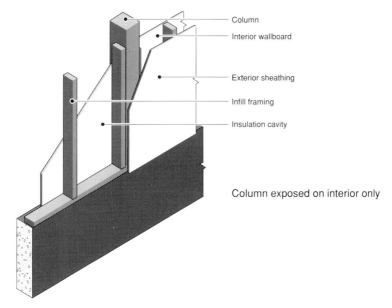

Column
Interior wallboard

Exterior sheathing

Infill framing

Insulation cavity

Column exposed on interior only

It may be desired for the exposed floor or roof decking to match the texture and colour of the beams which support it, or alternately, by using different stain colour, to be in contrast.

When used for floor decking, the decking is often overlaid with hardwood flooring or other flooring and constitutes the ceiling of the floor below. Finish flooring should be laid at right angles to the decking, using the same procedure followed as though laid conventionally over panel sub-flooring.

Being a good insulator, wood decking used for roofing provides a thicker wood insulating layer than plywood or OSB/waferboard sheathing. Therefore a deck roof requires less non-wood insulation than panel sheathed roofs or metal sheathed roofs. The amount of extra insulation required depends on climate, cost of heating, and the desired performance of the building.

Where the ceiling below is to be exposed, rigid insulation, commonly used with plank roofs, is usually laid on the upper side of the deck. For flat roofs, asphalt is often used to secure the insulation to the deck, and the membrane to the insulation. On steeper roofs (slopes exceeding 3 in 12), insulation is nailed to the deck between wood strapping. Wood panels are nailed to the strapping to serve as a nailing surface for shingles.

To be structurally efficient, the deck should distribute loads laterally between adjacent planks by means of tongue and groove joints and lateral nailing of the planks (see Section 4.4).

Wind Bracing
Wind bracing in light framing construction is provided by the shearwall action of framing and sheathing, acting in unison, or by the addition of diagonal bracing between the framing.

Because there are fewer framing members in post and beam construction than in light framing, loads are concentrated and special attention must be paid to wind bracing and uplift. Methods for ensuring structural adequacy include bracing, shearwall panels, rigid framing, and design of members to resist both horizontal and vertical forces.

Services
When decking is used in the place of joists or when stress-skin sandwich panels are used for walls in a post and beam building, special provision is required for running services.

This can be done by concealing services in prepared grooves behind posts and beams, or by specifying visible hardware which blends in with the wood finish.

Figure 6.9
Typical Post and Beam Roof Detail for a Low Slope Roof

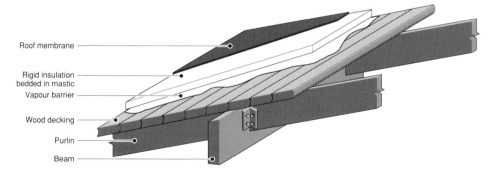

Roof membrane

Rigid insulation bedded in mastic

Vapour barrier

Wood decking

Purlin

Beam

Connections

A variety of heavy duty fasteners are available for post and beam connections (see Section 5). These include bolts, plates, split rings, shearplates, and glulam rivets. Because members and connections are usually purposely left exposed to view, it is important that connections not only be adequate for the applied loads, but that they be well proportioned, unobtrusive, and surface finished.

The selection of appropriate fasteners will be determined to a large extent by load transfer requirements. A certain degree of latitude is possible to provide for the most suitable appearance.

For timber joinery construction, it is usual not to use metallic fastenings of any sort but rather to use joint geometry and wooden pegs where required to pin joints together.

Timber Joinery

Timber joinery is the traditional form of post and beam construction. The origin of timber joinery in North America predates the availability of metal fasteners and of sawmill produced lumber. Therefore large hand hewn timbers were used, joined by shaping the members to fit together and to be retained in this position by means of wood pegs, or merely by joint geometry.

Timber joinery has enjoyed a revival in recent years where the technique has been used to create distinctive home designs. In some cases it has been used in commercial projects. It is a method of construction which is more labour intensive than contemporary post and beam construction but which offers a finished appearance demonstrating wood construction and workmanship in an artistic form.

Timber of either softwood or hardwood species is used for joinery work.

Contemporary post and beam construction and timber joinery differ in the following ways:

Post and Beam:
- timber, glulam, parallel strand lumber (PSL) and laminated veneer lumber (LVL) are used for main members

- shop preparation of connections is possible

- metal fasteners are used for speed, economy, and strength

Timber Joinery:
- hardwood or softwood timber is used for main members

- precise on site preparation of joints is usually required

- fastening is based on the interlocking of members by friction fit, and by the use of wooden pegs

A framing plan for a timber joinery building is shown in Figure 6.10 (→ 326). Timber joinery develops lateral stability from distributing loads by using knee braces in most bays. Because adjoining members must fit into each other rather than abut, due care is required in designing members and joints and in planning an erection sequence which allows the pieces to be assembled without placing undue stress on any point.

Like the conventional form of post and beam construction, infill panels are required to complete the building envelope. These may be prefabricated sandwich panels or may be conventional framing and sheathing.

Engineering design codes in North America provide design criteria for metallic connections but do not provide guidance for joinery connections because performance is so directly affected by workmanship.

Therefore, small timber joinery buildings will continue to rely on the building experience of those competent in this type of work. For larger buildings, engineering analysis from first principles will be required.

6

Structural Wood Systems

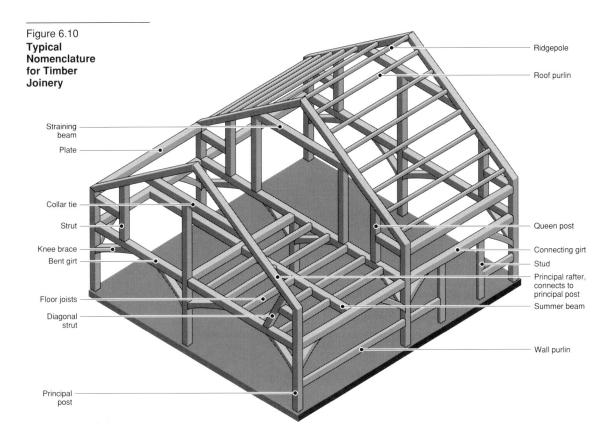

Figure 6.10
**Typical
Nomenclature
for Timber
Joinery**

Labels (clockwise): Ridgepole, Roof purlin, Queen post, Connecting girt, Stud, Principal rafter, connects to principal post, Summer beam, Wall purlin, Principal post, Diagonal strut, Floor joists, Bent girt, Knee brace, Strut, Collar tie, Plate, Straining beam

General Guidelines for Post and Beam Construction

- Post and beam construction is a dramatic method of using wood as a construction material. Large members of many shapes are available which can be finished to become major focal attractions of the building.

- If infill panels are used to make the framework visible from both the exterior and the interior, caulking must be provided. It must be capable of accommodating seasoning changes in the columns and beams.

- Resistance to lateral loads in the form of diagonal bracing or infill shearwall must be provided.

- Consider how electrical and other services will be carried in walls, ceiling and roofs.

- Prepare members in advance for connection as much as possible. Large shop equipment offers accuracy not always possible with site equipment.

- Finishing of members with stain and varnish before erection should be considered for economy and quality.

- Where sawn timber is used, consider the moisture content of the material, moderate the rate of drying by keeping initial heating levels low, and allow for shrinkage.

- For all heavy members, provide as much protection as possible from the weather during installation. Particular attention is required where uncoated fasteners might rust and stain the wood members.

References

Building Construction Materials and Methods, H.G. Miller, McMillan of Canada, 1980

The Timber-Frame Home, Tedd Benson, Taunton Press, 1989

Wood Engineering and Construction Handbook, Keith E. Flaherty and Thomas G. Williamson, McGraw Hill Publishing, 1989

Wood Design Manual, Canadian Wood Council, 1990

6

Structural Wood Systems

6.4 Shearwalls and Diaphragms

Structural Wood Systems

Introduction

Buildings are subject to lateral loads from winds and earthquakes, and must be sufficiently rigid to support vertical loads.

Wood frame construction offers an effective method of resisting lateral building loads because of light weight, strong fastening systems, and alternate load paths. Recent examples of this performance are Hurricane Hugo in the southeast United States in 1989, and the Loma Prieta earthquake in the San Francisco Bay area of California in 1989.

In post and beam construction, diagonal bracing or non-rotating connections are required to resist lateral loads. Conventional framing relies on the combination of shearwalls and diaphragms to resist lateral loads.

Shearwalls and diaphragms are combinations of framing members and sheathing designed to give strength and rigidity to walls and roofs.

The term shearwall is used to describe a wall where the attachment of sheathing to framing has been designed to resist in-plane racking forces.

The term diaphragm is used to describe a horizontal plane such as a framed floor or roof which has been designed to transfer lateral loads outwardly to shearwalls, which then transfer the loads to the foundation.

Although particularly effective in stiffening conventionally framed buildings, shearwall effects in infill panels, used for building closure between the columns in post and beam construction, can supplement or supplant diagonal bracing. Similarly, diaphragm action from panels or decking affixed to roof and floor purlins in a post and beam building can supplement or supplant cross bracing.

In small buildings such as houses, adequate lateral resistance may be provided by conventional framing techniques and additional stiffening resulting from interior partitions and even by the attachment of gypsum wallboard. For larger buildings, and buildings of all sizes in high earthquake risk areas, lateral forces can be substantial and special features must be incorporated into the building design to ensure adequacy.

In many types of wood construction, shearwalls and diaphragms are effective and economical means of stiffening because the building envelope is made to perform the dual function of enclosing and of providing structural rigidity.

The purpose of this section is to give a basic understanding of why shearwalls and diaphragms are required and how they function.

The Performance of Wood Shearwalls and Diaphragms

Whether in lateral loading, cyclical over several hours, as would result from hurricane conditions, or in severe short term loading as would result from a seismic event, wood shearwalls and diaphragms perform well.

There are several good reasons for this demonstrated performance.

First, wood frame construction is lightweight in relation to steel and masonry construction. Earthquake forces are unique in the lateral acceleration they impart to everything in their path. The inertia of each obstacle, such as a building, resists movement to a degree dependent upon its mass. The lighter a building is, the easier it is to manage the forces from this acceleration.

Second, earthquakes are highly unpredictable in intensity and direction, and in how the loads they impart are carried through a building. Shearwall and diaphragm construction counters unpredictability by using a vast number of small nail connectors which provide many load paths, unlike other types of construction which accumulate and transfer larger loads.

Third, wood can, for short periods of time, endure stresses which exceed those of normal service conditions, and therefore it has reserve strength. Structural wood panel diaphragms maintain high stiffness and strength and if pushed to their ultimate capacity, tend to yield gradually while continuing to carry high loads, rather than exhibit brittle failure.

Last, nails are ductile fasteners which, when used in lumber, permit some movement in a building when subjected to sudden lateral loading. So, while providing the rigidity required for good building performance in ordinary circumstances, the nail to wood interface, when subjected to strong lateral loads, also makes the

building somewhat flexible, rather than rigid.

Lateral Building Loads

Wall design must make allowance for the tendency of a building to rack (go out of square) from its own weight and from imposed loads such as snow. Shearwalls and diaphragms provide building stiffness to counter the tendency of a building to rack, due to lateral loading such as wind, earthquake, or an unbalanced load from soil pressure or bulk storage (see Figure 6.11 below). The effect of vertical loads is aggravated when sway is induced by the primary lateral forces acting on the structure.

Figure 6.11
**Causes of
Building
Racking**

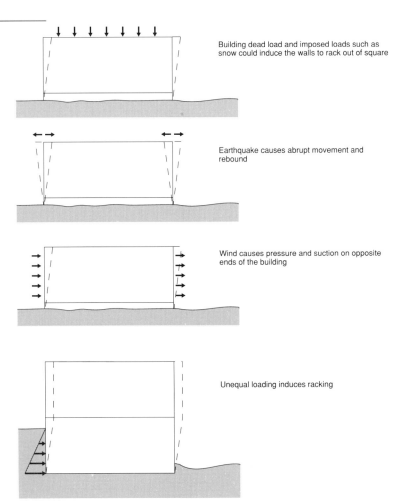

Building dead load and imposed loads such as snow could induce the walls to rack out of square

Earthquake causes abrupt movement and rebound

Wind causes pressure and suction on opposite ends of the building

Unequal loading induces racking

In addition to strength requirements, diaphragms and shearwalls must be designed to meet serviceability criteria so that deflections at specified loads are limited to values that do not cause distress to non-structural elements such as glazing and wall finishes, or make the structure susceptible to vibration.

The requirements for shearwalls and diaphragms vary greatly across North America and are most demanding in areas prone to earthquakes and high winds. Reference should be made to local code requirements for design criteria for these factors.

Shearwall and Diaphragm Action

In simple terms, a shearwall acts like a large flat vertical cantilever beam extending from the foundation and resisting lateral loads. A diaphragm acts like a large flat horizontal beam whose reactions are transferred to the walls which support it.

Lateral loads may or may not be normal to a building face. For a simple case where the end of a building is loaded laterally, Figure 6.12 (→ 332, 333) shows how shearwalls function, how diaphragms function, and how the two interact to stiffen a building.

The wall on which the wind acts is supported by the roof and foundation, and transfers one half the total wind load to roof level. The roof diaphragm transmits the load to the end shearwalls, which in turn transfer the load to the foundations.

Floor and roof diaphragms are designed to distribute lateral loads on the structure to the shearwall elements, which in turn carry the loads to the foundations. In addition to vertical shearwalls and horizontal diaphragms, a combined diaphragm/shearwall effect can be obtained in sloped or curvilinear building components.

Smaller buildings may be of adequate stiffness merely by following code requirements for small buildings which are based on past experience and testing.

Where specifically designed, shearwalls and diaphragms must be able to resist all lateral loads. Decking and sheathing must be adequately fastened to supporting members (studs, joists, trusses, beams, columns and walls) so that they transfer lateral loads to perimeter members. Openings in shearwalls and diaphragms must be adequately reinforced with framing members and connections to transfer forces to the rest of the shearwall or diaphragm.

Wind suction and vertical acceleration caused by sudden lateral loading can cause uplift forces at the roof/wall (diaphragm/shearwall) interface and at the wall/ foundation (shearwall/foundation) interface. For this reason, diaphragms must be suitably connected to the shearwalls, and the building must be fastened to the foundation to resist uplift loads and lateral shear forces.

For large buildings, it may be necessary to utilize one or more interior partitions to provide shearwall action to keep transferred loads to a manageable size. In large buildings without interior partitions, such as warehouses, exterior shearwalls can be bolstered by, for example, doubling the sheathing or using diagonal bracing. This may be accomplished by installing plywood or OSB/waferboard sheathing over the framing and installing the gypsum wallboard finish over the sheathing. The addition of supplementary shearwalls requires careful analysis to estimate the amount of lateral load which is transferred to each shearwall.

Because of the relative flexibility of wood diaphragms, it is often assumed that shearwalls are subjected to loads in proportion to their tributary areas. The designer should, however, keep in mind the effect of diaphragm stiffness on the way in which loads are carried in a structure and provide adequate horizontal diaphragm stiffness elements. This is particularly important for asymmetrical shearwall layouts.

6

Structural Wood Systems

Figure 6.12
**Shearwall and
Diaphragm
Action**

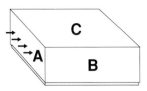

A- Endwall against which wind pressure
    (or earthquake force) acts.
B- Sidewalls (parallel to wind) which provide
    shearwall action in this example.
C- Roof provides diaphragm action.

Wind pressure causes A to hinge at the foundation.
To resist this, force must be applied along the side of A.

The load transfer from A tends to make
B go out of square or rack.

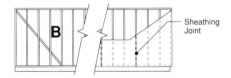

To resist the tendency to rack, B must be reinforced with
interior bracing, or a nailing spacing for the sheathing must
be used which permits the sheathing and framing
to resist racking.

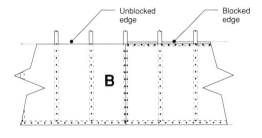

Installing blocking between the framing members at
sheathing edges increases resistance to racking by
increasing the perimeter where nailing can be used
to transfer load.

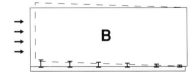

If B acts as a shearwall, the wind load from A may
cause the upwind corner of B to lift. The connection
of B to the foundation must be designed to resist uplift
and horizontal shear.

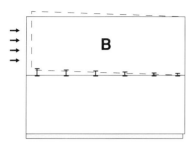

For multi-storey buildings, it is necessary to ensure that hold down continuity extends into upper storeys.

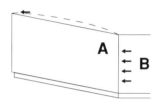

With the sides of A restrained by shearwall action in B, there is still a tendency for A to deflect its weak upper edge.

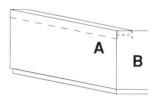

A beam on edge (or diaphragm (see below)) could be used to strengthen the upper edge of A with the reactions from the beam being transferred to the shearwall B.

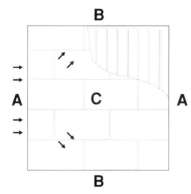

The roof sheathing and roof framing can be designed as a diaphragm (C) which acts like a deep beam in resisting the lateral pressure from A and transferring the load to the B walls.

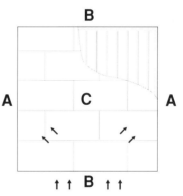

If the wind shifts to act on B, the A walls provide shearwalll action and the roof acts as a diaphragm by transferring loads to the A walls.

Materials for Shearwalls and Diaphragms

Framing Materials

Dimension lumber and light frame trusses are the most commonly used framing materials for shearwall and diaphragm design, but other wood members may be used in combination with sheathing to develop resistance to lateral loads.

Prefabricated wood I-joists, laminated veneer lumber (LVL) and parallel strand lumber (PSL) are other wood products common to wood frame construction. The materials used for post and beam construction, timber, glulam, LVL and PSL may also be used as purlins, combined with sheathing to resist lateral loading.

Panel Sheathing

Plywood and OSB/waferboard panels are used extensively in wood frame construction to provide shearwall and diaphragm action.

Strength of panel product diaphragms and shearwalls is dependent on the thickness of the panel, the nailing pattern, the nail holding ability of the framing material, and whether or not blocking is used to increase the nailed perimeter. In addition, strength is greater when the joints between panels are staggered so that there is not a continuous joint.

Increased shearwall capacity can be obtained by applying sheathing to both sides of framing.

Softer materials such as fibreboard and gypsum wallboard can add supplementary stiffening effect. However, for severe loading conditions, such as might result from earthquake loads, it is recommended that the strengthening effect of these materials be considered as a reserve rather than as primary resistance to such loads.

This is because the nail fasteners may tend to abrade these soft materials during normal cyclical loading, and result in too much loss of rigidity when a large loading occurs.

Lumber Boards and Decking

Boards used for shearwalls and for diaphragms should be at least 19mm (1" nom.) thick and 140mm (6" nom.) wide. Boards are usually limited to applications where the spacing of supports is 600mm (2') or less.

Board sheathing can be laid transversely to supporting members. Increased strength is obtained by placing the boards diagonal to the framing. Still more strength can be obtained by attaching a second layer of board sheathing diagonally opposite to the first layer.

Plank decking (lumber 38 to 89mm (2" to 4" nom.) thick, 127mm (5") and wider) is a stress graded lumber product, often used as a diaphragm material available in many species, sizes and shapes. Its thickness gives it the capacity to carry hefty floor and roof loads. It may also provide diaphragm resistance to lateral loads, and it may have the advantage of providing additional fire safety, by meeting the minimum size requirements of floor and roof materials for Heavy Timber construction.

Decking is usually laid transverse to supporting members, such as beams or purlins, in a controlled random pattern (see Section 4.4). It can also be laid diagonally to the support members to improve diaphragm strength.

Connections

Shearwalls and diaphragms effectively transfer lateral forces down to the foundation. All components must be suitably fastened together for the structure to act as an effective unit.

Whether the sheathing materials are boards or panels, the nail connection between sheathing and framing is the essential means of load transfer. This is why the capacity of a panel sheathed wall increases as the nail to nail spacing decreases. Loss of strength, due to splitting in the framing member, is a possibility when the nail spacing is less than 50mm (2"). Close nailing patterns are facilitated by mechanical nailing.

Figure 6.13
**Arrangements
and Relative
Strength of
Shearwalls**

Board sheathing comparison based on 19 x 140mm (1" x 6" nom.) boards with two 63 mm (2-1/2") nails per board per support.

Relative
Strength

6

Structural Wood Systems

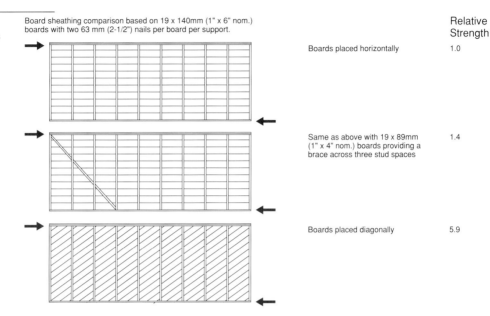

Boards placed horizontally   1.0

Same as above with 19 x 89mm
(1" x 4" nom.) boards providing a
brace across three stud spaces   1.4

Boards placed diagonally   5.9

Panel sheathing comparison based on unsanded plywood or OSB panels with edges supported by 38mm (2" nom.) or wider framing. Framing is Douglas Fir-Larch with a perimeter nail spacing of 100mm (4") and an intermediate support nail spacing of 300mm (12").

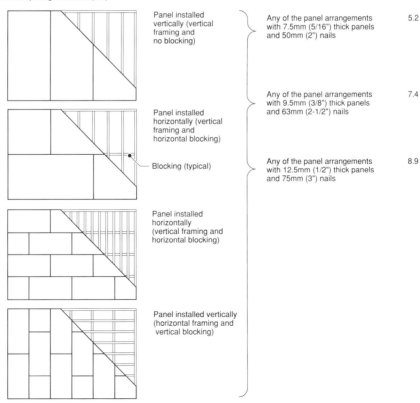

Panel installed
vertically (vertical
framing and
no blocking)

Any of the panel arrangements
with 7.5mm (5/16") thick panels
and 50mm (2") nails   5.2

Panel installed
horizontally (vertical
framing and
horizontal blocking)

Any of the panel arrangements
with 9.5mm (3/8") thick panels
and 63mm (2-1/2") nails   7.4

Blocking (typical)

Panel installed
horizontally
(vertical framing and
horizontal blocking)

Any of the panel arrangements
with 12.5mm (1/2") thick panels
and 75mm (3") nails   8.9

Panel installed vertically
(horizontal framing and
vertical blocking)

Note:
Code allowances for sheathing types varies. Consult local code for specific strengths.

Figure 6.14
Panel Arrangements and Relative Strengths of Diaphragms

This comparison is based on Douglas Fir-Larch framing, unsanded plywood or OSB panels, 38mm (2" nom.) framing members, 100mm (4") nail spacing at diaphragm boundary and at continous panel edges parallel to load, all other nail spacing at 150mm (6"), all edges blocked.

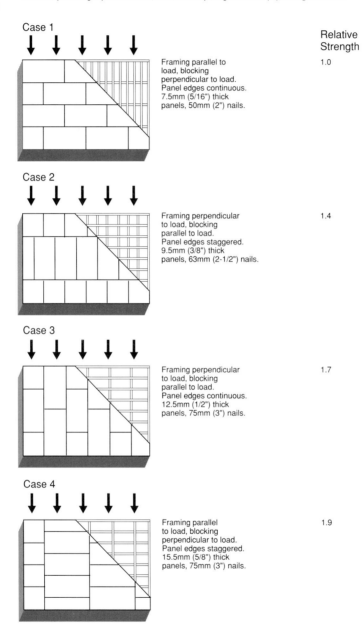

Case 1

Relative Strength

Framing parallel to load, blocking perpendicular to load. Panel edges continuous. 7.5mm (5/16") thick panels, 50mm (2") nails.

1.0

Case 2

Framing perpendicular to load, blocking parallel to load. Panel edges staggered. 9.5mm (3/8") thick panels, 63mm (2-1/2") nails.

1.4

Case 3

Framing perpendicular to load, blocking parallel to load. Panel edges continuous. 12.5mm (1/2") thick panels, 75mm (3") nails.

1.7

Case 4

Framing parallel to load, blocking perpendicular to load. Panel edges staggered. 15.5mm (5/8") thick panels, 75mm (3") nails.

1.9

Note:
Code strength allowances vary. Consult local codes for specific strengths and other configurations.

The nailing perimeter of a panel can be maximized by installing blocking between framing members so that all panel edges and ends are supported. This increases the load capacity of the building element.

Board sheathing relies on the resistance to turning created by the nails installed at each board to framing interface. The resistance to turning is most affected by the distance between the two nails which is dependent upon the width of the boards used. For this reason, the capacity of board sheathing is not significantly increased by additional nailing.

Because a shearwall acts like a cantilever beam extended from the foundation, lateral load tends to rotate the base of the cantilever resulting in uplift forces, and tends to push the wall base across the foundation. For these reasons, wall units must be capable of resisting lateral shear and uplift forces.

The uplift forces place vertical sections in tension between the foundation and roof and therefore tie down connections must be continuous from the roof down. For light loads, the sheathing can be used to transfer loads (see Figure 6.15 below) across the header space discontinuity created by platform framed floor sections.

6

Structural Wood Systems

Figure 6.15
Resisting Uplift of Shearwalls

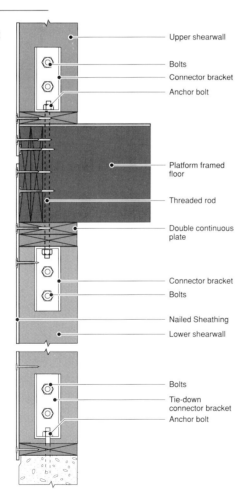

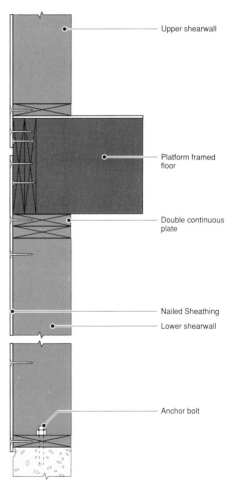

For heavy uplift load and for interior applications where panel sheathing is not used, tie-down connector brackets at select locations can be used to tie the building to the foundation.

Panel sheathing nailing is used to tie structure to foundation for light uplift load conditions.

For heavier loadings, it may be necessary to use tie-down connector brackets as shown in Figure 6.15 (→ 337) to make the vertical members between floors act as a continuous tensile member when resisting uplift. Such connectors should be tightened after seasoning of the floor joists just prior to enclosing the walls to take up any gap resulting from shrinkage in the horizontal lumber.

Proportions for Shearwalls and Diaphragms

Shearwalls and diaphragms are effective means of providing rigidity to wood structured buildings. Their effectiveness is based on design, but from experience, some practical limitations to the building proportions have been established.

Because the shearwall is likened to a cantilever beam fixed at the foundation, there is a practical limit to the height of a shearwall in relation to its length. While these values may vary with particular engineering standards, the Table below offers some practical values as a general guide.

In a similar vein, diaphragms are likened to a beam loaded from the side. Practical limitations have been established for the maximum slenderness the beam should have. In other words, there is a practical limit to the width to length ratio for diaphragm action. Again, these values as shown in the Table below, may vary according to the engineering standards in use and are presented as a general guide.

These guidelines indicate the basic geometric proportions which are most suitable for reinforcement by shearwall and diaphragm action. As the values show, most building arrangements fall within the guidelines, except for long and narrow buildings or high and squat buildings.

Use with Other Types of Building Materials

Wood shearwalls and diaphragms are more flexible than many other building materials. This causes some limitation in the use of wood to provide rigidity for concrete and masonry walls.

Although strong enough, a wood shearwall may deflect more than a high concrete or masonry wall can tolerate without cracking. This difference in flexibility initially led to a guideline confining their use to bracing one storey buildings with concrete or masonry walls.

Shearwall Height-to-Length Dimension Ratios

Material	Maximum height-to-length ratios
Diagonal board sheathing, one side	2 to 1
Plywood and OSB/waferboard, blocked and nailed all edges and ends	3.5 to 1
Plywood and OSB/waferboard, no blocking at intermediate joints	2 to 1

Note:
For multi-storey buildings, the values are the ratio of total wall height to the length of a given side.

Diaphragm Width-to-Length Dimension Ratios

Material	Maximum width-to-length ratio
Diagonal board sheathing, one side	3 to 1
Plywood and OSB/waferboard, blocked and nailed all edges and ends	4 to 1
Plywood and OSB/waferboard, no blocking at intermediate joints	4 to 1

For bracing two-storey buildings with masonry or concrete walls, the following guidelines may be appropriate for wood shearwalls:

- Wall heights should not exceed 3.66m (12').

- Horizontal diaphragms should not be cantilevered from one shearwall. They should be fixed as a minimum to two opposing shearwalls.

- Deflections of horizontal and vertical diaphragms should not permit per-storey deflections of supported masonry or concrete walls to exceed 0.005 times each storey height.

- Panel sheathing in horizontal diaphragms should have all unsupported edges blocked. Panel sheathing for both storeys of vertical shearwalls should have all unsupported edges blocked and for the lower storey walls should have a minimum sheathing thickness of 12.7mm (1/2").

- There should be no out-of-plane horizontal offsets between the first and second storeys of plywood shearwalls.

Although these factors may vary according to the North American engineering standards in effect in particular areas, the preceeding information is a general guide.

Openings

The rigidity of a building is reduced by window, door, skylight, and other openings. Openings in diaphragms and shearwalls can have a marked effect on structural performance so additional framing and connections may be needed to permit shear transfer around openings. If large openings such as industrial doors divide a shearwall into a number of smaller elements, design must allow for distribution of forces to independent shearwall sections.

Openings may also make a building asymmetrical (see Figure 6.16 below) and thereby affect its ability to resist lateral force from a given direction. In this situation, torsion is introduced and the building has a tendency to twist when subjected to lateral forces.

Weaker shearwalls may be bolstered by increasing panel thickness, edge nailing at closer spacings, or by affixing panels to both sides of the framing.

In some buildings, it may be difficult to create shearwall action. For example, airplane hangars (many of which were built of wood during World War II and are still in service) are characterised by one end which is almost entirely a door opening. In such a case, the only possible shearwall location is at the wall facing the open end. To provide resistance to lateral forces at the open end, it is necessary to design diagonal bracing around the opening to approximate the rigidity afforded by the shearwall at the opposing end.

6

Structural Wood Systems

Figure 6.16
Effects of Large Openings on Shearwalls

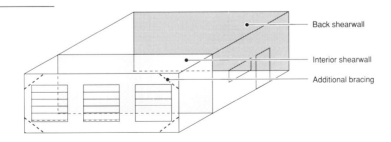

Back shearwall

Interior shearwall

Additional bracing

Large freight doors in this building reduce the wall area available for shearwall action.
Additional bracing, increased sheathing thickness and nailing density, or interior shearwalls may be required.

Guidelines for Shearwalls and Diaphragms

- Nailing patterns are critical to shearwall and diaphragm performance. Ensure that the contractor is aware of the higher density nailing patterns required, and inspect for performance.

- Larger buildings may require mechanical connections between floors to provide uplift resistance.

References

Engineering data in Earthquake Economics, Federal Reserve Board of San Francisco

Plywood Construction Manual, the Council of the Forest Industries of British Columbia

Shear Resistance of Wood Frame Buildings, A.T. Hansen, National Research Council of Canada, 1985

Wood Engineering and Construction Handbook, Keith F. Flaherty and Thomas G. Williamson, McGraw-Hill Publishing Company, 1987

Wood Design Manual, Canadian Wood Council, 1990

6.5   Bearing Stud Walls

Introduction

A bearing stud wall combines the primary separating or enclosing function of an interior or exterior partition with the role of transmitting vertical loads to the foundation. As well, a stud wall can transmit vertical, bending and lateral (see Shearwalls and Diaphragms, Section 6.4) loads in which case it behaves structurally as a load bearing wall, a beam, and as a shearwall.

Bearing walls have traditionally been constructed from stone, concrete, block, brick and other types of masonry materials. However, this rigid form of construction does not lend itself readily to future alterations such as the addition of openings for windows and doors. Bearing stud walls are a viable alternative for light-frame structures to concrete or masonry block walls.

A bearing stud wall is a versatile structural element which can be easily designed and pre-fabricated to suit many different architectural applications (see Figure 6.17 below).

Each framing member of a bearing stud wall behaves as a column in transferring vertical loads. The nailing of sheathing to framing members greatly enhances the column strength of each member by providing restraint from lateral displacement. Blocking between the studs can further improve the ability of long slender stud members to be effective columns.

Materials for Bearing Stud Walls

Bearing stud walls used in residential construction are typically comprised of 38 x 89mm (2" x 4" nom.) or 38 x 140mm (2" x 6" nom.) studs. They are, most commonly, of Stud grade lumber and sheathed with plywood or OSB/waferboard. Building codes provide requirements for the minimum stud size, the maximum stud spacing, and the maximum laterally unsupported wall height.

Spacings are usually 410mm (16") but 610mm (24") spacings are also used. These spacings have been based more on past experience with successful building practice and less on rigorous engineering analysis.

Bearing stud wall systems used in commercial applications are similar to those found in residential construction but member sizes must usually be larger to accommodate larger loads. Typical lumber dimensions are 38 x 140mm (2" x 6" nom.), 38 x 184mm (2" x 8" nom.), or 38 x 235mm (2" x 10" nom.) studs usually of No.1 or No.2 grade. These systems must be

6

Structural Wood Systems

Figure 6.17
Structural Applications of Bearing Stud Walls

Curvilinear Wall

Opening

Wood bearing stud walls are easily adapted to suit slopes, curves and openings.

engineered to ensure that the stud sizes, stud spacings, stud heights and top and bottom plates are adequate to resist the larger loads encountered in these types of applications.

For commercial buildings, sheathing thickness for bearing stud walls is usually specified in building codes and is usually governed by the minimum thickness required to span between the studs without distortion. If, however, the bearing wall is additionally required to perform as a shearwall, sheathing thickness, nail length, and nail spacing must be designed to ensure that adequate in-plane shear resistance is provided (see Section 6.4).

Although not specifically designed for this type of application, vertically oriented wood I-joists can be used successfully as stud wall systems. Similarly, laminated veneer lumber (LVL) and parallel strand lumber (PSL), used as top and bottom plates, can also be substituted for dimension lumber.

Uses for Load Bearing Stud Walls

Stud walls used as interior bearing walls are often of platform-frame construction. In this type of application, the roof trusses and floor joists can either be top- or bottom-chord bearing. In Figure 6.18 below, both trusses and joists are shown as bottom-chord bearing.

Top-chord supported trusses have less tendency to rotate and therefore require less lateral restraint in the form of cross bracing.

Bottom-chord supported trusses require more cross bracing but tend to lessen the height of bearing wall required to provide a given ceiling height. Because the strength of any column (or stud wall) of a given cross section reduces as its length increases, the labour and material cost for providing additional bracing for top-chord supported trusses may be offset by savings

Figure 6.18
Interior Load Bearing Studwall

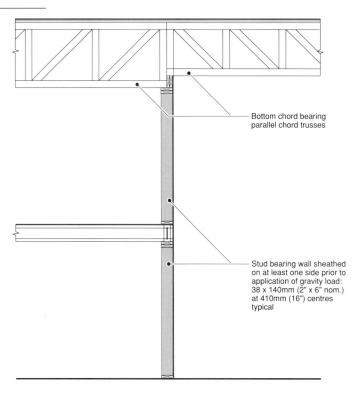

Bottom chord bearing parallel chord trusses

Stud bearing wall sheathed on at least one side prior to application of gravity load: 38 x 140mm (2" x 6" nom.) at 410mm (16") centres typical resulting from shorter and more effective bearing stud walls. For most interior commercial applications of this type, 38 x 140mm (2" x 6" nom.) studs at 410mm (16") centres are adequate.

Stud walls used as exterior bearing walls must be designed for both gravity loads and wind loads (see Figure 6.19 below) perpendicular to the face of the wall. For commercial buildings exposed to moderate snow and wind loads, a single 38 x 184mm (2" x 8" nom.) stud wall at 410mm (16") centres is usually acceptable for heights of up to 6m (20'). For more severe loading conditions, the stud size may have to be increased and the stud spacing may have to be reduced.

In situations where the stud wall is required to resist wind load only, or where snow and wind loads are light, 38 x 140mm (2" x 6" nom.) studs may be found to be sufficient.

When a wall performs an enclosing function, with gravity loads being resisted by separate grids of interior and exterior columns, the load bearing capacity of the wall is not utilized to its full potential. A bearing stud wall system maximises use of the structural capacity of the framing studs by performing both enclosing and load-bearing functions, resulting in larger column-free areas.

6

Structural Wood Systems

Figure 6.19
Gravity and Wind Loads on Exterior Load Bearing Studwall

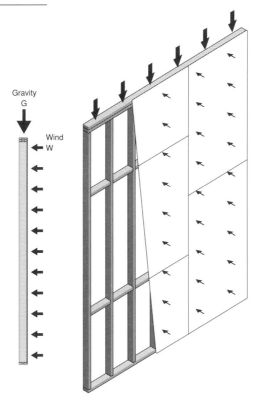

Gravity G

Wind W

General Guidelines for Bearing Stud Walls

- For residential applications, most bearing stud walls can be framed with 38 x 89mm (2" x 4" nom.) and 38 x 140mm (2" x 6" nom.) studs.

- For commercial applications in exterior load bearing walls, use 38 x 184mm (2" x 8" nom.) No.1 or No.2 studs spaced at 410mm (16") for preliminary sizing.

- For commercial applications in interior load bearing walls, use 38 x 140mm (2" x 6" nom.) No.1 or No.2 studs spaced at 410mm (16") for preliminary sizing.

- For both residential and commercial applications, kiln dried framing material for bearing stud walls offers best performance.

References

Design of Wood Structures, 2nd Edition, Donald E. Breyer, McGraw-Hill Book Company, 1988

Wood Design Manual, Canadian Wood Council, 1990

6.6 Composite Panels

Introduction

When framed together, sheathing and load bearing members act in composite to provide strength and rigidity. In comparison to an I-beam, the sheathing is the flange and the framing member is the web. This composite action occurs with many wood product combinations and accounts for the efficiency of shearwalls, bearing walls and other systems.

Composite panels are factory made combinations of wood sheathing products and wood framing materials. For some composite panels, foam takes the place of the sheathing or core.

There are three main types of composite panels: 1) Plywood stressed-skin panels, 2) Non-structural sandwich panels and 3) Structural sandwich panels.

Plywood Stressed-Skin Panels

Composition

The plywood stressed-skin panel is an engineered composite system of plywood panels (flanges) and 38mm (2" nom.) framing lumber (webs) glued together to behave as a structural composite unit. As such, it is capable of carrying higher loads than lumber and plywood acting individually (see Figure 6.20 below).

The plywood panels are applied with the grain of the face veneers parallel to the lumber webs. Plywood stressed-skin panels can be either two sided or one sided as shown in Figure 6.21 (→ 346). The two sided panel provides maximum strength and an interior surface which is ready to finish. The one sided panel, while not as strong as the two sided panel, facilitates the installation of electrical and mechanical services.

6

Structural Wood Systems

Figure 6.20
**Typical
Plywood
Stressed-Skin
Panel**

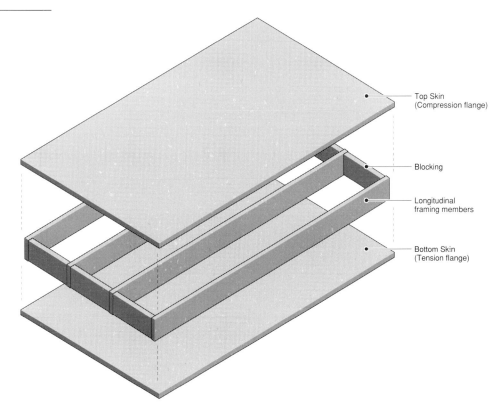

Top Skin
(Compression flange)

Blocking

Longitudinal
framing members

Bottom Skin
(Tension flange)

Figure 6.21
Cross Section of Plywood Stressed-Skin Panels

Plywood Stressed-Skin Panel (2 sided)

Plywood Stressed-Skin Panel (1 sided)
(Useful where access for electrical and plumbing services is necessary)

Figure 6.22
Examples of Plywood Stressed-Skin Panel Applications

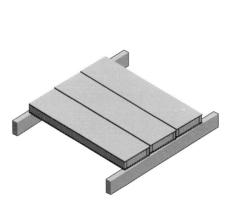
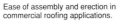

Ease of assembly and erection in
commercial roofing applications.

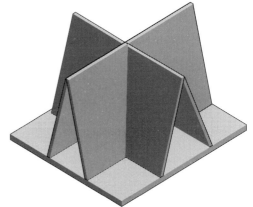

Unusual roof forms for all types of buildings.

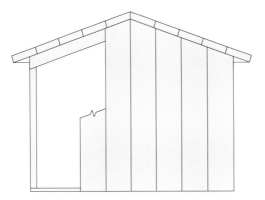

Pre-fabricated plywood stressed-skin panels used as
exterior wall enclosures and as roof panels reduce on-site
construction time and labour costs relative to on site construction.

Clear spans range from 2.4m (8') to 7.2m (24'). To maintain continuity for long spans, longitudinal framing members must be fingerjoined and plywood panels must be scarf-joined or butt-joined with splice plates. Headers and blocking are also required for added rigidity and lateral stability.

Applications
Used in wall, roof and floor construction, plywood stressed-skin panels can be designed to conform to varying architectural and structural requirements (see Figure 6.22 opposite). If thermal or acoustic properties are important, insulation can be installed in the voids with venting provided by drilling several small holes in the end blocking.

Advantages
Since plywood stressed-skin panels result in less overall weight for roof and floor systems, they are easy to erect. Prefabrication of panels permits convenient stacking for transportation and also eliminates on-site waste.

Usually prefabricated under shop conditions, stressed-skin panel buildings can be erected quickly, resulting in early building closure even during poor construction weather. The modular units can also be disassembled easily, making plywood stressed-skin panels well suited for buildings which must be capable of being relocated.

Non-Structural Sandwich Panels

Composition
Non-structural sandwich panels are assembled using a rigid foam core centre with exterior and interior sheathing bonded to each face. The rigid core centre is usually urethane or expanded polystyrene (EPS) and the sheathing materials plywood, OSB/waferboard or gypsum wallboard.

Non-structural sandwich panels are capable of withstanding lateral wall loads usually encountered in residential construction.

During assembly, sheathing materials are offset by 19mm (3/4"), creating a foam tongue along one side and a sheathing-faced groove along the other. Panels are fastened to the frame with spikes that penetrate at least 51mm (2") into the wood framing members. Nails are usually spaced 305mm (12") centre to centre.

6

Structural Wood Systems

Figure 6.23
Non-Structural Sandwich Panels

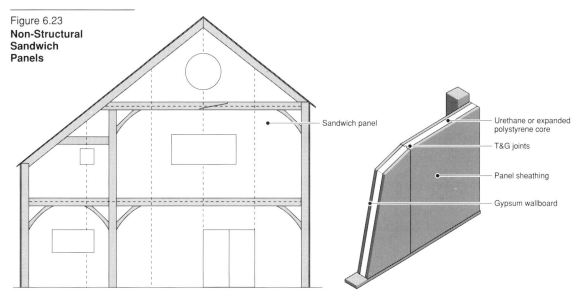

Sandwich panel

Urethane or expanded polystyrene core

T&G joints

Panel sheathing

Gypsum wallboard

Typical timber-frame structure showing locations of non-structural sandwich panels

Composition of non-structural sandwich panels

There are many types of non-structural sandwich panels, and they are known by several local names to builders. Some of these names are: stress-skin panels (not to be confused with plywood stressed-skin panels), laminated building panels, curtain-wall panels, foam-core panels, or pre-formed wall and roof panels.

Applications

Non-structural sandwich panels are used predominantly as enclosure systems for timber joining construction as shown in Figure 6.23 (→ 347). The attachment of the sandwich panel to the outside face of the frame effectively insulates the building while also providing exterior sheathing and interior gypsum wallboard surfaces.

Advantages

Non-structural sandwich panels are very good insulators due to the continuity of insulation. They can also provide moisture, thermal, acoustic and fire resistance. Some resistance to racking is also provided.

In post and beam construction, gypsum wallboard faced panels abut the post and beam frame, eliminating the need to scribe the gypsum wallboard to fit between the posts, and eliminating damage to the gypsum wallboard through dimensional changes. Once panel erection is complete, taping and crack filling are all that is needed to finish the interior.

One of the major advantages of this system is its flexibility. For example, in planning for doors and windows, rough openings can be cut before or after wall raising without the need for framing around the openings.

Structural Sandwich Panels

Composition

Structural sandwich panels may be used as a substitute for conventional framing. Typically, these panels consist of plywood or OSB/waferboard bonded to both faces of a foam core using construction adhesive, rated for structural use. These panels are also usually reinforced on the panel edges by 38mm (2" nom.) lumber framing members similar to plywood stressed-skin panels.

Recently, structural sandwich panels, consisting of a series of prefabricated wood I-joists or kiln dried lumber bonded to infill panels of expanded polystyrene (EPS) (see Figure 6.24 opposite), have also become available. Plastics other than EPS may be used.

Applications

These panels can be designed for many applications such as bearing walls, founda-tions, floors, and roofs.

Advantages

Due to their light-weight, high strength, and easy transportability, these types of panels are easy to erect and can be advantageous in many residential and commercial applications.

Figure 6.24
**Typical
Structural
Sandwich
Panel
Construction**

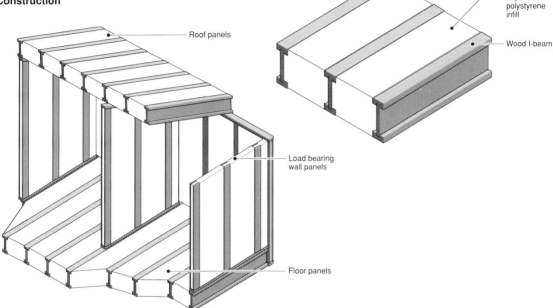

General Guidelines for Composite Panels

Plywood Stressed-Skin Panels
- Face grain of plywood is typically oriented parallel to the webs.

- Top plywood skin should be no less than 9.5mm (3/8") for roof applications and no less than 12.5mm (1/2") for floor applications.

- Webs should be spaced at about 410mm (16").

- For long panels, plywood must be scarf-joined and wood members must be fingerjoined.

Sandwich Panels (Non-Structural and Structural)
- Exterior skin should be strong , have good nail-holding capability for application of siding and trim, and should be an acceptable moisture barrier.

- Furring strips on exterior panels may be required in order to achieve proper nail penetration; typically 38mm (1-1/2") is required for application of wood siding.

- The panel should have good tensile resistance and serve as an air/vapour barrier.

References

Douglas Fir Plywood Stressed-Skin Panels, Council of Forest Industries of British Columbia

Fine Homebuilding Magazine, No. 62, pp. 52-57, No. 64, pp. 10-12., The Taunton Press, September 1990

Nascor-III System, CANO Structures Inc.

The Timber-Frame Home, Tedd Benson, The Taunton Press, Inc., 1989

Wood Design Manual, Canadian Wood Council, 1990

6.7   Permanent Wood Foundations

Introduction

A permanent wood foundation (PWF) is a wood foundation system made of pressure treated wood members and pressure treated plywood sheathing.

Current technology for building wood foundations is based on 30 years of service experience. The PWF system offers good service potential for residential and commercial buildings. It may be used where a full basement or a partial basement is required (see Figure 6.25 below).

The PWF method provides a reliable foundation which can be easily insulated for maximum comfort and energy conservation. The permanency of PWF performance is based on the following key design requirements as shown in Figure 6.26 (→ 352):

•   Superior wall and sub-floor drainage to keep the water level well below the basement floor level.

•   Moisture barrier and sealing to keep moisture from contacting the wood.

•   High quality pressure-treated lumber and plywood to resist decay from any moisture which transgresses the moisture barrier and to resist insect attack.

•   Lateral support from the basement floor and main floor framing to provide structural stability.

Advantages of Permanent Wood Foundations

Cost
Depending on local labour and material costs, PWFs are often more economical than concrete foundations. The cost advantage of wood foundations is most likely to be apparent if the foundation is to be finished as a living or work area. This is due to the insulation quality of wood, and the ability of the stud framed wood foundation to serve the double purpose as structure and as support for insulation and interior wall finishes.

Because the materials and skills required to construct a wood foundation are essentially the same as those required for wood framing above grade, some additional cost and schedule advantages may result.

Prefabrication
The major wall sections can be made on site or can be premanufactured to be assembled on site. This feature permits progress during periods of inclement weather.

Comfort
In either finished or unfinished applications, the insulating quality of wood does not foster condensation of room moisture on foundation surfaces.

In addition, the extra geotechnical provisions required of wood foundations resulting in drainage of external moisture away from the foundation walls, and the provision of a watertight membrane on the exterior ensures that PWF basements remain dry and comfortable.

Figure 6.25
Typical Arrangements for Permanent Wood Foundations

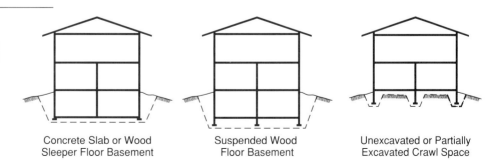

Concrete Slab or Wood
Sleeper Floor Basement

Suspended Wood
Floor Basement

Unexcavated or Partially
Excavated Crawl Space

Figure 6.26
**Key Design
Requirements
for PWFs**

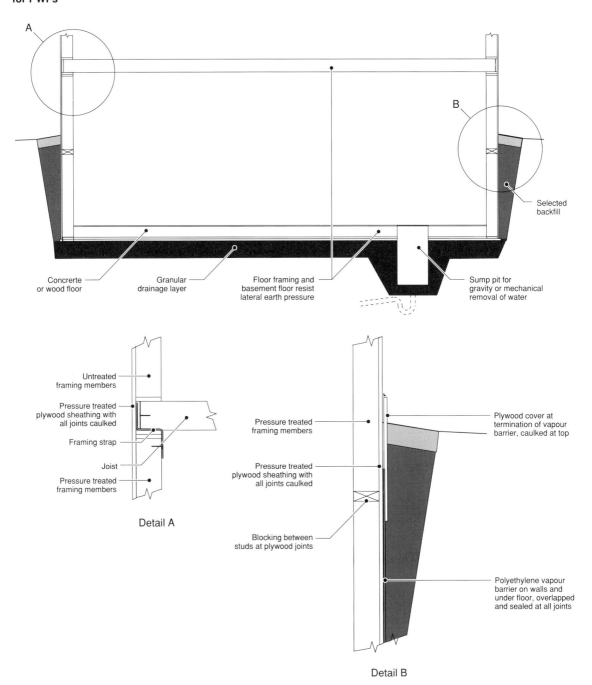

A

B

Selected
backfill

Concrerte
or wood floor

Granular
drainage layer

Floor framing and
basement floor resist
lateral earth pressure

Sump pit for
gravity or mechanical
removal of water

Untreated
framing members

Pressure treated
plywood sheathing with
all joints caulked

Framing strap

Joist

Pressure treated
framing members

Detail A

Pressure treated
framing members

Pressure treated
plywood sheathing with
all joints caulked

Blocking between
studs at plywood joints

Plywood cover at
termination of vapour
barrier, caulked at top

Polyethylene vapour
barrier on walls and
under floor, overlapped
and sealed at all joints

Detail B

Figure 6.27
Foundation Wall Panels

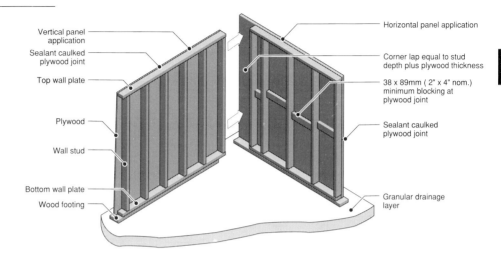

Vertical panel application

Sealant caulked plywood joint

Top wall plate

Plywood

Wall stud

Bottom wall plate

Wood footing

Horizontal panel application

Corner lap equal to stud depth plus plywood thickness

38 x 89mm (2" x 4" nom.) minimum blocking at plywood joint

Sealant caulked plywood joint

Granular drainage layer

Note:
Foundation walls can be built in place or be prefabricated

Maximization of Floor Area

Often, it is required that a foundation become a finished work area or living area. Wood foundations maximize usable floor space because the structure serves as the support as well as the housing for insulation.

Affixing framing to a concrete wall for the purpose of insulating and finishing results in a loss of floor space of 0.1 to 0.18 m^2/m (0.3 to 0.5 ft^2/linear foot) of floor perimeter. For a 12 x 18m (40' x 60') foundation, this space loss can be up to $7m^2$ (70 ft^2) depending on the degree of insulation provided.

Materials for Permanent Wood Foundations

Lumber

Lumber used in a PWF is grade stamped to indicate the quality of the lumber. All structural members in a PWF should be No.2 or better (see Section 3.2).

PWF lumber must also bear a qualification stamp indicating that the lumber meets preservative retention requirements. Lumber used for a PWF is required to have a higher degree of preservative retention than preserved wood used for other purposes and the designer must ensure

that material of this quality is specified and incorporated into the work.

Information on the types and properties of preservatives is in Section 9.4. A sample stamp for PWF material indicating the Canadian treatment standard is shown in Figure 6.28 (→ 354).

As much as possible, cutting of treated wood should take place prior to treating. Where it is necessary to make field adjustments, care must be taken to ensure exposed lumber is field treated in accordance with manufacturer's recommended practice.

Plywood

Plywood used as exterior wall sheathing in Canadian permanent wood foundations conforms to *CSA Standard O121-M, Douglas Fir Plywood*, or *CSA Standard O151-M, Canadian Softwood Plywood* and bears the appropriate grade stamp (see Section 4.2). It is unsanded exterior type plywood with at least four plies and is limited to the following species: western hemlock, amabilis fir, grand fir, and coastal Douglas fir.

Other species do not accept pressure treatment chemical in amounts adequate for this application, and therefore may not be used as plywood sheathing for permanent wood foundations. Plywood panels marked "COFI Exterior DFP-Hem Fir" or "COFI Exterior CSP-Hem Fir" meet both the strength and treatability requirements for PWFs.

Plywood suitable for PWF use bears a stamp (see Figure 6.28 below) indicating that the required treatment retention has been achieved.

The plywood is strongest with the face grain perpendicular to the studs. The thickness of the plywood which is required depends on the height of backfill and the orientation of the plywood in relation to the studs.

Nails and Staples
Nails, staples, and metal connectors used in the construction of PWFs must be corrosion resistant. The use of stainless steel or hot-dipped galvanized nails is required in some jurisdictions. If staples are used to attach the plywood sheathing they must be stainless steel. Requirements should be checked before specifying fasteners.

Framing Anchors and Straps
Framing anchors and straps in contact with treated materials are hot-dipped galvanized and used wherever the magnitude of loads is such that it is impractical to transfer the loads through nailing alone. A typical framing strap is made of 20 gauge galvanized metal, at least 38 x 400mm (2" x 16") fastened to the wood with 76mm (3") nails.

Sealants
Sealants are required to caulk all plywood to plywood joints. The sealants must be capable of providing a watertight seal, have a long expected service life without drying or hardening, and, ideally, be workable even at low temperatures. The sealant should also be compatible with the treated wood and exterior moisture barrier .

Moisture Barriers
A moisture barrier must be affixed to the plywood foundation walls. Good design requires that moisture barriers be compatible with the treated wood, have good adhesion to the PWF sheathing and be overlapped a minimum of 150mm (6") at each joint.

Polyethylene is the standard form of moisture barrier used in PWFs. Some builders first coat the PWF wall with an emulsion-type damp-proofing, then press polyethylene into the coating. Others use durable proprietary types of coatings or sheet materials.

The adhesive or sealant used to attach polyethylene to the top of the exterior wall must form a durable bond between the polyethylene and the treated plywood and be compatible chemically with the polyethylene.

Granular Drainage Layer
Granular material used in the drainage system is crushed stone or other coarse pit run gravel containing not more than 10 percent of fine material that will pass a 4mm (5/32") sieve and no material should be larger than 40mm (1-1/2"). It should form a firm base and be lightly tamped to provide a good working surface and uniform support for wall footing plates.

Basement Floor

The footings and floor may be constructed of concrete or preserved wood. The preserved wood floor may be suspended from the walls or may be supported by preserved wood sleepers resting on the

Figure 6.28
Facsimile of Qualification Stamp for PWF Materials (Canada)

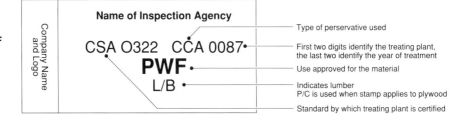

granular drainage layer as shown in Figure 6.29 (→ 356) depending on local building code requirements.

Member Sizing

The size of vertical members is dependent on the height of soil backfill which induces bending, and on the axial dead loads from snow and building materials above the foundation. Tables (see References) are available in Canada and in the United States from which the required member sizing and plywood thickness can be determined. For complex, nonstandard, or heavily loaded buildings, design should be verified for engineering properties.

Special Requirements

The main contributing factor to the dryness of PWF basements is the free-draining backfill and the below floor granular drainage layer and sump which quickly drain water away from the foundation.

The excavated area should slope to a point near its centre where the sump is to be installed. The sump is drained by gravity with a 100mm (4") diameter drain, or a sump pump when this is not possible.

Supporting Masonry Veneer

Masonry veneer exterior cladding may be supported on either a knee wall or on top of the main foundation wall as shown in Figure 6.30 (→ 357). Loadings resulting from masonry veneer walls may exceed the standard loadings listed in foundation wall selection tables, in which case the member sizing should be engineered.

Insulation

Wood foundation walls can be easily and economically insulated to improve heating economy and general comfort for basements used as living quarters. The stud space permits easy installation of batt type insulation. In addition, the thermal resistance of the minimum plywood sheathing thickness, 12.5mm (1/2"), contributes effectively to the total insulating value of the wall.

A PWF may also be insulated on the exterior using an inorganic, moisture resistant rigid insulation installed against the exterior face of the PWF after the moisture barrier is in place. The insulation can be installed below grade to a depth suiting the specific frost penetration and climatic conditions of a region.

Above grade the insulation should extend at least up to the top of the foundation wall. The exposed portion of the insulation between the siding and grade is supported and protected with treated plywood, asbestos-cement board or other suitable material.

Finishes

That portion of wood foundation walls which extends above the ground line may be left as exposed treated plywood or may be finished in a number of ways.

Treated plywood used for exterior wall sheathing may be painted or stained.

Alternately, a cement parging may be applied to the above ground portion of the foundation.

Siding installed over sheathing in the upper part of the building may be continued down over the foundation wall to the minimum permissible ground clearance for the siding used or the top edge of the plywood foundation may be used as the starting point for exterior wall cladding.

Services

The foundation wall studs should not be drilled or notched. Therefore, plumbing, heating or air conditioning services should not be installed in the exterior walls of permanent wood foundations.

Where duplex outlets or other wiring must be placed in exterior walls, the wiring to each outlet box should be run vertically within a single stud space and pass through a hole drilled in the top plates which need not be treated. The hole should be sealed to conserve vapour barrier continuity.

6

Structural Wood Systems

Figure 6.29
Types of Basement Floors for Permanent Wood Foundations

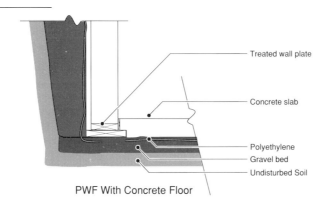

Treated wall plate

Concrete slab

Polyethylene
Gravel bed
Undisturbed Soil

PWF With Concrete Floor

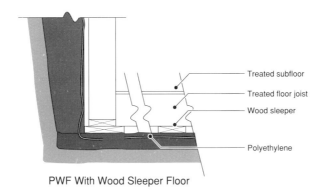

Treated subfloor

Treated floor joist

Wood sleeper

Polyethylene

PWF With Wood Sleeper Floor

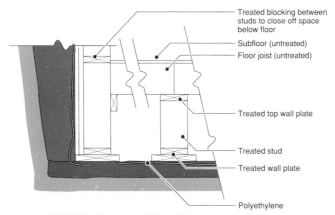

Treated blocking between studs to close off space below floor

Subfloor (untreated)
Floor joist (untreated)

Treated top wall plate

Treated stud

Treated wall plate

Polyethylene

PWF With Suspended Wood Floor

Figure 6.30
Support of Masonry Veneer

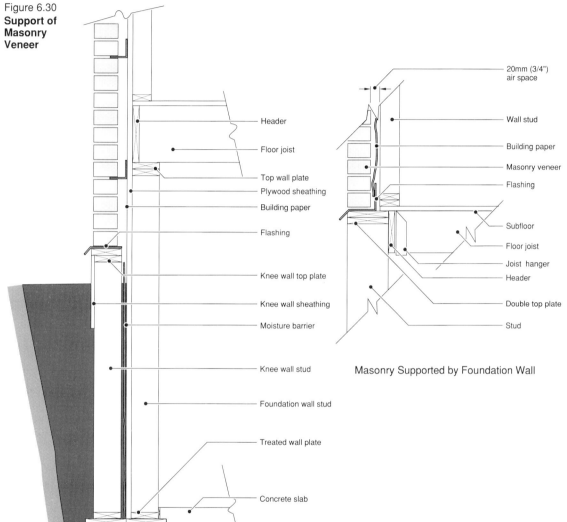

Header

Floor joist

Top wall plate

Plywood sheathing

Building paper

Flashing

Knee wall top plate

Knee wall sheathing

Moisture barrier

Knee wall stud

Foundation wall stud

Treated wall plate

Concrete slab

Polyethylene

Gravel bed

20mm (3/4") air space

Wall stud

Building paper

Masonry veneer

Flashing

Subfloor

Floor joist

Joist hanger

Header

Double top plate

Stud

Masonry Supported by Foundation Wall

Masonry Supported by Knee Wall

General Guidelines for Permanent Wood Foundations

- PWF basements can be insulated to a high level within the volume of the foundation walls. They are easily finished and insulated without additional framing or strapping required.

- A PWF can be prefabricated and can be installed in poor weather.

- PWF construction may provide schedule coordination advantages by employing the same trades for foundation and superstructure construction.

- Refer to local code requirements for member sizing and obtain engineering design and certification for applications which fall outside the code norm.

- Ensure that the wood materials carry a grade stamp indicating their suitability for PWF applications and verify the quality of materials incorporated into the work.

References

Datafiles WB-3 and WB-4, Canadian Wood Council, 1987

Permanent Wood Foundations, Gary J. Gibson, Sure-West Publishing Inc., 1990

Permanent Wood Foundation System Manual: Design, Fabrication, Installation, National Forest Products Association, 1987

The Permanent Wood Foundation System: Basic Requirements, Technical Report No. 7, National Forest Products Association, 1987

Wood Design Manual, Canadian Wood Council, 1990

Exterior Wood Products

7

Wood products,
left natural or
preservative-
treated, are
used extensively
for exterior
siding and
landscape
architectural
features.

Board and
batten vertical
siding lends a
traditional
character to this
contemporary
building.

Built in the early
1900s, this
elegant hotel
complex has
exterior walls of
interlocking logs.

Enduring the test of time, bevel siding (top) shows little sign of aging after 150 years.

Siding and trim of different colours accent the exterior of this office complex.

Striated and stained plywood panels clad the exterior of this commercial building.

A naturally-occurring construction material, wood is well-suited for making the transition between building and green space.

Patios, decks, balconies and boardwalks - good detailing and careful selection of species and protective coating offer good service for all these applications.

Imaginative cantilever deck detailing and sidewalls of cedar shingles demonstrate the versatility of wood for building exteriors.

Board and batten, a traditional siding method, casts strong vertical shadows on this contemporary building.

Patterned cedar
shingles and
nautical detailing
(opposite)
prepare this
dwelling for its
east coast
exposure.

Form, colour
and texture
blend to
exemplify the
versatility of
wood as an
exterior building
material.

Wood Shingles & Shakes

Vinyl and aluminium siding have their merits. But based on appearance, wood siding knows no equal.

Eastern white cedar shingles are manufactured in several grades.

1. A (extra)
2. B clear
3. Clear wall
4. 2nd clear
5. Undercourse

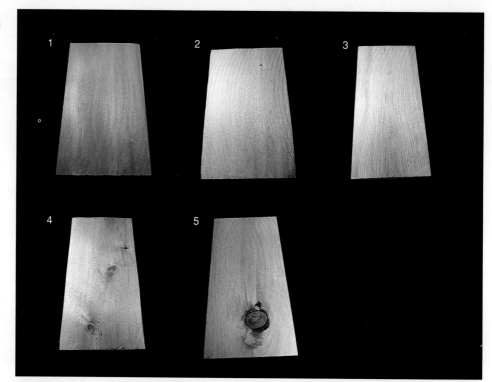

Several types of western red cedar shingles and shakes are manufactured

1. Split and resawn cedar shake
2. Certigrade cedar shingle
3. Certi-sawn taper-sawn cedar shake
4. Straight split and taper split cedar shakes
5. Rebutted and rejointed shingle and machine groove shakes
6. Fancy butt shingles
7. Hip and ridge units of split shakes, sawn shakes and shingles

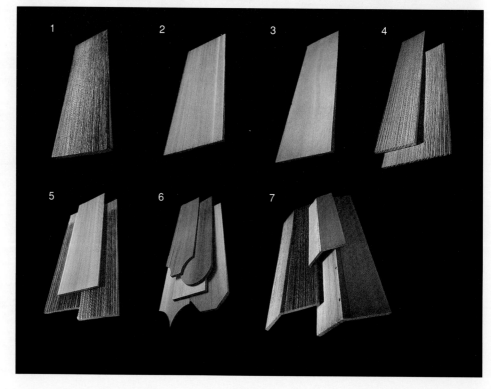

7.1   General Information

This section describes the solid and panel wood products which are used for exterior roof and wall finishes, and products used for landscape architecture in and around buildings.

With knowledge of the wood products available, their characteristics, and an understanding of the methods available for protecting wood, designers can specify products which provide good appearance and performance characteristics for exterior applications.

The products covered in this section are as follows:

7.2   Solid Wood
       Siding
       Shingles and Shakes
       Landscaping

7.3   Panel Products
       Softwood Plywood
       Specialty Panels

7

Exterior Wood Products

7.2   Solid Wood

Introduction

Solid wood products have been used extensively over the ages for wall siding (cladding), roofing, and for landscaping features.

Many of the softwood grades described here for exterior use are also appropriate for interior use as panelling, ceiling and other special finishes. Refer to Section 8 for more information.

Siding

Wood siding, with its natural texture, colour and grain, adds beauty and insulating value (approximately R1 depending on species and thickness) to residential and commercial buildings. The many patterns and finishes available with wood siding offer design flexibility and unlimited potential for innovation.

Species
Several Canadian softwood species are used for siding, the most common being western red cedar, eastern white cedar, eastern white pine, jack pine, lodgepole pine, red pine, Douglas fir, and spruce. The appearance characteristics of these species are shown in the Table below. The species which perform best in siding applications are those which are light weight and have a grain most suited for painting or staining.

Western red cedar is a popular siding because of its excellent dimensional stability, natural resistance to decay, workability, attractive weathering tone when left to weather naturally, and its ability to hold coatings and stain.

Grades
Siding is manufactured to span a short distance, usually 410mm (16"), and therefore is not stress graded as a structural product but rather, is graded based on appearance of the best face. The reverse face usually has characteristics approximately one grade lower than the best face.

For all Canadian softwood species, boards graded as Select Merchantable are recommended for exterior (or interior) uses where high quality appearance is a requirement. In addition to the Select Merchantable grade which applies to all species, there are two grade categories commonly used for exterior finish work which are limited to specific species. These are eastern red and white pine, and western red cedar.

For eastern red and white pine, the three grade categories most suited for exposure are Select (B and Better, C, and D) and Common (1, 2, and 3). Select grade is clear, or almost clear, depending on the grade level, and Common usually contains knots. For some applications, a knotty appearance is preferred and the 1, 2, and 3 Common grades contain knots which are tight and not subject to loosening or loss during service.

Western red cedar is available in several categories and grades suitable for both exterior and interior applications. It is available dressed or rough, and kiln dried, air dried, or green.

7

Exterior Wood Products

Typical Canadian Softwoods for Exterior Use	Species	Characteristics
	Western red cedar	Reddish brown, highly resistant to decay, seasons well, resists warping and twisting, used for siding, decking, shingles and shakes
	Eastern white cedar	Blond to reddish brown, fine texture, light weight, highly resistant to decay, comparatively soft, used mainly for shingles
	Eastern white pine	Light colour, easy to pattern, relatively soft
	Jack pine/ lodgepole pine	Light colour, medium hardness, often used as pressure treated wood
	Eastern red pine	Light red colour, otherwise similar to jack pine and lodgepole pine
	Douglas fir	Even grain, weathers well, hard durable softwood
	Spruce	Off white to pale yellow, medium strength, low decay resistance, not easily pressure treated

The major grade categories, grades, and principal characteristics for western red cedar siding are as follows:

Finish, Paneling, Ceiling, and Drop Siding
This category is usually dressed four sides and kiln dried. In order of descending quality, the grades are:

- Clear Heart: highest quality for top quality appearance, many pieces are absolutely clear.

- A: also very good appearance but allows some small imperfections.

- B: good appearance, many pieces have a fine appearance on one side and larger or more numerous growth characteristics on the back side.

Bevel Siding
This category is made from resawing kiln dried surfaced lumber on a bevel to produce two bevelled pieces. This category is often used for exterior siding. The grades are:

- Clear Heart: intended for highest quality applications, exposed width is all heartwood and free from imperfections

- A: very good appearance with some small imperfections permitted.

- B: this grade, permitting small imperfections and two or less cutouts, is a good quality siding where a painted surface is required

- Rustic: this grade has a rough finish on the better side and is used as a sidewall covering where a rustic appearance is desired.

Tight Knotted Stock Dressed or Rough Knotty Paneling and Sidings
Knots and other markings are the distinguishing characteristics of this grade category.

- Select Knotty: good quality siding with a knotty appearance, knots are tight and small.

- Quality Knotty: larger knots are permitted and some may be loose or unsound.

Knotty Bevel Siding
This is like the preceding grade category except that the siding is bevelled. The grades for this category are Select Knotty and Quality Knotty with characteristics similar to those in the preceding category.

Sizes
Wood siding is usually produced in random lengths of 1.8 to 5m (6' to 16') and in widths of 89 and 140mm (4" and 6" nom.). Western red cedar is also produced in wider widths of 190mm (8" nom.), 240mm (10" nom.), and 290mm (12" nom.) and is available in lengths up to 7.2m (24'). Standard thickness are 12.5, 15.9 and 19mm (1/2", 5/8", and 3/4"). Other thicknesses are available upon request.

Patterns
There are four main methods for joining siding to keep out moisture. Shiplap and tongue and groove edges provide an interlocking edge. Bevel siding relies on overlap or shiplap to join adjacent pieces. The fourth method involves using a batten to cover the joint between the adjacent boards. Many siding patterns are manufactured which make use of these jointing methods. Some typical ones are shown in Figure 7.1 opposite.

Some siding patterns, especially the non-curvilinear types, can be used on either the vertical or horizontal. When used on the horizontal, the overlap or joint must be arranged so that a drip notch effect is provided. Some sidings are smooth and rough on opposing faces and either side can be used as the finished face depending upon the texture desired. Bevel siding is generally available with either a rough or a finished surface and is applied horizontally.

Board and batten siding is applied vertically with the battens (wood strips) covering the gaps between the boards.

Nailing patterns, as shown in Figure 7.2 (→ 374), should be used which allow the wood siding to adjust to changing moisture conditions without splitting. Galvanized, stainless steel, or aluminum nails prevent rust stains on siding where nail heads are left exposed.

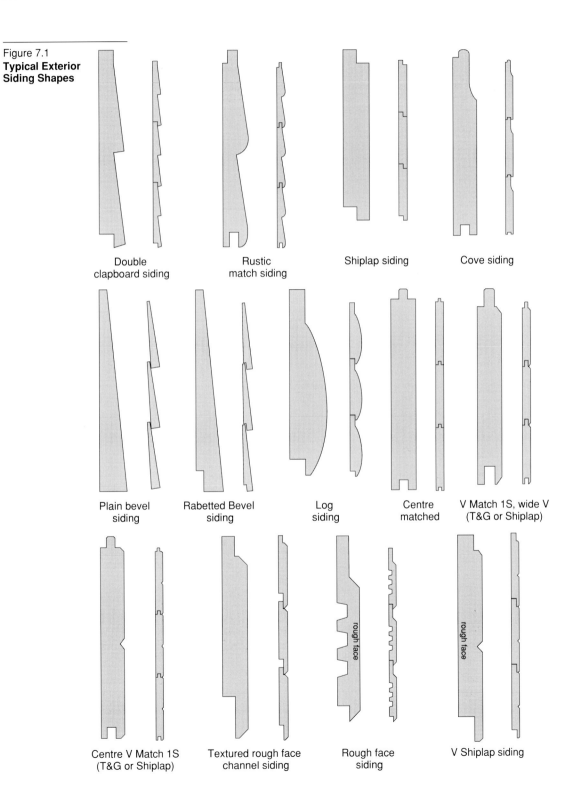

Figure 7.1
**Typical Exterior
Siding Shapes**

Double
clapboard siding

Rustic
match siding

Shiplap siding

Cove siding

Plain bevel
siding

Rabetted Bevel
siding

Log
siding

Centre
matched

V Match 1S, wide V
(T&G or Shiplap)

Centre V Match 1S
(T&G or Shiplap)

Textured rough face
channel siding

Rough face
siding

V Shiplap siding

rough face

rough face

7

Exterior Wood Products

Figure 7.2
**Typical Nailing
Patterns for
Wood Siding**

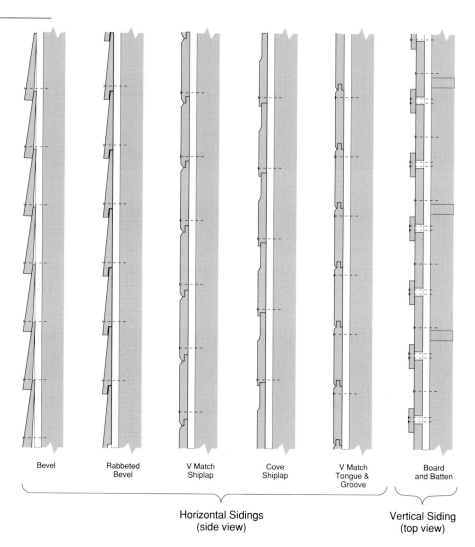

| Bevel | Rabbeted Bevel | V Match Shiplap | Cove Shiplap | V Match Tongue & Groove | Board and Batten |

Horizontal Sidings
(side view)

Vertical Siding
(top view)

Factory Finished Wood Siding

Some sidings are now available pressure treated and pre-stained to increase service life. This eliminates the need to finish the siding after installation.

The stain is applied either during or after the pressure treatment process and covers both the front and back of the siding. This finish is durable for many years and the wood can be restained when necessary.

Vertical Siding

When applying siding vertically, install 38 x 89mm (2" x 4" nom.) horizontal blocking between the studs as extra support for nailing. For siding up to 12.5mm (1/2") in thickness install the blocking on 600mm (2') centres, floor to ceiling. For thicker siding, install blocking on 1200mm (4') centres.

Shingles and Shakes

Cedar shingles and shakes have a long history of enduring performance in North America. This performance can be seen on the exterior of many older homes and agricultural buildings. The colouring which cedar products develop as they weather over time is the reason why this historic building product is often favoured as the cladding for contemporary buildings.

Shingles are manufactured by sawing and therefore have a relatively smooth surface. Shakes (except for taper-sawn shakes) are made by splitting the wood along the grain and therefore shakes have at least one face which is striated.

Shingles are made from eastern white cedar and western red cedar, and shakes are made from western red cedar.

Both products may be used for application to sidewalls and roofs. Selecting between shingles and shakes is based on the appearance desired.

Cedar has a high natural resistance to decay. Therefore, for light and moderate exposures, cedar shingles and shakes can be left to weather naturally, can be bleached to accelerate and balance colour change, or can be stained. Again, the choice is dependent on the appearance desired.

Grade selection has a bearing on the appearance and durability of the completed installation. There are several grades of shakes and shingles available for both western red cedar and eastern white cedar.

Western Red Cedar Shingles and Shakes

Western red cedar shingles and shakes are graded in accordance with CSA O118.1-83, *Western Red Cedar Shingles and Shakes* as follows:

Shingles
- No.1 Blue Label: premium grade of shingles for roofs and sidewalls which is made entirely from heartwood, is 100 percent clear (defect free), and has 100 percent edge-grain.

- No.2 Red Label: good grade for many applications with at least 250mm clear on 400mm (10" on 16") shingles, 275mm on 450mm (11" on 18") shingles, and 400mm on 600mm (16" on 24") shingles. Flat grain and limited sapwood are permitted in this grade.

- No.3 Black Label: utility grade for economy applications and secondary buildings with at least 150mm clear on 400 and 450mm (6" on 16" and 18")

shingles, and at least 250mm on 600mm (10" on 24") shingles.

- No.4 Green Label (Undercoursing): utility grade for starter course undercoursing.

Shakes
- Premium Grade: best grade of shakes made entirely from heartwood, having 100 percent edge grain, and defect free. Suited for roof and sidewall applications where high quality appearance is important.

- No.1 (Blue Label): good quality shakes made of heartwood which can contain up to 3.2mm (1/8") sapwood along one edge and which are predominately edge grained. Suited for roof and sidewall applications where high quality appearance is important.

- No.2 Grade (Sidewall or Red Label): shakes having good appearance similar to No.1 but flat grain is permitted. Use is restricted to sidewall applications.

In addition to the three grades, shakes are manufactured in the four following types:

- Resawn: (available in Premium and No.1) shakes have split faces and sawn backs to provide taper suitable for roofs and sidewalls.

- Taper-split: (available in Premium and No.1) shakes have two split faces and a natural taper. The natural shingle-like taper is achieved by reversing the block end-for-end with each split.

- Taper-sawn: (available in Premium, No.1, and No.2) shakes are sawn on both sides like shingles but are installed in the manner recommended for shakes.

- Straightsplit: (available in No.1 only) shakes are produced by machine or in the same manner as tapersplit shakes except that by splitting from the same end of the block, the shakes acquire the same thickness throughout.

Canadian western red cedar shingles and shakes are graded to Canadian Standards Association rules, and inspected by the

7

Exterior Wood Products

Figure 7.3
**Sample Grade
Stamps for
Shakes and
Shingles**

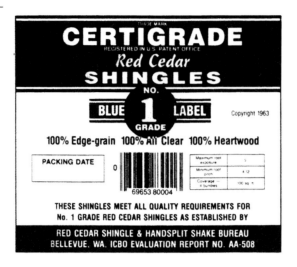

joint Canada-US organization called the Cedar Shingle & Shake Bureau. Some sample grade stamps for the bureau are shown in Figure 7.3 (opposite).

Eastern White Cedar Shingles

Eastern white cedar shingles are graded in accordance with CSA O118.2-81, *Eastern White Cedar Shingles* as follows:

- A (extra): the highest grade eastern shingle made from 100 percent heartwood with no defects, light brown in colour, suited for roofs and sidewalls where a high quality appearance is required.

- B (clear): a good quality grade made mostly from heartwood. Sound knots not closer than 180mm (7") from the butt which are not visible for normal exposure distances, are permitted. Used on sidewalls and for roofs having a slope of at least 4/12.

- C (2nd clear): this grade has a brownish tint and allows some defects. It is used for interior applications and for exterior applications on secondary buildings.

- Clear Wall: this shingle is almost white and contains no, or few, knots. It is used for interior applications and for secondary buildings for exterior exposure.

- Undercourse: this utility grade frequently contains knots. It is used for undercoursing on double course applications and for shimming in carpentry work.

Special Manufacturing for Shingles

The term "rebutted-rejointed" refers to shingles which have been machined to produce parallel edges and square corners. The appearance of these shingles may be preferred by the designer for some applications. In addition, rebutted-rejointed shingles are available with one side sanded to provide a refined, finished appearance.

Shingles may be ordered with fancy end cuts. Various combinations can be used to provide accents to roofs and sidewalls. The most frequently used end cuts are shown in Figure 7.4 below, and others are available by special order.

7

Exterior Wood Products

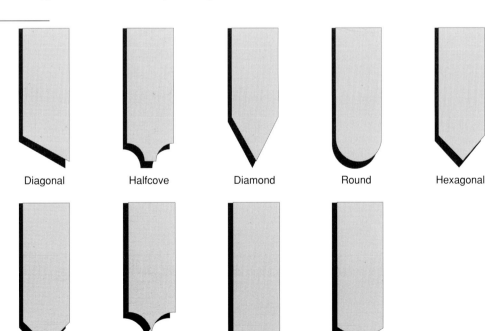

Figure 7.4
Fancy End Cuts for Shingles

Diagonal   Halfcove   Diamond   Round   Hexagonal

Octogonal   Arrow   Square   Fish-scale

Shingles are also available with uniform parallel machine grooves which give a texture resembling, but more regular than, shakes.

Decay Resistance

Exterior sidewalls of cedar shingles or shakes do not usually require a preservative treatment to insure long service life. The majority of cedar roofs remain untreated and are known to provide excellent service.

A surface chemical treatment is desirable where conditions very conducive to deterioration occur, such as areas where climate combines heat and humidity for considerable portions of the year, for roofs of low pitch or slope, or for roofs kept moist by the debris from closely overhanging trees.

For surface treatment, clear wood preservatives containing mildew and decay resisting chemicals are applied by brush or spray. Surface treatments are not permanent and should be applied at approximately five-year intervals, depending upon the products used.

In areas of low humidity, excessive drying may cause cracking. Commercial oil based preservatives will prevent excessive dryness and therefore prolong the natural resilience of cedar.

Where temperature and humidity levels are conducive to wood decay, such as in the southeast United States, it is recommended that chromated copper arsenate (CCA) pressure treated cedar shingles and shakes be used on roofs.

The pressure-treatment is permanent and will extend the service life of the roof. Most CCA treated shingles and shakes are available with a 30-year warranty. (See Section 9 for information on chemical preservatives). CCA treatment produces a dark grey colour with a tinge of light green which dissipates after a few months of exposure.

Fire-Retardant Cedar Shakes and Shingles

No.1 grade western red cedar shingles and shakes are available pressure-impregnated with fire retardants to meet testing standards developed by Underwriters' Laboratories and adopted by the National Fire Protection Association. The chemicals used are suited for exterior application fire-retardant treatment and provide long term protection.

Exposure Lengths

The length of shake or shingle which can be expose to the weather is dependant upon the quality of the material and the slope angle of the surface to be covered.

The recommended exposure lengths for both western red cedar shingles and shakes as shown in Tables 7.1 and 7.2 ($\rightarrow$ 383, 384) and eastern white cedar shingles as shown in Tables 7.3 ($\rightarrow$ 384) are dependant upon the quality (grade) of the product and on whether a product is used for sidewall or roof applications.

Sidewall Installation

There are several methods for installing shingles and shakes as shown in Figure 7.5 ($\rightarrow$ 379, 380). Each must ensure adequate overlap which varies according to the length of product used. Corner details for shakes and shingles are shown in Figure 7.6 ($\rightarrow$ 381).

Roof Installation

Shingles and shakes may be applied over spaced sheathing of 19 x 89mm or 19 x 140mm (1" x 4" nom. or 1" x 6" nom.) boards or over solid sheathing.

Solid sheathing, such as plywood or OSB/ waferboard, may be required to meet code requirements for seismic conditions. It is also recommended in areas where wind-driven snow is a concern.

The method of roofing felt installation differs for shingles from that of shakes as shown in Figure 7.7 ($\rightarrow$ 382).

Figure 7.5
Sidewall Patterns for Shakes and Shingles

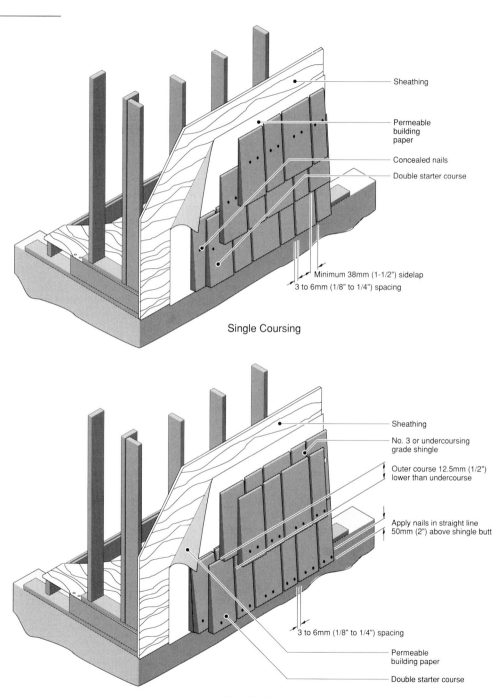

Sheathing

Permeable building paper

Concealed nails

Double starter course

Minimum 38mm (1-1/2") sidelap
3 to 6mm (1/8" to 1/4") spacing

Single Coursing

Sheathing

No. 3 or undercoursing grade shingle

Outer course 12.5mm (1/2") lower than undercourse

Apply nails in straight line 50mm (2") above shingle butt

3 to 6mm (1/8" to 1/4") spacing

Permeable building paper

Double starter course

Double Coursing

Figure 7.5
continued
**Sidewall
Patterns for
Shakes and
Shingles**

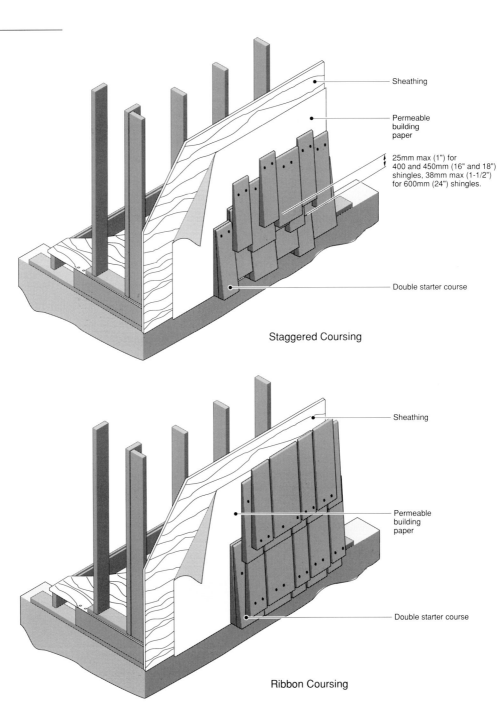

Sheathing

Permeable
building
paper

25mm max (1") for
400 and 450mm (16" and 18")
shingles, 38mm max (1-1/2")
for 600mm (24") shingles.

Double starter course

Staggered Coursing

Sheathing

Permeable
building
paper

Double starter course

Ribbon Coursing

Figure 7.6
**Corner Details
for Shingles
and Shakes**

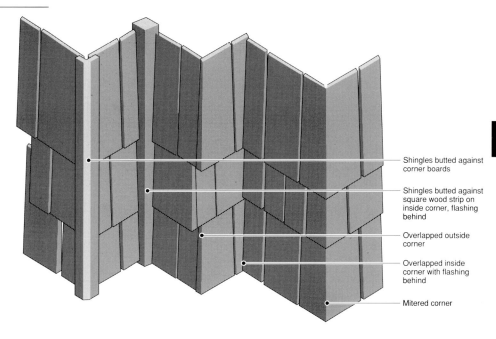

Shingles butted against
corner boards

Shingles butted against
square wood strip on
inside corner, flashing
behind

Overlapped outside
corner

Overlapped inside
corner with flashing
behind

Mitered corner

Landscaping

In addition to the wood products which are used to protect building exteriors and to enhance appearance, there are many uses for wood products in landscape architecture. Landscape features such as decks, stairs, boardwalks, fencing, retaining walls, and site furnishings can add significantly to the appearance of a building.

Three basic types of wood products are most often used in landscape construction. These are:

- Dimension lumber, as framing support members for decking and, on the flat, as decking.

- Boards as decking material or for fencing.

- Timber as structural members for posts, beams, and as crib members for retaining walls.

Durability of Wood

Deck and other horizontal surfaces encounter weather exposure to sun, water, and ponding. For this reason, materials and protective coatings must be carefully selected to ensure serviceability.

Cedar has a high degree of natural decay resistance and is therefore highly recommended for applications where exposure is severe. In addition, cedar is a straight grained wood not prone to warping.

For horizontal decking, cedar offers good performance, as does preservative treated wood. Other softwood species which have not been preservative treated can also offer good service when properly surfaced with paint or stain (see Section 9). Care should be taken to specify seasoned wood so that cracking and cupping, which can trap and hold water, does not occur.

Direct ground contact is one of the most destructive environments for wood. For this reason, all wood members within 200mm (8") of the ground, including cedar members, should be preservative treated to ensure long service life.

Figure 7.7
**Application
Details for
Shingle and
Shake Roofing**

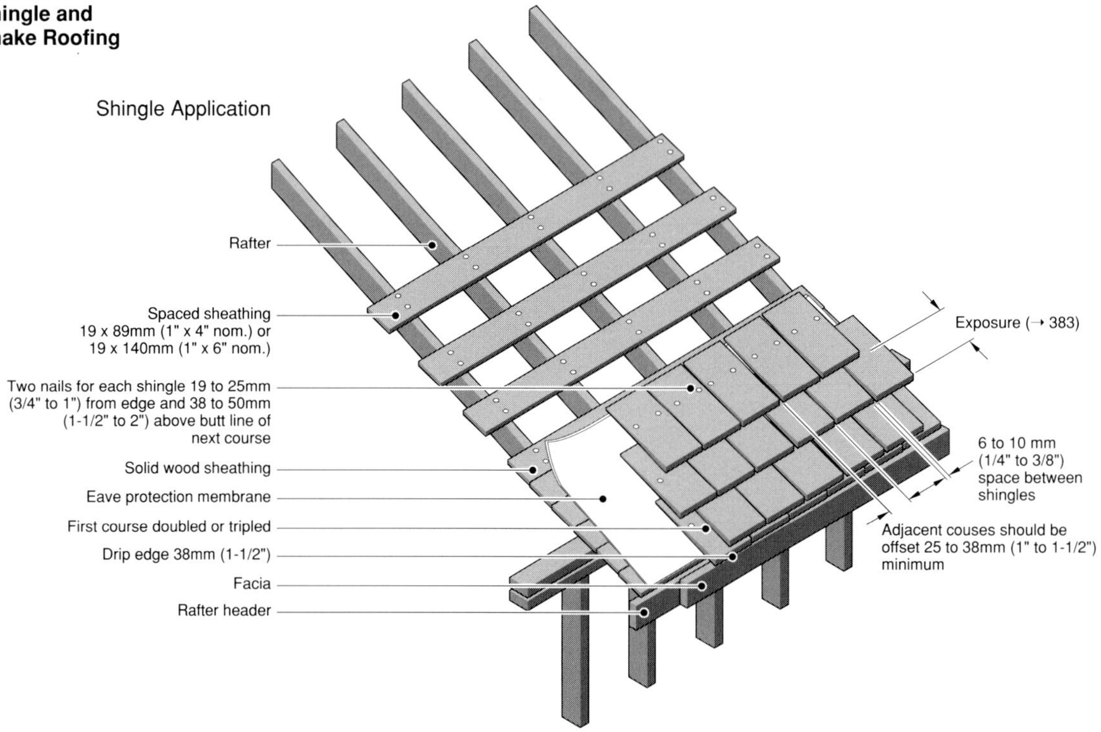

Shingle Application

Rafter

Spaced sheathing
19 x 89mm (1" x 4" nom.) or
19 x 140mm (1" x 6" nom.)

Two nails for each shingle 19 to 25mm
(3/4" to 1") from edge and 38 to 50mm
(1-1/2" to 2") above butt line of
next course

Solid wood sheathing

Eave protection membrane

First course doubled or tripled

Drip edge 38mm (1-1/2")

Facia

Rafter header

Exposure (→ 383)

6 to 10 mm
(1/4" to 3/8")
space between
shingles

Adjacent couses should be
offset 25 to 38mm (1" to 1-1/2")
minimum

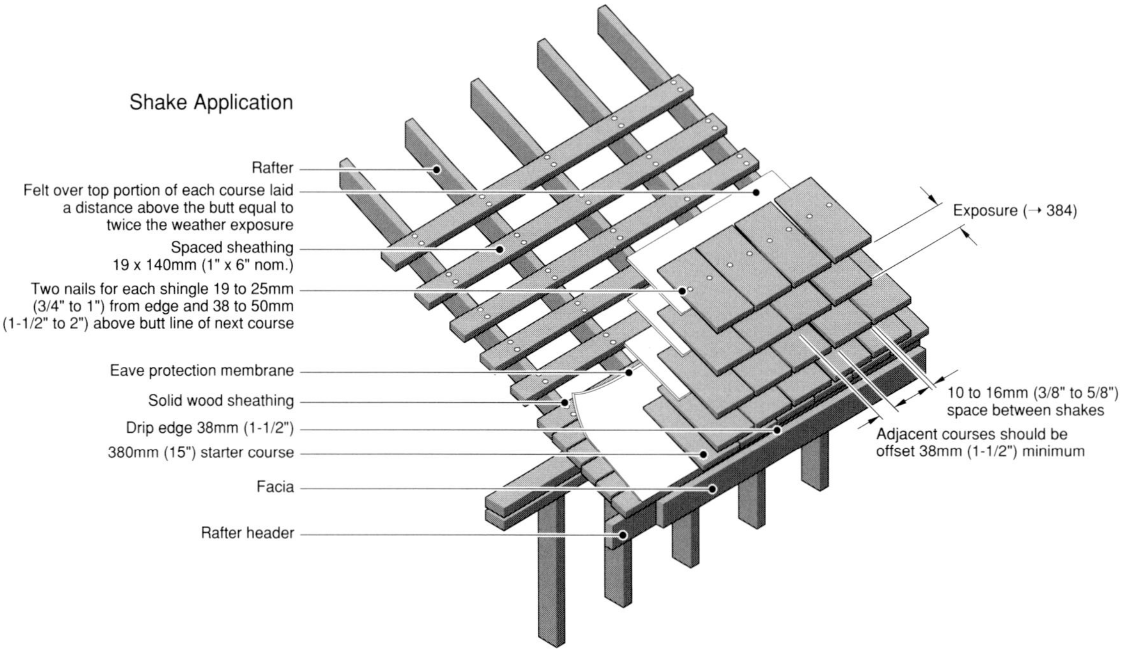

Shake Application

Rafter

Felt over top portion of each course laid
a distance above the butt equal to
twice the weather exposure

Spaced sheathing
19 x 140mm (1" x 6" nom.)

Two nails for each shingle 19 to 25mm
(3/4" to 1") from edge and 38 to 50mm
(1-1/2" to 2") above butt line of next course

Eave protection membrane

Solid wood sheathing

Drip edge 38mm (1-1/2")

380mm (15") starter course

Facia

Rafter header

Exposure (→ 384)

10 to 16mm (3/8" to 5/8")
space between shakes

Adjacent courses should be
offset 38mm (1-1/2") minimum

Reference Tables

Table 7.1
Recommended Maximum Exposure for Western Red Cedar Shingles

Application	Shingle length mm	in.	Grade	Recommended maximum exposed shingle length mm	in.
Roof (minimum slope 1 in 3)	400	16	No.1 Blue Label	125	5
			No.2 Red Label	100	4
			No.3 Black Label	90	3-1/2
	450	18	No.1 Blue Label	140	5-1/2
			No.2 Red Label	115	4-1/2
			No.3 Black Label	100	4
	600	24	No.1 Blue Label	190	7-1/2
			No.2 Red Label	165	6-1/2
			No.3 Black Label	140	5-1/2
Roof (minimum slope 1 in 4)	400	16	No.1 Blue Label	95	3-3/4
			No.2 Red Label	90	3-1/2
			No.3 Black Label	75	3
	450	18	No.1 Blue Label	110	4-1/4
			No.2 Red Label	100	4
			No.3 Black Label	90	3-1/2
	600	24	No.1 Blue Label	145	5-3/4
			No.2 Red label	140	5-1/2
			No.3 Black Label	125	5
Exterior sidewall (double-coursed) [1]	400	16	No.1 Blue Label	305	12
	450	18	No.1 Blue Label	355	14
	600	24	No.1 Blue Label	405	16
Exterior sidewall (single-coursed)	400	16	No.1 Blue or No.1 Red Label	190	7-1/2
	450	18	No.1 Blue or No.1 Red Label	215	8-1/2
	600	24	No.1 Blue or No.1 Red Label	290	11-1/2

Note:
1. Also requires an undercourse layer of No.4 grade or better shingles.

Reference Tables continued

Table 7.2
Recommended Maximum Exposure for Western Red Cedar Shakes

| Application | Shake length [1] | | Recommended maximum exposed shake length | | | |
| | | | Two-ply Roof | | Three-ply Roof | |
	mm	in.	mm	in.	mm	in.
Roof (minimum slope 1 in 3)	450	18	190	7-1/2	140	5-1/2
	600	24	255	10	190	7-1/2

| Application | Shake Type | Shake length [2] | | Recommended maximum exposed shake length | | | |
| | | | | Single-course | | Double-course | |
		mm	in.	mm	in.	mm	in.
Sidewall	Resawn	450	18	215	8-1/2	355	14
	Straight-split	450	18	215	8-1/2	405	16
	Resawn	600	24	290	11-1/2	510	20
	Taper-split	600	24	290	11-1/2	510	20

Notes:
1. Premium or No.1 Grade only
2. Premium or No.1 or Sidewall Grades

Table 7.3
Recommended Maximum Exposure for Eastern White Cedar Shingles

| Application | Shingle length | | Grade | Recommended maximum exposed shingle length | |
	mm	in.		mm	in.
Roof (minimum slope 1 in 3)	400	16	A (Extra)	125	5
			B (Clear)	100	4
	450	18	A (Extra)	140	5-1/2
			B (Clear)	115	4-1/2
Roof (minimum slope 1 in 4)	400	16	A (Extra)	100	4
			B (Clear)	90	3-1/2
	450	18	A (Extra)	105	4-1/8
			B (Clear)	100	4
Exposed sidewall (double-coursed)	400	16	All grades except undercourse	305	12
	450	18	All grades except undercourse	355	14
Exposed sidewall (single-coursed)	400	16	All grades except undercourse	190	7-1/2
	450	18	All grades except undercourse	215	8-1/2

7.3   Panel Products

Softwood Plywood

All grades of Douglas Fir Plywood (DFP) and Canadian Softwood Plywood (CSP) are made with adhesives suitable for exterior applications, both for sheathing (unsanded grades) and for finished surfaces (sanded grades) (see Section 4.2).

Sheathing grades of plywood make an economical cladding with a pleasing rustic appearance especially when the plywood is stained with a heavy bodied stain and the joints are covered with battens or mouldings.

The sanded softwood plywood grades, Good Two Sides (G2S) and Good One Side (G1S) are suited for applications where high quality finish is required. For exterior applications such as soffits where only one side is usually exposed to view, G1S is used extensively because the sanded surface has a good appearance when painted or stained.

Medium Density Overlaid plywood is an exterior type plywood protected with a weather resistant overlay of phenolic or melamine resin and cellulose fibres. MDO plywood has a smooth durable surface ideal for paint coatings which gives a low maintenance finish.

Other specialty grades of plywood are manufactured for use as finish siding in either panel form or cut and applied as lap or bevel siding. As part of the manufacturing process, one of the following surface treatments is applied to the exposed face:

• Brushed Face: machine brushing removes the softer springwood so that the harder summerwood stands out in relief to give a durable textured finish.

• Grooved Face: both standard and MDO plywood is available with grooved patterns. Patterns range from fine-line grooves at equidistant spacings to randomly spaced wide grooves.

Exposed edges of plywood should be sealed with two coats of exterior primer or aluminum-based paint to prevent moisture migration through the panel edges.

Specialty siding plywood is available in several edge patterns for application including tongue and groove, shiplap, bevel edge, and flat butt, where battens are to be used to cover joints. The joints between panels can be left narrow to be concealed, or can be left wide and be covered with battens to accentuate the joints.

Specialty Panels

Hardboard is a highly compacted wood fibre product which has been used extensively as a residential siding product. When sealed with a resin coating, a durable finish results which resists moisture and holds paint well.

New siding products have been introduced which have oriented strandboard (OSB) as a substrate for an exposed face resin coating which imparts colour and simulated wood grain texture to the panels. For example, one manufacturer produces panels with channel groove and plain patterns in panels 1220mm (4') wide by 2.1, 2.4, 2.7, 3.6, and 4.9m (7', 8', 9', 12' and 16') long, and offers a 25 year warranty for the substrate and a 5 year guarantee for the prime coat.

7

Exterior Wood Products

General Guidelines for Exterior Wood Products

- Many wood products are available which offer good service and good, if not exceptional, appearance potential for exterior siding and roofing.

- The major products to choose from are: solid wood siding, cedar shingles and shakes, and regular or textured plywood.

- Many stock patterns are available for exterior siding, designed to shed water well and to provide bold patterns visible from a distance. Custom patterns are also available by special order.

- Because of natural resistance to decay, western red cedar and eastern white cedar perform well in exterior applications.

- Where service conditions allow wood to dry after wetting, the cedars especially, and other species to a lesser degree, can be left to weather naturally where a silver gray natural colour is desired. In all other cases, wood surfaces should be protected by coating or by pressure treating (see Section 9).

- Use fasteners which will not cause rust staining of the wood (see Section 5).

References

CSA O188.1 Western Red Cedar Shingles, Handsplit Western Red Cedar Shakes, and Machine Grooved Shakes, Canadian Standards Association (see Information Sources), 1980

CSA O188.2 Eastern White Cedar Shingles, Canadian Standards Association (see Information Sources), 1981

Landscaping with Wood, Canadian Wood Council, 1991

New Roof Construction, and, Exterior and Interior Walls, Red Cedar Shingle and Shake Bureau (see Information Sources), 1990

Standard Grading Rules for Canadian Lumber, National Lumber Grades Authority, 1990

Western Red Cedar – The Elegant Softwood, Council of Forest Industries of British Columbia, 1990

Interior Wood Products

8

For interior finish work, wood products offer infinite possibilities.

Wood trusses,
plank decking
and siding,
illuminated by
clerestory
window light,
create a bright,
inviting space.

The brilliant
colours of
modern retailing
and the variable
colour and
texture of wood
create
interesting
contrasts.

Sequence matched hardwood panels, both planar and curved, embellish this building interior.

Even when used in small amounts, wood adds elegance.

Structure, function and beauty are reflected in the use of stained and painted wood for this ceiling.

Softwood plywood with battens, stained light green, grace the stairwell of this office building.

The contrast of
two different
wood species
and the grain
matching of the
dominant
species proclaim
craftsmanship
and attention to
detail.

Premium quality sequence-matched hardwood plywood, suitably stained and finish coated, exemplifies wood as a decorative material.

Any building,
including those
where flame-
spread rating is
regulated, can
use architectural
woodwork to
enhance interior
spaces.

Hardwood
flooring and
plywood, slightly
different in finish
colour,
distinguish this
residential
hallway.

No two pieces of wood are exactly alike in colour or grain pattern. This unique characteristic is used effectively to provide a random pattern of colour for this ceiling.

The warmth and beauty of wood merges with the ornamental detailing of cast iron to create a stunning handrail.

Wood Species

Canadian wood species offer a
remarkable range of colour, texture and
pattern.

Ash
white flat cut

Ash
white quarter
stripe

Aspen

Beech

Birch
white

Butternut

Cedar
western red

Cherry
figured

Cherry
flat cut

Elm

Fir
Douglas

Hemlock
western

Hickory

Maple
birds eye

Maple
curly

Maple
flat cut

Maple
quartered

Oak
burl

Oak
red flat cut

Oak
red quartered

Oak
white flat cut

Oak
white quartered

Oak
white rift cut

Pine
knotty

Pine
white

Spruce

Walnut
figured stripe

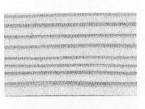  

Walnut
flat cut

Walnut
plain stripe

Walnut
premium burl

Interior wood
finishes can be
carefully
matched or
effectively
contrasted.

8.1   General Information

This section describes the variety of wood products used as interior finishing in applications such as trim, panelling, and architectural woodwork.

The products described are as follows:

8.2   Solid Wood
       Hardwood Lumber
       Hardwood Flooring
       Softwood Lumber
       Softwood Flooring

8.3   Panel Products
       Hardwood Plywood
       Softwood Plywood
       Specialty Panels

Wood products offer a unique opportunity to create warmth and character in living and work interiors. This applies for wood frame buildings and it also applies for high rise buildings where wood products can be used to add distinctiveness to boardrooms, elevators, lobbies and other areas where good appearance is paramount. For most code requirements, wood products used for architectural woodwork can add beauty while meeting flame spread requirements (see Section 10).

Architectural woodwork associations (see Information Sources) in Canada and the US have developed quality grades for specifying casework, doors, frames, and architectural woodwork. These quality grades indicate not only the quality of lumber which must be used for a certain application but also the quality of workmanship relative to the matching of wood colour and grain, the concealment of fasteners, and the sanding and coatings.

The information published by these associations simplifies the specifying and attaining of high quality wood finish and the reader is encouraged to refer to the information published by these associations to supplement the basic product information in this section.

8

Interior Wood Products

References

Building Construction Materials and Methods, H.G. Miller, McMillan of Canada, 1980

The Timber-Frame Home, Tedd Benson, Taunton Press, 1989

Wood Engineering and Construction Handbook, Keith E. Flaherty and Thomas G. Williamson, McGraw Hill Publishing, 1989

Wood Design Manual, Canadian Wood Council, 1990

6

Structural Wood Systems

6.4 Shearwalls and Diaphragms

Introduction

Buildings are subject to lateral loads from winds and earthquakes, and must be sufficiently rigid to support vertical loads.

Wood frame construction offers an effective method of resisting lateral building loads because of light weight, strong fastening systems, and alternate load paths. Recent examples of this performance are Hurricane Hugo in the southeast United States in 1989, and the Loma Prieta earthquake in the San Francisco Bay area of California in 1989.

In post and beam construction, diagonal bracing or non-rotating connections are required to resist lateral loads. Conventional framing relies on the combination of shearwalls and diaphragms to resist lateral loads.

Shearwalls and diaphragms are combinations of framing members and sheathing designed to give strength and rigidity to walls and roofs.

The term shearwall is used to describe a wall where the attachment of sheathing to framing has been designed to resist in-plane racking forces.

The term diaphragm is used to describe a horizontal plane such as a framed floor or roof which has been designed to transfer lateral loads outwardly to shearwalls, which then transfer the loads to the foundation.

Although particularly effective in stiffening conventionally framed buildings, shearwall effects in infill panels, used for building closure between the columns in post and beam construction, can supplement or supplant diagonal bracing. Similarly, diaphragm action from panels or decking affixed to roof and floor purlins in a post and beam building can supplement or supplant cross bracing.

In small buildings such as houses, adequate lateral resistance may be provided by conventional framing techniques and additional stiffening resulting from interior partitions and even by the attachment of gypsum wallboard. For larger buildings, and buildings of all sizes in high earthquake risk areas, lateral forces can be substantial and special features must be incorporated into the building design to ensure adequacy.

In many types of wood construction, shearwalls and diaphragms are effective and economical means of stiffening because the building envelope is made to perform the dual function of enclosing and of providing structural rigidity.

The purpose of this section is to give a basic understanding of why shearwalls and diaphragms are required and how they function.

The Performance of Wood Shearwalls and Diaphragms

Whether in lateral loading, cyclical over several hours, as would result from hurricane conditions, or in severe short term loading as would result from a seismic event, wood shearwalls and diaphragms perform well.

There are several good reasons for this demonstrated performance.

First, wood frame construction is lightweight in relation to steel and masonry construction. Earthquake forces are unique in the lateral acceleration they impart to everything in their path. The inertia of each obstacle, such as a building, resists movement to a degree dependent upon its mass. The lighter a building is, the easier it is to manage the forces from this acceleration.

Second, earthquakes are highly unpredictable in intensity and direction, and in how the loads they impart are carried through a building. Shearwall and diaphragm construction counters unpredictability by using a vast number of small nail connectors which provide many load paths, unlike other types of construction which accumulate and transfer larger loads.

6

Structural Wood Systems

Third, wood can, for short periods of time, endure stresses which exceed those of normal service conditions, and therefore it has reserve strength. Structural wood panel diaphragms maintain high stiffness and strength and if pushed to their ultimate capacity, tend to yield gradually while continuing to carry high loads, rather than exhibit brittle failure.

Last, nails are ductile fasteners which, when used in lumber, permit some movement in a building when subjected to sudden lateral loading. So, while providing the rigidity required for good building performance in ordinary circumstances, the nail to wood interface, when subjected to strong lateral loads, also makes the

building somewhat flexible, rather than rigid.

Lateral Building Loads

Wall design must make allowance for the tendency of a building to rack (go out of square) from its own weight and from imposed loads such as snow. Shearwalls and diaphragms provide building stiffness to counter the tendency of a building to rack, due to lateral loading such as wind, earthquake, or an unbalanced load from soil pressure or bulk storage (see Figure 6.11 below). The effect of vertical loads is aggravated when sway is induced by the primary lateral forces acting on the structure.

Figure 6.11
Causes of Building Racking

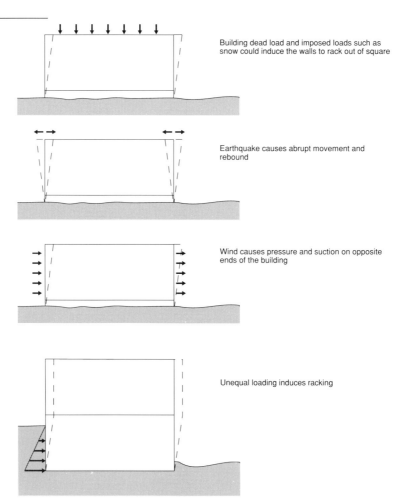

Building dead load and imposed loads such as snow could induce the walls to rack out of square

Earthquake causes abrupt movement and rebound

Wind causes pressure and suction on opposite ends of the building

Unequal loading induces racking

In addition to strength requirements, diaphragms and shearwalls must be designed to meet serviceability criteria so that deflections at specified loads are limited to values that do not cause distress to non-structural elements such as glazing and wall finishes, or make the structure susceptible to vibration.

The requirements for shearwalls and diaphragms vary greatly across North America and are most demanding in areas prone to earthquakes and high winds. Reference should be made to local code requirements for design criteria for these factors.

Shearwall and Diaphragm Action

In simple terms, a shearwall acts like a large flat vertical cantilever beam extending from the foundation and resisting lateral loads. A diaphragm acts like a large flat horizontal beam whose reactions are transferred to the walls which support it.

Lateral loads may or may not be normal to a building face. For a simple case where the end of a building is loaded laterally, Figure 6.12 (→ 332, 333) shows how shearwalls function, how diaphragms function, and how the two interact to stiffen a building.

The wall on which the wind acts is supported by the roof and foundation, and transfers one half the total wind load to roof level. The roof diaphragm transmits the load to the end shearwalls, which in turn transfer the load to the foundations.

Floor and roof diaphragms are designed to distribute lateral loads on the structure to the shearwall elements, which in turn carry the loads to the foundations. In addition to vertical shearwalls and horizontal diaphragms, a combined diaphragm/shearwall effect can be obtained in sloped or curvilinear building components.

Smaller buildings may be of adequate stiffness merely by following code requirements for small buildings which are based on past experience and testing.

Where specifically designed, shearwalls and diaphragms must be able to resist all lateral loads. Decking and sheathing must be adequately fastened to supporting members (studs, joists, trusses, beams, columns and walls) so that they transfer lateral loads to perimeter members. Openings in shearwalls and diaphragms must be adequately reinforced with framing members and connections to transfer forces to the rest of the shearwall or diaphragm.

Wind suction and vertical acceleration caused by sudden lateral loading can cause uplift forces at the roof/wall (diaphragm/shearwall) interface and at the wall/foundation (shearwall/foundation) interface. For this reason, diaphragms must be suitably connected to the shearwalls, and the building must be fastened to the foundation to resist uplift loads and lateral shear forces.

For large buildings, it may be necessary to utilize one or more interior partitions to provide shearwall action to keep transferred loads to a manageable size. In large buildings without interior partitions, such as warehouses, exterior shearwalls can be bolstered by, for example, doubling the sheathing or using diagonal bracing. This may be accomplished by installing plywood or OSB/waferboard sheathing over the framing and installing the gypsum wallboard finish over the sheathing. The addition of supplementary shearwalls requires careful analysis to estimate the amount of lateral load which is transferred to each shearwall.

Because of the relative flexibility of wood diaphragms, it is often assumed that shearwalls are subjected to loads in proportion to their tributary areas. The designer should, however, keep in mind the effect of diaphragm stiffness on the way in which loads are carried in a structure and provide adequate horizontal diaphragm stiffness elements. This is particularly important for asymmetrical shearwall layouts.

6

Structural Wood Systems

Figure 6.12
**Shearwall and
Diaphragm
Action**

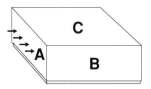

A- Endwall against which wind pressure
    (or earthquake force) acts.
B- Sidewalls (parallel to wind) which provide
    shearwall action in this example.
C- Roof provides diaphragm action.

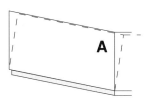

Wind pressure causes A to hinge at the foundation.
To resist this, force must be applied along the side of A.

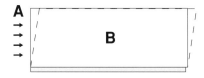

The load transfer from A tends to make
B go out of square or rack.

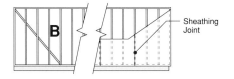

Sheathing
Joint

To resist the tendency to rack, B must be reinforced with
interior bracing, or a nailing spacing for the sheathing must
be used which permits the sheathing and framing
to resist racking.

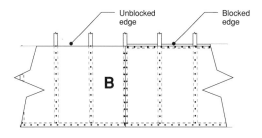

Unblocked
edge

Blocked
edge

Installing blocking between the framing members at
sheathing edges increases resistance to racking by
increasing the perimeter where nailing can be used
to transfer load.

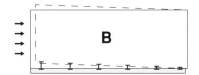

If B acts as a shearwall, the wind load from A may
cause the upwind corner of B to lift. The connection
of B to the foundation must be designed to resist uplift
and horizontal shear.

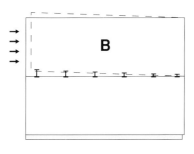

For multi-storey buildings, it is necessary to ensure that hold down continuity extends into upper storeys.

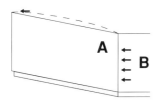

With the sides of A restrained by shearwall action in B, there is still a tendency for A to deflect its weak upper edge.

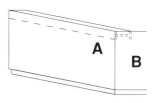

A beam on edge (or diaphragm (see below)) could be used to strengthen the upper edge of A with the reactions from the beam being transferred to the shearwall B.

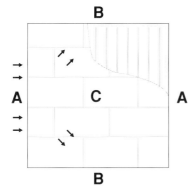

The roof sheathing and roof framing can be designed as a diaphragm (C) which acts like a deep beam in resisting the lateral pressure from A and transferring the load to the B walls.

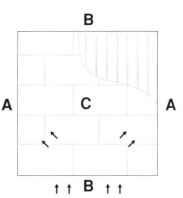

If the wind shifts to act on B, the A walls provide shearwalll action and the roof acts as a diaphragm by transferring loads to the A walls.

Materials for Shearwalls and Diaphragms

Framing Materials

Dimension lumber and light frame trusses are the most commonly used framing materials for shearwall and diaphragm design, but other wood members may be used in combination with sheathing to develop resistance to lateral loads.

Prefabricated wood I-joists, laminated veneer lumber (LVL) and parallel strand lumber (PSL) are other wood products common to wood frame construction. The materials used for post and beam construction, timber, glulam, LVL and PSL may also be used as purlins, combined with sheathing to resist lateral loading.

Panel Sheathing

Plywood and OSB/waferboard panels are used extensively in wood frame construction to provide shearwall and diaphragm action.

Strength of panel product diaphragms and shearwalls is dependent on the thickness of the panel, the nailing pattern, the nail holding ability of the framing material, and whether or not blocking is used to increase the nailed perimeter. In addition, strength is greater when the joints between panels are staggered so that there is not a continuous joint.

Increased shearwall capacity can be obtained by applying sheathing to both sides of framing.

Softer materials such as fibreboard and gypsum wallboard can add supplementary stiffening effect. However, for severe loading conditions, such as might result from earthquake loads, it is recommended that the strengthening effect of these materials be considered as a reserve rather than as primary resistance to such loads.

This is because the nail fasteners may tend to abrade these soft materials during normal cyclical loading, and result in too much loss of rigidity when a large loading occurs.

Lumber Boards and Decking

Boards used for shearwalls and for diaphragms should be at least 19mm (1" nom.) thick and 140mm (6" nom.) wide. Boards are usually limited to applications where the spacing of supports is 600mm (2') or less.

Board sheathing can be laid transversely to supporting members. Increased strength is obtained by placing the boards diagonal to the framing. Still more strength can be obtained by attaching a second layer of board sheathing diagonally opposite to the first layer.

Plank decking (lumber 38 to 89mm (2" to 4" nom.) thick, 127mm (5") and wider) is a stress graded lumber product, often used as a diaphragm material available in many species, sizes and shapes. Its thickness gives it the capacity to carry hefty floor and roof loads. It may also provide diaphragm resistance to lateral loads, and it may have the advantage of providing additional fire safety, by meeting the minimum size requirements of floor and roof materials for Heavy Timber construction.

Decking is usually laid transverse to supporting members, such as beams or purlins, in a controlled random pattern (see Section 4.4). It can also be laid diagonally to the support members to improve diaphragm strength.

Connections

Shearwalls and diaphragms effectively transfer lateral forces down to the foundation. All components must be suitably fastened together for the structure to act as an effective unit.

Whether the sheathing materials are boards or panels, the nail connection between sheathing and framing is the essential means of load transfer. This is why the capacity of a panel sheathed wall increases as the nail to nail spacing decreases. Loss of strength, due to splitting in the framing member, is a possibility when the nail spacing is less than 50mm (2"). Close nailing patterns are facilitated by mechanical nailing.

Figure 6.13
Arrangements and Relative Strength of Shearwalls

Board sheathing comparison based on 19 x 140mm (1" x 6" nom.) boards with two 63 mm (2-1/2") nails per board per support.

Relative Strength

6

Structural Wood Systems

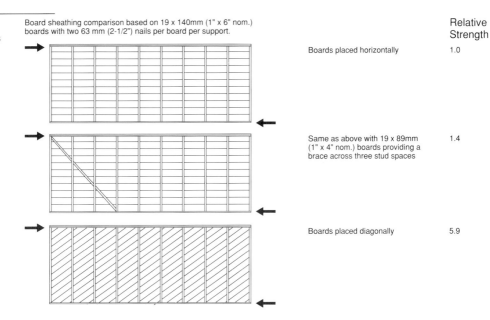

Boards placed horizontally   1.0

Same as above with 19 x 89mm (1" x 4" nom.) boards providing a brace across three stud spaces   1.4

Boards placed diagonally   5.9

Panel sheathing comparison based on unsanded plywood or OSB panels with edges supported by 38mm (2" nom.) or wider framing. Framing is Douglas Fir-Larch with a perimeter nail spacing of 100mm (4") and an intermediate support nail spacing of 300mm (12").

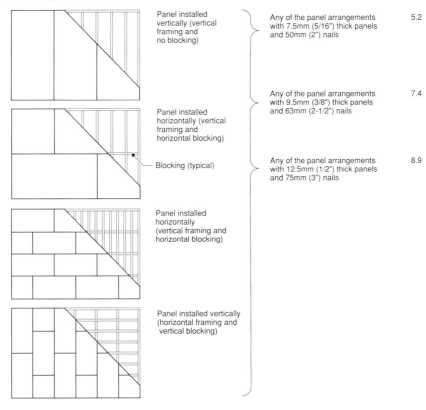

Panel installed vertically (vertical framing and no blocking)

Panel installed horizontally (vertical framing and horizontal blocking)

Blocking (typical)

Panel installed horizontally (vertical framing and horizontal blocking)

Panel installed vertically (horizontal framing and vertical blocking)

Any of the panel arrangements with 7.5mm (5/16") thick panels and 50mm (2") nails   5.2

Any of the panel arrangements with 9.5mm (3/8") thick panels and 63mm (2-1/2") nails   7.4

Any of the panel arrangements with 12.5mm (1/2") thick panels and 75mm (3") nails   8.9

Note:
Code allowances for sheathing types varies. Consult local code for specific strengths.

Figure 6.14
**Panel
Arrangements
and Relative
Strengths of
Diaphragms**

This comparison is based on Douglas Fir-Larch framing, unsanded plywood or OSB panels, 38mm (2" nom.) framing members, 100mm (4") nail spacing at diaphragm boundary and at continous panel edges parallel to load, all other nail spacing at 150mm (6"), all edges blocked.

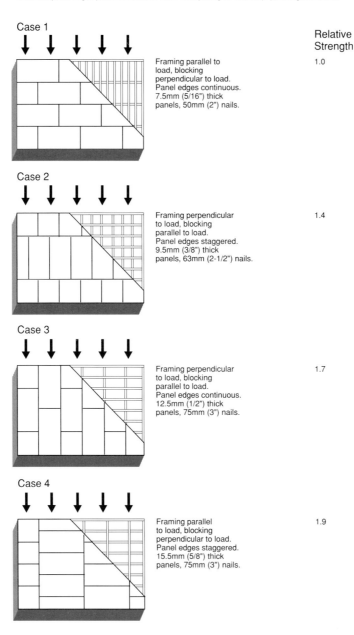

Case 1

Relative
Strength

Framing parallel to
load, blocking
perpendicular to load.
Panel edges continuous.
7.5mm (5/16") thick
panels, 50mm (2") nails.

1.0

Case 2

Framing perpendicular
to load, blocking
parallel to load.
Panel edges staggered.
9.5mm (3/8") thick
panels, 63mm (2-1/2") nails.

1.4

Case 3

Framing perpendicular
to load, blocking
parallel to load.
Panel edges continuous.
12.5mm (1/2") thick
panels, 75mm (3") nails.

1.7

Case 4

Framing parallel
to load, blocking
perpendicular to load.
Panel edges staggered.
15.5mm (5/8") thick
panels, 75mm (3") nails.

1.9

Note:
Code strength allowances vary. Consult local codes
for specific strengths and other configurations.

The nailing perimeter of a panel can be maximized by installing blocking between framing members so that all panel edges and ends are supported. This increases the load capacity of the building element.

Board sheathing relies on the resistance to turning created by the nails installed at each board to framing interface. The resistance to turning is most affected by the distance between the two nails which is dependent upon the width of the boards used. For this reason, the capacity of board sheathing is not significantly increased by additional nailing.

Because a shearwall acts like a cantilever beam extended from the foundation, lateral load tends to rotate the base of the cantilever resulting in uplift forces, and tends to push the wall base across the foundation. For these reasons, wall units must be capable of resisting lateral shear and uplift forces.

The uplift forces place vertical sections in tension between the foundation and roof and therefore tie down connections must be continuous from the roof down. For light loads, the sheathing can be used to transfer loads (see Figure 6.15 below) across the header space discontinuity created by platform framed floor sections.

6

Structural Wood Systems

Figure 6.15
Resisting Uplift of Shearwalls

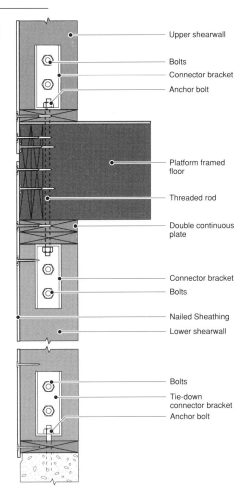

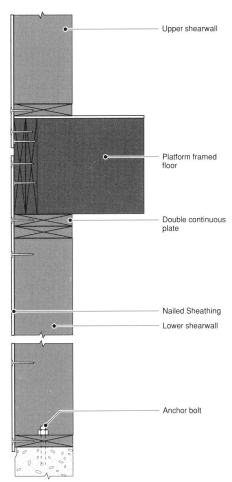

For heavy uplift load and for interior applications where panel sheathing is not used, tie-down connector brackets at select locations can be used to tie the building to the foundation.

Panel sheathing nailing is used to tie structure to foundation for light uplift load conditions.

For heavier loadings, it may be necessary to use tie-down connector brackets as shown in Figure 6.15 (→ 337) to make the vertical members between floors act as a continuous tensile member when resisting uplift. Such connectors should be tightened after seasoning of the floor joists just prior to enclosing the walls to take up any gap resulting from shrinkage in the horizontal lumber.

Proportions for Shearwalls and Diaphragms

Shearwalls and diaphragms are effective means of providing rigidity to wood structured buildings. Their effectiveness is based on design, but from experience, some practical limitations to the building proportions have been established.

Because the shearwall is likened to a cantilever beam fixed at the foundation, there is a practical limit to the height of a shearwall in relation to its length. While these values may vary with particular engineering standards, the Table below offers some practical values as a general guide.

In a similar vein, diaphragms are likened to a beam loaded from the side. Practical limitations have been established for the maximum slenderness the beam should have. In other words, there is a practical limit to the width to length ratio for diaphragm action. Again, these values as shown in the Table below, may vary according to the engineering standards in use and are presented as a general guide.

These guidelines indicate the basic geometric proportions which are most suitable for reinforcement by shearwall and diaphragm action. As the values show, most building arrangements fall within the guidelines, except for long and narrow buildings or high and squat buildings.

Use with Other Types of Building Materials

Wood shearwalls and diaphragms are more flexible than many other building materials. This causes some limitation in the use of wood to provide rigidity for concrete and masonry walls.

Although strong enough, a wood shearwall may deflect more than a high concrete or masonry wall can tolerate without cracking. This difference in flexibility initially led to a guideline confining their use to bracing one storey buildings with concrete or masonry walls.

Shearwall Height-to-Length Dimension Ratios

Material	Maximum height-to-length ratios
Diagonal board sheathing, one side	2 to 1
Plywood and OSB/waferboard, blocked and nailed all edges and ends	3.5 to 1
Plywood and OSB/waferboard, no blocking at intermediate joints	2 to 1

Note:
For multi-storey buildings, the values are the ratio of total wall height to the length of a given side.

Diaphragm Width-to-Length Dimension Ratios

Material	Maximum width-to-length ratio
Diagonal board sheathing, one side	3 to 1
Plywood and OSB/waferboard, blocked and nailed all edges and ends	4 to 1
Plywood and OSB/waferboard, no blocking at intermediate joints	4 to 1

For bracing two-storey buildings with masonry or concrete walls, the following guidelines may be appropriate for wood shearwalls:

- Wall heights should not exceed 3.66m (12').

- Horizontal diaphragms should not be cantilevered from one shearwall. They should be fixed as a minimum to two opposing shearwalls.

- Deflections of horizontal and vertical diaphragms should not permit per-storey deflections of supported masonry or concrete walls to exceed 0.005 times each storey height.

- Panel sheathing in horizontal diaphragms should have all unsupported edges blocked. Panel sheathing for both storeys of vertical shearwalls should have all unsupported edges blocked and for the lower storey walls should have a minimum sheathing thickness of 12.7mm (1/2").

- There should be no out-of-plane horizontal offsets between the first and second storeys of plywood shearwalls.

Although these factors may vary according to the North American engineering standards in effect in particular areas, the preceeding information is a general guide.

Openings

The rigidity of a building is reduced by window, door, skylight, and other openings. Openings in diaphragms and shearwalls can have a marked effect on structural performance so additional framing and connections may be needed to permit shear transfer around openings. If large openings such as industrial doors divide a shearwall into a number of smaller elements, design must allow for distribution of forces to independent shearwall sections.

Openings may also make a building asymmetrical (see Figure 6.16 below) and thereby affect its ability to resist lateral force from a given direction. In this situation, torsion is introduced and the building has a tendency to twist when subjected to lateral forces.

Weaker shearwalls may be bolstered by increasing panel thickness, edge nailing at closer spacings, or by affixing panels to both sides of the framing.

In some buildings, it may be difficult to create shearwall action. For example, airplane hangars (many of which were built of wood during World War II and are still in service) are characterised by one end which is almost entirely a door opening. In such a case, the only possible shearwall location is at the wall facing the open end. To provide resistance to lateral forces at the open end, it is necessary to design diagonal bracing around the opening to approximate the rigidity afforded by the shearwall at the opposing end.

6

Structural Wood Systems

Figure 6.16
Effects of Large Openings on Shearwalls

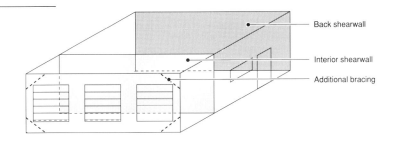

Large freight doors in this building reduce the wall area available for shearwall action.
Additional bracing, increased sheathing thickness and nailing density, or interior shearwalls may be required.

Guidelines for Shearwalls and Diaphragms

- Nailing patterns are critical to shearwall and diaphragm performance. Ensure that the contractor is aware of the higher density nailing patterns required, and inspect for performance.

- Larger buildings may require mechanical connections between floors to provide uplift resistance.

References

Engineering data in Earthquake Economics, Federal Reserve Board of San Francisco

Plywood Construction Manual, the Council of the Forest Industries of British Columbia

Shear Resistance of Wood Frame Buildings, A.T. Hansen, National Research Council of Canada, 1985

Wood Engineering and Construction Handbook, Keith F. Flaherty and Thomas G. Williamson, McGraw-Hill Publishing Company, 1987

Wood Design Manual, Canadian Wood Council, 1990

6.5   Bearing Stud Walls

Introduction

A bearing stud wall combines the primary separating or enclosing function of an interior or exterior partition with the role of transmitting vertical loads to the foundation. As well, a stud wall can transmit vertical, bending and lateral (see Shearwalls and Diaphragms, Section 6.4) loads in which case it behaves structurally as a load bearing wall, a beam, and as a shearwall.

Bearing walls have traditionally been constructed from stone, concrete, block, brick and other types of masonry materials. However, this rigid form of construction does not lend itself readily to future alterations such as the addition of openings for windows and doors. Bearing stud walls are a viable alternative for light-frame structures to concrete or masonry block walls.

A bearing stud wall is a versatile structural element which can be easily designed and pre-fabricated to suit many different architectural applications (see Figure 6.17 below).

Each framing member of a bearing stud wall behaves as a column in transferring vertical loads. The nailing of sheathing to framing members greatly enhances the column strength of each member by providing restraint from lateral displace-

ment. Blocking between the studs can further improve the ability of long slender stud members to be effective columns.

Materials for Bearing Stud Walls

Bearing stud walls used in residential construction are typically comprised of 38 x 89mm (2" x 4" nom.) or 38 x 140mm (2" x 6" nom.) studs. They are, most commonly, of Stud grade lumber and sheathed with plywood or OSB/waferboard. Building codes provide requirements for the minimum stud size, the maximum stud spacing, and the maximum laterally unsupported wall height.

Spacings are usually 410mm (16") but 610mm (24") spacings are also used. These spacings have been based more on past experience with successful building practice and less on rigorous engineering analysis.

Bearing stud wall systems used in commercial applications are similar to those found in residential construction but member sizes must usually be larger to accommodate larger loads. Typical lumber dimensions are 38 x 140mm (2" x 6" nom.), 38 x 184mm (2" x 8" nom.), or 38 x 235mm (2" x 10" nom.) studs usually of No.1 or No.2 grade. These systems must be

Figure 6.17
Structural Applications of Bearing Stud Walls

Curvilinear Wall

Opening

Wood bearing stud walls are easily adapted to suit slopes, curves and openings.

engineered to ensure that the stud sizes, stud spacings, stud heights and top and bottom plates are adequate to resist the larger loads encountered in these types of applications.

For commercial buildings, sheathing thickness for bearing stud walls is usually specified in building codes and is usually governed by the minimum thickness required to span between the studs without distortion. If, however, the bearing wall is additionally required to perform as a shearwall, sheathing thickness, nail length, and nail spacing must be designed to ensure that adequate in-plane shear resistance is provided (see Section 6.4).

Although not specifically designed for this type of application, vertically oriented wood I-joists can be used successfully as stud wall systems. Similarly, laminated veneer lumber (LVL) and parallel strand lumber (PSL), used as top and bottom plates, can also be substituted for dimension lumber.

Uses for Load Bearing Stud Walls

Stud walls used as interior bearing walls are often of platform-frame construction. In this type of application, the roof trusses and floor joists can either be top- or bottom-chord bearing. In Figure 6.18 below, both trusses and joists are shown as bottom-chord bearing.

Top-chord supported trusses have less tendency to rotate and therefore require less lateral restraint in the form of cross bracing.

Bottom-chord supported trusses require more cross bracing but tend to lessen the height of bearing wall required to provide a given ceiling height. Because the strength of any column (or stud wall) of a given cross section reduces as its length increases, the labour and material cost for providing additional bracing for top-chord supported trusses may be offset by savings

Figure 6.18
Interior Load Bearing Studwall

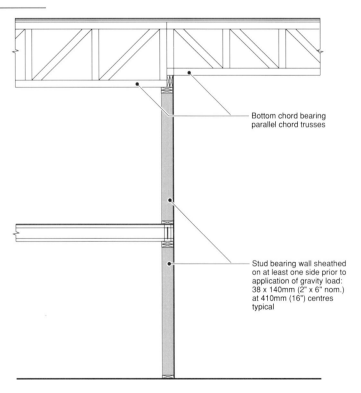

Bottom chord bearing parallel chord trusses

Stud bearing wall sheathed on at least one side prior to application of gravity load: 38 x 140mm (2" x 6" nom.) at 410mm (16") centres typical

General Guidelines for Interior Wood Products

- For clear finishes, both hardwoods and softwoods offer unique colour and appearance characteristics.

- Final appearance is governed by wood quality, workmanship, and finish coating (see Section 9).

- The review of hand samples is recommended to ensure wood quality, trim, and coatings will meet project requirements.

References

Architectural Woodwork Quality Standards: Guide Specifications and Quality Certification Program, Architectural Woodwork Institute (see Information Sources), 1989

Canadian Woods – Their Properties and Uses, E.J. Mullins and T.S. McKnight, University of Toronto Press, 1981

Quality Standards for Architectural Woodwork, Architectural Woodwork Manufacturers Association of Canada (see Information Sources), 1991

Wood Handbook: Wood as an Engineering Material, Agricultural Handbook 72, United States Department of Agriculture, 1987

8

Interior Wood Products

Protecting and Finishing Wood

9

Paint, solid stain and detailing combine to protect the wood products in this simple window detail.

Lightly stained
structural
members and
uncoated
western red
cedar panelling
provide
contrasting hues
in this
interpretation
centre.

Stained, painted
and uncoated
wood surfaces,
dappled by late
afternoon
shadows,
beckon the
visitor to this
world exposition
exhibit.

Painting adds distinction to wood while protecting it from the elements. Cedar shingles, with a natural resistance to sun and moisture, weather to a uniform silver hue.

Properly protected by paint, wood building materials, like the stonework they accent, will provide years of service.

Shade and high annual rainfall can create unfavourable conditions. Preservative treatment ensures lasting performance in these applications.

Left to weather naturally, timbers and framing acquire different hues depending on their exposure to water and sunlight.

Solid Stains (Exterior)

Solid stains hide grain but accent wood texture.
Many other colours are available.

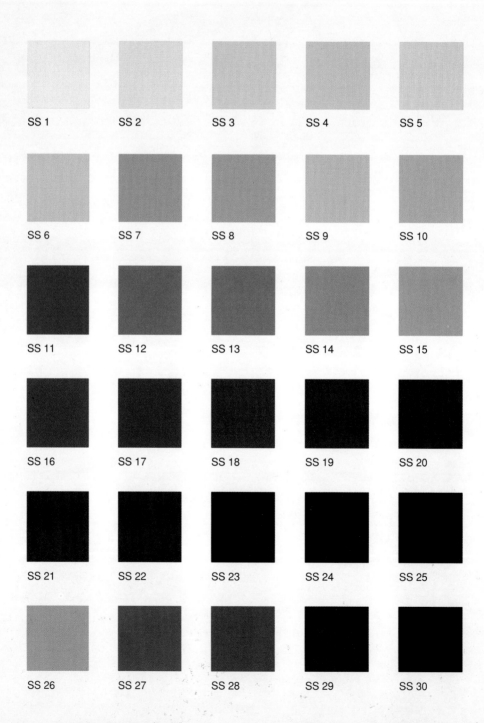

SS 1   SS 2   SS 3   SS 4   SS 5

SS 6   SS 7   SS 8   SS 9   SS 10

SS 11   SS 12   SS 13   SS 14   SS 15

SS 16   SS 17   SS 18   SS 19   SS 20

SS 21   SS 22   SS 23   SS 24   SS 25

SS 26   SS 27   SS 28   SS 29   SS 30

Semi-Transparent Stains (Exterior)

Semi-transparent stains allow grain and texture
to show. Many other colours are available.

STS 1	STS 2	STS 3	STS 4	STS 5
STS 6	STS 7	STS 8	STS 9	STS 10
STS 11	STS 12	STS 13	STS 14	STS 15
STS 16	STS 17	STS 18	STS 19	STS 20
STS 21	STS 22	STS 23	STS 24	STS 25
STS 26	STS 27	STS 28	STS 29	STS 30

Stains (Interior)

Stains for interior fine finish applications accent
wood grain and adjust colour. The appearance of
the stain colours shown is dependent on the wood
species used. Many other colours are available.

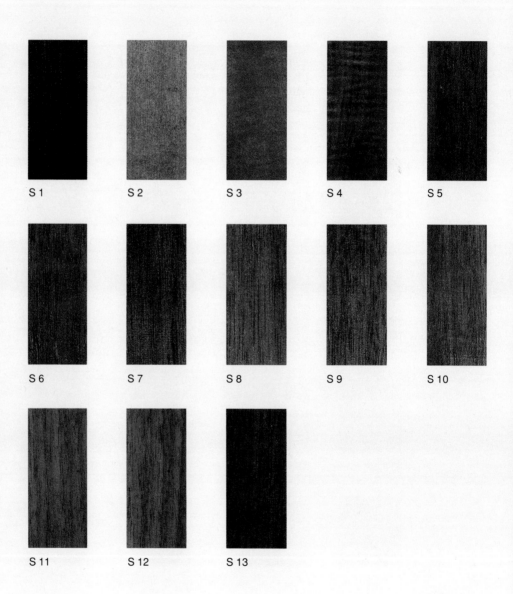

S 1 S 2 S 3 S 4 S 5

S 6 S 7 S 8 S 9 S 10

S 11 S 12 S 13

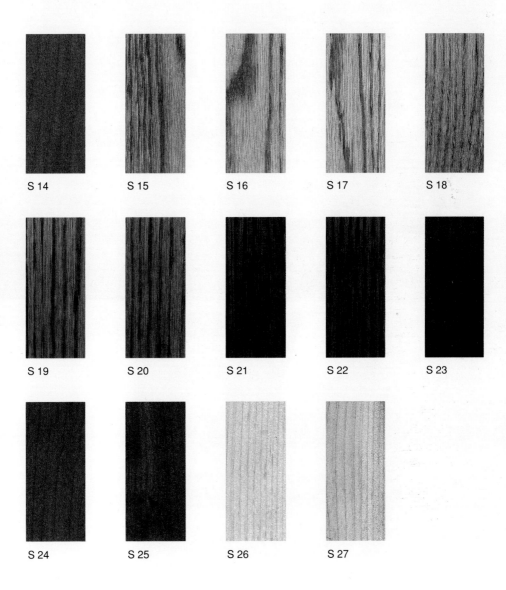

S 14

S 15

S 16

S 17

S 18

S 19

S 20

S 21

S 22

S 23

S 24

S 25

S 26

S 27

Whether used
formally or
informally, wood
creates
environments
that bring people
together in
beauty and
comfort.

9.1   General Information

To sustain service life and appearance, there are various methods and materials for protecting wood products from insect attack, fungi attack, dirt, ultra-violet light, wetting, fire and abrasion.

The methods employed for protection will depend upon the type of wood product, the way in which it is used, and the degree of severity and type of hazard which it will encounter during its service life.

The methods for protecting wood products presented in this section are:

9.2   Protection by Detailing

9.3   Coatings

9.4   Preservative-Treated Wood

9.5   Fire-Retardant Treatment and Coating

At times, wood astounds us by the length of time it can withstand the attacks of nature. Rail fences, marine pilings, sunken sailing ships and building facades left totally neglected sometimes endure for centuries. By the same token, the home-owner is sometimes dismayed by the speed with which the home built wood deck deteriorates.

Three methods of protection covered in this section involve varying degrees of intervention to the natural defences of wood to decay and deterioration. The first section, Protection by Detailing, focuses on the basic principals of distancing wood from the most pervasive destructive agent, decay.

The application of coatings to wood products provides a degree of protection in addition to what is often the primary goal, that of enhancing tone and grain, and adjusting colour.

For the most demanding service conditions, preservative treating offers a means for improving the resistance to decay and insect attack for those wood species which do not have sufficient natural resistance, and for improving resistance to fire.

9

Protecting and Finishing Wood

9.2   Protection by Detailing

Wood products offer good service life potential when sound techniques are used in the choice of materials and methods of installation.

The initial line of defence against deterioration for wood products used in applications exposed to the elements, is a method of installation which facilitates shedding water, protecting edge grain, and giving access to air for drying between wettings.

There are many examples in North America and throughout the world of old buildings built of wood which have never had the benefit of chemical preservative or even a coating of paint or stain. For example, covered bridges, barns, and the cedar shingle houses of Atlantic fishing communities demonstrate the durability of wood used in this fashion. Religious complexes in Tibet, royal palaces in China, churches in Russia, theatres in England and railway stations in Switzerland have stood for centuries, defying extreme climates and extensive use. Such buildings have been left to weather naturally, but have benefited from design details which have enabled them to resist the elements well.

Many books are available which demonstrate details for wood exteriors. Some details are good and some violate time tested principles which risk foreshortening the life expectancy of the products used. This section is intended not to be a collection of all possible details for wood but rather to illustrate the mechanisms of water movement in a building exterior and to show some examples of how these mechanisms can be arrested through detailing.

Water Penetration

Water can enter a building exterior by several means described by elementary physics such as gravity, surface tension, pressure differential, momentum, and capillary action as shown in Figure 9.1 (→ 442).

By understanding these mechanisms, the designer is challenged to design joints and arrange members so that these mechanisms are not given an opportunity to function.

As an additional precaution, a wind screen wall offers a vertical wall cavity through which any moisture which does penetrate can escape. While many agree that a wind screen is good design practice, the additional cost of the screen is accepted infrequently.

Selection of Material

Species and quality have a significant impact on the resistance of wood products to deterioration. For example, the cedars (see Section 7) contain natural chemical protection against decay and insect attack.

Irregularities such as knots and splits offer opportunity for the entrapment of water and a decrease in resistance against deterioration. Selecting dry, high quality lumber for exterior applications is a good investment in long term performance.

Design Details

The illustrations in Figures 9.2 (→ 443), 9.3 (→ 444), 9.4 (→ 445), and 9.5 (→ 446) are meant to be self explanatory in showing some of the ways the detailing of a contemporary residential or commercial building offsets the water penetration mechanisms described.

9

Protecting and Finishing Wood

Figure 9.1
Types of Water Penetration and Prevention for Siding

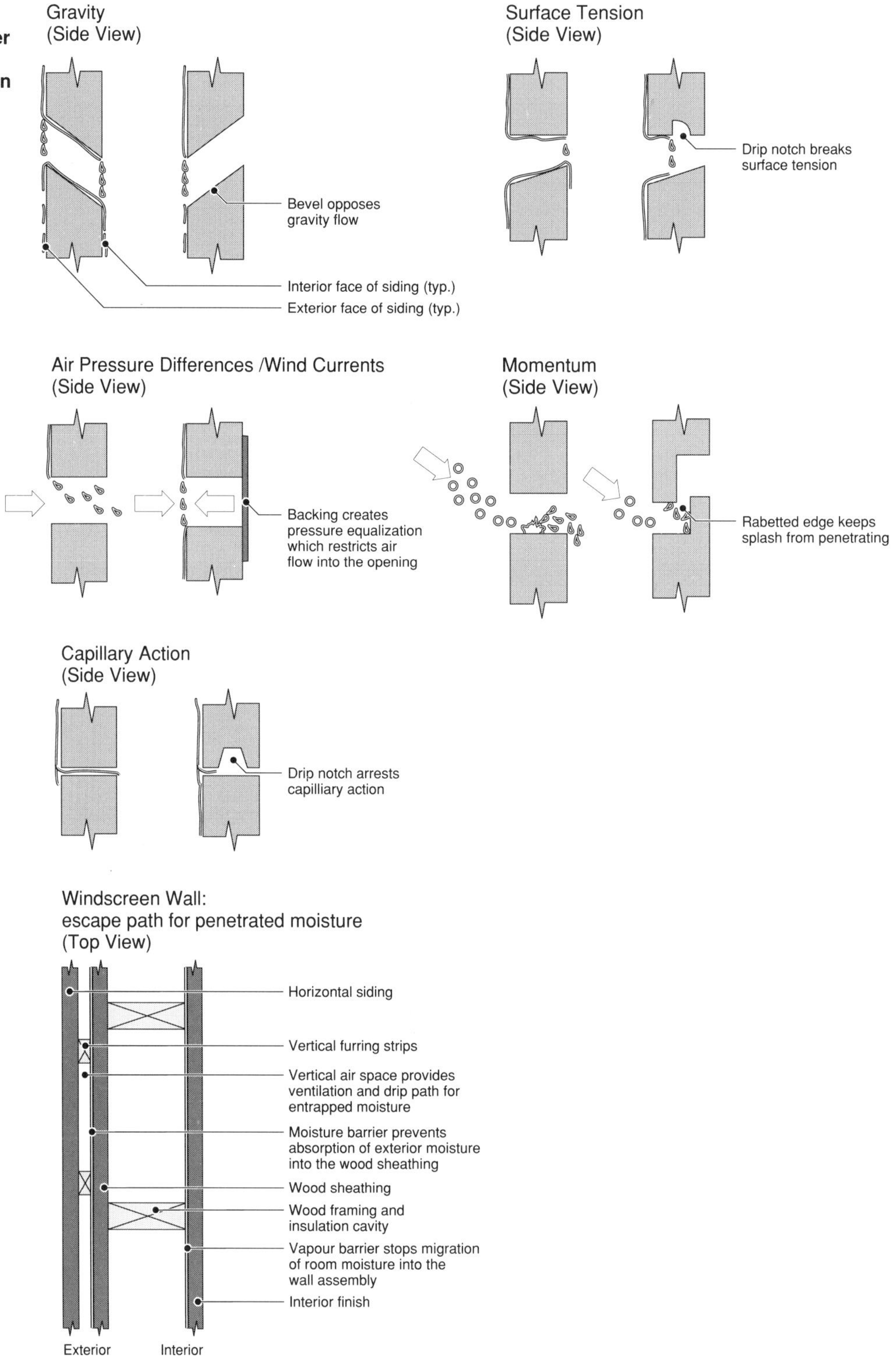

Gravity
(Side View)

Bevel opposes gravity flow

Interior face of siding (typ.)
Exterior face of siding (typ.)

Surface Tension
(Side View)

Drip notch breaks surface tension

Air Pressure Differences /Wind Currents
(Side View)

Backing creates pressure equalization which restricts air flow into the opening

Momentum
(Side View)

Rabetted edge keeps splash from penetrating

Capillary Action
(Side View)

Drip notch arrests capilliary action

Windscreen Wall:
escape path for penetrated moisture
(Top View)

Horizontal siding

Vertical furring strips

Vertical air space provides ventilation and drip path for entrapped moisture

Moisture barrier prevents absorption of exterior moisture into the wood sheathing

Wood sheathing

Wood framing and insulation cavity

Vapour barrier stops migration of room moisture into the wall assembly

Interior finish

Exterior   Interior

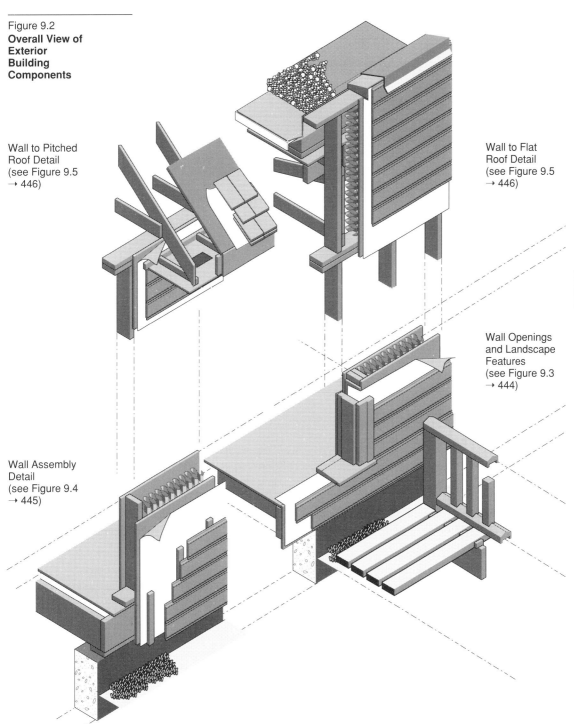

Figure 9.2
**Overall View of
Exterior
Building
Components**

Wall to Pitched
Roof Detail
(see Figure 9.5
→ 446)

Wall to Flat
Roof Detail
(see Figure 9.5
→ 446)

Wall Openings
and Landscape
Features
(see Figure 9.3
→ 444)

Wall Assembly
Detail
(see Figure 9.4
→ 445)

9

Protecting and Finishing Wood

Figure 9.3
**Typical Details
for Openings
and Landscape
Features**

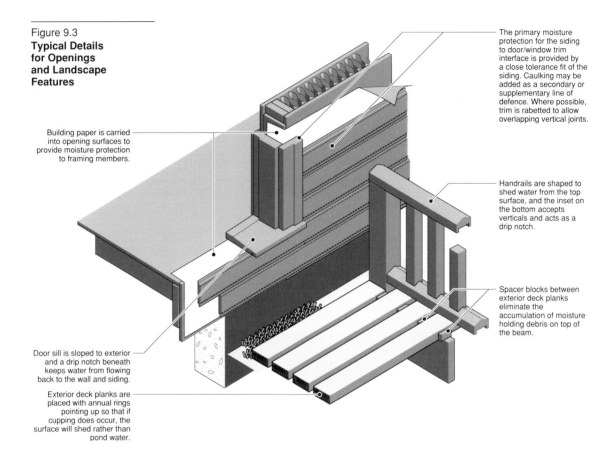

The primary moisture protection for the siding to door/window trim interface is provided by a close tolerance fit of the siding. Caulking may be added as a secondary or supplementary line of defence. Where possible, trim is rabetted to allow overlapping vertical joints.

Building paper is carried into opening surfaces to provide moisture protection to framing members.

Handrails are shaped to shed water from the top surface, and the inset on the bottom accepts verticals and acts as a drip notch.

Spacer blocks between exterior deck planks eliminate the accumulation of moisture holding debris on top of the beam.

Door sill is sloped to exterior and a drip notch beneath keeps water from flowing back to the wall and siding.

Exterior deck planks are placed with annual rings pointing up so that if cupping does occur, the surface will shed rather than pond water.

Figure 9.4
**Typical Details
for Wall
Assemblies**

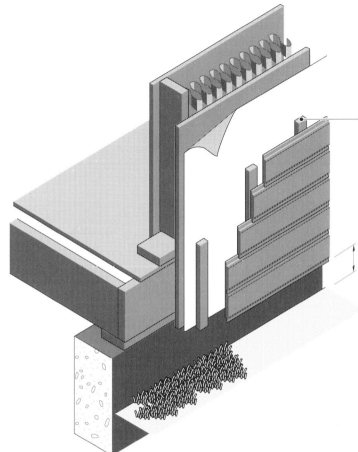

In areas frequently prone to
wind driven rain, installing siding
over vertical furring strips allows
any moisture which permeates
the siding to drip away or dry
through evaporation.

200mm (8") minimum siding
to ground spacing reduces
splashing from the ground onto
the siding.

9

Protecting and Finishing Wood

Figure 9.5
**Typical Details
for Pitched and
Flat Roofs**

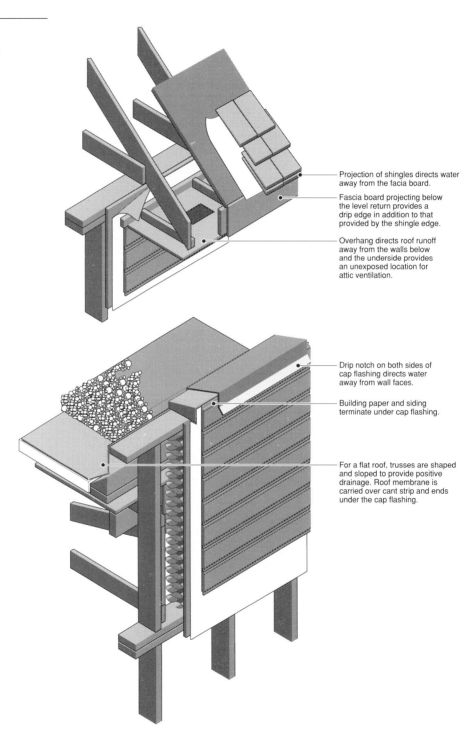

Projection of shingles directs water
away from the facia board.

Fascia board projecting below
the level return provides a
drip edge in addition to that
provided by the shingle edge.

Overhang directs roof runoff
away from the walls below
and the underside provides
an unexposed location for
attic ventilation.

Drip notch on both sides of
cap flashing directs water
away from wall faces.

Building paper and siding
terminate under cap flashing.

For a flat roof, trusses are shaped
and sloped to provide positive
drainage. Roof membrane is
carried over cant strip and ends
under the cap flashing.

General Guidelines for Detailing Wood Exteriors

- Generally, the fewer defects in the grade selected, the better the resistance of wood products used for exterior applications.

- Select a product grade in combination with a finish coating to provide the appearance required as well as good service life at reasonable cost.

- Select a siding pattern and arrangement (vertical or horizontal) which will suit site conditions with regard to ability to self-clean wind-carried dirt.

- In many cases, primary weather seal is dependent upon quality workmanship to provide a good fit between siding and trim. Caulking is a convenient means for providing additional protection but of course is not an alternative to good workmanship.

- There are many fastener materials (see Section 5.2) which do not cause rust staining of wood products. For appearance sake, conceal fasteners whenever possible or at the least, select fasteners which will be unobtrusive.

- In particular, protect end grain from wetting.

References

Canadian Wood Frame House Construction, Canada Mortgage and Housing Commission, 1989

Roofs – Design, Application and Maintenance, Maxwell C. Baker, Multiscience Publications Limited, 1980

Structural Uses of Wood in Adverse Environments, Robert W. Meyer and Robert M. Kellogg, van Nostrand Reinhold Company, 1982

The Professional Handbook of Building Construction, John Wiley and Sons, 1986

9

Protecting and Finishing Wood

9.3   Coatings

Introduction

The grain, texture, colour and variety of wood products are admired universally. Throughout the ages, numerous methods of coating, colouring, or otherwise altering the appearance of wood have been devised.

The choice of coatings and coating techniques available for wood products can seem overwhelming. As well, terminology applied inconsistently between one manufacturer and another adds needlessly to the confusion.

This section explains the properties and applications for the major wood coatings, these being paint, varnish, stain and lacquer. This section is not intended to be exhaustive but rather, by providing pertinent information, to help the specifier communicate with the relevant industry specialists. It is organized as follows:

- General Information about Coatings

- Exterior Coatings

- Interior Coatings – General Purpose

- Interior Coatings – Fine Finishes

For interior coatings, the distinction between general purpose and fine finish is sometimes unclear. For this section, the term general purpose is used to describe coatings for interior applications such as trim, doors, wall and ceiling board panelling, and floors where a painted surface or a good quality transparent surface is required. The term "fine finish" is used to describe coating treatments for architectural woodwork where an exceptional appearance is required. Although beyond the scope of this book, fine finish techniques and products also apply to furniture and cabinetry.

For more detailed information and for information on less frequently used products or techniques, refer to the references listed at the end of the section.

Coatings provide varying degrees of protection to wood products by retarding moisture fluctuation, reducing the effect of ultra violet light, or by providing increased resistance to abrasion. These products also perform the function of accentuating wood grain and texture or giving partial or full colour to wood surfaces.

General Information about Coatings

Composition
Wood coatings (paint, varnish, stain, and lacquer) have three major components:

- Solvent

- Pigment

- Resin

The proportion of these components and their chemical composition varies with the type of product and its end use. In some clear finish products, pigment may be specialized or may be absent altogether.

The role of each component is as follows:

Solvent
The solvent in a coating product thins the pigment/resin mixture to application viscosity. During the drying process the solvent evaporates and has no effect on the physical properties of the cured paint film.

Water and mineral spirit solvents are the types of solvent in the majority of coatings used for wood products. Water solvent is more environmentally benign than mineral spirit solvent. More and more water solvent products, including paint, varnish, stain, and even lacquer, are becoming available.

9

Protecting and Finishing Wood

Pigment
The primary purpose of pigment in a coating is to provide colour and hiding ability, but some pigments are used to make sanding easier, to control gloss level, or simply to act as a filler. There are many different types of pigments, but most fall into one of the following categories:

- Titanium Dioxide: Titanium dioxide is the principle pigment used in paint to give hiding ability. It makes the paint white. The amount used in a product controls the degree of hiding ability.

- Colour Pigments: Used by themselves or in conjunction with titanium dioxide, colour pigments provide colour and opacity to paint. Colour pigments, dispersed in a glycol solvent in the tinting machines used by paint stores, provide custom tints to water based or solvent based products.

- Extender Pigments: Extender pigments, such as clay, are primarily used to control the gloss of a product by changing the pigment to resin ratio. As the amount of pigment is increased, the gloss level decreases. When the pigment to resin ratio reaches a level where there is not enough resin to cover the pigment completely, the resulting coating will no longer have any level of gloss and will be flat.

- Rust Inhibiting Pigments: Rust inhibiting pigments are used in conjunction with other pigments in metal primers to provide corrosion protection.

Resin
The type of resin used in a formulation gives the coating product most of its physical characteristics such as adhesion and durability. Resin is the film forming ingredient and binds the pigment particles together after the paint has dried.

The type of resin used is what gives the product its name.

Alkyd, latex and polyurethane are the resins used most frequently in modern wood coatings. Nitrocellulose is used most often for lacquer.

As the resin content increases, the gloss increases, and the durability increases, but the ability of the coating to conceal imperfections decreases.

For this reason, a low pigment to resin content coating would be desired where a lot of wear is anticipated, and a high ratio of pigment to resin latex coating where it is necessary to mask flaws in the prepared surface.

Types of Coatings
The most used coatings for wood are paint, varnish, stain and lacquer. Their basic characteristics are shown in Figure 9.6 (opposite).

Paint
Paint is a coating which provides solid colour to wood and other materials.

The vast majority of paints applied to wood products use alkyd or latex as their principal resin ingredients.

Properties such as gloss, sheen, hardness, durability (including ability to be scrubbed without burnishing), and hiding ability are attained by adjusting the pigment to resin ratio.

Gloss is the ability of a coating to reflect light. Generally, the higher the gloss of a paint coating, the more washable and wear resistant it is.

Colour is controlled by the colouring pigment. The suitability of the paint for exterior or interior application is determined by the chemical composition of the resin. Resin for exterior paint provides the flexibility to accommodate temperature and dimensional changes in the wood, and permeability to allow the movement of water without blistering the paint.

Varnish
Varnish is a clear coating used as a topcoat over natural or stained wood for interior trim and architectural woodwork. It has some exterior applications.

Most varnishes contain a resin combining alkyd with polyurethane. They have recently become available as a water reducible polyurethane product.

Varnish is like paint but, because it is used as a clear finish, lacks hiding pigment. However, extender pigment may be used to establish the desired gloss level.

Stain
Stain is a coating with a high solvent content which causes the stain to be absorbed into the cell openings of the wood surface. The degree to which a stain penetrates can be adjusted for specific applications. Although some stains penetrate to the extent that they leave no surface residue, most leave some surface coating, in addition to penetrating into the wood. Therefore they are described generally as a type of coating.

Stains are specially formulated to meet the specific requirements of exterior, interior general purpose and interior fine finish applications.

For exterior applications, stain is usually used alone but in some instances may be topcoated with exterior quality varnish. When used alone, stain is used to alter the colour of the wood and to provide a degree of protection from sun and water.

For interior general purpose and fine finish applications, stain is used to alter the colour of wood and to accent grain and texture. A transparent topcoat is applied to seal the surface.

9

Protecting and Finishing Wood

Figure 9.6
General Composition of Wood Coatings

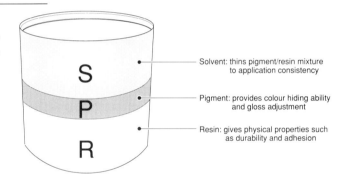

Solvent: thins pigment/resin mixture to application consistency

Pigment: provides colour hiding ability and gloss adjustment

Resin: gives physical properties such as durability and adhesion

Paint
• Used to colour and protect wood in interior and exterior applications
• Contains pigment for colour
• Two basic types: alkyd (oil based) and latex (water based)
• Resin adjustment gives special properties to suit interior or exterior applications
• Primers and sanding sealers are types of paints

Varnish
• Used to provide clear protective coating, mostly for interior applications
• Polyurethane is the most common resin for interior use and is marketed under several tradenames
• Alkyd varnish is used for exterior applications and contains an ultra-violet inhibitor
• Some new polyurethane varnishes are water reducible
• Pigment is lacking in varnish, or if present, is used to control gloss for interior varnish and to inhibit ultra-violet light penetration

Stain
• Used to colour interior wood and to colour and protect exterior wood
• General purpose stains may be alkyd or latex resin based
• Special stains are made for fine finishing and may be mineral spirit or water based

Lacquer
• Used in fine finishing to protect and topcoat wood
• Main types are standard, catalyzed, and acrylic lacquer
• Solvent may be petrochemical or water based

Lacquer
Lacquer is a fast drying protective topcoating used for fine finishing of architectural woodwork and furniture. It is normally used as a transparent finish, like varnish, to display the wood grain, but it is also available in solid colours.

Alkyd and Latex Coatings
Most paints, varnishes, and stains used for the interior and exterior protection of wood walls, trim, and other general purposes can be categorized generally as having either an alkyd or a latex resin base.

Alkyd Coatings
Alkyd resins or so-called oil resins are used for the manufacture of general purpose paint, varnish, and stain.

Early oil paints used linseed oil as the resin and mineral spirits as the solvent. They were soft and slow drying as a consequence.

Oil paint was developed which used alkyd blended with linseed oil as the resin. Alkyd formulations dry faster, have better durability relative to early oil paints, and retain most of the flexibility of the soft early oil paints. Polyurethane resins may also be blended with alkyd to produce polyurethane paints, or polyurethane alone may be used as the resin.

Alkyd paints containing a large amount of linseed oil give paint flexibility properties which are important for use as exterior primers and paints.

Increasing the amount of alkyd while reducing the amount of linseed oil, results in a hard interior/exterior enamel desirable for high wear surfaces. Mixing alkyd and polyurethane resins increases the hardness further, giving a polyurethane enamel. Enamel is a paint having a high degree of durability and therefore a fairly high gloss level.

Latex Coatings
Latex formulations contain latex as the resin, water as the solvent, and pigments, such as titanium dioxide, extender pigments, and colour pigments similar to those found in alkyd paints.

Latex is used as the resin for paint, varnish, and solid stains, but not for semi-transparent stains.

Latex resin is comprised of small spheres of plastic material suspended in the water solvent. As the paint dries, the spheres coalesce to form a film that covers the painted surface.

The amount of resistance the finished surface has to abrasion by wear and scrubbing is dependant upon the extent to which the pigment is covered by latex. As the latex resin content increases relative to the pigment, the durability increases but the hiding power of the coating to conceal subsurface irregularities decreases.

Latex resin becomes hard when cooled. Therefore proper application and initial cure temperature of at least 10°C (50°F) is essential to the formation of a strong film.

Exterior and interior latex coatings differ in the type of latex used for the resin. Acrylic latex is the most used resin for exterior products. More economical latex resin called PVA is commonly used for interior applications. For high quality interior paint, a blend of PVA and acrylic, or straight acrylic is used.

Acrylic has better adhesion qualities than PVA. Acrylic latex paint would therefore bond better to an alkyd paint than would a PVA resin latex.

Comparison of Alkyd and Latex Coatings
Most alkyd paints contain some vegetable oils such as linseed oil that have a tendency to yellow over time. Because latex coatings do not contain any oil, they have better gloss and colour retention.

Latex coatings dry faster and give off less noxious odour than alkyd coatings, and cleanup is effected with water rather than the spirit or oil based solvents used with alkyd paints.

Acrylic latex paints have better gloss and colour retention than alkyd paints. Flat latex paint tends to be more durable on exterior surfaces than alkyd finishes because the latex is permeable and allows the moisture content of wood to adjust rather than blister the paint. However this is not the case for gloss latex paints which have a permeability similar to alkyds.

Alkyd coatings are still preferred for trim such as doors, door frames, and baseboards because they are harder, and flow better thereby leaving fewer brush marks than latex coatings.

The primary differences between alkyd and latex coatings are summarized in the Table below.

Because latex coatings are so much more acceptable to the environment when compared to oil based products, it is expected that their use will continue to increase. Continuing research and development will lead to latex coatings which match or exceed in all respects the performance of alkyd based coatings.

Application
Proper surface preparation is essential to a successful coating finish.

Whether the application is commercial or residential, the application temperature is critical. In general, coatings should be applied at temperatures above 10°C (50°F) to surfaces which are dry, clean, and dust free.

Alkyd paints applied at temperatures lower than 10°C (50°F) dry slowly. Therefore the surface is left vulnerable to accumulate airborne dust. If made wet before drying, alkyd paint may lose its gloss.

For latex paint, proper film formation will not take place at low application temperatures. The paint will dry but film formation will not have taken place, reducing adhesion and durability, and giving poor adhesion to the subsequent coat. This could result in peeling at a later date.

Exterior Coatings

The durability of exterior coatings is dependent on the ability of the coating to permit the movement of moisture and in so doing avoid blistering. It is also dependent on the ability of the coating to exclude the ultra-violet portion of sunlight which causes the coating to deteriorate.

Pigmented coatings resist ultra-violet light penetration and endure better than unpigmented coatings. Figure 9.7 (→ 454) shows the expected service life of exterior coatings and the effect of pigment content.

Some typical exterior wood finishes are shown in the Table on page 454.

Wood products treated with water borne wood preservatives can be coated using the same products and techniques as for untreated materials. As for all wood products used for exterior applications, performance will be best if the moisture content of the material is less than 19 percent (S-Dry).

Products
Paint
Primers are used as a first coat on new exterior wood surfaces to ensure adhesion between wood and topcoats. Primers are available in alkyd or latex formulations to condition new wood to accept the finish coats.

9

Protecting and Finishing Wood

Comparison of Alkyd and Latex Coatings	Latex	Alkyd
	Better colour and gloss retention	Better adhesion to previously painted surfaces
	Better exterior durability	Better abrasion resistance
	Fast dry and short recoat interlude	Better flow and levelling properties (fewer brush and roller marks)
	Water clean-up	Better resistance to mildew
	Less odour and very low solvent emissions	Clean-up with solvents

Figure 9.7
Lasting Ability of Exterior Coatings

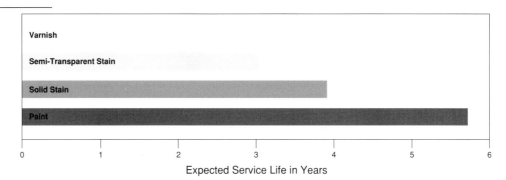

Varnish

Semi-Transparent Stain

Solid Stain

Paint

0   1   2   3   4   5   6

Expected Service Life in Years

Typical Exterior Coating Applications

Type of Coating	Application	Primer	Topcoat	Notes
Paint (latex)	Walls & vertical surfaces	1 coat alkyd or latex primer	2 coats latex	
	Horizontal surfaces		2 coats alkyd enamel	
Varnish	All surfaces	(stain if desired)	5 coats varnish	high maintenance requirement
Stain (solid hide)	Vertical surfaces only	1 coat stain (alkyd or latex)	1 coat stain (alkyd or latex)	
Stain (semi-transparent)	All surfaces		1 coat stain (alkyd)	

Gloss Levels for Exterior Paint

Type	Gloss
Alkyd Paint:	Gloss and semi-gloss
Latex Paint:	Gloss, semi-gloss, satin, and flat

If a painted surface is desired, it is important that primers be applied to new wood as quickly as possible after installation. As the wood weathers, it takes on a grey appearance. This grey patina can seriously affect adhesion of paint and must be removed by sanding before priming takes place.

Exterior finish coats are available in alkyd and latex products. Alkyd paints perform better than latex on doors and trim whereas latex paints have superior gloss and colour retention on siding.

Exterior alkyds differ from interior alkyds in that they contain a higher level of vegetable oil (soya or linseed) which makes them softer and more flexible for use on wood siding. As wood takes on or loses moisture dimensional changes occur and the coating must be able to move with the wood.

Exterior paints are available in several gloss levels for both alkyd and latex paints. These are shown in the Table above.

The satin and flat latex paints are more permeable to moisture than the alkyd and high gloss exterior latex paints and therefore blister less.

Varnish
The most common varnish made for exterior use is alkyd resin based.

It contains some extender pigment in the form of a screening agent which is capable of eliminating some ultra-violet light infiltration, but contains no colour pigment.

The pigment is not capable of excluding all ultra-violet light. The light which does penetrate breaks down the varnish resin and the rate of degradation increases with time. As the varnish deteriorates, the gloss fades.

Once the gloss of an exterior varnish has diminished to a semi-gloss level, sanding and recoating should take place. If degradation is allowed to proceed, the coating will crack and fail and complete removal, surface sanding, and replacement will be required.

As a result, exterior grade varnishes are high maintenance finishes requiring four to five initial coats and an annual new coat.

Exterior varnish (spar varnish) is available only in high gloss.

Surface dirt impedes the ability of the gloss finish to reflect light. Therefore, good maintenance practice includes keeping exterior varnish surfaces clean to extend the service life of exterior varnish.

Stain
Stains for exterior applications are available in a wide variety of colours and formulations. Exterior stains are available as solid stains (alkyd and latex) and semi-transparent stains (alkyd only).

Solid hide stains, due to additional pigmentation, give better protection but hide the grain pattern while allowing the texture of the wood to show through. Solid hide latex stains have much better colour retention than solid hide solvent based products but do not perform well on horizontal surfaces such as decks.

Semi-transparent stains offer some protection to the wood and a considerable amount of grain show-through.

Interior Coatings – General Purpose

Paint, varnish, and stain are used on trim and flooring for general purpose interior applications. For interior applications, the first coat is called the undercoat, and the finish coat is called the topcoat. Some typical general purpose interior finishes are shown in the Table below.

The difference between an interior general purpose finish and a fine finish may at times be subtle. A section for fine finishes follows (→ 457), to outline some products and techniques for architectural woodwork quality finishing.

9

Protecting and Finishing Wood

Typical Interior – General Purpose Coating Applications	Type of Coating	Application	Special Treatment	Undercoat	Topcoat	Notes
	Paint	Woodwork and trim		1 coat alkyd	2 coats alkyd	2 coats alkyd is typical
	Varnish	General purpose	Stain if desired		3 coats polyurethane	
		Hardwood and softwood flooring	Stain if desired	1 coat polyurethane diluted 20%	2 coats polyurethane	
		Gymnasium floor	Stain if desired	1 coat polyurethane diluted 20%	1 coat polyurethane, line painting, 2 coats polyurethane	
	Lacquer	Non-wearing surfaces	Stain if desired, sanding sealer		2 coats lacquer	Spray application

Products

Paint

Interior trim should be undercoated prior to application of the topcoats. Undercoats are alkyd paint coatings designed for use as a first coat on new wood for interior applications where a painted surface is required. Undercoats are formulated to seal the wood surface but are soft enough to allow easy sanding in preparation for topcoating with alkyd or latex products.

Alkyd sanding sealers are alkyd paint coatings used as a preparation coat for a clear alkyd varnish. Like undercoats, sanding sealers allow smooth sanding but differ from undercoats in that they contain no hiding pigment.

Alkyd sanding sealers are not compatible with polyurethane products which perform so well on floors. Therefore sanding sealers are used mostly as a preparation coat on vertical surfaces.

Topcoats for interior use are available in several gloss levels (see Table below).

The best topcoats for wood trim are eggshell, semi-gloss and gloss products in either alkyd or latex formulations. For high wear areas such as doors, alkyd topcoats are superior to latex for the following reasons:

- Better adhesion to previously painted surfaces

- Better flow and levelling properties (fewer brush marks)

- Better abrasion resistance

Varnish

Varnish, like lacquer, is used in interior applications where a transparent finish accentuating wood grain is desired.

Varnish can be used as a general purpose coating for large areas like hardwood floors. It may also be used as a topcoat for the fine finishing of architectural woodwork.

Varnish for interior applications is available in three gloss levels for interior use: gloss, satin and flat.

Gloss varnish is a coating with resin and solvent, but without pigment. To reduce gloss, flat and satin varnishes contain some inert extender pigments which are transparent when the varnish dries.

Alkyd and latex varnish can be placed over a sanding sealer but a polyurethane varnish cannot. Preparation for polyurethane is usually made by diluting the first coat 20 percent with mineral spirits to gain additional penetration.

Polyurethane varnish is highly recommended for floors because of its hardness and resistance to abrasion.

Stain

Stains applied to interior wood products are usually the first step in a finishing system and give colour to the wood. Interior stains contain a lot of solvent and penetrate into the wood surface.

Interior stains are the transparent type that allow the beauty of the wood grain to show through. Stains are made using several types of solvents, including water. More information on specialized stains for architectural woodwork is found in Interior Coatings – Fine Finishes (→ 457).

Care must always be exercised to ensure the stain used will be compatible with the topcoats which follow. It is recommended that stain and topcoats be applied to samples to ascertain final appearance.

Gloss Levels for Interior Paint	Type	Gloss
	Alkyd Paint	Gloss, semi-gloss, eggshell, and flat
	Latex Paint	Gloss, semi-gloss, eggshell, satin, and flat

Note:
The terms velvet and pearl are sometimes used to describe satin.

Lacquer

Lacquer is a fast drying topcoat. It is usually used for fine finishing and therefore is covered in detail later in this section.

Interior Coatings – Fine Finishes

Fine finishing differs from general purpose finishing in the amount of surface sanding and filling performed, the quality of the topcoats applied and the degree of workmanship. Fine finishes are applied to surfaces where a very high quality appearance is required.

For wood products used as decorative materials, this usually means that a transparent finish is required so that the unique texture and grain of wood are displayed. Fine finishes are applied to softwood and hardwood solid and panel wood materials for architectural woodwork such as panelling, doors and windows, and casework, and for furniture.

The Table below shows the finishing qualities of some woods used frequently for architectural woodwork.

Depending on the nature of the project, fine finishing of architectural woodwork may be done on site or it may be done in a shop, with final touch-up only on site.

A fine finish is comprised of stain (where desired), wood filler (where required), sanding sealer, and topcoats. It is important that the finisher select products for these functions which are chemically compatible with each other.

9

Protecting and Finishing Wood

Coating Qualities of Various Wood Species

Name	Relative Surface Hardness	Grain	Finish
Ash	Hard	Open	Filler recommended
Alder	Soft	Close	Stains well
Aspen	Soft	Close	Paints well
Basswood	Soft	Close	Paints well
Beech	Hard	Close	Poor for paint, takes varnish well
Birch	Hard	Close	Stains and varnishes well
Cedar	Soft	Close	Paints well. Finishes well with varnish
Cherry	Hard	Close	Takes all finishes well
Chestnut	Hard	Open	Filler recommended. Not suitable for paint finish
Cottonwood	Soft	Close	Good for paint finish
Cypress	Hard	Close	Takes paint or varnish well
Elm	Hard	Open	Filler recommended. Not suitable for paint finish
Fir	Soft	Close	Can be painted, stained or left natural
Gum	Soft	Close	Can be finished with variety of finishes
Hemlock	Soft	Close	Paints fairly well
Hickory	Hard	Open	Filler recommended
Mahogany	Hard	Open	Filler recommended. Takes all finishes well
Maple	Hard	Close	Takes any type finish
Oak	Hard	Open	Filler recommended
Pine	Soft	Close	Takes any type finish
Spruce	Soft	Close	Can be painted, stained or left natural
Teak	Hard	Open	Filler recommended
Walnut	Hard	Open	Filler recommended. Takes all finishes well

Notes:
1. Open grain is associated with varying pore sizes between springwood and summerwood.
2. Close grain is associated with woods having overall uniform pore sizes.

Fine finishing usually involves the provision of hand samples by the finisher to the specifier for advance approval of colour, tone, and gloss characteristics for the species of wood specified.

Fine finishing is a complex topic with a vast variety of products and methods. Some of the most common and straightforward techniques are listed in the Table below. For more detailed information, the reader is advised to consult a reputable architectural woodwork specialist or contact the technical associations in Canada and the US which specialize in architectural woodwork (see Information Sources).

In sequence of application, fine finishing usually involves filler (optional), stain, sanding sealer, and topcoats.

Preparation

Proper sanding is crucial to fine finishing. Effort spent staining, finishing, and rubbing may be disappointing unless the surface has been properly prepared. All finish sanding should be with the grain. Only by sanding with the grain can maximum smoothing be achieved with minimum waste of wood and effort.

Products

While some of the stains and polyurethanes used for general finishing are also used for fine finishing, there are other products such as filler, stain, sanding sealer, and lacquer which are used specifically for architectural finishes. These are described here in more detail.

Fillers

The physical structure of hardwoods differs from that of softwoods. Sap conveying vessels in hardwoods appear as pores in sawn lumber.

The sizes of the pores in wood vary between species as shown in the Table on page 457. In hardwoods such as oak, chestnut and ash, there is a great difference in the pores of summerwood and springwood. Species having this variety of pore size are said to open grained. Species having small uniform sized pores are said to be close grained.

Examples of woods with close grain and tight pores are maple, birch, cherry and pine. Examples of woods with open grain are walnut, oak, elm and ash.

Close grain woods do not usually require a filler, even if a varnish is used. Open grain woods required to have a smooth varnish or lacquer finish should be filled with a wood paste filler.

When a filler is used, it can be mixed with stain so that its colour will match the wood. The filling and staining is then done simultaneously.

Wood flooring, which was discussed as a general purpose application, is not usually filled. Varnish used alone produces a good finish on hardwood floors.

Stain

Stains used in the finishing of architectural woodwork are: pigmented wiping stains, and non-grain raising (NGR) stains.

Typical Interior – Fine Finish Coating Applications	Type of Coating	Application	Special Treatment	Undercoat	Topcoat	Notes
	Varnish	For high quality applications	Stain or stained filler if required	1 coat polyurethane diluted 20%	2 coats polyurethane	Use filler for open grain woods
	Lacquer	For high quality applications	Oil stain or stained filler if required		2 coats standard or catalyzed lacquer	Use filler for open grained woods

Note:
For detailed information on fine finishing refer to:
1. Architectural Woodwork Manufacturers Association of Canada
2. Architectural Woodwork Institute (US)
   (see Information Sources)

The species of wood, the desired undertone colour, the desired artistic effect, the filler and the selected topcoat are the considerations which affect the selection of the appropriate type of stain.

The staining of open pore woods is quite different from the staining of close pore woods. A greater amount of stain will be accepted into open pore woods and can result in mottled appearance. Fillers, less concentrated stain solution, and fast removal of excess stain by wiping can be used to ensure uniform staining for open grain woods.

Pigmented wiping stains, often called oil stains, are probably the most versatile stains available. They can be applied by any method, including spraying or dipping. They are known also as uniforming stains because they must be wiped or uniformed for best results. The colour is supplied by a pigment. Depending on the nature of this pigment, some long-lasting results can be achieved.

Penetrating dye stains are liquid dye stains, applied by brush, spray or cloth. The transparency of these stains emphasizes the natural beauty of hardwoods and softwoods. They may have a base of alcohol, water, lacquer or oil.

Sanding Sealers
A sanding sealer is a product applied by spray or brush after the wood has been stained, or stained and filled. It is applied to seal the minute pores of the wood, seal in the filler, seal the stain, facilitate sanding, and form a bond between the wood and the following coats.

Both alkyd and lacquer sanding sealers are manufactured. They should be used with a topcoat which is chemically compatible with the sealers.

Topcoats
Lacquer: Lacquers are fast drying, high quality coatings used for architectural woodwork such as wall panelling. The furniture manufacturing industry makes extensive use of lacquer.

Lacquer is usually used as a clear finish to amplify the grain and texture of fine woods. Clear gloss lacquer does not contain pigment, and satin lacquers have inert extender pigments for gloss adjustment.

The two main types of lacquer are standard and catalyzed.

Standard lacquer uses nitrocellulose as the resin. Nitrocellulose may be modified with other resins and plasticizers to enhance durability. It can be obtained in several different gloss levels. It has good resistance to rapid temperature change but little or no water resistance, or chemical resistance to household and reagent type chemicals. It dries very quickly and is relatively easy to repair if damaged.

Catalyzed lacquer contains some nitrocellulose, but it is modified with a converting resin and other plasticizing modifiers. The performance and chemical resistance properties of this product are superior to standard lacquer. It dries very quickly, is relatively easy to repair if damaged and is used where exposure to wetting or high humidity is a possibility.

A third type of lacquer, acrylic lacquer, which is water reducible, has been available for some time. Water solvent lacquers are more benign to the environment than the non-water solvent types. The technology for water solvent lacquer is still evolving and performance has not yet matched that of the standard and catalyzed lacquers.

Lacquers harden by evaporation of highly volatile solvent. The typical dry to touch time for standard and catalyzed lacquer is ten minutes. The water solvent lacquers have a dry-to-touch time of about thirty minutes.

Lacquer dries much faster than varnish and several coats can be applied in rapid succession. This very fast drying time reduces the chances of dust contamination during drying. The stains, and sanding sealers made especially for lacquer finishes are also fast drying.

9

Protecting and Finishing Wood

Lacquer darkens wood the least of all the topcoat finishes but it is not as durable as varnish and not as resistant to water.

Pigmented lacquers are solid coloured coatings, like paint, but they exhibit the fast drying characteristics of lacquer. Pigmented lacquers are also known as lacquer enamels and are used whenever a solid colour finish is desired. Manufactured in a variety of colours and sheens, they may be intermixed to create other shades or colours, and can be matched to paint colour numbers.

A primer surfacer is used as sanding primer where a solid colour lacquer (pigmented) topcoat will be applied.

Lacquer is applied best under shop conditions where specialized equipment for application, and an environment which controls dust and provides ventilation for worker safety, are present. Site touch-up is possible but must be done carefully to ensure a good product and safety for building occupants.

Varnish: The varnishes suitable for general purpose finishes are also used in the fine finishing of architectural woodwork.

Varnish is slower drying than lacquer, with overnight drying between coats usually required. The slower drying time increases the risk of dust settling on the surface. Varnish, particularly the polyurethane varnishes, provides a harder surface than lacquer and is more resistant to water drip marking and alcohol.

Oils: Tung oil and Danish oil are sometimes used for natural finishing but they do not provide a great deal of protection and they are susceptible to water marking and washout. Oils have for the most part been replaced by lacquer and varnish.

Wax: Wax may be used over the topcoat to adjust gloss and to provide a wearing surface. If applied directly to wood having no topcoat, it eliminates the ability to apply a topcoat at a later date.

General Guidelines for Coatings

General

- Moisture content of wood surface should be below 12 to 14 percent.

- Surface must be clean and dry to ensure proper adhesion. Without good adhesion, qualities such as durability will be diminished.

- Knots and pitch streaks should be treated with a knot sealer or shellac before the finish is applied to prevent the wood resins from bleeding through the topcoat.

- Recoating: Alkyds can be placed over top of latex coatings. Latex does not adhere well to an alkyd surface, especially in a damp environment and if the alkyd is glossy. However, a flat latex will perform adequately over a flat alkyd.

- Flat finishes (latex and alkyd) mar easily but conceal surface defects well and are suited for ceilings and low traffic areas.

- Satin finishes (latex only) are more washable than flat finishes and are suitable for use on walls and ceilings and moderate traffic areas.

- Eggshell finishes (alkyd or latex) wash well, have good resistance to burnishing (especially alkyds), and have a low enough sheen to minimize most surface defects. They are excellent paints for walls in commercial and residential applications.

- Semi-gloss (alkyd or latex) enamels are durable coatings which are the standard for doors, frames and trim.

- Gloss finishes (alkyd or latex) are used in areas of heavy wear and heavy traffic, such as walls in manufacturing plants or entrance doors on most buildings.

Exterior
- Softwood products are used extensively on exterior surfaces. Generally, the lowest density softwoods, such as cedar, hold finishes best.

- Prefinished wood products are available with factory applied decorative finishes which use spray or pressure treatment. The major advantages are quality control, controlled application conditions, and long service life of the product.

- For new wood surfaces, use an exterior wood primer in alkyd or latex prior to the finish coat.

- CCA pressure treated lumber must be permitted to season after the application of water borne preservative, before coating with alkyd or latex products.

- Use a polyurethane floor enamel for painted walk areas such as decks.

- Do not use latex stains on horizontal surfaces such as decks. Latex stains used on deck surfaces do not penetrate and the stain will wear through very quickly. Use semi-transparent alkyd stain to penetrate the wood and let the beauty of the wood show through.

- Stain is superior to paint for fencing because there is so much exposed end grain which acquires and loses water readily. Stain protects while allowing movement to take place, thus avoiding peeling.

- For vertical surfaces, solid hide latex stain will last longer than solid hide alkyd stain. It will not last as long as paint which provides a heavier layer.

- Glulam is usually factory sealed. It may be stained and coated like other wood products. Refer to Section 3.3 for information on appearance grades of glulam.

- Plywood edges should be sealed with a coat of exterior primer, or aluminum-based paint. Plywood faces should be primed and topcoated with at least one coat of paint.

- A heavy stain should be used when a stained finish is desired for plywood. A recoat should be applied after the first six months of service. (Prestained specialty plywood siding products in a variety of colours are available from some manufacturers (see Section 7)).

Interior – General Purpose
- Interior trim: An alkyd semi-gloss has better durability than a latex semi-gloss and leaves fewer brush marks.

- Floors: Polyurethane coatings give good wear-resistant coating for wood flooring.

Interior – Fine Finishes
- For hardwood and softwood plywood and solid wood mouldings, request hand samples demonstrating colour and texture resulting from the effect of filler, sealer, stain, and topcoats.

References

Canadian Woods: Their Properties and Uses, E.J. Mullins and T.S. McNight, University of Toronto Press, 1981

Complete Book of Wood Finishing, Robert Scharff, McGraw-Hill, 1974

Paint Handbook, Guy E. Weismantel, McGraw Hill, 1981

Quality Standards for Architectural Woodwork, Architectural Woodwork Manufacturers Association of Canada, 1991 (see Information Sources)

Fine Finishing, Architectural Woodwork Institute, (see Information Sources), 1989

Architectural Woodwork Quality Standards, Guide Specifications and Quality Certification, Architectural Woodwork Institute, (see Information Sources), 1989

9

Protecting and Finishing Wood

9.4   Preservative-Treated Wood

Preservative-treated wood is wood which has been surface coated or impregnated by means of pressure with chemicals which improve resistance to damage from decay and insect attack.

Preservative-treatment processes do not alter the basic characteristics of wood but do provide much improved service life for wood building materials in severe service conditions.

For a wood preservative to function effectively it must be applied under controlled conditions, to specifications known to ensure that the preserved wood will perform in service. The Canadian Standards Association (CSA) publishes a wood preserving standard containing these specifications. *CSA Standard O80-M Wood Preservation* gives detailed requirements which are particular to Canadian wood species and also adopts certain standards of the American Wood-Preservers' Association (AWPA).

The ease by which a species can be treated is a function of the cell biology and the process used. Canada has an abundant variety of wood species. Some species are more difficult to pressure-treat than others.

Process

Most preservative-treatments are applied using the full-cell pressure method by which wood is placed in a pressure vessel and a vacuum is applied to draw air from the wood cells. The preservative solution is admitted to the cylinder and is first drawn into the cells by the vacuum. Then pressure of 690 to 1380 kPa (100 to 200 psi) is applied to force additional preservative into the wood as shown in Figure 9.8 (→ 464). A final vacuum is then applied to remove excess surface chemical.

For all types of preservative-treatment, the quantity of preservative which can be forced into the cells and be retained depends in part upon the moisture content of the wood. The amount of water present in the cell cavities at the time of treatment influences the influx of preservative.

For this reason, the moisture content of the raw wood material is an important aspect of quality control.

For waterborne preservatives (see Types of Preservatives → 465), the moisture content of lumber to be treated should be in the low (15 to 25 percent) range to permit easy entry of preservative, and chemical reaction with the cell wall. If there is excess cell water present, rebound pressure will have the effect of expelling preservative from the cells once the process pressure abates.

In order to enhance the penetration of wood preservatives, the moisture content of the wood is reduced by a conditioning process. This can be achieved by air-seasoning, kiln drying, or by a process carried out in the treatment cylinder for example by the application of steam and subsequent vacuum, or by boiling under a vacuum in the presence of the treating solution.

To avoid release of excess chemical after treatment, time should be allowed at the place of manufacture for the fixation of chemical into the wood cell walls to take place. Once the set period has finished, the waterborne preservative is chemically affixed to the cell walls.

Retention of Preservative

Retention, usually expressed as kilograms of preservative per cubic metre of wood (pounds per cubic foot), is the amount of preservative retained in the wood after completion of the treating cycle and is one measure of the degree of protection provided.

Plywood can be penetrated by preservatives more readily than solid wood of the same species because the veneer cutting process opens the wood grain. These minute fissures are hard to detect with the naked eye but are readily penetrated by preservative under pressure.

9

Protecting and Finishing Wood

Figure 9.8
**Manufacture of
Pressure-
Treated Wood**

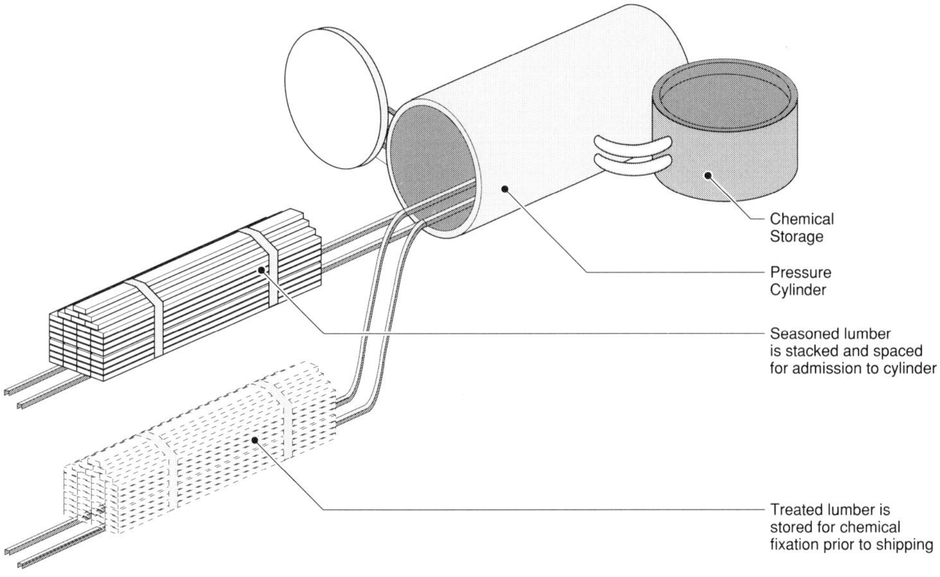

Chemical
Storage

Pressure
Cylinder

Seasoned lumber
is stacked and spaced
for admission to cylinder

Treated lumber is
stored for chemical
fixation prior to shipping

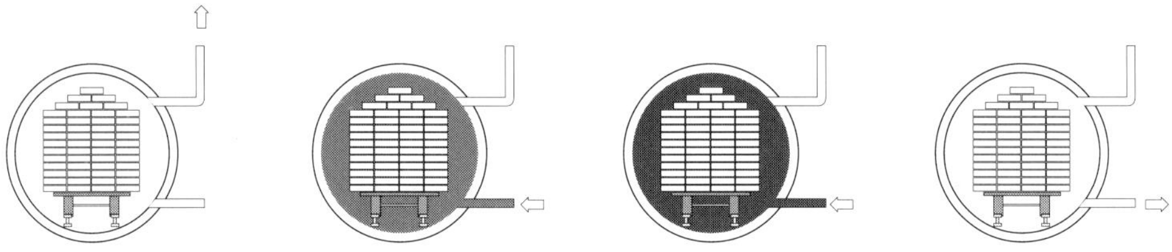

Lumber is loaded,
cylinder is sealed and
a vacuum is applied.

Cylinder is filled
with chemical

Pressure is applied

Cylinder is drained
and lumber is removed

Figure 9.9
**Cross Section
of Preservative
Treated
Lumber**

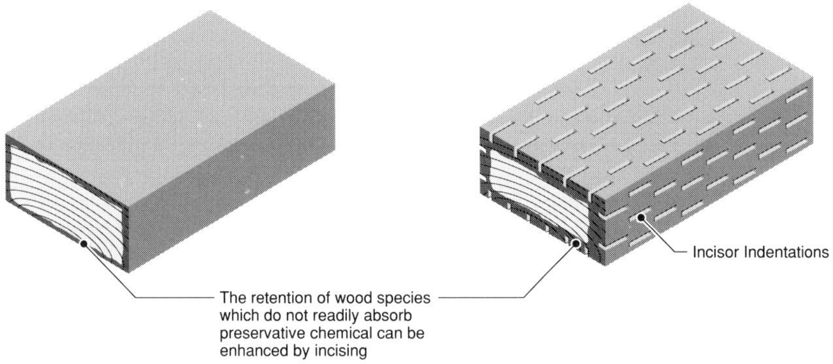

Incisor Indentations

The retention of wood species
which do not readily absorb
preservative chemical can be
enhanced by incising

Non-Incised Lumber   Incised Lumber

Penetration of Preservative

Penetration is the depth to which preservative chemicals are forced into the wood. It is an indication of the amount of protection provided. The amount of penetration is determined by the qualities of the species and the treating process. The greater the depth of penetration, the less likely it is that the protected boundary of pressure-treated wood will be breached.

In some cases the penetration of chemical can be improved by incising the surfaces of lumber with knives to create artificial openings through which chemical preservative can enter the wood (see Figure 9.9 opposite). With new incising technology the appearance of a board is not substantially altered by incising.

Types of Preservatives

Preservatives may be classified broadly into three groups:

1. Waterborne inorganic compounds are water soluble chemicals used to protect against insects and decay. The water evaporates leaving the chemical affixed to the wood cell walls.

2. Creosote or creosote solutions are oil-based distillates of coal tar used to protect against insects and decay. Creosote occupies the cell cavities of wood fibre.

3. Oilborne chemicals are organic chemicals dissolved in a suitable petroleum oil carrier. They are used to protect against insects and decay. These chemicals occupy the cell cavities of wood fibre.

Waterborne Preservative
There are two types of waterborne preservatives in current use. The most common one is chromated copper arsenate (CCA) which is easily identified by the green coloration it imparts to wood (brown coloured formulations are also available). The other is ammoniacal copper arsenate (ACA).

Both these chemicals are mixtures of stable metal oxides dissolved in water. CCA is an aqueous solution of copper, chrome, and arsenic while ACA is an aqueous solution of copper arsenate and ammonium hydroxide.

Copper acts as a fungicide to give the chemicals resistance to decay. The arsenate is toxic to wood destroying insects such as termites.

CCA and ACA affix chemically to the wood fibre by uniting with wood sugars to render wood unsuitable as food to insects and fungi. The copper in the preservative also deters the formation of moss on the treated wood surface in damp climates.

CCA and ACA treated wood do not release excess chemical when properly treated and produce a clean dry surface, which is odourless.

The treating process does not obscure the natural grain of the wood. Treated surfaces may be stained or painted. Treated wood can also be left uncoated, in which case it will acquire a driftwood grey colour.

Creosote
Creosote is a distillate of coal tar produced by the high temperature carbonization of bituminous coal. Creosote is primarily composed of liquid and solid aromatic hydrocarbons as well as some tar acids and tar bases, which provide protection against destructive insects and organisms. It is not often used in building construction.

Oilborne Preservative
Pentachlorophenol, or penta, is the normally used oilborne preservative. Penta pressure-treated wood is highly resistant to fungi and insect attack, but because of its petroleum base, is not usually associated with building construction. It is used as a preservative for applications such as utility poles.

9

Protecting and Finishing Wood

Finishing

Wood pressure-treated with waterborne preservatives may be painted or stained provided the moisture content after treating is reduced to at least 20 percent. The colour imparted to the wood by the preservative may affect the final shade of any stains used.

Wood that has been treated with creosote, creosote solutions or oilborne preservatives cannot be stained successfully, or painted.

Water-repellent preservative finishes contain waxes, oils, resins, preservatives and, sometimes, pigments. The waxes, oils and resins make the wood surface repellent to water while the preservatives impart mildew and decay resistance to the wood. Pigments add colour and protect the wood surfaces from destruction by ultra-violet light. Finish life is related to the pigmentation and ranges from two to four years. One application of a preservative finish is usually sufficient. Maintenance is simple. The surface is cleaned and washed before a new coat of finish is applied.

Applications

The waterborne preservatives are the chemicals most used for building construction. These chemicals are used to provide protection for plywood, parallel strand lumber (PSL), glulam, dimension lumber and timbers used for wood foundations, roofing accessories, facias and soffits, structural members in exposed locations,

and for any other building application where wood is exposed to damaging conditions, including landscape features.

Creosote and oilborne preservative-treated wood products are not usually associated with building construction because of odour and appearance but rather find use in heavy industrial applications such as in dock and railroad construction.

Effect of Preservatives on Wood Strength

Acid salts can lessen the strength of wood if they are present in large concentrations. The concentrations used in preservative-treatments of wood are sufficiently small so that they do not affect the strength properties under normal use conditions.

However, engineering codes require that a slight reduction in engineering properties be made to account for loss of strength and stiffness due to incising of pressure-treated wood.

Field Cutting

In preparing a project specification, it is advisable to have all the wood pieces sized, drilled, notched and trimmed to finish dimensions, prior to pressure-treating. Should field fabrication be unavoidable, adequate field treatment of all exposed surfaces must be performed, using an acceptable brush-on preservative, to restore the integrity of the preservative-treatment.

Figure 9.10
Facsimile of Canadian Wood Preservers Bureau Stamp

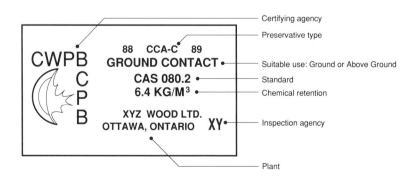

Handling Practices for Preservative-Treated Wood

- Wear gloves when handling preservative-treated wood to avoid direct skin contact.

- Avoid frequent or prolonged inhalation of sawdust from treated wood by wearing a mask or by performing cutting operations outdoors.

- When power-sawing and machining, wear goggles to protect eyes from flying particles.

- Wash exposed areas thoroughly after skin contact, and before eating or drinking.

- Do not dispose of treated wood by burning.

- Treated wood used for patios, decks, and walkways should be free of surface preservative residues.

Quality Control

Canadian preservative-treated wood is manufactured to CSA standards. To ensure that the specified degree of protection will be provided by a product, it should bear a quality assurance grade stamp (see Figure 9.10 opposite). The stamp indicates that the product meets standards for retention and penetration, and that wood moisture content at the time of treatment was conducive to acceptance of chemical preservative.

General Guidelines for Preservative-Treated Wood

- Use preservative-treated wood for damp conditions especially in proximity to the ground and where insect attack is a risk.

- Minimize the field cuts after pressure-treatment. Apply two coats of preservative-treatment to protect field cuts.

- Verify that the chemical retention specified for a project is delivered to the jobsite.

References

Wood Preservation, Canadian Institute of Treated Wood, 1990

Treated Wood Guidelines, Canadian Institute of Treated Wood, 1990

Waterborne Wood Preservatives, Canadian Institute of Treated Wood, 1990

Wood Design Manual, Canadian Wood Council, 1990

9

Protecting and Finishing Wood

9.5 Fire-Retardant Treatment and Coating

Introduction

Where flame-spread ratings of 75 or less are stipulated in building codes, most lumber and plywood must be treated or coated to reduce flame spread over the surface of the material. The two most common methods of reducing the flame-spread rating are by pressure-impregnation with water-borne salts and by surface coating with fire-retardant chemicals.

This section describes the chemical means used to reduce flame spread on wood products. For detailed information on the importance of flame-spread rating to building construction, refer to Section 10.

Fire-Retardant Treated Lumber and Plywood

Fire-retardant treated wood (FRTW) is material which has been pressure impregnated with special chemicals which improve the performance of wood products in a fire. The pressure-treating process for injecting fire-retardant chemicals into wood and plywood products is essentially the same as that for preservative-treatment as shown in Figure 9.8 (→ 464).

Fire-retardant chemical treatments retard the spread of flame and limit smoke production from wood in fire situations. FRTW can meet the most restrictive requirements for flame-spread rating and smoke developed-classification in the North American building codes.

Fire-retardant treatment of wood enhances the fire performance of the products by reducing the amount of heat released during the initial stages of fire. The treatments also reduce the amount of flammable volatiles released during fire exposure. This results in a reduction in the rate of flame spread over the surface. When the flame source is removed, treated wood ceases to char.

During a fire, fire-retardant chemicals begin to react when temperatures reach a point slightly below the point where wood will ignite. Nonflammable gases and water vapour are formed and released at a slow steady rate thereby insulating the wood fibres from temperatures that would cause them to burn.

To be an acceptable fire-retardant treated product in Canadian jurisdictions, wood products must be labelled by an accredited testing agency, such as Underwriters' Laboratories of Canada. A sample label is shown in Figure 9.11 (→ 470). In the US, similar labelling and certification requirements apply.

FRTW is suitable for indoor applications where the humidity is not expected to exceed 60 percent for long periods of time. FRTW should be protected from excessive moisture and weather during transit, storage, and erection. While some wetting might be expected during installation, frequent wetting or ponding is unacceptable. In general, FRTW requires more care in installation than would normally be considered good practice for non-FRTW products.

FRTW products are used in many interior applications, such as millwork and panelling, where the code requirements for flame spread are most restrictive. The building codes of North America also permit the use of fire-retardant treated lumber and plywood for roof and floor trusses, beams, interior roof decks, and for interior load-bearing and non-load bearing partitions.

FRTW is generally restricted to interior use because of the possibility that the protective salts will leach out of the materials if they are exposed to the weather. For exterior applications where codes specifically require FRTW products, exterior grade treatments are available for wood products which are capable of meeting accelerated weathering test requirements.

FRTW products used in areas where the material is exposed to weather or high humidity, are treated with special non-leaching chemicals similar to those used for FRTW shakes and shingles. An accelerated weathering test (ASTM D2898) exposes FRTW to regular wetting and drying cycles to represent actual long-term outdoor conditions. In order to qualify for exterior use, FRTW must still achieve a flame-spread rating of 25 after undergoing this accelerated weathering.

9

Protecting and Finishing Wood

Figure 9.11
Panel Markings for Fire-Retardant Treated Lumber and Plywood

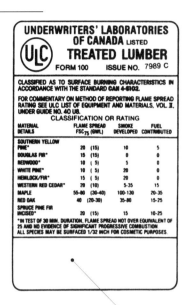 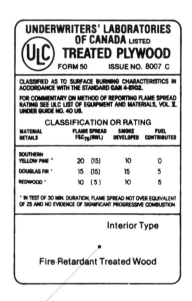

Manufactuers Name, Address and Product Name

The fire-retardant treatment of wood does not generally interfere with the adhesion of decorative paint coatings unless the treated wood has an increased moisture content. The finish characteristics of particular products should be discussed with the manufacturers of the treated wood.

In the United States, where the use of FRTW products has been extensive, the combination of temperature, humidity, and certain fire-retardant chemical formulation has led to deterioration of the products in certain climatic zones, particularly in plywood used in roof assemblies.

This problem has been specific to certain chemical formulations. Some of the latest generation fire-retardant chemicals and processes have been formulated to prevent this degradation from taking place while continuing to meet the fire-safety requirements of the building codes. In selecting FRT wood products, the designer should review the documented performance of those products under consideration.

Fire-Retardant Coatings

In addition to chemical impregnation by pressure-treating, the burning characteristics of wood products can be reduced by applying specially formulated coatings to wood surfaces. These coatings, are generally used for architectural woodwork applications where appearance is important.

Fire-retardant coatings are available in clear and white finishes. Where a solid colour finish is required, one or two coats of alkyd paint can be applied over the clear or white fire-retardant coating with only a small increase in the flame-spread rating.

The reaction of these coatings to fire and the actual mechanism of protection varies according to the composition of the coating. Some of the basic mechanisms of protection are as follows:

- Insulation: thick coatings insulate the treated material against high temperatures.

- Crust formation: the coating melts under the action of heat, covering the treated material with an impermeable insulating crust that deprives the wood of oxygen.

- Heat absorption: the coating absorbs the heat and maintains the temperature of the protected surface below its ignition temperature.

- Intumescent insulation: the coating swells when heated to form a thick insulating layer that delays the spread of flame and the transmission of heat to the protected surface.

Like FRTW products, wood products protected by fire-retardant coatings, because of their reduced flame-spread rating, can be used in areas where untreated wood products cannot be used. However, most fire-retardant coatings are not suitable for use in high humidity or exterior applications.

Fire-retardant coatings are manufactured as proprietary products subjected to extensive fire testing. For specifications on rate of coverage and properties, a manufacturer should be consulted.

These products can be applied by brush, roller, or sprayer. Because fire-retardant coatings are high viscosity (thick) liquids, they should be maintained at room temperature, especially when spray applied, to ease application. Where appearance is important, two light coats, by reducing sagging, are superior to one heavy coat and provide the required flame-spread characteristics.

Fire-retardant coatings can be used for new construction, and for rehabilitation projects, to give surfaces burning characteristics which meet modern requirements. For previously uncoated surfaces, the normal surface preparation required for paint, stain, varnish, and lacquer will ensure good adhesion and performance. For prefinished panels and for previously painted, waxed or otherwise coated surfaces, light sanding is required followed by application of an undercoat specially formulated to provide the adhesion between the surface and subsequent fire-retardant coating.

9

Protecting and Finishing Wood

General Guidelines for Fire-Retardant Treatment and Coating

- Specify FRTW plywood products which have been treated with chemicals exhibiting proven performance over the past 15 years by consulting organizations such as the National Association of Home Builders (NAHB).

- Consult the manufacturer concerning the effect on non-exterior FRTW products of rain wetting and specify construction procedures for storage and handling which maintain the integrity of the fire-retardant chemicals.

- For fire-retardant coatings, ensure the surface to be coated is clean and dry. For previously coated surfaces, sand lightly and apply a specially formulated undercoat in advance of the fire-retardant coating application.

- For fire-retardant coated surfaces where appearance is important, apply the coating in two light layers while meeting the recommended application rates of the manufacturer. Final colour can be obtained by applying up to two coats of alkyd paint over the clear or white fire-retardant coating.

References

Wood and Fire Safety, Canadian Wood Council, 1991

Product Guide for Fire-Retardant Wood Applications, Dricon, Koppers Company Limited, 1989

Homebuilders Guide to Fire-Retardant Treated Plywood, NAHB National Research Center, 1990

Design for
Fire Safety

10

10.1 General Information

This section provides general information for North American building code regulations on fire safety in buildings which are constructed with wood products. It deals with loadbearing and non-loadbearing wood building components and the use of wood as an interior finish material. The main topics are as follows:

10.2 Wood Construction

10.3 Protection Against Fire Spread

10.4 Fire Resistance

There are four model building codes in North America. They are called model codes because they form the basis for most provincial, state, and municipal building codes (see Figure 10.1 below) regulating construction of buildings. These are:

- *National Building Code of Canada (NBCC)* published by the National Research Council of Canada (NRCC)

- *Uniform Building Code (UBC)* published by the International Conference of Building Officials (ICBO)

Figure 10.1
North American Building Codes

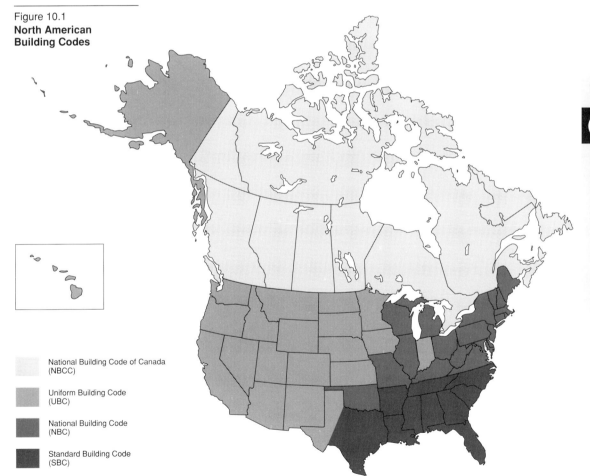

National Building Code of Canada (NBCC)

Uniform Building Code (UBC)

National Building Code (NBC)

Standard Building Code (SBC)

10

Design for Fire Safety

- *National Building Code (NBC)* published by Building Officials and Code Administrators (BOCA)

- *Standard Building Code (SBC)* published by Southern Building Code Congress International (SBCCI)

The *National Building Code of Canada (NBCC)* applies to all buildings and has nine parts, two of which, Parts 3 and 9, contain fire safety requirements. Part 9 applies to houses and other buildings of three storeys or less, up to 600m² (6,450 ft²) in area except for those containing assembly, institutional, or high hazard industrial occupancies. Part 3 applies to all buildings which are outside the scope of Part 9.

In the US, the three model codes apply to buildings of all sizes and any kind of occupancy. However, all these reference the *One and Two Family Dwelling Code* published by the Council of American Building Officials (CABO). This code applies to single family detached, duplexes, and townhouses/rowhouses which are vertically separated and have separate exits.

In both countries, the fire safety requirements contained in the codes for these smaller buildings follow the same principle as those used for large buildings, but are less restrictive in general to allow flexibility in design of a single family unit.

The four model building codes have many differences between them in their approach to designing for fire safety. This section provides general information on fire safety applying to all the codes. For specific information, the reader is directed to the codes themselves.

There are two publications which provide extensive discussion on the code requirements for fire safety and how wood construction can meet those requirements.

These are:

- *Wood and Fire Safety* published by the Canadian Wood Council

- *Code Conforming Wood Design* published by the National Forest Products Association (US)

North American building codes are based on certain fundamental principles and assumptions which differ in some respects from their counterparts in other parts of the world.

The North American approach to fire safety is predicated on the fact that fire-resistant design alone cannot ensure an acceptable level of safety. It considers, among other things, that the content of buildings, generally not subject to building regulations, can create a fire hazard far greater than the actual building construction components.

In Canada and the US, building codes are to a large extent based on prescriptive requirements but in recent years have been moving toward a more performance-based approach. Prescriptive means limitations are imposed dependent upon material characteristics. Prescriptive requirements state exactly which materials and construction can be used, and therefore offer very little flexibility.

Performance-based regulations would allow any materials to be used as long as their behaviour in a fire meets defined criteria. In other words, it is not whether a material is combustible or noncombustible which is of prime importance, but rather how it performs in meeting acceptable levels of safety.

Fire protection engineering research and building system behaviour in fire conditions form the basis for many of the performance-based changes to the North American codes. This research evaluates the expected level of safety provided by various building systems.

Increasing emphasis is being given to adopting a performance-based approach to fire safety which uses fire-risk and fire-hazard assessment models, which are in many cases computer-based. The Society of Fire Protection Engineers and the National Fire Protection Association are two of the leading organizations directing activities in this developing engineering field.

The minimum fire safety requirements for building construction are based on the characteristics of each type of occupancy and an assessment of their impact on life safety. Factors considered are the range of activities and location of occupants during 24-hour and seven-day weekly periods, the response capabilities of occupants, occupancy fire hazards, and expected fire loading all affect life safety.

In its simplest terms, fire protection is required for three objectives:

- Structural stability under fire conditions

- Protection against fire spread

- Safe means of egress

Structural stability under fire conditions is characterized by the fire-resistance rating assigned to the structural assembly. The codes relate fire-resistance ratings to the intended occupancy, size, and type of the structure. The rating is the major fire safety factor affecting structural design choices in wood.

Protection against fire spread is achieved in several ways within the codes. The main emphasis is on providing fire separations which form fire compartments within a building to isolate the fire. Regulations specify the use of automatic sprinkler systems where it is felt that the "passive" fire protection provided by the fire separations must be supplemented by "active" fire protection of sprinklers.

In addition, the flammability or flame-spread rating of interior finishes is controlled to limit the growth and spread of a fire, especially in critical areas such as exit routes. Such regulations have a significant impact on the use of interior finishes.

Providing safe means of egress is accomplished through the requirements for exit routes which specify maximum travel distances, location, and minimum width of exits. Provisions for detection and alarm systems assure that the movement of people in case of a fire will be initiated early to reduce the threat for loss of life or injury.

The following sections discuss the code requirements related to structural stability and preventing fire spread. These issues are the ones which have the greatest impact on the use of wood products in construction. Requirements for egress and the provision of fire alarm systems are a matter of concern for all types of construction. These topics are addressed only on the basis of the impact they have on the use of wood products.

Before discussing specific fire safety requirements, background information is provided on the code development process in North America.

Code Development Process

All of the model codes are published regularly. In Canada, the NBCC is published in a five year cycle, usually with only one interim update. The US codes, the UBC, NBC, and SBC, are published in a three year cycle, with regular annual updates.

The NBCC is a model code and its contents are determined by the Associate Committee. Appointed by the National Research Council and composed of approximately 30 leading Canadian citizens in the field of construction, the Associate Committee gives policy guidance to a number of Standing Committees, which in turn are responsible for the technical aspects of one or more parts of the code.

10

Design for Fire Safety

Each Standing Committee is structured to ensure an appropriate mix of expertise by drawing from every major sector of the construction industry. The members are appointed on the strength of their knowledge and professional interest, not as direct representatives of a particular industry, association, or interest group.

With support from the technical codes and standards, and research sections within the National Research Council of Canada (NRCC), the committees consider code issues. At least twice during the five-year cycle, proposed changes to the Code are drafted and public input is sought. Once the code is published, the provinces must pass legislation to adopt the revisions officially.

All three model codes in the US follow the same procedure but with a different committee structure and a shorter cycle. Each of the building code groups for the UBC, NBC, and SBC codes has a Code-Change Committee responsible for the technical requirements of the codes. The committees are comprised solely of building officials.

The committees review annually various proposals for code changes and publish recommendations for handling these proposals. The proposals are published for public comment and then the committee reassesses their recommendations. At the annual general meeting of each of the groups, a final decision on the adoption of the proposed changes is determined by ballot of the voting members of the organization. The changes adopted are published in annual updates to the basic code.

10.2   Wood Construction

Wood is a natural resource. It is also a building material which has remarkable qualities of strength and beauty. Despite its ability to burn once its ignition temperature has been reached, wood can be used structurally and decoratively to meet the performance requirements for fire safety.

As in the case of buildings of noncombustible materials like concrete and steel, there have been serious fires in wood buildings. At times, the reaction of legislators to catastrophic fires in wood buildings has been to limit the use of Wood-Frame construction in favour of fire-resistive materials.

Experience shows, however, that even materials that do not sustain fire do not guarantee the safety of a structure. In other words, much more than relative combustibility must be considered to provide fire safe buildings.

Steel, for instance, quickly loses its strength when heated. Its yield point decreases significantly as it absorbs heat, thereby endangering stability of the structure. An unprotected, conventional open web steel joist system will fail in less than 10 minutes under standard fire exposure test methods, while a conventional wood joist floor system exposed to similar fire conditions can last up to 15 minutes. Even reinforced concrete is not immune to fire. Though concrete structures rarely collapse, the structural integrity of concrete is impaired as the concrete spalls at higher temperatures and the steel reinforcement is weakened.

The challenge to building code officials, designers, and the legislators who determine the content of the building codes, is in the application of building materials. Building materials must be selected and applied in a fashion which protects occupants and fire fighters from all the hazards posed in fires by providing structural stability, protection against fire spread, and safe means of egress. Wood construction can be used in various ways to meet these requirements.

Structural Systems in Wood

In Canada, structural systems in wood are designated as Wood-Frame or Heavy Timber construction. In the US, a third type called Noncombustible-Wall Wood-Joist construction is permitted in addition to Wood-Frame and Heavy Timber construction.

These three types of construction have important differences according to the size of the wood members, methods of assembly, and the way in which they must be combined with other materials to achieve fire-safe conditions.

The regulations for minimum fire-resistance ratings for each type of construction will vary depending on the building size and occupancy. In all the codes there are provisions for most construction types to be used with no assigned fire-resistance rating. Obviously these cases would apply only for very small buildings.

Table 10.1 (→ 485 to 492) gives examples of the size of buildings of wood construction permitted by the four model codes. Except as noted, the heights and areas listed from the NBCC (Canada) apply to buildings sprinklered and constructed of protected Wood-Frame (3/4 hour) and both protected (3/4 hour) and unprotected Noncombustible construction as well as Heavy Timber construction. The values listed for the US codes apply only to buildings sprinklered and constructed of protected Wood-Frame construction (one hour) except as noted.

Wood-Frame Construction
Wood-Frame construction, as it is referred to in the building codes, is basically the light framing discussed in detail in Section 6.2. It is an economical, safe, and reliable method of construction for residential and commercial buildings in Canada and the US.

10

Design for Fire Safety

Though the structure of a modern wood frame building is made entirely of wood, protective finishes such as gypsum wallboard can be applied to the framing to provide increased fire resistance to the passage of heat and flame. Through the use of appropriate materials and construction methods, wood frame assemblies can be made to resist the effects of a fire for up to two hours.

The length of time which wood-frame floor and wall assemblies can be expected to resist the effects of fire is determined by testing, and assemblies with varying amounts of fire resistance, from 45 minutes to two hours, can be constructed. This allows Wood-Frame construction to be used for buildings of any occupancy, according to most of the model codes.

Heavy Timber Construction
Heavy Timber construction uses wood sections of large dimension which have a greater inherent resistance to fire. Wood has a very low thermal conductivity. The burned section of the wood surface helps protect and insulate unburnt wood below the charred layer. The unburnt portion of a thick member only suffers a loss of 10 to 15 percent of its strength as a result of the higher temperatures in a fire.

Hence, a wood member with a large cross-section could burn for an hour or more before its size is reduced to the point where it can no longer carry its assigned loads.

The North American model building codes recognize the increasing structural integrity of wood members in fire situations as dimensions of the members increase. Also, advantages follow from placing limitations on the minimum thickness of wood floors and roofs and by the avoidance of concealed spaces under floors and roofs. Both solid sawn and glulam members qualify under this definition provided that they have the minimum sizes required as shown in Table 10.2 (→ 493).

In Canada, Heavy Timber construction includes buildings with interior and exterior walls of Wood-Frame, or Noncombustible construction. In the US, exterior walls are required to be of Noncombustible construc-

tion with some exceptions allowing the use of fire-retardant treated wood framing. Interior walls can be either Wood-Frame or Noncombustible.

To meet code regulations, wood elements in Heavy Timber construction are required to be arranged in solid masses, with essentially smooth flat surfaces, to avoid thin sections and sharp projections. This is to reduce to a minimum the surfaces which can be exposed to fire.

In addition to minimum size requirements, other code requirements are intended to ensure that the advantages of this type of construction are not affected by poor assembly. When these conditions are met, the NBCC in Canada usually considers Heavy Timber construction as equivalent to 45-minute rated Wood-Frame construction. Thereby maximum building heights and areas permitted for the two types of construction are similar.

In the US codes, Heavy Timber construction is defined separately and assigned maximum building area and height limits. As a result, such buildings can be built larger in area by at least 30 to 40 percent, and up to 3 storeys more in height than traditional protected Wood-Frame construction.

All the codes specify particular details with regard to the continuity of beams and columns, as well as with metal connections. Specific requirements in the code should be observed.

Floors in Heavy Timber construction are usually constructed with solid sawn planks. When laid flat, they should be tongue and groove, or splined. Splined planks are held together by strips of wood (called splines) which are inserted into grooves cut into opposing edges of abutting planks to form a continuous joint.

Planks laid on edge must be spiked together (see Section 4.4). Planks must be laid so that joints occurring in the middle of a span are staggered. A continuous line of end joints is permissible only over points of support, such as a beam.

Figure 10.2
**Examples of
Floor Decks in
Heavy Timber
Construction**

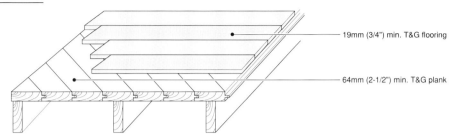

19mm (3/4") min. T&G flooring

64mm (2-1/2") min. T&G plank

Tongue and Groove (T&G) Plank

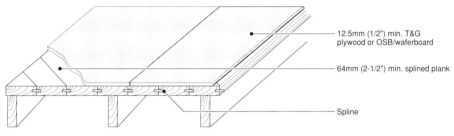

12.5mm (1/2") min. T&G
plywood or OSB/waferboard

64mm (2-1/2") min. splined plank

Spline

Splined Plank

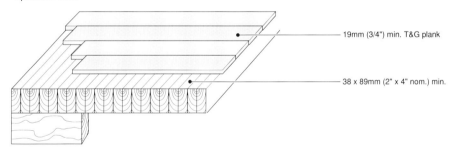

19mm (3/4") min. T&G plank

38 x 89mm (2" x 4" nom.) min.

Spiked Plank on Edge

10

Design for Fire Safety

All plank floors must be covered by tongue and groove lumber laid across or diagonally, or by plywood, particleboard, or OSB/waferboard having thicknesses stipulated in the individual codes. A 12 to 15mm (1/2" to 5/8") clearance to end walls must be provided to allow for expansion, and the gap between flooring and the wall must be fire-stopped at top or bottom with lumber or plywood. Figure 10.2 (opposite) shows some typical details of Heavy Timber floor deck construction.

Roof decks may be constructed of solid sawn planks assembled in the same way as floors, or of tongue and groove plywood suitable for exterior applications. Minimum thicknesses apply in both cases. In all other respects, Heavy Timber construction is subject to the requirements pertaining to

roof coverings and concealed spaces as provided for in other types of construction.

Noncombustible-Wall Wood-Joist
All three US codes specifically define and regulate a type of construction which combines combustible and noncombustible materials. This type of construction permits buildings with exterior walls of noncombustible materials, used in combination with wood floor and roof assemblies. Provisions are made with this type of construction to permit assemblies having zero fire-resistance rating as well as one-hour fire-resistance ratings. Like Heavy Timber construction, using one-hour rated Noncombustible-Wall Wood-Joist construction results in increased area and height allowances in comparison to protected Wood-Frame construction.

Wood in Noncombustible Construction

The North American building codes require that some buildings be entirely of Noncombustible construction. This requires the use of noncombustible materials for the structure and certain assemblies. The requirements for Noncombustible construction limit but do not preclude the use of combustible materials.

Wood is perhaps the most prevalent combustible material used in noncombustible buildings. It may be used for nailing or furring strips for the attachment of interior finishes, or for fascia and canopies, cant strips, roof curbs, roof sheathing and coverings, millwork, cabinets, counters, window sash, doors, flooring, studs and even as wall finishes. Its use in certain types of buildings, such as tall buildings, is slightly more limited in areas such as exits, corridors and lobbies. Even then, wood products protected by fire-retardant treatments and some types of fire-retardant coatings can be used to meet code requirements.

The following brief descriptions of some of the uses permitted in such buildings gives some indication of the versatility of wood products.

Wood Furring
Wood is particularly useful as a nailing base for different types of cladding and interior finishes. Most codes allow wood furring strips to be used to attach interior finishes, such as gypsum wallboard, provided the strips are fastened to or recessed into noncombustible backing, and any concealed space created by the wood elements is blocked off by fire stops.

Roofs
In the installation of roofing, wood cant strips, roof curbs, nailing strips, and similar components may be used. In Canada, wood roofs of Heavy Timber construction are permitted in any noncombustible building two storeys or less in height when the building is protected by a sprinkler system arranged, upon activation, to transmit a signal to the fire department.

In the US codes, heavy timber and fire-retardant treated wood roof assemblies are permitted, typically in one- and two-storey noncombustible structures, where there is a minimum clearance from the floor to the roof of at least 6m (20'), or in some cases where no fire-resistance rating is otherwise required for the roof assembly.

In Canada, the NBCC requires buildings, of a size required to be noncombustible, to have roof coverings of Class A, B or C (see Fire Spread Between Buildings, → 496). This allows the use of fire-retardant treated wood shakes and shingles on sloped roofs. Most US codes also make provisions for similar use of wood roof coverings. However, there are usually restrictions on the size of the building and its location relative to the property line.

Combustible Cladding and Fascias
New requirements in the 1990 NBCC in Canada relax rules on the use of combustible claddings and supporting assemblies on certain types of noncombustible buildings. Specifically, the use of wall assemblies containing both combustible cladding elements and non-loadbearing wood framing members is allowed (see Figure 10.3 opposite) with certain restrictions.

In the US, the SBC permits fire-retardant treated wood framing in exterior non-loadbearing walls where separation from the lot line exceeds 9m (30').

In Canada, use of fire-retardant treated wood decorative cladding is also permitted on first floor canopy fascias, provided the material meets flame-spread limits after undergoing accelerated weathering tests. In the US, exterior wood trim and veneers are permitted on all noncombustible buildings with limits specified on the height to which the materials can be installed.

Millwork
Wood millwork such as interior trim, doors, and door frames, show windows and frames, aprons and backing, handrails, shelves, cabinets and counters can also be used in Noncombustible construction. It is not necessary to restrict their use because they contribute minimally to the overall fire hazard.

Figure 10.3
**Wood Frame
Wall for
Noncombustible
Construction**

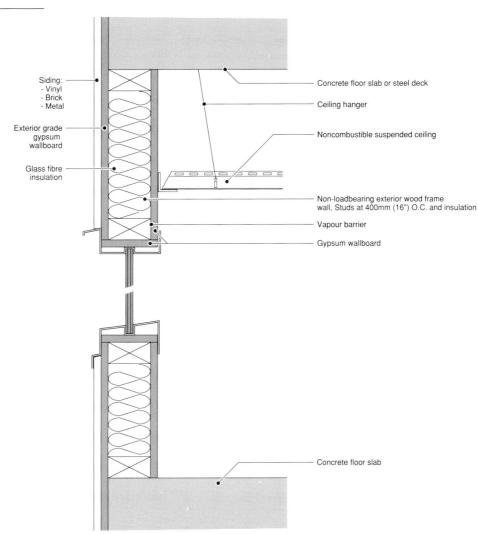

Siding:
- Vinyl
- Brick
- Metal

Exterior grade
gypsum
wallboard

Glass fibre
insulation

Concrete floor slab or steel deck

Ceiling hanger

Noncombustible suspended ceiling

Non-loadbearing exterior wood frame
wall, Studs at 400mm (16") O.C. and insulation

Vapour barrier

Gypsum wallboard

Concrete floor slab

Notes:
1. Example of wood frame non-loadbearing exterior wall section permitted in buildings required to be of
   Noncombustible construction.
2. Siding and exterior grade gypsum wallboard can be replaced with exterior grade, fire-retardant treated wood
   siding when phenolic foam insulation is used in the stud cavities.

10

Design for Fire Safety

Flooring

Combustible finished flooring such as wood strip or parquet is allowed in any building. Wood supports for flooring are also permitted providing they are applied directly to or set into a noncombustible floor slab and the concealed spaces are fire stopped. Most codes specify maximum height and minimum fire stopping requirements for the concealed space created. This allows the use of wood joists or wood trusses, with the latter providing more flexibility for running building services within the spaces.

Wood Partitions

In Canada, other than in institutional buildings, non-loadbearing solid lumber partitions at least 38mm (2" nom.) thick and wood-framed partitions are permitted within unsprinklered fire compartments that are not more than 600m² (6,450 ft²) in area or within sprinklered storeys with no compartment area limits. These partitions must not be fire separations as required by the Code. In the US, similar partition arrangements are permitted without specific limitations except that fire-retardant treated wood framing must be used.

Wood Finishes

The use of interior finishes is mostly regulated by restrictions on their flame-spread rating. Wood finishes may be used extensively in noncombustible buildings on walls and partitions within tenant suites, and to a lesser extent in areas such as exits and lobbies. Many wood products meet the maximum flame spread limits of 150 or 200 imposed by the codes. Where stricter flame-spread rating requirements apply, such as in a corridor, wood qualifies as an interior finish if it is fire-retardant treated, or protected by a fire-retardant coating.

Reference Tables

Table 10.1a
Maximum Building Area per Floor (sprinklered) National Building Code of Canada (NBCC – 1990 Edition)

Occupancy Group	Division	Use	Building Height (Storeys)	Access Condition	Maximum Building Area [1,2] m² per floor	sq. ft. per floor
A		**Assembly**				
	1	Performing Arts [3]	1	A	Determined by Occupant Load	
	2	Other (Schools, Restaurants)	2	A	1,600	17,200
				B	2,000	21,500
				C	2,400	25,800
			1	A	3,200	34,400
				B	4,000	43,100
				C	4,800	51,700
	3	Arenas	1	A	4,800	51,700
				B	6,000	64,600
				C	7,200	77,500
	4	Outdoor Viewing (no FRR)	-		Determined by Occupant Load	
B		**Institutional**				
	2	Hospitals, Nursing Homes	2	A	1,600	17,200
			1	A	2,400	25,800
C		**Residential**				
		Apartments, Hotels, Motels, Houses	3	A	1,200	12,900
				B	1,500	16,100
				C	1,800	19,400
			2	A	1,800	19,400
				B	2,250	24,200
				C	2,700	29,100
			1	A	3,600	38,800
				B	4,500	48,400
				C	5,200	56,000
C		**Residential (1 hr FRR)**				
		Apartments, Hotels, Motels, Houses	4 [5]	A	1,200	12,900
				B	1,500	16,100
				C	1,800	19,400
			3	A	1,600	17,200
				B	2,000	21,500
				C	2,400	25,800
			2	A	2,400	25,800
				B	3,000	32,300
				C	3,600	38,800
			1	A	4,800	51,700
				B	6,000	64,600
				C	7,200	77,500
D		**Business and Personal Services**				
		Offices	3 [6]	A	3,200	34,400
				B	4,000	43,100
				C	4,800	51,700
			1	A	9,600	103,300
				B	12,000	129,200
				C	14,400	155,000

Footnotes (→ 486)

Reference Tables continued

Table 10.1a continued Maximum Building Area per Floor (sprinklered) National Building Code of Canada (NBCC – 1990 Edition)

Occupancy Group	Division	Use	Building Height (Storeys)	Access Condition	Maximum Building Area [1,2] m² per floor	sq. ft. per floor
E		**Mercantile [4]**				
		Stores, Supermarkets	3 [6]	A	1,600	17,200
				B	2,000	21,500
				C	2,400	25,800
			1	A	4,800	51,700
				B	6,000	64,600
				C	7,200	77,500
F		**Industrial**				
	1	High Hazard	1	A	1,600	17,200
				B	2,000	21,500
				C	2,400	25,800
	2	Medium Hazard [7]	4	A	1,600	17,200
				B	2,000	21,500
				C	2,400	25,800
			1	A	6,400	68,900
				B	8,000	86,100
				C	9,600	103,300
	3	Low Hazard [7]	4	A	2,400	25,800
				B	3,000	32,300
				C	3,600	38,800
			1	A	9,600	103,300
				B	12,000	129,200
				C	14,400	155,000

Access Conditions:

A. Facing one street or access route.
B. Facing two streets or access routes [8].
C. Facing three streets or access routes [9].

Notes:
1. Table based on building being sprinklered. If building is not sprinklered, the maximum building area is halved except as noted.
2. In general, buildings described can be of Wood-Frame construction and are required to have 45-minute fire-resistance rating (FRR), or be of Heavy Timber construction (exceptions noted).
3. Occupancy load less than 300.
4. Buildings over 1500m² (16,100 ft²) must be sprinklered.
5. Buildings must be sprinklered.
6. For 2 storey buildings add 50 percent to maximum area permitted per floor.
7. For maximum area per floor in 3 and 2 storey buildings take total area permitted for all floors combined and divide by number of storeys.
8. A building is considered to face 2 streets when not less than 50 percent of the building perimeter is located within 15m (49') of the street(s) or access route(s).
9. A building is considered to face 3 streets when not less than 75 percent of the building perimeter is located within 15m (49') of the street(s) or access route(s).

Reference Tables continued

Table 10.1b
**Maximum
Building Area
per Floor
(sprinklered)
Uniform
Building Code
(UBC – 1988
Edition)**

Occupancy Group	Division	Use	Building Height (Storeys)	Access Condition	Maximum Building Area [1,2] sq. ft. per floor
A		**Assembly** [3,4]			
	2 and 2.1	Performing Arts [3], Arenas [5]	2	A	42,000
			1	A	63,000
	3 [4]	Schools (beyond 12th grade with more than 50 persons), Churches, Restaurants	3 [6]	A B C	7,000 10,500 14,000
			2	A B C	21,000 31,500 42,000
			1	A B C	31,500 47,250 63,000
B		**Business**			
	2	Mercantile, Offices, Light Industrial, Storage	4 [6]	A B C	7,000 10,500 14,000
			3	A B C	18,667 28,000 37,333
			2 [7]	A B C	28,000 42,000 56,000
			1 [7]	A B C	42,000 63,000 84,000
E		**Educational**			
		Schools (more than 50 students)	3 [6]	A B C	10,470 15,700 20,930
			2	A B C	31,400 47,100 62,800
			1	A B C	47,100 70,650 94,200

Footnotes (→ 488)

Reference Tables continued

Table 10.1b continued
Maximum Building Area per Floor (sprinklered) Uniform Building Code (UBC – 1988 Edition)

Occupancy Group	Division	Use	Building Height (Storeys)	Access Condition	Maximum Building Area [1,2] sq. ft. per floor
I		**Institutional** [8]			
	1	Hospitals, Nursing Homes (non-ambulatory)	2	A	5,200
				B	7,800
				C	10,400
			1	A	15,600
				B	23,400
				C	31,200
	2	Nursing Homes (ambulatory), Children's Custodial Homes (6 years and older)	3	A	3,467
				B	5,200
				C	6,933
			2	A	10,400
				B	15,600
				C	20,800
			1	A	15,600
				B	23,400
				C	31,200
R		**Residential** [6]			
	1	Hotels, Apartment Houses	4	A	5,250
				B	7,875
				C	10,500
			3	A	14,000
				B	21,000
				C	28,000
			2	A	21,000
				B	31,500
				C	42,000
			1	A	31,500
				B	47,250
				C	63,000

Access Conditions:
Percent of building perimeter facing street or unoccupied space at least 30' wide with the latter accessible by a posted fire lane at least 18' wide.

A. Minimum 1 side access to public way or yard.
B. Separation on 2 sides (minimum 60' clearance).
C. Separation on 3 sides (minimum 60' clearance) or separation on 4 sides (minimum 40' clearance).

Notes:
1. Based on building being sprinklered. For non-sprinklered conditions, refer to the Code.
2. Values apply to Wood-Frame construction with 1-hr fire-resistance rating (Type V). See Code for increases permitted for Noncombustible-Wall Wood-Joist (Type III-1 hr) and Heavy Timber (Type IV).
3. Occupant load less than 1000 with a stage.
4. Occupant load less than 300 without a stage.
5. Occupant load more than 300 without a stage.
6. Sprinklers permit extra storey – no floor area increases permitted for sprinklers.
7. Unlimited area permitted when separation on 4 sides is at least 60'.
8. See Code for mandatory sprinkler requirements.

Reference Tables continued

Table 10.1c
Maximum Building Area per Floor (sprinklered) National Building Code (NBC – 1990 Edition)

Occupancy Group	Division	Use	Building Height (Storeys)	Access Condition	Maximum Building Area [1,2] sq. ft. per floor
A		**Assembly** [3,4]			
	1 and 3	Theatres (with stages), Art Galleries, Libraries, Restaurants	2 or 1	A B C	26,775 31,237 40,162
	2	Night Clubs, Dance Halls, Assembly Halls, (no stages)	2 or 1	A B C	7,650 8,925 11,475
	4	Churches	2 or 1	A B C	45,900 53,550 68,850
B		**Business** [3]			
		Offices, Banks, Police Stations, Post Offices, Schools (less than 50 persons)	4 or 3	A B C	27,540 35,190 50,490
			2 or 1	A B C	45,900 53,550 68,850
E		**Educational** [3]			
		Schools, Colleges, Child Day Care Centres [5] (more than 50 persons)	2 or 1	A B C	45,900 53,550 68,850
F		**Industrial** [3,4]			
	1	Food Processing, Printing, Woodworking, Manufacturing	3	A B C	18,360 23,460 33,660
			2 or 1	A B C	30,600 35,700 45,900
	2	Foundry, Metal Fabrication, Ice Manufacturing	4 or 3	A B C	27,540 35,190 50,490
			2 or 1	A B C	45,900 53,550 68,850
I		**Institutional** [4] **(more than 6 persons)**			
	1	Board and Care, Group Homes, Drug Centres	4 or 3	A B C	16,065 20,527 24,990
			2 or 1	A B C	26,775 31,237 40,162
	2	Hospitals, Nursing Homes, Detoxification Facilities	2 or 1	A B C	22,950 26,775 34,425
	3	Prisons, Jails, Reformatories, Correctional Centres	2 or 1	A B C	19,125 22,312 28,687

Footnotes (→ 490)

Reference Tables continued

Table 10.1c continued
Maximum Building Area per Floor (sprinklered) National Building Code (NBC – 1990 Edition)

Occupancy Group	Division	Use	Building Height (Storeys)	Access Condition	Maximum Building Area [1,2] sq. ft. per floor
M		**Mercantile** [3,4]			
		Retail Stores, Shops, Service Stations, Markets	3	A	18,360
				B	23,460
				C	33,660
			2 or 1	A	30,600
				B	35,700
				C	45,900
R		**Residential** [3,4]			
	1 and 2	Hotels, Motels, Boarding Houses, Multi-Family Dwellings	4 or 3	A	18,360
				B	23,460
				C	33,660
			2 or 1	A	30,600
				B	35,700
				C	45,900
S		**Storage** [3,4]			
	1	Storage of Goods (moderate hazard)	2 or 1	A	26,775
				B	31,237
				C	40,162
	2	Storage of Goods (low hazard)	4 or 3	A	27,540
				B	35,190
				C	50,490
			2 or 1	A	45,900
				B	53,550
				C	68,850

Access Conditions:
Percent of building perimeter facing street or unoccupied space at least 30' wide with the latter accessible by a posted fire lane at least 18' wide.

A. 25 percent
B. 50 percent
C. 100 percent

Notes:
1. Table is based on building being sprinklered. For non-sprinklered conditions, refer to the Code.
2. Values apply to Wood-Frame construction with 1 hour fire-resistance rating (Type 5A). See Code for increases permitted for Noncombustible-Wall Wood-Joist (Type 3A-1 hour) and Heavy Timber (Type 4).
3. Using Type 3A and Type 4 construction permits significant increases in building height and area.
4. See Code for mandatory sprinkler requirements.
5. For occupant load less than 50 persons, increase of one storey on height limitations is permitted.

Reference Tables continued

Table 10.1d
**Maximum
Building Area
per Floor
(sprinklered)
Standard
Building Code
(SBC – 1988
Edition)**

Occupancy Group	Division	Use	Building Height (Storeys)	Access Condition	Maximum Building Area [1,2] sq. ft. per floor
A		**Assembly**			
	1	Large Assembly [3] (more than 1000 persons, no working stage), Theatres, Auditoriums, Churches	2	A	12,000
				B	16,000
				C	24,000
			1	A	36,000
				B	40,000
				C	48,000
	2	Small Assembly (50 to 1000 persons without working stage), Theatres, Auditoriums, Churches, Restaurants	2	A	7,500
				B	10,000
				C	15,000
			1	A	22,500
				B	25,000
				C	30,000
B		**Business**			
		Office, Small Restaurants, Schools (beyond 12th grade), Banks, Libraries	3	A	13,500
				B	18,000
				C	27,000
			2	A	27,000
				B	31,500
				C	40,500
			1	A	40,500
				B	45,000
				C	54,000
E		**Educational**			
		Schools (through 12th grade), Child Care Facilities	3	A	12,000
				B	16,000
				C	24,000
			2	A	24,000
				B	28,000
				C	36,000
			1	A	36,000
				B	40,000
				C	48,000
F		**Factory-Industrial** [4]			
		Assembly, Packaging, Processing, Manufacturing	2	A	15,000
				B	20,000
				C	30,000
			1 [5]	A	45,000
				B	50,000
				C	60,000
I		**Institutional**			
		Unrestrained-Hospitals, Nursing Homes	1	A	22,500
				B	25,000
				C	30,000
		Restrained-Jails, Detention Centres, Reformatories	3	A	15,000
				B	17,500
				C	22,500
			2	A	15,000
				B	17,500
				C	22,500
			1	A	22,500
				B	25,000
				C	30,000

Footnotes (→ 492)

Reference Tables continued

Table 10.1d continued
Maximum Building Area per Floor (sprinklered) Standard Building Code (SBC – 1988 Edition)

Occupancy Group	Division	Use	Building Height (Storeys)	Access Condition	Maximum Building Area [1,2] sq. ft. per floor
M		**Mercantile [4]**			
		Stores, Markets, Shopping Centres	3	A	9,000
				B	12,000
				C	18,000
			2	A	18,000
				B	21,000
				C	27,000
			1 [5]	A	27,000
				B	30,000
				C	36,000
R		**Residential [4]**			
		Hotels, Motels, Apartments	4	A	10,500
				B	14,000
				C	21,000
			3	A	21,000
				B	24,500
				C	31,500
			2	A	21,000
				B	24,500
				C	31,500
			1	A	31,500
				B	35,000
				C	42,000
S		**Storage**			
		Low and Moderate Hazard Basic Commodity Storage	2	A	9,000
				B	12,000
				C	18,000
			1 [5]	A	27,000
				B	30,000
				C	36,000

Access Conditions:
Percent of building perimeter facing street or public space at least 30' wide.

A. 25 percent
B. 50 percent
C. 100 percent

Notes:
1. Table based on building being sprinklered. For non-sprinklered conditions, refer to the Code.
2. Values apply to Wood-Frame construction with 1 hour fire-resistance rating (Type VI) except where noted otherwise. See Code for increases permitted for Noncombustible-Wall Wood-Joist (Type V-1 hour) and Heavy Timber (Type III).
3. Values shown are for building Type V-1 hour construction.
4. Using Type V and Type III construction permits significant height and area increases.
5. Unlimited area permitted when separation on four sides is at least 60'.

Reference Tables continued

Table 10.2
Minimum Dimensions of Wood Elements in Heavy Timber Construction

Jurisdiction	Supported Assembly	Structural Element	Solid Sawn (width x depth)		Glulam (width x depth) (actual)		Round	
			mm	in. (nom.)	mm	in. (nom.)	mm	in. (nom.)
NBCC	Roofs only	Columns	140 x 191	6 x 8	130 x 190	5 x 7-1/2	180	7
		Arches supported on the tops of walls or abutments	89 x 140	4 x 6	80 x 152	3 x 6	-	-
		Beams, girders and trusses	89 x 140	4 x 6	80 x 152	3 x 6	-	-
		Arches supported at or near the floor line	140 x 140	6 x 6	130 x 152	5 x 6	-	-
	Floors, floors plus roofs	Columns	191 x 191	8 x 8	175 x 190	7 x 7-1/2	200	8
		Beams, girders, trusses and arches	140 x 241 or 191 x 191	8 x 10 or 8 x 8	130 x 228 or 175 x 190	5 x 9 or 7 x 7-1/2	-	-

Jurisdiction	Supported Assembly	Structural Element	Solid Sawn and Glulam (width x depth) in. (nom.)
UBC, NBC and SBC	Roofs only	Columns	6 x 8
		Arches supported on the tops of walls or abutments	4 x 6
		Beams, girders and trusses	4 x 6
		Arches supported at or near the floor line	6 x 8 (lower half) / 6 x 6 (upper half)
	Floors, floors plus roofs	Columns	8 x 8
		Beams, girders	6 x 10
		Trusses and arches	8 x 8

10.3   Protection Against Fire Spread

General

It is necessary to determine the area and height of a building in order to apply the requirements of the codes which stipulate the type of construction and the level of fire protection required for fire separations and fire suppression based upon occupancy.

Building area, or floor area, as it is sometimes referred to in some US codes, is usually considered to include the greatest horizontal area of a building above grade within the outside surface of exterior walls, or within the outside surface of exterior walls and the centreline of firewalls. Firewalls, or area separation walls in some US codes, may be used to reduce a building's defined area.

Part of a building, separated from the rest by firewalls, is typically permitted to be classified as a separate building for the purposes of fire protection. This can mean using Wood-Frame construction instead of some form of Noncombustible or mixed construction. The economies of building with wood can often more than offset the cost of the firewalls.

Determining building height in storeys or metres (feet) is slightly more complex because it is dependant on the location of grade. All the codes refer to grade as the lowest level of the average finished ground adjacent to each side of a building. However, each code handles the setting of grade elevation somewhat differently. On a relatively flat lot, this is fairly simple, but it can become far more difficult for large buildings on irregular lots or on lots with sloping grades.

Once grade has been established, it can be determined which floor level constitutes the first storey of the building. From that determination, building height is established. The calculation of building height sometimes excludes rooftop enclosures.

Mezzanines are also discounted as storeys in building height if their floor area is not more than a certain percentage of the area of the floor area below and have no visual obstruction above or below them. Criteria for these exclusions are contained in the individual codes. Limits to visual obstructions ensure that occupants of the mezzanine will be alerted to a life-threatening situation at the same time as the occupants of the floor area below. The critical issues are how quickly the occupants will become aware of a fire and, once notified, how well they can safely evacuate the area.

The use of a space, a group of rooms, a floor or an entire building for the same purpose is referred to as an occupancy, which relates to the use or intended use of a building or part thereof for the shelter or support of persons, animals or property. Each type of occupancy is subject to requirements concerned with flame-spread, fire alarms, exits and fire separation which are particular to that occupancy.

Major occupancy is the principal occupancy for which a building, or part thereof, is used or intended to be used and shall be deemed to include the subsidiary occupancies which are an integral part of the principal occupancy.

For example, a school may contain, in addition to classrooms, offices, a gymnasium, an auditorium, a cafeteria and laboratories. All of these uses could be considered as related to the principal use of the building, which is education.

The dividing line between what constitutes a major occupancy and a subsidiary occupancy will not always be clear-cut.

10

Design for Fire Safety

Generally, all the codes require that the entire building be constructed according to the rules of whichever major occupancy in the building warrants the most restrictive requirements. However, each of the codes addresses subsidiary occupancies differently with the intent of ensuring that the level of safety is adequate and that occupancies are protected against the hazards presented by other occupancies contained in the same building.

The construction requirements of the codes are usually ordered first by occupancy, then height and area, the accessibility to the building and whether or not the building is sprinklered. For any building, several construction alternatives may be available and the designer may choose the one which is the least restrictive.

For instance, in Canada a three-storey office building with an area of 4,000m² (43,100 ft²) facing two streets could be regulated under three different Articles: as Group D (Business and Personal Services), up to three storeys, as Group D, up to six storeys, or as Group D, any height, any area.

Under the first option, the maximum size for a building of that height facing two streets is set at 2,000m² (21,500 ft²), but if it is sprinklered, the area can be doubled to 4,000m² (43,100 ft²). In this case the building could be entirely of Wood-Frame construction, having a 45-minute fire-resistance rating for major assemblies, or be of mixed construction incorporating Heavy Timber and unprotected Noncombustible construction along with the 45-minute rated Wood-Frame construction.

Under the second option, the building would have to be of Noncombustible construction, with a fire-resistance rating of one hour, but it would not be required to be sprinklered.

Under the third option, it would be Noncombustible construction, with a fire-resistance rating of two hours. Obviously, the third option would probably not be considered unless there were plans to enlarge the building in the near future, but the first two options are viable.

The owner would have to weigh the costs and benefits of providing the sprinkler system and Combustible construction having 45-minute fire-resistance ratings, or a mixed construction type, against those of providing Noncombustible construction having one-hour fire-resistance ratings. On the other hand, the building could also be divided by a firewall into two separate buildings of equal area, the resulting reduced area making available the first option of Wood-Frame construction without sprinklers.

The following sections discuss specific fire safety requirements, such as flame-spread ratings limits for interior finishes, and fire-resistance rating requirements for major structural components. The minimum requirements, as noted above, generally are determined on the basis of building size and occupancy.

Fire Spread Between Buildings

A fire in one building is always a threat to neighbouring buildings. To reduce this risk, the number and size of openings in the building face can be limited, or buildings can be required to be noncombustible, or to be clad with noncombustible siding, or to be separated by a clear space.

Most code requirements for spatial separation of buildings are based on British and Japanese studies performed during postwar years. In Canada most of the data on the relationship between separation between buildings and tolerable radiation levels evolved from experiments referred to as the St. Lawrence Burns conducted in the winter of 1958. The findings served as the basis for the NBCC requirements that are still applied today.

Spatial separation, though a primary means of attaining the objective of preventing fire spread between buildings, is not always the most practical method. In major urban areas where land is expensive, large set-backs from property lines will have a serious economic impact on a project. In such cases it is common to combine spatial separation with control on the amount and size of openings in the exterior wall in order to prevent fire spread between buildings.

The clear space which must be maintained around the building is referred to as the limiting distance or fire separation distance. It is usually measured from the building face to the property line, the centre line of a street or public thoroughfare, or an assumed line between two buildings. For a given limiting distance or fire separation distance, the percentage of unprotected openings permitted to be used in a wall is determined by the height and width of the building face.

Some codes use the term unprotected opening to refer to doors, windows or other openings in a building face that are not protected with a closure or protective device which may be a fire door, a fire window or fire shutter. The individual codes state the maximum allowable unprotected openings permitted in an exterior wall.

Where the percentage of permitted unprotected openings is restricted due to proximity to the property line, the balance of the wall must have some fire endurance to ensure that, during a fire, the radiating area does not increase as a result of failure of the wall itself. The requirements for the wall to have a fire-resistance rating or for the use of Noncombustible construction and cladding become less stringent as the permitted area of unprotected openings increases.

In Canada, the fire-resistance rating for an exterior wall assembly is required from the inside of the building only. A fire-resistance rating from the outside is not required, regardless of the limiting distance specified or the percent of unprotected openings permitted.

In the US, the fire-resistance rating requirements for exterior walls differ. With the following noted exceptions, all three codes require a fire-resistance rating from both the inside and the outside faces of an exterior wall. In the SBC and NBC, the fire-resistance rating is not required from the outside when the fire separation distance is greater than 1.5m (5 ft.). These requirements, being more stringent than those in Canada, often result in the need for application of exterior grade gypsum wallboard on the exterior side of the wall.

The requirements for clear space between buildings affects the area of openings permitted. It also can affect the type of wall construction and exterior cladding permitted. Specific details on the requirements of individual codes should be reviewed to ensure that limits are not exceeded.

In a building equipped with automatic sprinklers, the cooling effect from the water discharged by the sprinklers will usually control fire spread and radiation levels. Therefore, in such buildings, the codes typically allow the permitted area of unprotected openings to be increased. Consequently, the designer can use sprinkler protection to reduce limiting distance or, for a given limiting distance, to increase the amount of unprotected openings.

Roof coverings have often been contributing factors where fire spreads across roof tops from building to building. Most roof coverings, even today, are combustible by the very nature of the materials used for making them waterproof. The objective of the building codes is to minimize the risks associated with a roof covering, based on its location and use.

10

Design for Fire Safety

The main types of wood products used for roof covering include wood shingles and shakes (see Section 7.2). In Canada both are tested for performance under external fire exposure by independent laboratories in accordance with CAN/ULC-S107. The US codes use either ASTM E-108 or NFPA 257 as a reference for testing roof coverings. All three test methods are essentially the same.

The fire-test standards classify roof coverings in accordance with their performance. Those that perform well under severe fire-test exposures are Class A; under moderately severe exposures, Class B, and under less severe exposure, Class C.

The NBCC (Canada) permits roof coverings that meet the Class C rating to be used for any building regulated by Part 3 of the Code, including any noncombustible building, regardless of height or area. Class A or B ratings can be met with fire-retardant treated wood shakes and shingles with some form of fire-resistant under-decking.

The US code requirements vary. The UBC generally requires Class A or B roof coverings for all buildings, except for some buildings two storeys or less in height and less than 558m^2 (6000 ft^2) in area. The NBC requires Class A or B on all Type 1 Noncombustible construction but permits Class A, B, or C on all other types. The SBC requires Class A or B roof coverings on any building located within a fire district while permitting any class in buildings outside the district.

The Class C rating can be met easily using fire-retardant treated wood shakes or shingles with no special underlay. All of the model codes make provisions for the use of non-rated roof coverings but usually only for small residential or non-industrial buildings.

In the case of fire-retardant treated wood shakes and shingles, accelerated weathering tests are carried out to ensure that the effects of fire-retardant treatment will not be reduced by continuous exposure to weather. Wood shingles and shakes protected by a fire-retardant coating cannot meet all the requirements of a Class C rating because of the severity of the extreme accelerated weathering tests.

It is important that, when approving a roof covering, results of all individual types of fire tests required by the Standard are provided. These individual tests include the spread of flame, burning brand, intermittent flame, and flying brand tests.

Fire Walls/Area Separation Walls

A firewall or area separation wall is a building element used to subdivide a building. Each separated portion is considered as a separate building for the purpose of determining the minimum fire protection requirements. A designer may take a large building area requiring Noncombustible construction and divide it by these walls, so that each section is small enough to permit the use of Wood-Frame construction. These walls are also sometimes used as a party wall separating two properties built on the lot line.

A firewall separating adjoining buildings which share a common lot line, is expected to protect the second property during the time taken by a fire to burn itself out on the first property. Depending on the occupancies it separates, a firewall may require a fire-resistance rating of two or four hours (in the SBC, all firewalls must have a 4-hour fire-resistance rating). To withstand prolonged fire exposure from either side without collapsing, a firewall is required to be constructed so that adjoining construction on the fire exposed side can collapse without affecting it. In essence, the firewall must be a free-standing structure.

In the UBC, reference is made to an area separation wall which is a type of firewall. In this code the wall can be either Noncombustible or Combustible construction. Framing of adjoining construction is not regulated except where parapets have been omitted.

Where firewalls must be made of masonry or concrete, wood roof constructions can be used effectively with parapeted firewalls. Wood floors can be framed into firewalls provided that the thickness of the masonry or concrete necessary for the required fire resistance is maintained. Joist connections and supports must be designed so that the collapse of the floor during a fire will not cause the collapse of the firewall. Two examples of such construction are shown in Figure 10.4 (→ 500).

Building codes usually require that a firewall extend through all storeys from the basement slab up through the roof where it must form a parapet above the roof surface. The required height of the parapet varies from code to code usually depending on whether the wall requires a two- or four-hour rating.

Sprinkler Systems

Automatic sprinkler protection is a proven means of safeguarding property from fire, but like any other fire protection system, it must be installed and maintained properly to ensure proper function when a fire occurs. The model codes require that sprinkler systems, where required, be designed, installed and tested in accordance with the Standard NFPA 13, *Installation of Sprinkler Systems.* Two other standards, NFPA 13D and NFPA 13R, for residential occupancies, can be used where specifically permitted.

Neither of these residential standards, with life safety as the priority, requires sprinklers to be installed in areas where it has been shown statistically that fires originating in such spaces do not cause a large number of deaths or injuries. As a result, sprinklers are not required in unused concealed spaces such as attics and floor spaces or some small closets and washrooms. Therefore, the cost of installing sprinklers in residential properties, using these standards, is reduced significantly, especially for Wood-Frame construction.

Sprinkler systems are usually installed throughout a building but in some cases the codes require only a specific floor area or space to be sprinklered depending on the hazard being protected or the nature of the fire safety issue. For example, the NBCC (Canada) requires sprinkler protection in all linen and refuse chutes even though the building may not otherwise be protected by sprinklers.

The design Standard NFPA 13, for commercial buildings and large residential buildings, requires sprinklers to be installed throughout a building, including most concealed spaces containing combustible materials or exposed combustible surfaces. There are, however, many instances where sprinkler protection is waived for these concealed spaces, even in buildings of Wood-Frame construction. Such buildings, which do not have sprinklers installed in these specific combustible concealed spaces, are still considered fully sprinklered under the code requirements.

The minimum water supply required for a sprinkler system depends on the building occupancy, the construction type, and the design approach used to size the system branch lines and feed mains. The most popular, the hydraulic design approach described in NFPA 13, calculates flow rates and pressure losses in the system, usually reducing the water supply requirements substantially from that required by the traditional pipe schedule approach, especially for sprinkler systems protecting Wood-Frame buildings.

10

Design for Fire Safety

Figure 10.4
**Wood Members
Affixed to
Noncombustible
Firewalls**

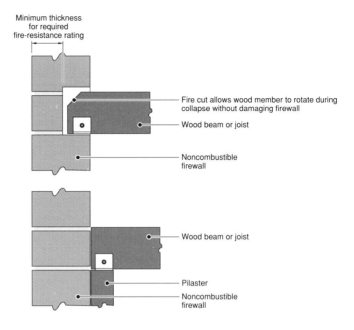

Minimum thickness
for required
fire-resistance rating

Fire cut allows wood member to rotate during collapse without damaging firewall

Wood beam or joist

Noncombustible firewall

Wood beam or joist

Pilaster

Noncombustible firewall

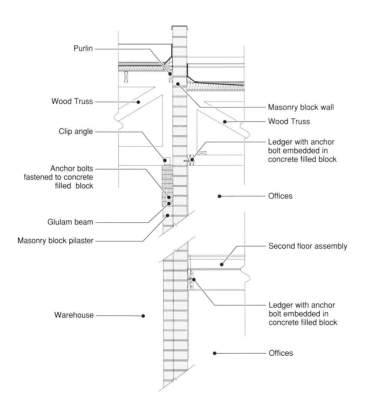

Purlin

Wood Truss

Clip angle

Anchor bolts fastened to concrete filled block

Glulam beam

Masonry block pilaster

Warehouse

Masonry block wall

Wood Truss

Ledger with anchor bolt embedded in concrete filled block

Offices

Second floor assembly

Ledger with anchor bolt embedded in concrete filled block

Offices

All the building codes relax many passive fire protection requirements, such as fire-resistance ratings for assemblies or flame-spread ratings for finishes, in buildings protected by an automatic sprinkler system. This relaxation is based on the fact that sprinklers can extinguish the fire, or at least control it, until the fire department can take over fire extinguishing operations.

In deciding to sprinkler a building, sprinkler installation costs can be weighed against savings resulting from the relaxation of passive fire protection requirements, while still maintaining or enhancing occupant safety. The underlying principle in this case is that a sprinkler system provides a level of fire safety at least equal to that which would be expected if only the passive fire protection requirements were met. An automatic sprinkler system, properly installed and maintained, ensures a high level of fire safety for occupants at all times.

Installing automatic sprinklers can change fire protection requirements in several areas. Each building code varies as to the specific requirements that may be relaxed or waived entirely. Some examples are:

- Wood framing can be used in partitions in certain buildings in lieu of noncombustible framing.

- The number of exits can be reduced by permitting increased travel distances.

- Flame-spread rating limits on interior finishes are reduced thereby permitting greater use of wood finishes.

- The area or height of a building can be increased without increasing the level of fire resistance or changing the construction type to that otherwise required for the larger-sized building.

- The fire-resistance rating can be waived for roof assemblies.

- The fire-resistance ratings can be waived for interior fire separations, or the rating can be reduced.

The examples shown in Figure 10.5a to 10.5d ($\rightarrow$ 502 to 505) show possible changes to building sizes for each of the model codes by installing sprinklers in buildings with business occupancies built with Wood-Frame construction.

The design and installation of sprinkler systems is complex, since the requirements vary with building construction type and occupancy. Designers and installers must have extensive, specialized knowledge.

The National Fire Protection Association's (NFPA) *Automatic Sprinkler Systems Handbook* and *Fire Protection Handbook* provide extensive background and explanation on the design and use of all types of automatic sprinkler systems. These documents should be used by all sprinkler system designers in order to interpret the standards for sprinkler systems installed to meet fire safety requirements in the building codes.

10

Design for Fire Safety

Figure 10.5a
Effect of Access and Sprinklers on Building Height and Area: NBCC (1990) Group D Business and Personal Service

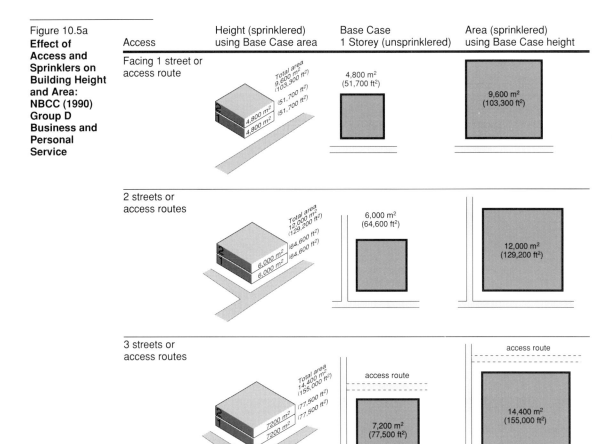

Access	Height (sprinklered) using Base Case area	Base Case 1 Storey (unsprinklered)	Area (sprinklered) using Base Case height
Facing 1 street or access route	Total area 9,600 m² (103,300 ft²); (51,700 ft²); (51,700 ft²); 4,800 m²; 4,800 m²	4,800 m² (51,700 ft²)	9,600 m² (103,300 ft²)
2 streets or access routes	Total area 12,000 m² (129,200 ft²); (64,600 ft²); (64,600 ft²); 6,000 m²; 6,000 m²	6,000 m² (64,600 ft²)	12,000 m² (129,200 ft²)
3 streets or access routes	Total area 14,400 m² (155,000 ft²); (77,500 ft²); (77,500 ft²); 7200 m²; 7200 m²	access route; 7,200 m² (77,500 ft²)	access route; 14,400 m² (155,000 ft²)

Notes:
1. Comparison based on Wood-Frame (3/4 hour), Noncombustible (unprotected), or Heavy Timber construction.
2. Minimum street width is 9m (30'). Minimum access route width is 6m (20').

Figure 10.5b
Effect of Access and Sprinklers on Building Height and Area: UBC (1988) Group B Business

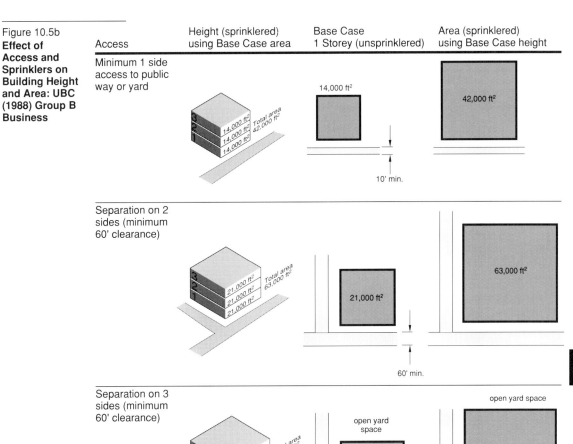

	Access	Height (sprinklered) using Base Case area	Base Case 1 Storey (unsprinklered)	Area (sprinklered) using Base Case height
	Minimum 1 side access to public way or yard	3 — 14,000 ft² / 2 — 14,000 ft² / 1 — 14,000 ft² / Total area 42,000 ft²	14,000 ft² / 10' min.	42,000 ft²
	Separation on 2 sides (minimum 60' clearance)	3 — 21,000 ft² / 2 — 21,000 ft² / 1 — 21,000 ft² / Total area 63,000 ft²	21,000 ft² / 60' min.	63,000 ft²
	Separation on 3 sides (minimum 60' clearance)	3 — 28,000 ft² / 2 — 28,000 ft² / 1 — 28,000 ft² / Total area 84,000 ft²	open yard space / 28,000 ft²	open yard space / 84,000 ft²

Notes:
1. Comparison based on Protected Wood Frame (V-1 hour) construction.
2. Open yard space must lie within property line limits.
3. Separation on 4 sides with minimum 40' clearance each side permits similar building sizes.

10

Design for Fire Safety

Figure 10.5c
**Effect of
Access and
Sprinklers on
Building Height
and Area: NBC
(1987) Group B
Business**

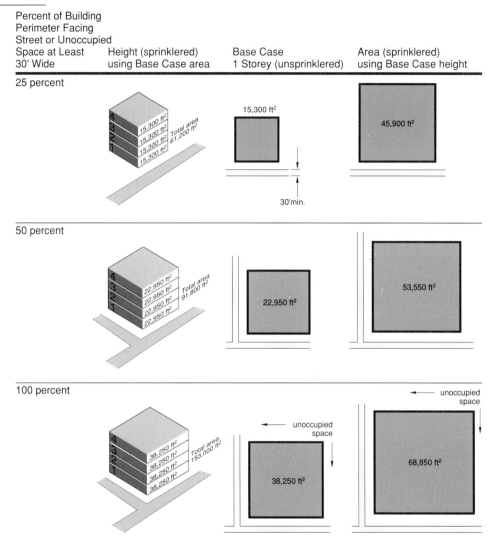

Percent of Building Perimeter Facing Street or Unoccupied Space at Least 30' Wide	Height (sprinklered) using Base Case area	Base Case 1 Storey (unsprinklered)	Area (sprinklered) using Base Case height
25 percent	15,300 ft² / 15,300 ft² / 15,300 ft² / 15,300 ft² Total area 61,200 ft²	15,300 ft² 30' min.	45,900 ft²
50 percent	22,950 ft² / 22,950 ft² / 22,950 ft² / 22,950 ft² Total area 91,800 ft²	22,950 ft²	53,550 ft²
100 percent	38,250 ft² / 38,250 ft² / 38,250 ft² / 38,250 ft² Total area 153,000 ft²	unoccupied space 38,250 ft²	unoccupied space 68,850 ft²

Notes:
1. Comparison based on Protected Wood-Frame (5A-1 hour) construction.
2. Unoccupied space must be accessible by a posted fire lane at least 18' wide.

Figure 10.5d
**Effect of
Access and
Sprinklers on
Building Height
and Area: SBC
(1988) Group B
Business**

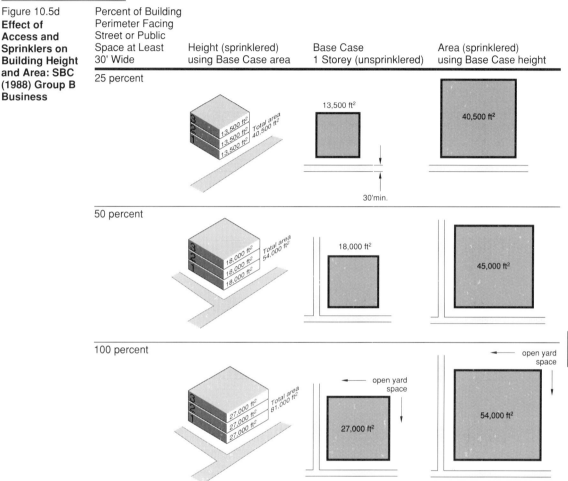

Percent of Building Perimeter Facing Street or Public Space at Least 30' Wide	Height (sprinklered) using Base Case area	Base Case 1 Storey (unsprinklered)	Area (sprinklered) using Base Case height
25 percent	13,500 ft² / 13,500 ft² / 13,500 ft² Total area 40,500 ft²	13,500 ft² 30'min.	40,500 ft²
50 percent	18,000 ft² / 18,000 ft² / 18,000 ft² Total area 54,000 ft²	18,000 ft²	45,000 ft²
100 percent	27,000 ft² / 27,000 ft² / 27,000 ft² Total area 81,000 ft²	open yard space 27,000 ft²	open yard space 54,000 ft²

10

Design for Fire Safety

Notes:
1. Comparison based on Protected Wood Frame (VI-1 hour) construction.
2. Open yard space must lie within property line limits.

Flame-Spread Ratings

General
Once a fire starts in a building, the rate at which it grows will have a significant impact on the safety of the occupants, and the time available for their escape. This will depend largely on the flammability of building contents and materials. In an attempt to control the fuel present, building codes restrict the flammability of all interior finishes in a building, as well as that of other materials which may be contained within concealed spaces.

This section discusses briefly the tests used to measure surface-burning characteristics for interior finishes, specific code requirements relating to interior finishes, and fire-retardant treated wood. Alternative flame-spread rating values for common building products are listed as well as values for frequently used wood products.

Fire Test for Interior Finishes
The need to control the flammability of building contents and materials was highlighted by a number of major fires, mostly in the 1940s and 1950s, which resulted in extensive loss of life and property.

This prompted regulatory authorities throughout North America to determine means of classifying materials by fire tests in accordance with at least two essential fire properties: surface flame-spread and smoke generated.

Materials are tested in a furnace to determine their fire properties. The test furnace is usually referred to as "the Steiner tunnel" or just "the tunnel" because of its shape.

During the test, which lasts 10 minutes for common materials used for interior finishes, the distance the flame front travels in the tunnel is observed.

The test is a relative assessment of the flammability of a material because the flame-spread measured on a specific product is evaluated against two products which serve to calibrate the apparatus: inorganic reinforced cement board and red oak, which are arbitrarily assigned a flame-spread rating of 0 and 100 respectively. The lower the flame-spread rating of a material, the more the material inhibits the spread of fire along its surface.

At the vent end of the tunnel, a photo-electric device measures the opacity of the smoke, providing an indication of the amount of smoke released from the burning material.

All tested materials are compared to the two reference materials and the results of the tests provide what is termed the flame-spread rating and the smoke-developed classification.

In Canada, information is contained in Chapter 2 of the Supplement to the NBCC on the flame-spread rating and smoke-developed classification of building materials. Information in the Supplement is provided only for generic materials for which extensive fire-test data is available. For instance, lumber, regardless of species, and Douglas fir, poplar, and spruce plywood of a thickness not less than those listed are assigned a flame-spread rating of 150.

Most surface coatings such as paint and wallpaper are usually less than 1mm (1/28") thick and will not contribute significantly to the overall rating. This is why the Supplement to the NBCC assigns the same flame-spread and smoke-developed rating to materials such as plywood, lumber and gypsum wallboard whether they are unfinished or covered with paint, varnish or cellulosic wallpaper as shown in Table 10.3 (→ 511).

Specific flame-spread ratings and smoke-developed classifications on wood products and product type by species are given in Tables 10.4 and 10.5 (→ 512). The flame-spread rating for untreated western red cedar is 73 and its smoke-developed classification is 98. Similar values are seen with some of the spruce and fir species. Because of their favourable fire performance, western red cedar and other species with a flame-spread rating below 75 can be used for interior finishes in some building applications where other products would not be recommended. Information on proprietary and fire-retardant materials is available from listings published by fire testing laboratories or the manufacturer.

Code Requirements for Interior Finishes
The North American building codes generally state that any material that forms part of the building interior and is exposed is considered to be an interior finish. In most cases this includes interior wall and ceiling finishes, flooring, carpeting, doors, trim, windows, and lighting elements. Provisions are made however in each of the codes for excluding certain minor building components which in many cases include some trim, moulding and doors.

When a surface finish such as paint, wallpaper, wood veneer, fabric or plastic is applied to a substrate such as plaster, gypsum wallboard or plywood, the surface finish is considered as the interior finish and is regulated. However, for some coatings, such as paint or wallpaper, when less than 1mm (1/28") in thickness, the flame-spread rating of the substrate may continue to govern, depending on the model code in effect.

Special fire-retardant coatings (see Section 9.5) can reduce substantially the flame-spread rating of an interior surface. These coatings are particularly useful for reducing the flame-spread rating of wood finish materials to acceptable levels. They are especially useful for those areas, such as exits, in both new and existing buildings requiring a flame-spread rating no greater than 25.

Although flooring is regulated, the model codes permit the use of finish wood flooring in almost all areas of a building. The specific code should be consulted to determine where limitations apply.

The level of code requirements for flame-spread ratings is relative to the importance of a space as a means of escape. Therefore, the restrictions increase in proportion to the importance of the space as a link to safety, and to the number of occupants in the building.

Obviously, maximum protection will be required in the exit stairway, since a fire in the exit would jeopardize all occupants of the building, while a fire in a corridor would hamper the evacuation of occupants on one floor alone. Less stringent requirements would apply in a room.

The flame-spread requirements apply equally to Combustible and Noncombustible construction because they concern the rate of fire spread along interior finishes, and not the structural fire resistance of the structure. In some buildings, such as high-rise structures, further restrictions are imposed on interior finishes.

The US codes set the maximum flame-spread rating for interior wall and ceiling finishes in most buildings at 200, which can be met by most wood products. In Canada the NBCC maximum limit is 150, with some exceptions. This means that many wood products may be used as interior finishes without special requirements for fire-retardant treatments or coatings. Where code requirements for flame-spread rating are set at 75, such as for assembly occupancies, there are several wood species, such as western red cedar, which can be used with no special treatment.

Flame-spread ratings are used to regulate the use of interior finish materials to reduce the probability of rapid fire spread. Smoke-developed classifications are used in conjunction with flame-spread ratings to regulate the use of interior finish materials where the potential to generate smoke or control smoke movements is of major fire safety importance.

10

Design for Fire Safety

In Canada, regulating products on the basis of their smoke-developed classification (SDC) only applies in high-rise buildings and to materials located in return air plenums. The SDC limits vary depending upon where the products are used. In the US, all three codes require all interior finishes to have a SDC of not greater than 450. Most wood products typically have a SDC less than 300 and therefore can meet these requirements. Using fire-retardant treated wood or fire-retardant coatings allows the use of wood finishes where more restrictive limits apply.

Fire-Retardant Treated Wood

Fire-Retardant Treated Wood (FRTW) is wood or wood product which has been impregnated with fire-retardant chemicals under high pressure.

FRTW products burn at a slower rate than untreated wood products. The treatment reduces surface-burning characteristics such as flame-spread, rate of fuel contribution and smoke contribution. To dispel any myths that may still exist, the treatment does not, as some believe, make the wood noncombustible. The concept of noncombustibility stems from certain earlier building codes which equated a 25 flame-spread rating to noncombustibility. Although manufactured by the same pressure process, FRTW contains different chemicals than products known as preservative treated wood. The products are not interchangeable.

In Canada, FRTW must have a flame-spread rating of not more than 25. When FRTW is specified in the US codes, it must meet similar FSR requirements but with an extended fire-test duration of 30 minutes compared to the 10 minutes normally required for other interior finishes.

Because FRTW has a flame-spread rating of not more than 25, it qualifies as an interior finish for any application since the most restrictive flame-spread rating in the building codes is 25.

Fire-retardant coatings applied to wood can also be used to reduce the flame-spread rating of the finish to less than 75 or 25.

FRTW must be identified by a label (see Section 9.5) from an independent testing laboratory which indicates that the necessary tests have been carried out and production controls maintained. These laboratories provide lists of tested materials, which are useful reference documents for locating sources of supply.

Access for Firefighting

It is vital that a building be arranged so that any fire can be reached quickly. Access and egress facilities must be provided and maintained to permit fire department personnel to reach the site, evaluate and suppress the fire in the building and to reach those people who may be exposed to the fire.

Almost all buildings must be accessible from a street or an access route on the property. For larger buildings, the access routes must be adjacent to the principal entrance and must meet certain minimum width requirements, as well as requirements for access to or from thoroughfares, quality of travel surfaces and, in some cases, turn-around limits. Figure 10.6 (opposite) shows an example of the requirements in Canada for access to buildings for fire department use.

The allowable heights and areas for buildings are determined according to the amount of firefighting access provided. A building facing three streets, or with clear or unoccupied space on three sides, can have a greater building area or building height than one facing only a single street. Obviously, with the greater amount of access provided the risk is reduced. Consequently, the fire safety requirements, such as construction type restrictions, are relaxed. The information contained in the examples in Figures 10.5a to 10.5d (→ 502 to 505) as well as Table 10.1 (→ 485 to 492) shows the impact on the building size resulting from the amount of access around the outside of a building for firefighting purposes.

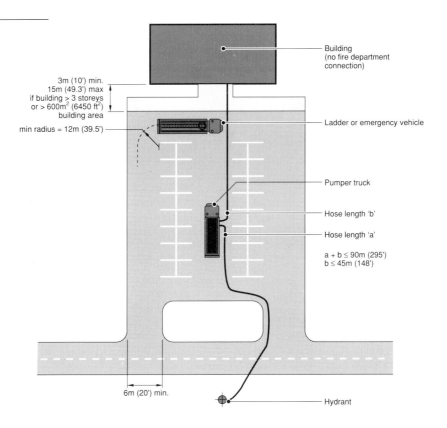

Figure 10.6
Example of Building Access Requirements (Canada)

3m (10') min.
15m (49.3') max
if building > 3 storeys
or > 600m² (6450 ft²)
building area
min radius = 12m (39.5')

Building
(no fire department
connection)

Ladder or emergency vehicle

Pumper truck

Hose length 'b'

Hose length 'a'

a + b ≤ 90m (295')
b ≤ 45m (148')

6m (20') min.

Hydrant

10

Design for Fire Safety

Fire Separations and Fire Compartments

A fire separation is a construction assembly that acts as a barrier against the spread of fire. The rated fire separations, that is, the building floors and interior walls, are the basic components of a fire compartment.

A fire compartment or fire area is an enclosed space in a building that is separated from all other parts of the building by fire separations having a required fire-resistance rating.

The codes contain requirements intended to limit the combustibility and flammability of building materials which should limit fire growth. However, because little control exists over the flammability of building contents (such as furniture and furnishings), these restrictions cannot ensure that a fire will not become fully developed at some time. Requirements for fire separa-

tions, fire compartments, and fire-resistance are intended to provide passive fire protection for the occupants of a building.

Code requirements for passive fire protection systems in the form of minimum fire-resistance ratings and compartments, combined in some cases with active protection in the form of automatic sprinklers, provide for a degree of structural stability and limited fire growth. This is intended to ensure building occupants time to evacuate and also allow for fire department entry.

A fire separation must, in most cases, have fire-resistance and continuity. In all cases, a fire separation must be designed to remain in place and restrict the passage of smoke and fire for a long enough period to ensure that occupants can leave the area or in some cases, until a sprinkler system is activated that will control and usually suppress the fire.

The North American codes require fire separations to be constructed as continuous elements. However, floors and interior walls of a building must have openings to allow for the passage of people and building services. It is critical that these openings be protected so that the continuity of the fire separations and the compartments are maintained.

Fire rarely spreads from one compartment to another by burning through floors or walls. Usually, it bypasses these physical barriers through concealed spaces in ceilings or attics, heating, ventilating and air-conditioning ducts, holes made through fire separations for the passage of electrical wires or open doors. Each opening in a fire separation must therefore be protected by a barrier or fire stopped with materials that will withstand smoke and hot fire gases for a specified period.

Openings such as doorways and holes for the passage of building services must be protected with closures such as doors, shutters, fire dampers, wired glass or glass blocks. Such devices or assemblies must be rated for fire exposure in accordance with specific test standards, depending on the type of closure.

The codes impose limits on the size of openings permitted in fire separations and, in some cases, limit the number of openings in the fire separation.

To be effective, closures must remain closed, or close automatically under fire conditions. Because size makes doors a particular concern, the codes generally require self-closing devices on every door in a fire separation. Such protection cannot be over-emphasized in occupancies such as hotels and apartment buildings. A suite door left open could allow hot fire gases and smoke to fill a corridor.

In certain cases, the codes allow hold-open devices which hold the door open until a fusible link fails, or until a smoke detector or fire alarm system gives a signal. Fusible links are often used in industrial buildings where a guillotine or sliding shutter will be activated to close an opening. Schools, hotels and commercial facilities often use an electromagnetic device which releases the door on a signal from a fire alarm system or detector. The codes specify conditions for use of each type of device.

Wood doors can be designed to meet the requirements for closures in certain fire separations. Most codes permit the use of 20-minute rated solid-core wood doors to be used in any fire separation required to have a fire-resistance rating of not more than one-hour.

Concealed spaces must be given special consideration to ensure that they will not act as flues through which a fire may burn or smoke may spread undetected.

Fire stopping or draft stopping in concealed spaces is installed to limit the spread of smoke and hot fire gases. For these applications, most codes permit the use of solid lumber or wood panel products such as plywood, OSB/waferboard, or particleboard. Minimum spacing of the stops as well as maximum thicknesses of the materials are specified in each of the codes.

Reference Tables

Table 10.3
**Assigned
Flame-Spread
Ratings and
Smoke
Developed
Classifications
in NBCC
(Canada)**

Materials	Applicable Standard	Minimum Thickness mm	in.	Unfinished [3] FSR [4]	SDC [4]	Paint or Varnish not More than 1.3mm (1/20") Thick, Cellulosic Wallpaper not more than 1 Layer FSR [4]	SDC [4]
Hardwood or softwood flooring [3]	-	-	-	300	300		
Gypsum wallboard	CSA A82.27	9.5	3/8	25	50	25	50
Lumber	None	16	5/8	150	300	150	300
Douglas fir plywood [1]	CSA O121	11	7/16	150	100	150	300
Poplar plywood [1]	CSA O153	11	7/16	150	100	150	300
Plywood with spruce face veneer [1]	CSA O151	11	7/16	150	100	150	300
Douglas fir plywood [1]	CSA O121	6	1/4	150	100	150	300
Fibreboard low density	CSA A247	11	7/16	> 150	100	150	300
Hardboard Type 1 Standard	CGSB-11.3	9 6	11/32 1/4	150 150	> 300 300	[2] 150	[2] 300
Particleboard	CAN3-O188.1	12.7	1/2	150	300	[2]	[2]
Waferboard	CAN3-O188.1	-	-	[2]	[2]	[2]	[2]

Notes:
1. The flame-spread ratings and smoke developed classifications shown are for those plywoods without a cellulose resin overlay.
2. Insufficient test information available.
3. Wood flooring unfinished or finished with a spar or urethane varnish coating.
4. FSR – Flame-Spread Rating; SDC – Smoke-Developed Classification

Source: NBCC Supplement

Reference Tables continued

Table 10.4
Flame-Spread Ratings and Smoke Developed Classifications of Solid Wood Products

Species [4]		Flame-Spread Ratings	Smoke-Developed Classification	Source
Birch	Yellow	105 - 110	-	UL
Cedar	Western red	70	-	HPMA
		73	98	CWC
	Pacific coast yellow	78	90	CWC
Fir	Amabilis (pacific silver)	69	58	CWC
Fir	Douglas	70 - 100	-	UL
Hemlock	Western	60 - 75	-	UL
Maple	(flooring)	104	-	CWC
Oak	Red or white	100	100	UL
Pine	Eastern white	85	122	CWC
	Lodgepole	93	210	CWC
	Ponderosa	105 - 230	-	UL
	Red	142	229	CWC
	Western white	75	-	UL
Poplar		170 - 185	-	UL
Spruce	Northern	65	-	UL
	Sitka	74	74	CWC
	Western white	100	-	UL
Walnut		130 - 140	-	UL
Shakes	Western red cedar	69	-	HPMA
Shingles	Western red cedar 12.5mm (1/2" actual)	49	-	HPMA

Notes:
1. CWC: Canadian Wood Council – *Wood and Fire Safety*
2. UL: Underwriters' Laboratory – UL527, May 1971, Test Report 645197
3. HPMA: Hardwood Plywood Manufacturers Association, Test Reports 202, 203, 335, 337, 592, 596.
4. Values listed are for lumber, 19mm (1" nom.) thickness, except as noted.

Table 10.5
Flame-Spread Ratings for Panel Products

Product	Thickness mm	in.	Flame-Spread Rating [1]
Aspen plywood	6.4	1/4	196
Birch plywood	6.4	1/4	115 - 185
	4.8	3/16	170 - 190
	4.0	5/32	160 - 195
Cherry plywood	6.4	1/4	160
Hickory plywood	6.4	1/4	140
Lauan plywood	6.4	1/4	99 - 141
Maple plywood	6.4	1/4	155
Oak plywood	6.4	1/4	125 - 185
Pine plywood	6.4	1/4	120 - 140
Walnut plywood	6.4	1/4	138 - 160

Note:
1. Source: Hardwood Plywood Manufacturers Association

10.4   Fire-Resistance

Fire-Resistance Ratings

The previous section included descriptions of fire separations used to protect against fire spread and those which form fire compartments within a building. A fire-resistance rating is the time that a material or assembly of materials will withstand the passage of flame, and the transmission of heat when exposed to fire under specified conditions of test and performance criteria. Walls and floors built to act as fire separations must be designed to resist the effects of fire for a certain time based on the expected severity of the fire in a compartment.

Fire severity is based in part upon the amount of fuel present in a fire, which varies with occupancy. For example, the fuel available in a fire in an office building may be significantly greater than the amount of fuel available in a residential fire. For this reason, the fire-resistance ratings of the assemblies also vary from occupancy to occupancy. In addition to the expected fire severity in an occupancy, other factors, such as exit travel distance and the mobility of occupants for a given occupancy were taken into consideration in determining the fire-resistance ratings required by the building codes.

Since the early 1920s, the conventional way of establishing fire-resistance rating has been to subject a representative sample of the construction assembly to a standard fire test performed in a special furnace as shown in Figure 10.7 (→ 514). The test methods and furnaces date back to the end of the last century.

Representative samples of the assemblies are tested. Test assemblies are large enough to simulate the floor or wall enclosing a small room; for instance, floor specimens must be almost 17m² (180 ft²) and walls must be slightly over 9m² (100 ft²) in area.

Horizontal assemblies are tested for fire exposure from the underside only, because a fire in the room or space below presents the most severe threat. Similarly, the fire-resistance rating is required from the underside of the assembly only.

Walls are tested for fire exposure from one side only. However, partitions or interior walls required to have a fire-resistance rating must be rated equally from each side and therefore must be designed symmetrically since a fire could develop on either side of the assembly.

Most wood-stud wall assemblies are tested and listed as loadbearing which allows them to be used in both loadbearing and non-loadbearing applications. Wood-stud wall assemblies can be designed to meet fire-resistance rating requirements up to two hours. Most steel-stud wall assemblies are tested and listed as non-loadbearing because they are used primarily in non-loadbearing applications in noncombustible buildings.

In Canada, exterior walls only require rating for fire exposure from within a building regardless of how close the building is to the property line. The requirement for symmetry in fire-rated interior wall assemblies does not apply to exterior wall assemblies because fire exposure from the exterior of a building is not likely to be as severe as that from a fire in an interior room or compartment.

In the US, all three codes require the fire-resistance rating for exterior walls to be provided from both sides except that in the SBC and NBC, the rating is not required from the outside where the fire separation distance is greater than 1.5m (5').

The test and acceptance criteria for fire-resistance is essentially the same in Canada and the US. The tests in both countries are essentially identical. The test measures the ability of an assembly to restrict the passage of heat or flame and to stay in place for a specified time during a fire.

10

Design for Fire Safety

Figure 10.7
Fire Test Furnace for Walls

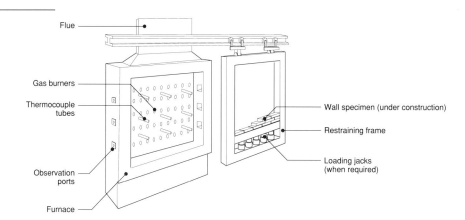

Flue

Gas burners

Thermocouple tubes

Wall specimen (under construction)

Restraining frame

Loading jacks (when required)

Observation ports

Furnace

The fire test provides a measure of the fire-resistance of the entire assembly, not that of its individual components. In other words, the fire-resistance test is designed to assess an assembly as a complete system, whether it is of combustible or noncombustible construction. Designers must conform to every essential detail of the tested assemblies for the results to be applicable. Even a slight modification, such as type or spacing of fasteners, could necessitate testing a new specimen to ensure that the proposed modification will not have a detrimental effect on the fire-resistance of the assembly.

For buildings incorporating wood frame structural components in Canada, the code refers to three types of construction, while in the US all three codes each contain provisions for up to six types. The major differences between the types of construction are the materials used for the main structural components (combustible vs. noncombustible) and the fire-resistance rating required (0, 3/4, 1, or 2 hrs.).

In most of these construction types, floor, roof and mezzanine assemblies require a fire-resistance rating, but there are exceptions. For example, in Canada in office buildings three storeys or less in building height, the floor, mezzanine and roof assemblies are permitted to be of unrated noncombustible construction while combustible construction requires a 45-minute fire-resistance rating, or be of Heavy Timber construction. The limits on building height and area are the same for all three types of construction.

In the US codes, the height and area limits vary significantly from one type of construction to another. For buildings incorporating wood frame floors and walls, the minimum fire-resistance ratings range from zero to two hours. Obviously, the larger buildings will require the higher fire-resistance ratings.

Fire-Resistance of Sample Assemblies

A multitude of fire-resistance tests have been conducted over the last 70 years by North American laboratories. Results are available through:

• Underwriters' Laboratories of Canada

• Warnock Hersey Professional Services Ltd.

• Underwriters' Laboratories Incorporated

• Factory Mutual Research Corporation

In addition, manufacturers of construction products publish results of fire-resistance tests on assemblies incorporating their proprietary products.

Two of the model codes, the NBCC in Canada and the SBC in the US, list specific descriptions of fire-rated assemblies. Detailed information on a large number of tested assemblies with different fire-resistance ratings is also contained in the *Building Construction Lists* published by Underwriters' Laboratories of Canada (ULC) and Underwriters' Laboratories Inc. (ULI) in the US.

Examples of the type of information contained in the ULC listings are shown in Figures 10.8 below and 10.9 (→ 516). The listings are useful because they offer custom solutions to designers, but at the same time they may limit innovation because designers are tempted to use assemblies which have already been tested, rather than pay to have new assemblies assessed. Fire-resistance ratings developed in accordance with the US standard, ASTM E119 are acceptable both in Canada and the US.

Figure 10.8
Listed Wood Joist Floor Assembly

ULC Design No. M503
Unrestrained Assembly Rating: 2h

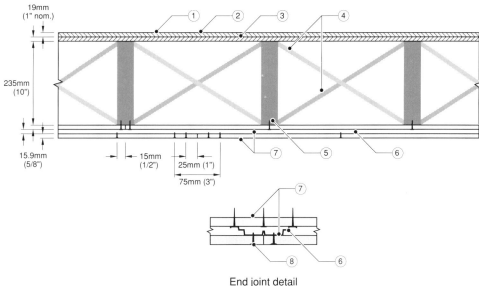

End joint detail

Combustible Construction
(Finish Rating - 75 minutes)

10

Design for Fire Safety

1. Finish Flooring: 19 x 89mm (1" x 4") T & G flooring laid perpendicular to joists or 15.5mm (5/8") select sheathing grade T & G phenolic bonded Douglas Fir plywood with face grain perpendicular to joists and joints staggered.
2. Building Paper (optional): Commercial sheathing material, 0.25mm (0.10") thick.
3. Sub-flooring: 19 x 140mm (1" x 6") T & G boards laid diagonally to joists or 12.5mm (1/2") unsanded sheathing grade phenolic bonded Douglas Fir plywood with face grain perpendicular to joists and joints staggered.
4. Bridging: 19 x 64mm (1" x 3").
5. Wood Joists: 38 x 235mm (2" x 10") spaced 400mm (16") O.C., firestopped.
6. Furring Channel: Resilient, formed of 0.5mm (0.021") electrogalvanized steel as shown, spaced 600mm (24") O.C. perpendicular to joists. Channels overlapped at splice 38mm (1-1/2") and fastened to each joist with 63mm (8d) common nails. Minimum clearance of channels to walls, 20mm (3/4"). Additional pieces 1500mm (60") long placed immediately adjacent to channels at end of joints of second layers; ends to extend 150mm (6") beyond each side of end joint.
7. Gypsum Wallboard: (Guide No. 40U18.23). 15.9mm (5/8") thick, 1200mm (48") wide. First layer of wallboard installed with long dimension perpendicular to joists and end joints of boards located at the joists. Nailed to joists with uncoated 63mm (8d) box nails spaced 180mm (7") O.C. All nails located 15mm (1/2") minimum distance from the edges and ends of the board. Second layer of wallboard secured to furring channels by 25mm (1") long wallboard screws. Second layer installed with long dimension perpendicular to the furring channels and centre line of boards located under a joist and so placed that the edge joint of this layer is not in alignment with the end joint of the first layer. Secured to furring channels with wallboard screws 300mm (12") O.C. with additional screws 75mm (3") from side joints. End joints of wallboard fastened at additional furring channels as shown in end-joint detail. All screws located 25mm (1") minimum distance from edges of boards.
   ATLANTIC GYPSUM, a division of the Lundrigans-Comstock Limited
   DOMTAR INC.
   GEORGIA PACIFIC CORPORATION
   WESTROC INDUSTRIES LIMITED
8. Wallboard screws: Type S Phillips self-drilling and self-tapping 25mm (1") long.
9. Joint System (not shown): Paper tape embedded in cementitious compound over joints and exposed nail heads covered with compound, with edges of compound feathered out.

(Reprinted by permission of Underwriters' Laboratories of Canada)

Figure 10.9
**Listed Wood
Stud Wall
Assembly**

Design No. U301
Assembly Rating: 2h

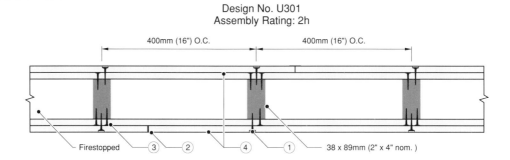

Bearing Wall - Combustion Construction
(Finish Rating - 66 minutes)

1. Nailheads: Exposed or covered with joint finisher.
2. Joints: Exposed or covered with tape and joint finisher.
3. Nails: 51mm (1-7/8", 6d), cement-coated flathead.
4. Gypsum Wallboard: (Guide No. 40U18.23),15.9mm (5/8") thick applied in two layers. Base layer placed vertically with joints butted over studs and nailed to studs 150mm (6") O.C. Face Layer applied horizontally with joint finisher cement and nailed 300mm (12") O.C. temporarily to base layer until cement sets. All joints in face layers staggered with joints in base layers and with joints on opposite sides.

Canadian Gypsum Company, Limited
Domtar Inc.

Reprinted by permission of Underwriters' Laboratories of Canada

Calculation Methods for Fire-Resistance Ratings

General
Fire-resistance ratings can be determined by calculation methods in lieu of using standard fire test results. The methods are adopted in Canada in the NBCC and in the US in the UBC and SBC for Wood-Frame, wall, floor, and roof assemblies and in the NBCC and NBC for Heavy Timber columns and beams. They involve the use of simple calculation procedures which are based on extensive fire-test results carried out on Wood-Frame and Heavy Timber assemblies.

Calculation of Fire-Resistance of Light Frame Assemblies
The most practical method uses procedures given for calculating the fire-resistance rating of light Wood-Frame wall, floor and roof assemblies based on generic descriptions of materials. This, the Component Additive Method, can be used when it

is clear that the fire-resistance rating of an assembly depends strictly on the specification and arrangement of materials for which nationally recognized standards exist. The method was developed in the early 1960s from an analysis of fire-test data. Since the assigned ratings must apply to all systems and products covered by the material standard description, the estimates are conservative.

The Component Additive Method can be used in Canada to assign a fire-resistance rating of up to 90 minutes. It is limited to 1 hour in the US codes. In both countries, the method can be applied to wood-stud walls and partitions, and to wood-joist floor and roof assemblies. In Canada, the method can also be used for wood truss roof and floor assemblies. The major structural components of Wood-Frame floor and roof assemblies include wood joists and metal plate-connected wood trusses, of both pitched and parallel chord design.

Wood studs, wood joists and wood framing members of trusses must not be less than 38 x 89mm (2" x 4" nom.). No data is currently available to support the application of this calculation method to assemblies incorporating wood trusses with metal-tube or bar webs, nor to prefabricated wood I-joists. Manufacturers of these products have proprietary listings of assemblies incorporating these elements with fire-resistance ratings ranging from 45 minutes to two-hours.

In applying the Component Additive Method, the fire-resistance rating of an assembly is calculated by adding the time assigned to the protective membrane (wallboard or ceiling membrane) on the fire side to the time assigned to the structural framing members. Additional time can be added when some types of insulation are provided within the assembly. Although resilient and drywall furring channels were not common when the calculation method was developed, they are now permitted in Canada for floor or roof assemblies, without reduction in assigned values.

Table 10.6 (→ 527) lists the time assigned to wallboard membranes used for walls and ceilings based on the ability of the membrane to stay in place during the standard fire test.

Table 10.7 (→ 527) lists the times assigned to various wood frame members, which are based on the time between the failure of the protective membrane on the fire side and the collapse of the assembly. Values are not assigned to wood studs spaced at 600mm (24") on centre due to lack of data. However, several of the codes contain lists of fire-resistance ratings for interior and exterior wall assemblies which can be used for these greater stud spacings. Also, there are proprietary fire ratings for the greater stud spacings available both in Canada and in the US.

For fire-resistance rated interior partitions, the NBCC in Canada requires ratings from both sides. The Component Additive Method assumes that the wall assembly will be symmetrical in design and will therefore have equivalent membrane protection on each side. If the membranes differ, the fire-resistance rating must be determined on the basis of the membrane assigned the lowest time. In this calculation, no contribution to the fire-resistance rating is assigned for the membrane(s) on the non-fire exposed side of the assembly, whether it is a partition, floor or roof, or exterior wall, because it is assumed that the unexposed membrane will collapse when the framing fails.

In Canada, exterior walls must be rated from the interior side only. The assembly need not be symmetrical, provided the sheathing and exterior cladding combination is listed in Table 10.8 (→ 527) or is a membrane listed in Table 10.6 (→ 527) that is assigned at least 15 minutes.

For floor and roof assemblies rated on the basis of fire exposure from below, the upper membrane (subfloor/finish floor; roof deck/covering) must consist of one of the combinations listed in Table 10.9 (→ 528) or a membrane in Table 10.6 (→ 527) assigned at least 15 minutes.

In Canada only, in using the Component Additive Method to determine the fire-resistance rating of a floor or roof assembly, a designer may choose a ceiling membrane that contributes all of the rating. The times assigned to gypsum wallboard differ where the fire-resistance rating of a ceiling is determined based on the contribution of the membrane only rather than on the complete assembly. Table 10.10 (→ 528) lists these values which apply only to assemblies with wood joists and wood trusses.

Specific details on important features such as fastener spacing and minimum penetration, as well as the orientation and joint support required for gypsum wallboard panels must be respected. A section on fire-resistance ratings for solid-wood floors, walls and roofs is listed in the Supplement to the NBCC and is useful when dealing with existing buildings having Heavy Timber construction elements.

10

Design for Fire Safety

Calculation Examples for Light Frame Assemblies

Following are examples of how to calculate the FRR of light wood-frame assemblies.

The examples are based on the approach used in Canada. In the US codes, the approach is similar but minor differences prevent a direct comparison.

Example 1

Determine the fire-resistance rating of an interior partition with 12.7mm (1/2") Type X gypsum wallboard (GWB) on both sides of wood studs spaced at 400mm (16") on centre.

From Table 10.6 (→ 527)

Time assigned to 12.7mm (1/2") Type X GWB	25

From Table 10.7 (→ 527)

Time assigned to wood studs	20
Fire-resistance rating of interior partition:	45 minutes

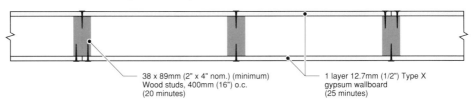

38 x 89mm (2" x 4" nom.) (minimum)
Wood studs, 400mm (16") o.c.
(20 minutes)

1 layer 12.7mm (1/2") Type X
gypsum wallboard
(25 minutes)

Example 2

Determine the fire-resistance rating of a wood stud exterior wall assembly with 15.9mm (5/8") Type X gypsum wallboard (GWB) on the interior side and plywood sheathing and wood shingle siding on txe exterior with the studs spaced at 400mm (16") on centre.

From Table 10.6 (→ 527)

Time assigned to 15.9mm (5/8") Type X GWB	40

From Table 10.7 (→ 527)

Time assigned to wood studs	20
Fire-resistance rating of exterior wall:	60 minutes

From Table 10.8 (→ 527)

Minimum thickness of plywood sheathing to be 7.5mm (5/16") exterior grade, plus wood shingle siding.

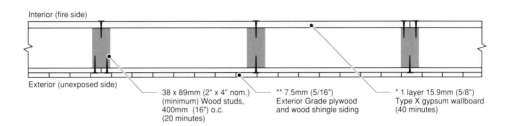

Interior (fire side)

Exterior (unexposed side)

38 x 89mm (2" x 4" nom.)
(minimum) Wood studs,
400mm (16") o.c.
(20 minutes)

** 7.5mm (5/16")
Exterior Grade plywood
and wood shingle siding

* 1 layer 15.9mm (5/8")
Type X gypsum wallboard
(40 minutes)

Notes to Example 2:

*   If the wall cavity is insulated with Mineral Fibre insulation (not fibreglass) having a mass
     of not less than 1.22 kg/m^2 (0.25 lbs/ft^2)of wall surface (15 minutes assigned contribu-
     tion) Type X GWB could be 12.7mm (1/2") thick (25 minutes) and still retain one hour
     assigned FRR.

**   This combination could be replaced by any membrane assigned at least 15 minutes in
     Table 10.6 (→ 527) or by any other membrane(s) described in Table 10.9 (→ 527).

Example 3

Determine the fire-resistance rating of a wood truss floor assembly with a ceiling of
15.9mm (5/8") Type X gypsum wallboard (GWB) and trusses spaced at 600mm (24") on
centre.

From Table 10.6 (→ 527)

     Time assigned to 15.9mm Type X GWB   40

From Table 10.7 (→ 527)

     Time assigned to wood trusses   5
                                                                    ───────────
     Fire-resistance rating of wood truss floor assembly: 45 minutes

10

Design for Fire Safety

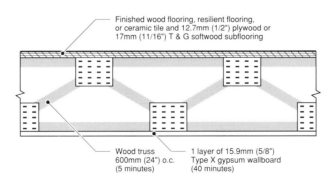

Finished wood flooring, resilient flooring,
or ceramic tile and 12.7mm (1/2") plywood or
17mm (11/16") T & G softwood subflooring

Wood truss
600mm (24") o.c.
(5 minutes)

1 layer of 15.9mm (5/8")
Type X gypsum wallboard
(40 minutes)

Example 4
Determine the fire-resistance rating of a wood joist floor assembly with a ceiling of 2 layers of 12.7mm (1/2") gypsum wallboard (GWB) and joists spaced at 400mm (16") on centre.

From Table 10.6 (→ 527)

Time assigned to two layers of 12.7mm (1/2") gypsum wallboard   50 *

From Table 10.7 (→ 527)

Time assigned to wood joists   10
                                                                                   _____

Fire-resistance rating of wood joist floor assembly   60 minutes

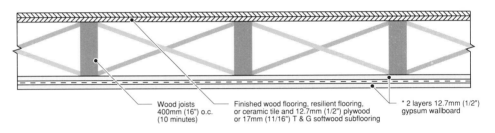

Wood joists
400mm (16") o.c.
(10 minutes)

Finished wood flooring, resilient flooring,
or ceramic tile and 12.7mm (1/2") plywood
or 17mm (11/16") T & G softwood subflooring

* 2 layers 12.7mm (1/2")
gypsum wallboard

Notes to Example 4:

* Wire mesh with 1.57mm (0.62") diameter wire and 25 x 25mm (1" x 1') openings must be fastened between the two sheets of wallboard.

Calculation of Fire-Resistance of Heavy Timber Columns and Beams

The NBCC in Canada and the National Building Code (NBC) in the US adopt a calculation method for determining the fire-resistance rating of Heavy Timber columns and beams. In Canada, the method can be used only with glulam members while in the US it is applicable to both glulam and solid sawn members.

Another major difference in the US is that there are requirements specified which detail minimum protection from fire exposure for the connectors and fasteners. There are no such requirements in the Canadian method. Again, due to minor differences in the two methods, only the Canadian values are shown. However, the principles behind the method referred to in the NBC in the US are in general the same.

When exposed to fire, wood undergoes thermal degradation and produces a layer of char. Under standard fire test conditions the constant across-grain char rate of most wood species is approximately 0.66 mm/minute (1/40"). This char layer acts as an insulator protecting the unburnt portion of the wood.

Studies on the combustion of wood products have produced models to calculate the fire-resistance rating of unprotected wood assemblies. They predict char depth, temperature distribution in the unburnt parts and strength properties of wood at elevated temperatures.

The Supplement to the NBCC in Canada and the NBC in the US include empirical equations for calculating the fire-resistance rating of glulam and solid sawn (US only) timber beams and columns. These equations were developed from theoretical predictions and validated by test results.

Under these procedures, beams and columns may be assigned a fire-resistance rating (FRR) based on exposure to fire from three or four sides. In Canada, the fire-resistance rating, in minutes, of glulam beams and columns is based on

$$FRR = m\,f\,B\left[4 - \frac{2B}{D}\right]$$

for beams exposed to fire on 4 sides;

$$FRR = m\,f\,B\left[4 - \frac{B}{D}\right]$$

for beams exposed to fire on 3 sides;

$$FRR = m\,f\,B\left[3 - \frac{B}{D}\right]$$

for columns exposed to fire on 4 sides;

$$FRR = m\,f\,B\left[3 - \frac{B}{2D}\right]$$

for columns exposed to 3 sides;

where

m = 0.1 for calculations in metric units and 2.54 for calculations in Imperial units.

f = the load factor shown in Figure 10.10 ($\rightarrow$ 522) to compensate for partial loading.

B = the full dimension of the smaller side of the beam or column in mm before exposure to fire as shown in Figure 10.11 ($\rightarrow$ 523).

D = the full dimension of the larger side of the beam or column in mm before exposure to fire as shown in Figure 10.11 ($\rightarrow$ 522).

The formula for columns or beams which may be exposed on three sides applies only when the unexposed face is the smaller side of a column; no experimental data exists to verify the formula when a larger side is unexposed. If a column is recessed into a wall or a beam into a floor, the full dimensions of the structural member must be used in calculations.

Comparisons of the calculated fire-resistance ratings with experimental results show the calculated values as conservative, being almost 30 percent underestimated in some cases. The predictions can be considered reasonably accurate since similar variations are seen in repeat fire tests.

In Canada, a designer may determine the allowable load on a beam or column by referring to CSA Standard CAN/CSA-O86.1-M89 *Engineering Design in Wood* or the Canadian Wood Council's *Wood Design Manual*.

In the US, this information is obtained from the National Forest Product Association *National Design Specification*.

10

Design for Fire Safety

Calculation Example for Heavy Timber

The following is an example of fire-resistance calculation of glulam beams:

Example 1

Determine the fire-resistance rating of a glulam beam exposed on three sides having dimensions of 175 x 380mm (6.9" x 15") and stressed to 80 percent of its factored bending moment resistance.

B = 175mm (6.9")

D = 380mm (15")

From Figure 10.10 ($\rightarrow$ 522), f = 1.075 for a beam designed to carry a factored load equal to 80 percent of factored bending moment resistance.

$$FRR = m \, f \, B\left[4 - \frac{B}{D}\right]$$

Metric:

$$FRR = 0.1 \times 1.075 \times 175 \times \left[4 - \frac{175}{380}\right]$$

Imperial:

$$FRR = 2.54 \times 1.075 \times 6.9 \times \left[4 - \frac{6.9}{15}\right]$$

Total fire-resistance rating = 66.6 minutes.

This beam could be used to support a one hour fire-resistance rated wood frame floor assembly such as the one shown in the Example 4 (→ 520). calculation, using the Component Additive Method.

Figure 10.10
Load Factor for Glulam Fire-Resistance Calculations (NBCC)

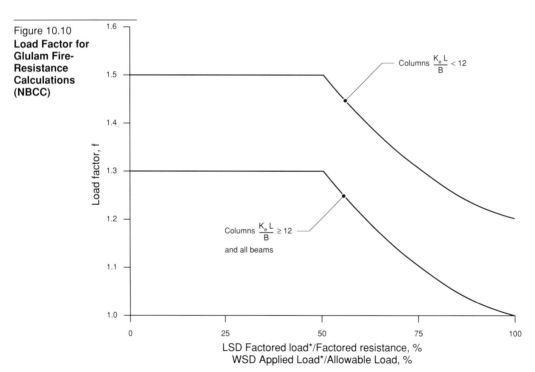

Notes:
1. K_e = Effective length factor
2. L = Unsupported length of a column in mm
3. B = Smaller side of a beam or column in mm (before fire exposure)
4. LSD = Limit States Design
   WSD = Working Stress Design
* In the case of beams, use bending moment in place of load.

Figure 10.11
Examples of Full Dimension Beams and Columns in Glulam Exposure Cases

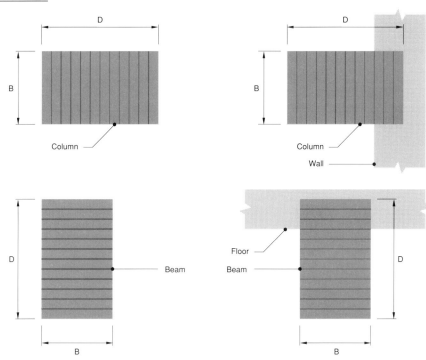

10

Design for Fire Safety

Extrapolation of Data from Fire-Resistance Tests

Although not specifically referenced in any of the North American building codes or fire-test standards, several documents have been written on how to extrapolate information from fire-test results.

Dr. Tibor Harmathy's *The Ten Rules of Fire Endurance* provides guidance on the impact made on the fire-resistance rating of materials and assemblies when the original product or assembly is altered in some way.

The document provides a means of assessing the fire endurance of various assemblies since it is impossible to test, prior to use, all assemblies used today. Harmathy's document was used by the NBCC committee that developed the Component Additive Method in the 1960s.

Harmathy's 10 rules are:

Rule 1
The thermal fire endurance of a construction consisting of a number of parallel layers is greater than the sum of the "thermal" fire endurance characteristics of the individual layers when exposed separately to a fire.

Rule 2
The fire endurance of a construction does not decrease with the addition of further layers.

Rule 3
The fire endurance of constructions that contain continuous air gaps or cavities is greater than the fire endurance of similar constructions of the same weight, but containing no gaps or cavities.

Rule 4
The farther an air gap or cavity is located from the exposed surface, the more beneficial is its effect on fire endurance.

Rule 5
The fire endurance of a construction cannot be increased by increasing the thickness of a completely enclosed air layer.

Rule 6
Layers of materials of low thermal conductivity are better utilized on the side of the construction on which fire is more likely to occur.

Rule 7
The fire endurance of asymmetrical constructions depends on the direction of heat flow.

Rule 8
The presence of moisture, if it does not result in explosive spalling, increases fire endurance.

Rule 9
Load-supporting elements, such as beams, girders and joists, yield higher fire endurances when subjected to fire endurance tests as part of a floor, roof, or ceiling assembly than they would when tested separately.

Rule 10
The load-supporting elements (beams, girders, joists, etc.) of a floor, roof or ceiling assembly can be replaced by such other load-supporting elements that, when tested separately, yield fire-endurance ratings of not less than that of the assembly.

Figure 10.12 (opposite) illustrates the 10 rules. The rules are not intended to replace more accurate design methods but may help in evaluating minor changes to the components of tested assemblies.

A more recent Canadian publication, *Criteria For Use in Extension Of Data From Fire Endurance Tests* (ULC Subject C263(e)-M1988) is based in part on Harmathy's rules. This document is useful in determining whether or not an assembly can meet fire-resistance rating requirements based on results of a test on an assembly which has been altered so that it differs slightly in design from the original which was tested.

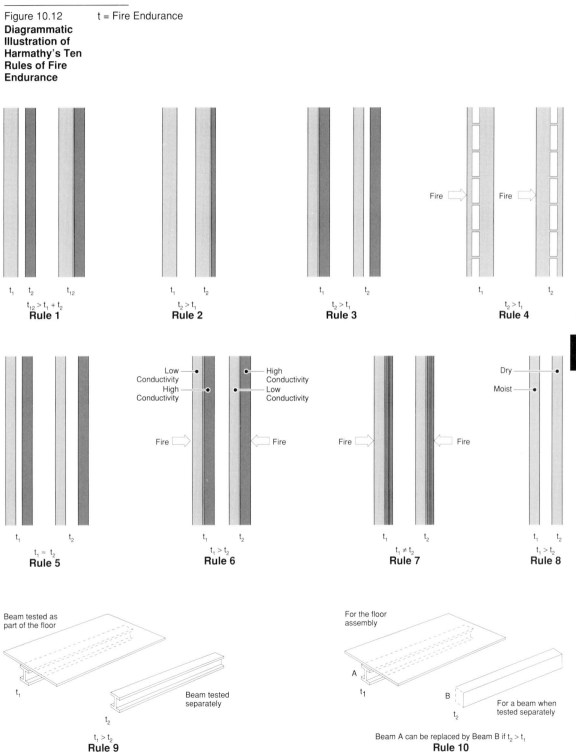

Figure 10.12   t = Fire Endurance

**Diagrammatic
Illustration of
Harmathy's Ten
Rules of Fire
Endurance**

t_1 t_2 t_{12}
$t_{12} > t_1 + t_2$
Rule 1

t_1 t_2
$t_2 > t_1$
Rule 2

t_1 t_2
$t_2 > t_1$
Rule 3

Fire ⇨   Fire ⇨

t_1 t_2
$t_2 > t_1$
Rule 4

t_1 t_2
$t_1 \approx t_2$
Rule 5

Low Conductivity
High Conductivity
High Conductivity
Low Conductivity
Fire ⇨   ⇦ Fire

t_1 t_2
$t_1 > t_2$
Rule 6

Fire ⇨   ⇦ Fire

t_1 t_2
$t_1 \neq t_2$
Rule 7

Dry
Moist

t_1 t_2
$t_1 > t_2$
Rule 8

10

Design for Fire Safety

Beam tested as
part of the floor

t_1

Beam tested
separately

t_2

$t_1 > t_2$
Rule 9

For the floor
assembly

A

t_1

B

For a beam when
tested separately

t_2

Beam A can be replaced by Beam B if $t_2 > t_1$
Rule 10

General Guidelines for Design for Fire Safety

- Building codes are moving away from arbitrary restrictions based strictly on combustibility and moving towards performance based requirements, which focus on how building systems actually behave in a fire. Building codes establish the parameters within which wood building systems meet fire safety performance requirements.

- Well executed building design using wood products provides structural stability under fire conditions, protection against fire spread, and safe means of egress.

- The four North American model codes provide many opportunities for the use of wood products in structural and decorative applications, while meeting accepted levels for life safety.

- Even in high-rise buildings where special measures are required to ensure life safety, wood products can be used for some structural applications and for most decorative applications.

- Passive fire protection for wood buildings is provided by using heavy timbers for structural components or fire resistant material such as gypsum wallboard to protect light frame structural elements.

- Active fire protection for wood buildings is provided by sprinkler and alarm systems which activate in response to fire.

- Wood buildings of large size can be constructed which rely solely on passive fire protection features. Significant increases in height and area are made possible when sprinkler protection to enhance passive protection measures is used.

References

Automatic Sprinkler Systems Handbook, Solomon, R.E, ed., Fourth Edition, National Fire Protection Association, Quincy, MA, 1989.

Code Conforming Wood Design, National Forest Products Association, 1989.

Criteria for Use in Extension of Data from Fire Endurance Tests, ULC Subject C263(e)-M1988, Underwriters Laboratories of Canada, 1988.

Fire Laboratory Listings, Warnock Hersey Professional Services Ltd., Mississauga, Ontario, 1989.

Fire Protection Handbook, 16th Edition, National Fire Protection Association, Quincy, MA, 1986.

Fire Resistance Design Manual, GA-600-88, Gypsum Association, Twelfth Edition, Washington, DC, 1988.

Fire Resistance Directory, Underwriters' Laboratories Inc., Northbrook, Illinois, 1989.

FM Specification Tested Products Guide, Factory Mutual Corporation, Norwood, MA, 1989.

Guideline on Fire Ratings of Archaic Materials and Assemblies, Rehabilitation Guideline #8, U.S. Department of Housing and Urban Development, Germantown, MD, 1980.

List of Equipment and Materials, Volume II Building Construction, Underwriters' Laboratories of Canada, Scarborough, Ontario, 1989.

Supplement to the National Building Code of Canada 1990, Associate Committee on the National Building Code, National Research Council of Canada, Ottawa, NRCC 30629, 1990.

Ten Rules of Fire Endurance Ratings, T.Z. Harmathy, Fire Technology, Vol.1, No.2, National Fire Protection Association, May 1965.

Wood and Fire Safety, Canadian Wood Council, Ottawa, 1991.

Wood Design Manual, Canadian Wood Council, Ottawa, 1990.

Reference Tables

Table 10.6 **Time Assigned for Contribution of Wallboard Membranes**	Description of Finish	Time minutes
	12.5mm (1/2") fibreboard	5
	8.0mm (3/8") Douglas Fir plywood phenolic bonded	5
	11.0mm (1/2") Douglas Fir plywood phenolic bonded	10
	14.0mm (5/8") Douglas Fir plywood phenolic bonded	15
	9.5mm (3/8") gypsum wallboard	10
	12.7mm (1/2") gypsum wallboard	15
	12.7mm (1/2") Type X gypsum wallboard	25
	15.9mm (5/8") gypsum wallboard	20
	15.9mm (5/8") Type X gypsum wallboard	40
	Double 9.5mm (3/8") gypsum wallboard	25
	12.7mm (1/2") and 9.5mm (3/8") gypsum wallboard	35
	Double 12.7mm (1/2") gypsum wallboard	40
	Double 12.7mm gypsum wallboard	50 [1]
	4.5mm (3/16") asbestos cement and 9.5mm (3/8") gypsum wallboard	40 [2]
	4.5mm (3/16") asbestos cement and 12.7mm (1/2") gypsum wallboard	50 [2]
	Composite 3mm (1/8") asbestos cement on 11mm fibreboard	20

Notes:
1. Wire mesh with 1.57mm (0.062") diameter wire and 25 x 25mm (1" x 1") openings must be fastened between the two sheets of wallboard.
2. Values shown apply to wall only.

Table 10.7 **Time Assigned for Contribution of Wood Frame Members**	Description of Frame	Time Assigned to Frame minutes
	Wood studs 400mm (16") on centre	20
	Wood floor and roof joists 400mm (16") on centre	10
	Wood roof and floor truss assemblies 600mm (24") on centre	5

Table 10.8 **Membrane on Exterior Face of Wood Stud Wall**	Sheathing	Exterior Cladding
	16mm (5/8") T & G lumber	Lumber siding
	7.5mm (5/16") Exterior grade plywood	Wood shingles and shakes
	12.7mm (1/2") Gypsum wallboard	6mm (1/4") plywood exterior grade
		6mm hardboard
		Metal siding
		Stucco on metal lath
		Masonry veneer
	None	9.5mm (3/8") exterior grade plywood

Reference Tables continued

Table 10.9 **Flooring or Roofing over Wood Joists or Trusses**	Type of Members	Structural Deck	Subfloor or Roof or Roofing	Finish Flooring Assembly
	Floor	Wood joists or trusses	12.5mm (1/2") plywood or 17mm (11/16") T & G softwood	Hardwood or softwood flooring on building paper. Resilient flooring, parquet floor, felted synthetic-fibre floor coverings, carpeting, or ceramic tile on 8mm (3/8") panel-type underlay
				Ceramic tile on 30mm (1-1/4") mortar bed
	Roof	Wood joists or trusses	12.5mm (1/2") plywood or 17mm (11/16") T & G softwood	Finish roofing material with or without insulation

Table 10.10 **Fire-Resistance Rating for Ceiling Membranes (Membrane Method of Calculation)**	Description of Membranes	Fire-Resistance Rating [1,2] minutes
	9.5mm (3/8") gypsum wallboard and 12.7mm (1/2") gypsum wallboard	30
	Double 12.7mm (1/2") gypsum wallboard	30
	15.9mm (5/8") Type X gypsum wallboard with at least 75mm mineral wool batt insulation above wallboard	30
	19mm (3/4") gypsum-sand plaster on metal lath	30
	Double 14.0mm (5/8") Douglas Fir plywood phenolic bonded	30
	Double 12.7mm (1/2") Type X gypsum wallboard	45
	25mm (1") gypsum-sand plaster on metal lath	45
	Double 15.9mm (5/8") Type X gypsum wallboard	60
	32mm (1 1/4") Gypsum-sand plaster on metal lath	60

Notes:
1. Values apply where the assembly fire-resistance rating is to be determined on the basis of the membrane only, not the complete assembly.
2. Values apply only to wood joist and wood truss assemblies.

Appendix

Index

Appendix

Index continued

Appendix

Index continued

Appendix

Index continued

Appendix

Index continued

Appendix

Glossary

Acrylic A synthetic resin used extensively for exterior latex paints and some high quality interior latex paints.

Additives Chemicals which are added to coatings in small amounts to alter the physical or chemical properties of the finish. For example, certain additives can reduce the drying time of alkyd (oil-based) finishes.

Adhesion The union between a coating film and the material with which it is in contact. The latter may be another film of paint (intercoat adhesion) or any other material such as wood.

Adhesive A substance capable of holding materials together by surface attachment. It is a general term and includes cements, mucilage, paste, and glue.

Adhesive, Cold-Setting An adhesive that sets at temperatures below 20°C (68°F).

Adhesive, Construction Any adhesive used to assemble primary building materials such as floor sheathing into components during building construction. The term is most commonly applied to elastomer-based, mastic-type adhesives.

Adhesive, Contact An adhesive which, while apparently dry to the touch, will adhere instantaneously to itself upon contact. The terms contact bond adhesive, or dry bond adhesive, are also used.

Adhesive, Gap-Filling Adhesive suitable for use where the surfaces to be joined may not be in close or continuous contact owing either to the impossibility of applying adequate pressure or to slight inaccuracies in matching mating surfaces.

Adhesive, Hot-Melt An adhesive that is applied in a molten state and forms a bond on cooling to a solid state.

Adhesive, Room-Temperature Setting An adhesive that sets in the temperature range of 20 to 30°C (68 to 86°F).

Adhesive, Working Life (pot life) The period of time during which an adhesive, after mixing with catalyst, solvent, or other compounding ingredients, remains suitable for use.

Alkyds Oil based coatings used in a wide variety of protective coatings, such as floor and deck paint enamels, wall and trim paints, stains, and varnishes.

Annual Growth Ring The layer of wood growth added each growing season to the diameter of the tree. In the temperate zone the annual growth rings of many species such as oaks and pines are readily distinguished because of differences in the cells formed during the early and late parts of the seasons.

Axial Force A push (compression) or pull (tension) acting along the length of a member, expressed in kilonewtons (pounds).

Axial Stress The axial force acting at a point along the length of a member divided by the cross-sectional area of a member, expressed in kilopascals (pounds per square inch).

Back Priming Application of paint to the back of woodwork and exterior siding to prevent moisture from getting into the wood, causing the grain to swell and the paint to peel.

Bark Pocket An opening between annual growth rings that contains bark. Bark pockets appear as dark streaks on radial surfaces and as rounded areas on tangential surfaces.

Beam A structural member loaded on its narrow face.

Bearing The contact area over which one structural element, such as a truss, is supported on another structural element such as a wall.

Bearing Stud Wall An exterior or interior wall designed to act as a structural element by transmitting vertical loads to the foundation.

Appendix

Glossary continued

Birdseye Small localized areas in wood with the fibres indented to form small circular or elliptical figures on the tangential surface which are used for decorative purposes. Sometimes found in sugar maple but only rarely in other hardwood species.

Bleeding The process of diffusion of a soluble coloured substance such as pitch from a knot through a paint or varnish coating, resulting in an undesirable staining or discolouration.

Blistering The formation of dome-shaped projections in paints or varnish films by local loss of adhesion to the underlying surface and lifting of the film. Usually caused by applying paint to a surface containing excessive moisture. It may also be caused by excessive heat, or by using paint with poor adhesive qualities.

Board A piece of lumber that is less than 38mm (2" nominal) in smaller dimension used for sheathing, formwork, or for further manufacture into trim and shaped products, such as siding.

Board Foot A unit of measurement of lumber represented by a board 1 foot long, 12 inches wide, and 1 inch thick or its cubic equivalent. In areas where metric measure has been implemented, the cubic metre may be used to measure timber harvest, but "board foot" remains the unit of measure for lumber production and sale.

Bond Failure Rupture of adhesive bond.

Bond Strength The unit load applied in tension, compression, flexure, cleavage, or shear, required to break an adhesive assembly, with failure occurring in or near the plane of the bond.

Bow A deviation from a straight line (a curve along the face of the piece of lumber) from end to end of a piece, measured at the point of greatest deviation.

Box Beam A built-up beam with solid wood flanges and plywood or woodbase panel product webs.

Brace, Lateral A continuous member connected to a truss chord to maintain the vertical position of the truss during construction.

Brace, Vertical Cross Members placed in a vertical plane between an X pattern between trusses to prevent rotation of the tops of the truss under load.

Broad-leaved trees Trees which shed their leaves in the autumn. Most broad-leaved or deciduous trees are hardwoods and have broad leaves.

Building Area The greatest horizontal area of a building above grade within the outside surface of exterior walls or within the outside surface of exterior walls and the centreline of firewalls.

Building Height The number of storeys contained between the roof and the floor of the first storey.

Burl Swirl or twist in wood grain usually occurring near a knot, valued as the source of highly-figured burl veneers used for ornamental purposes.

Camber An upward vertical displacement built into a truss or glued-laminated beam to offset deflection.

Cambium A thin layer of tissue between the bark and the wood in a tree which repeatedly subdivides to form a new wood and bark cells.

Cantilever The part of a truss or structural member that extends beyond its support.

Cell General term for the minute units of wood structure, including wood fibres, vessel segments and other elements.

Cellulose The carbohydrate that is the principal constituent of wood. It forms the framework of wood cells.

Chalking The formation of a powdery coating on the surface of a paint film caused by disintegration of the binding medium by action of the weather.

Appendix

Glossary continued

Characteristics Distinguishing features which, by their extent, number and character, determine the quality of a piece of lumber.

Check A lengthwise separation of the wood which extends across the rings of annual growth, usually resulting from stresses set up in wood during seasoning.

Chord, Bottom A horizontal or inclined member that establishes the lower edge of a truss, usually carrying combined tension and bending stresses.

Chord, Top An inclined or horizontal member that establishes the upper edge of a truss, usually carrying combined compression and bending stresses.

Clear Span Horizontal distance between interior edges of supports.

Combined Stress The combination of axial and bending stresses acting on a member simultaneously, such as occurs in the bottom chord (usually tension plus bending) of a truss.

Compression Failure Deformation of the wood fibres resulting from excessive compression along the grain either in direct end compression or in bending. In surfaced lumber, compression failures may appear as fine wrinkles across the face of the piece.

Concentrated Load Loading centred on a certain point (such as from roof-mounted equipment) as opposed to being equally distributed along the length of a member.

Conditioning The exposure of a wood to the influence of a prescribed atmosphere for a stipulated period of time, or until a stipulated relation is reached between material and atmosphere.

Connector, Timber Metal ring, plate, or grid embedded in the wood of adjacent members to increase the strength of the joint.

Cup A distortion of a board in which there is a deviation from a straight line across the width of the board.

Cure The setting of an adhesive by chemical reaction, usually accomplished by the action of heat or a catalyst with or without pressure.

Dead Load Any permanent load resulting from the weight of building materials or installed equipment.

Decay The decomposition of wood substance caused by the action of wood-destroying fungi, resulting in softening, loss of strength, weight, and often in change of texture and colour.

Decay, Brown Rot Wood decay in which the attack concentrates on the cellulose and associated carbohydrates rather than on the lignin, producing a light to dark brown friable residue and sometimes referred to as dry rot.

Decay, Heart Rot Any rot characteristically confined to the heartwood originating in the living tree.

Decay, Incipient The early stage of decay that has not proceeded far enough to soften or otherwise apparently impair the hardness of the wood. It is usually accompanied by a slight discolouration or bleaching of wood.

Decay, White-Rot Decay attacking both the cellulose and the lignin, producing a generally whitish residue that may be spongy or stringy.

Deflection Displacement of a member usually due to dead and live loads.

Delamination The separation of layers in laminated wood or plywood because of failure of the adhesive, either within the adhesive itself or at the interface between the adhesive and the wood.

Density The mass of wood substance enclosed within the boundary surfaces of a wood-plus-voids complex having unit volume. It is variously expressed as pounds per cubic foot, kilograms per cubic metre, or grams per cubic centimetre, at a specified moisture content.

Appendix

Glossary continued

Diaphragm A horizontal or nearly horizontal roof or floor structural element designed to resist lateral loads (wind and earthquake loads) and transmit these loads to the vertical resisting elements (shearwalls).

Dressed Size The cross-sectional dimensions of lumber after planing.

Dry, Air Process of drying or seasoning lumber naturally by exposure to air.

Dry, Kiln Process of drying or seasoning lumber naturally by placing the lumber in a kiln and exposing the lumber to heat for a prescribed period of time.

Edge Distance The distance from the edge of a member to the centre of the nearest fastening.

End Distance The distance measured parallel to the axis of a piece from the centre of a fastening to the square-cut end of the member (if the end of the member is not square-cut, a formula is used to calculate the end distance).

Equilibrium Moisture Content The moisture content at which wood neither gains nor loses moisture when surrounded by air at a specified relative humidity and temperature.

Extender A substance added to an adhesive to reduce the amount of primary binder required per unit area.

Extender Pigment A coating additive which imparts special properties (for example, to give exterior varnish protection from ultra-violet light degradation).

Factored Load The product of a specified load and its applicable load factor as used in Limit States Design.

Factored Resistance The product of resistance and its applicable resistance factor as applied in Limit States Design.

Fibre A long narrow, tapering wood cell closed at both ends.

Fibreboard A broad term including materials of widely varying densities manufactured by pressing wood fibres into panels sometimes used for sheathing.

Fibre Saturation Point The moisture content of wood, usually around 25-30 percent, at which the cell walls are saturated and the cell cavities are free of water.

Figure The pattern produced in a wood surface by annual growth rings, rays, knots, or irregular colouration.

Filler A substance used to fill the holes and irregularities in planed or sanded surfaces to decrease the porosity of the surface before applying finish coatings. As applied to adhesives, a filler is a substance added to an adhesive to improve its working strength or other properties.

Fine Finish Coatings of paint, varnish, lacquer, wax or other material applied to high quality wood surfaces to protect and enhance their durability and appearance.

Fine Woodwork Products such as trim, panelling used for architectural woodwork to provide a high quality decorative appearance to rooms.

Fingerjoin An end joint made up of several meshing wedges or fingers of wood bonded together with an adhesive. Fingers are sloped and may be cut parallel to either the wide or narrow face of the piece.

Fire Compartment An enclosed space in a building that is separated from all other parts of the building by enclosing construction. This provides a fire separation which has a required fire-resistance rating.

Fire-Resistance Rating The time in hours or minutes that a material or assembly of materials will withstand the passage of flame and the transmission of heat when exposed to fire under specified conditions of test and performance.

Fire-Retardant A chemical or preparation of chemicals used to reduce flammability or to retard the spread of a fire over the surface.

Appendix

Glossary continued

Fire-Retardant Coating A coating applied by brush, roller, or sprayer which reduces the burning characteristics of wood surfaces.

Fire-Retardant Treated Wood Wood or a wood product that has had its surface-burning characteristics, such as flame-spread, rate of fuel contribution and density of smoke developed, reduced by pressure treating with fire retardant chemicals.

Fire Separation A construction assembly that acts as a barrier against the spread of fire. (A fire separation may or may not have a fire-resistance rating.)

Firewall A type of fire separation of noncombustible construction that subdivides a building or separates adjoining buildings to resist the spread of fire and that has a fire-resistance rating as prescribed in the codes and has structural stability to remain intact under fire conditions for the required fire rated time.

Flame-Spread Rating An index or classification indicating the extent of spread of flame on the surface of a material, or an assembly of materials, as determined in a standard fire test as prescribed in the building codes.

Flaking Lifting of the paint from the underlying surface in the form of flakes or scales.

Light Framing The use of dimension lumber, trusses, and other small cross-section members to provide support and enclosure for a building.

Girder A large or principle beam used to support concentrated loads at isolated points along its length.

Glulam Structural wood product made by bonding together laminations of dimension lumber.

Glulam Rivet A nail-like oval shaped fastener used in combination with predrilled steel plates to connect glulam members (approved for use in Canada).

Gloss The degree of reflection of a coating film. Paints, varnishes, and lacquers having a lot of reflection are said to be glossy, while those having a low level of reflection are said to be flat.

Grade A classification of lumber or other wood products based on criteria of quality such as natural characteristics and strength.

Grade stamp A stamp placed on lumber to denote its grade.

Grain The direction, size, arrangement, appearance or quality of the fibre in wood or veneer.

Grain, Close-Grained Wood Structure of some hardwoods, such as birch and maple, having narrow, inconspicuous annual rings with little difference in pore size between springwood (early wood) and summerwood (late wood).

Grain, Cross A pattern in wood in which the fibre and other longitudinal elements deviate from a line parallel to the sides of the piece as a result of sawing or as a result of inconsistent grain direction as a growth characteristic.

Grain, Edge (quarter-sawn, quarter-cut) Terms referring to timber or veneer cut in a plan approximately at right angles to the annual rings.

Grain, Flat (flat-sawn, plain-sawn) Lumber that has been sawed parallel to the length of the log and approximately tangent to the growth rings.

Grain, Open-Grained Wood Structure of some hardwoods such as oak, chestnut and ash in which there is a distinctive difference in the pore sizes between springwood (early wood) and summerwood (late wood). The term coarse is also sometimes used to describe open grain woods.

Grain, Spiral-Grain An arrangement of the fibres in a piece of timber or veneer which results from their growth in a spiral direction around the trunk of the tree.

Appendix

Glossary continued

Green (unseasoned) Freshly sawed lumber, or lumber that has received no intentional drying. Wood that has become completely wet after immersion in water would not be considered green, but may be said to be in the green condition.

Hardboard A panel manufactured primarily from interfolded wood fibres consolidated under heat and pressure in a hot press and used, for example, in the manufacture of siding products.

Hardwood (deciduous) Trees One of the botanical groups of trees that have broad leaves, in contrast to the conifers or softwoods. The term does not necessarily refer to the actual hardness of the wood.

Header A single member composed of two or more wood members, securely fastened together and used to increase load carrying capability at wall or floor openings.

Heartwood The wood extending from the true centre to the sapwood, and whose cells no longer participate in the life processes of the tree. Heartwood may contain gums, resins, and other materials that usually make it darker and more decay resistant than sapwood.

Heavy Timber Construction A type of combustible construction in which a degree of fire safety is attained by placing limitations on the sizes of wood structural members and on thickness and composition of wood floors and roofs and by the avoidance of concealed spaces under floors and roofs.

Heel Point on truss at which the top and bottom chords intersect.

Honeycomb A cellular separation in the interior of a wood piece, usually along the wood grain, a result of internal stress. It normally occurs during kiln drying, particularly in white or red oak, when too much heat is applied too rapidly.

Intumescence The swelling of a fire-retardant coating when heated, resulting in the formation of low-density film which provides a degree of surface flame-spread resistance.

Importance Factor A factor applied to factored loads, other than dead load, to take into account the consequence of collapse as related to the use and occupancy of the structure, as in Limit States Design.

Joint, Butt An end joint formed by abutting the squared ends of two pieces.

Joint, End A joint made by bonding two pieces of wood together end to end, usually by finger or scarf joint.

Joint, Scarf An end joint formed by joining with adhesive the ends of two pieces that have ben tapered or bevelled to form sloping plane surfaces.

Joist One of a series of parallel beams used to support floor and ceiling loads, supported in turn by larger beams, girders, or bearing walls.

Joist A piece of dimension lumber 114 mm (6" nom.) or more in larger dimension, intended to be loaded on its narrow face.

Knot That portion of a branch or limb that has been surrounded by subsequent growth of the stem. The shape of the knot as it appears on a lumber surface depends on the angle of the cut relative to the long axis of the knot.

Knot, Loose A knot which is not held firmly in place by growth or position and which cannot be relied upon to remain in place.

Knot, Pin A knot that is not more than 12.5mm (1/2") in diameter.

Knot, Sound A knot that is solid across its face, at least as hard as the surrounding wood, and shows no indication of decay.

Laminate, Wood A product made by bonding layers of wood or other material to a wood substrate.

Laminated Veneer Lumber (LVL) A structural lumber product manufactured from veneers laminated so that the grain of all veneers run parallel to the axis of a member.

Appendix

Glossary continued

Latex A synthetic resin used in the manufacture of water soluble paint coatings. PVA and acrylic are two types of latex resins used to make latex coatings.

Level or Soffit Return Lumber filler placed horizontally from the end of an overhang to the outside wall to form a soffit.

Lignin The second most abundant constituent of wood after cellulose. It is the thin cementing layer between the wood cells.

Limit State A condition of a structure at which the structure ceases to fulfil the design function as applied in Limit States Design.

Live Load Any loading that is of a temporary nature such as snow, wind, earthquake, and construction loads.

Load Combination Factor A factor applied to the factored loads in Limit States Design, other than dead load, to take into account the reduced probability of a number of loads from different sources acting simultaneously as applied to Limit States Design.

Load Duration The period of continuous application of a specified load, or the aggregate of periods of intermittent applications of the same load.

Load Factor A factor applied to a specified load that, for the limit state under consideration, takes into account the variability of the loads and load patterns as applied to Limit States Design.

Lumber The product of the saw and planing mill not further manufactured than by sawing, resawing, passing lengthwise through a standard planing machine, cross-cutting to length, and grading.

Lumber, Boards Lumber that is less than 38mm (2" nom.) thick and 38mm (2" nom.) or more wide.

Lumber, Dimension Lumber 38 to 102mm (2" to 4" nom.) in smaller dimension.

Lumber, Dressed Sized The dimensions of lumber after being surfaced with a planing machine.

Lumber, Machine Stress-Rated (MSR) Lumber which has been mechanically evaluated to determine its stiffness and bending strength.

Lumber, Matched Lumber that is edge dressed and shaped to make a close tongue and groove joint at the edges or ends, when laid edge to edge, or end to end.

Lumber, Nominal Size The size of lumber after sawing and prior to surface finishing by planing.

Lumber, Patterned Lumber that is shaped to a pattern or to a moulded form in addition to being surface planed.

Lumber, Rough Lumber that has not been dressed (surfaced) but which has been sawed, edged, and trimmed.

Lumber, Shiplapped Lumber that is edge dressed to make a lapped joint.

Lumber, Sizes of For metric measure, lumber size is based on actual size rounded to the nearest millimetre. For Imperial measure, lumber size is usually expressed in terms of nominal size which is the size before surfacing. The dressed size is usually 12 to 19mm (1/2 to 3/4") less than the nominal or rough size. For example, a 2" x 4" stud after dressing measures about 1-1/2" x 3-1/2".

Lumber, Structural Lumber which has strength in relation to the anticipated structural end use, as a controlling factor in grading or selecting.

Lumber, Visually Stress-Graded Lumber Lumber that has been graded for strength based on visual appearance, as opposed to MSR lumber which is evaluated mechanically and checked visually.

Appendix

Glossary continued

Millwork Planed and patterned lumber for finish work in buildings, including items such as sash, doors, cornices, panelwork, and other items of interior or exterior trim, but not flooring or siding.

Mineral Spirits A petroleum derived solvent similar to gasoline, used primarily for thinning alkyd and other oil based coatings such as paint, stain, and varnish.

Moisture Content The amount of water contained in the wood, expressed as a percentage of the weight of the oven-dry wood.

Moulding A wood strip having a curved or projecting surface used for decorative purposes.

Noncombustible Construction That type of construction in which a degree of fire safety is attained by the use of noncombustible materials for structural members and other building assemblies.

Oriented Strandboard (OSB) A panel product, used for sheathing, made from strands with the face wafers oriented in the long direction of the panel to provide additional strength in that direction.

Overlay A thin layer of paper, plastic, film, metal foil, or other material bonded to one or both faces of panel products, or to lumber, to provide a protective or decorative face, or a base for painting.

Paint A coating containing enough pigment to create an opaque solid film after application as a thin layer.

Paint, Enamel A coating product characterized by ability to form a uniform hard film used for flooring and other high wear applications. Enamels may be obtained in a full range of colours and usually in gloss or semi-gloss.

Panel Point The point of intersection where the web or webs of a truss meet a chord.

Parallel Strand Lumber (PSL) A structural wood product made by gluing together long strands of wood which have been cut from softwood veneer.

Pith The small cylinder of primary tissue of a tree stem around which the annual rings form.

Pitch The accumulation of resin in wood.

Pitch Pocket An opening between growth rings which usually contains or has contained resin or bark or both.

Panel, Exterior A general term for plywood or OSB/waferboard, bonded with a type of adhesive that by systematic tests and service records has proved highly resistant to weather.

Panel, Interior A general term for a panel made from a type of adhesive which is not resistant to moisture and is therefore limited to uses where protection from moisture is provided.

Plywood A glued wood panel made up of thin layers of veneer with the grain of adjacent layers at right angles, or of veneer in combination with a core of lumber or of reconstituted wood.

Plywood, Standard Construction Panels constructed of pairs of plies that are balanced as to grain direction and thickness about the central ply or panel centreline, in which the grain of each ply is at right angles to at least one other ply.

Plywood, Modified Construction Panels which are not standard thickness or which have an even number of plies.

Plywood Stressed-Skin Panel A form of construction in which outer skins of plywood are applied over internal frame members to form a rigid structural element.

Polyurethane A paint and varnish resin which imparts good abrasion resistance and marketed under several trade names such as varathane, urethane, and durathane.

Appendix

Glossary continued

Post A timber with larger dimension not more than 51mm (2") greater than the smaller dimension and usually graded for use as a column.

Preservative Any substance effective in preventing the development and action of wood-rotting fungi, borers of various kinds, and harmful insects that cause the deterioration of wood.

Pressure-Treating The process of impregnating wood with preservative or fire retardant chemicals by placing the wood and chemical in a pressure chamber.

Pressure-Treating, Empty-Cell Process Pressure treating process in which back pressure from air drives out part of the injected preservative or chemical to leave the cell walls coated but the cell cavity mostly devoid of chemical.

Pressure-Treating, Full-Cell Process Pressure treating process in which a vacuum is drawn to remove air from the wood before admitting the preservation, resulting in a heavy absorption and retention of preservative due to the cells being almost filled.

Primer One or more preliminary base coats of paint system, applied prior to the application of finishing coats.

Rafter One of a series of structural members of a roof designed to support roof loads.

Raised Grain A roughened condition of the surface of dressed lumber in which the hard latewood is raised above the softer earlywood but not torn loose from it.

Rays Strip of cells extending radially within a tree and varying in height from a few cells in some species to 100mm (4") which cause an appealing grain pattern.

Resin An ingredient of coatings which acts as a binder and gives the coating physical properties such as hardness and durability.

Resin (natural) Inflammable, water-soluble, vegetable substances secreted by certain plants or trees, and characterizing the wood of many coniferous species.

Rip A cut made lengthwise in a wood member, parallel to the grain.

Sap The watery fluid that circulates through a tree carrying the chemical food that enables the tree to grow.

Sanding Sealer A preparation coating which seals the wood in preparation for topcoating and which is easy to smooth by sanding.

Sapwood The wood of pale colour near the outside of the log. Under most conditions sapwood is more susceptible to decay than heartwood.

Seasoning The process of drying lumber either naturally, or in a kiln, to a moisture content appropriate for the conditions and purposes for which it is to be used.

Service Condition, Dry A service condition in which the average equilibrium moisture content over a year is 15 percent or less and does not exceed 19 percent.

Service Condition, Wet All service conditions other than dry.

Sandwich Panel, Structural Panels made of parallel framing members separated by expanded polystyrene which act as structural units in resisting horizontal or vertical loads.

Sandwich Panel, Non-Structural A panel comprised of a foam core with plywood or OSB bonded to each face designed to enclose but not to be the main load-carrying elements.

Serviceability Limit States Those states which restrict the intended use and occupancy of the structure including deflection, joint slip, vibration, and permanent deformation as applied in Limit States Design.

Shake A separation along the grain usually occurring between the rings of annual growth.

Appendix

Glossary continued

Shake A western red cedar roofing and sidewall product made by splitting blocks of cedar, as opposed to shingles which are manufactured by sawing.

Shearwall A wall or partition designed to transfer lateral loads (wind and earthquake loads) from abutting walls and roof to the foundation.

Shrinkage The decrease in the dimension of wood resulting from a decrease of moisture content and generally occurring to the greatest extent between about 20 and 30 percent moisture content.

Slope (Pitch) The ratio of vertical rise to horizontal run for inclined members (generally expressed as 3/12, 4/12, 5/12 etc.).

Slope of grain The angle between the direction of the grain and the axis of a piece of lumber, expressed as a ratio.

Softwoods (conifers) One of the botanical groups of trees that in most cases have needlelike or scalelike leaves.

Solvents Volatile liquids used in paint, stain, varnish, and lacquer coatings which give the coating workability and which, upon evaporation, allow the resin to harden.

Specie A distinct sort or kind of tree having some characteristics or qualities in common that distinguishes it from other groups.

Species Group The combining of species into commercial groups because of their similarity in appearance and physical properties.

Springwood (early wood) The portion of the annual growth ring that is formed during the early part of the season's growth; it is usually less dense, lighter in colour, and weaker mechanically than summerwood.

Stain (natural) A discolouration on or in lumber, other than its natural colour.

Stain (chemical) A solution or suspension of colouring matter in a vehicle designed to penetrate a surface and colour the wood, without hiding surface characteristics and providing some protection.

Strength Limit States Those states concerning safety and including the maximum load-carrying capacity of the structural materials of the connection as they relate to Limit States Design.

Stud One of a series of vertical load bearing members used as supporting elements in walls and partitions.

Stud Wall System Combination of studs and sheathing panels or boards on one or both sides designed to bear vertical loads and to provide shearwall action.

Summerwood The portion of the annual growth that is formed after the springwood (early wood) formation has ceased. It is usually more dense and stronger mechanically than springwood (early wood).

Texture The relative size and arrangement of the wood cells.

Thermoplastic Glues and Resins Glues and resins that are capable of being repeatedly softened by heat and hardened by cooling.

Thermosetting Glues and Resins Glues and resins that are cured with heat but do not soften when subsequently subjected to high temperatures.

Timber A piece of lumber 140mm (5-1/2") or more in smaller dimension.

Timber Connector A metal ring or plate that, by being embedded in adjacent wood faces or in one wood face, acts in shear to transmit loads from one timber to another, or from a timber to a bolt and, in turn, to a steel plate or another connector.

Toughness A quality of wood which permits the material to absorb a relatively large amount of energy, to withstand repeated shocks, and to undergo considerable deformation before breaking.

Appendix

Glossary continued

Truss An assembly of members combined to form a rigid framework. All members are interconnected to form triangles. Light frame trusses are made from dimension lumber restrained by toothed plates. Heavy trusses are made for large members restrained by bolts and connectors or glulam rivets.

Truss Plate A light steel plate fastening, intended for use in structural lumber assemblies, that may have integral teeth of various shapes and configurations.

Twist Warping in which one corner of a piece twists out of the plane of the other three.

Varnish A paint coating which lacks pigment and which gives a transparent or translucent finish to wood.

Veneer, Rotary Cut Veneer cut in a lathe which rotates a log, chucked in the centre, against a knife.

Veneer, Sawed Veneer produced by sawing.

Veneer, Sliced Veneer that is sliced from a log with a knife.

Waferboard A mat-formed structural panel board made of wood wafers, randomly arranged and bonded together with a waterproof and boilproof binder.

Wood Preservative Means any suitable substance that is toxic to fungi, insects, borers, and other living wood-destroying organisms.

Wane Bark or lack of wood on the edge or corner of a piece of wood resulting from the piece being sawn from near the outer circumference of a sawlog.

Warp Any deviation from a true or plane surface. Warp includes bow, crook, cup and twist, and any combination of these.

Water Repellent A liquid that penetrates wood which retards changes in moisture content and in dimensions without adversely altering the desirable qualities of wood.

Water-Repellent Preservative A water repellent that contains a preservative, accomplishing the dual purpose of imparting resistance to attack by fungi or insects. It also retards changes in moisture content.

Weathering The mechanical or chemical disintegration and discolouration of the surface of wood caused by exposure to light, the action of dust and sand carried by winds, and the alternate shrinking and swelling of the surface fibres with the continual variation in moisture content, brought by changes in the weather.

Webs Members that join the top and bottom chords to form the triangular patterns that give truss action. They usually carrying tension or compression stresses.

Wood Cells (vessels) The basic units comprising wood having open ends and set one above the other so as to form continuous tubes. The openings of the vessels on the surface of a piece of wood are usually referred to as pores.

Wood I-joist, Prefabricated A structural wood member made by using adhesive to attach wood flanges (LVL, MSR, or high quality dimension lumber) to a plywood or OSB web.

Workability The degree of ease and smoothness with which wood can be worked.

Appendix

Information Sources

There are many specialists groups in Canada and the United States which offer technical information and assistance on the use of wood and wood products in building construction.

If you have a technical enquiry and are not sure who to call, contact the Canadian Wood Council in Canada or the National Forest Products Association in the United States for guidance.

Canada

Alberta Forest Products Associations (AFPA)
11710 Kingsway Avenue, Suite 104
Edmonton, AB T5G 0X5
Telephone: (403) 452-2841
Fax: (403) 455-0505

Wood Products : Consumer Information

Architectural Woodwork Manufacturers Association of Canada (AWMAC)
242-4299 Canada Way
Burnaby, BC V5G 1H3
Telephone: (604) 438-6616
Fax: (604) 438-6525

Architectural Woodwork

Association des manufacturiers de bois de sciage du Québec
(Québec Lumber Manufacturers Association)
5055, boul. Hamel ouest, bureau 200
Québec, QC G2E 2G6
Telephone: (418) 872-5610
Fax: (418) 872-3062

Lumber

Association provinciale de l'industrie de bois ouvré du Québec, Inc.
485 boul. Langelier, Suite 200
Québec, QC G1K 5P4
Telephone: (418) 529-7258

Doors, Windows, Mouldings

Bureau de Promotion des Industries du Bois (BPIP)
(Building products information)
5055, boul. Hamel ouest, bureau 200
Québec, QC G2E 2G6
Telephone: (418) 872-2424
Fax: (418) 872-3062

Wood Products : Consumer Information

Bureau de Promotion des Industries du Bois (BPIB)
(Wood Product Promotion Bureau)
Bleinheim Court
7 Beaufort Park, Woodlands Lane
Almondsbury
Bristol, UK
BS124NE
Telephone: 011 44 454 666 000
Fax: 011 04 54 666 080

Wood Products

Canadian Hardwood Plywood Association (CHPA)
27 Goulburn Avenue
Ottawa, ON K1N 8C7
Telephone: (613) 233-6205

Hardwood, Plywood

Canadian Home Builders Association
(CHBA)
200 Elgin Street, Suite 701
Ottawa, ON K2P 0G5
Telephone: (613) 230-3060
Fax: (613) 232-4635

Residential Building

Canadian Institute of Treated Wood (CITW)
75 Albert Street, Suite 506
Ottawa, ON K1P 5E7
Telephone: (613) 234-9456
Fax: (613) 234-1228

Treated Wood Consumer Information

Canadian Particleboard Association (CPA)
27 Goulburn Avenue
Ottawa, ON K1N 8C7
Telephone: (613) 233-6205

Particleboard

Appendix

Information Sources continued

Canadian Lumber Standards Accreditation Board (CLS)
1055 West Hastings Street
Suite 260
Vancouver, BC V6E 2E9
Telephone: (604) 687-2171
Fax: (604) 687-8036

Lumber Grading, Standards

Canadian Lumbermen's Association (CLA)
(Association canadienne de l'industrie du bois)
27 Goulbourn Avenue
Ottawa, ON K1N 8C7
Telephone: (613) 233-6205
Fax: (613) 233-1929

Wood Products

Canadian Standards Association (CSA)
178 Rexdale Boulevard
Rexdale, ON M9W 1R3
Telephone: (416) 747-4000
Fax: (416) 747-2473

Material and Design Standards

Canadian Wood Council
Suite 1550
55 Metcalfe Street
Ottawa, ON K1P 6L5
Telephone: (613) 235-7221
Fax: (613) 235-9911

Wood Products: Consumer Information
Codes and Standards
Wood Engineering

Canadian Wood Preservers' Bureau
c/o Canadian Institute of Treated Wood
75 Albert Street, Suite 506
Ottawa, ON K1P 5E7
Telephone: (613) 234-9456
Fax: (613) 234-1228

Treated Wood Certification and Inspection

Cariboo Lumber Manufacturers' Association (CLMA)
197 Second Avenue North, Suite 301
Williams Lake, BC V2G 1Z5
Telephone: (604) 392-7778
Fax: (604) 392-4692

Lumber

Cedar Shake & Shingle Bureau
515-116th Street NE
Suite 275
Bellevue, WA 98004
Telephone: (206) 453-1323

Shingles & Shakes

Central Forest Products Association, Inc. (CFPA)
P.O. Box 1169
Hudson Bay, SK S0E 0Y0
Telephone: (306) 865-2595
Fax: (306) 865-3302

Lumber

Council of Forest Industries of British Columbia (COFI)
1200-555 Burrard Street
Vancouver, BC V7X 1S7
Telephone: (604) 684-0211
Fax: (604) 687-4930 (Vancouver)

Lumber, Plywood: Consumer Information

COFI-London
Tileman House
131-133 Upper Richmond Road
London England SW15 2TR
Telephone: (01) 788-4446
Fax: (01) 789-0148

Lumber, Plywood

COFI-Tokyo
John Powles
COFI
Tameike Annex
1-5-15 Akasaka
Minato-KU
Tokyo 107, Japan
Fax: (011) 81-3-586-8804 (Japan)

Lumber, Plywood

COFI Northern Interior Lumber Sector (COFI-NILS)
400-1488 Fourth Avenue
Prince George, BC V2L 4Y2
Telephone: (604) 564-5136
Fax: (604) 564-3588

Lumber

Interior Lumber Manufacturers' Association (ILMA)
360,1855 Kirshner Road
Kelowna, BC V1Y 4N7
Telephone: (604) 860-9663
Fax: (604) 860-0009

Lumber

Laminated Timber Institute of Canada (LTIC)
c/o Western Archrib Structures
4315-92nd Avenue
Edmonton, AB T6B 3M7
Telephone: (403) 465-9771
Fax: (403) 469-1667

Glulam

Appendix

Information Sources continued

Maritime Lumber Bureau (MLB)
(Bureau du bois de sciage des Maritimes)
P.O. Box 459
Amherst, NS B4H 4A1
Telephone: (902) 667-3889
Fax: (902) 667-0401

Lumber

National Lumber Grades Authority (NLGA)
260-1055 West Hastings Street
Vancouver, BC V6E 2E9
Telephone: (604) 689-1563
Fax: (604) 687-8036

Lumber Grading

Ontario Lumber Manufacturers' Association (OLMA)
(Association des manufacturiers de bois
de sciage de l'Ontario)
55 University Avenue
Suite 325 P.O. Box 8
Toronto, ON M5J 2H7
Telephone: (416) 367-9717
Fax: (416) 362-3641

Lumber

Structural Board Association (SBA)
45 Sheppard Avenue East
Suite 412
Willowdale, ON M2N 5W9
Telephone: (416) 730-9090
Fax: (416) 730-9013

OSB/waferboard

Truss Plate Institute of Canada (TPIC)
c/o Gangnail Canada
100 Industrial Road
Bradford, ON L3Z2B7
Telephone: (416) 775-5337
Fax: (416) 775-9695

Truss Plates, Trusses

Underwriters' Laboratories of Canada (ULC)
7 Crouse Road
Scarborough, ON M1R 3A9
Telephone: (416) 757-3611
Fax: (416) 757-9540

Fire Standards

Western Wood Truss Association (WWTA)
3177-207A Atreet
Langley, BC V3A 4B5
Telephone: (604) 534-4138

Wood Trusses

United States

American Hardboard Association
520 N. Hicks Road
Palatine, IL 60067
Telephone: (708) 934-8800
Fax: (708) 934-8803

Hardboard

American Institute of Timber Construction (AITC)
11818 S.E. Mill Plain Boulevard
Suite 415
Vancouver, WA 98684
Telephone: (206) 254-9132
Fax: (206) 254-9456

Glulam

American Lumber Standards Committee (ALSC)
P.O. Box 210
Germantown, MD 20875-0201
Telephone: (301) 972-1700
Fax: (301) 540-8004

Lumber Grading

American Plywood Association (APA)
P.O. Box 11700
7011 S. 19th Street
Tacoma, WA 98411
Telephone: (206) 565-6600
Fax: (206) 565-7265

*Plywood, OSB, Waferboard, Structural panels,
Glulam*

American Society for Testing and Materials (ASTM)
1916 Race Street
Philadelphia, PA 19103
Telephone: (215) 299-5400
Fax: (215) 977-9679

Material Standards

American Wood-Preservers Association
P.O. Box 849
Stevensville, MD 21666
Telephone: (301) 643-4163
Fax: (301) 643-2708

Treated Wood: Standards & Specifications

American Wood Preservers Bureau (AWPB)
7962 Conell Court
P.O. Box 5283
Lorton, VA 22079
Telephone: (703) 339-6660
Fax: (703) 339-6711

Treated Woods: Certification & Inspection

Appendix

Information Sources continued

American Wood Preservers Institute
1945 Gallows Road
Suite 405
Vienne, VA 22182
Telephone: (703) 893-4005

Treated Wood: Environment and Legislation

Appalachian Hardwood Mfrs. Inc.
North Carolina National Bank Building
P.O. Box 427
164 South Main Street, Room 408
High Point, NC 27261
Telephone: (919) 885-4410
Fax: (919) 886-8865

Hardwood

Architectural Woodwork Institute
2310 Walter Reed Drive
Arlington, VA 22206-1199
Telephone: (703) 671-9100

Architectural Woodwork

California Redwood Association
405 Enfrente Dr.
Suite 200
Novato, CA 94949
Telephone: (415) 382-0662
Fax: (415) 382-8531

Redwood Lumber Products

Cedar Shake & Shingle Bureau
515-116th Street NE
Suite 275
Bellevue, WA 98004
Telephone: (206) 453-1323

Shingles & Shakes

Fine Hardwood Veneer Association (FHVA)
5603 West Raymond Street
Suite O
Indianapolis, IN 46241-4390
Telephone: (317) 244-3311

Hardwood Veneers

Hardwood Manufacturers Association (HMA)
2831 Airways Blvd., Suite 205
Memphis, TN 38132
Telephone: (901) 346-2222
Fax: (901) 346-2233

Hardwood Products

Hardwood Plywood Manufacturers Association (HPMA)
1825 Michael Faraday Drive
P.O. Box 2789
Reston, VA 22090-2789
Telephone: (703) 435-2900
Fax: (703) 435-2537

Hardwood, Plywood and Veneers

Maple Flooring Manufacturers Association
60 Revere Drive, Suite 500
Northbrook, IL 60062
Telephone: (708) 480-9138

Hardwood Flooring

National Association of Home Builders (NAHB)
1201 15th St. Northwest
Washington, DC 20005
Telephone: (202) 822-0200
Fax: (202) 822-0374

Residential Building

National Fire Protection Association
Batterymarch Park
Quincy, MA 02269
Telephone: (617) 770-3000
Fax: (617) 770-0700

Fire Standards
Sprinkler Standards
Fire Safety

National Forest Products Association
1250 Connecticut Ave. NW, Suite 200
Washington, DC 20036
Telephone: (202) 463-2700
Fax: (202) 463-2785

Lumber Products: Consumer Information
Codes and Standards
Wood Engineering

NFPA Field Staff

P. H. Billing
42W 223 Retreat Court
St. Charles, IL 60175-8274
Telephone: (708) 377-3230

Kenneth Bland, P.E.
Old Keene Road
P.O. Box 205
Troy, NH 03465
Telephone: (603) 242-3831

R.R. Walker, Senior District Manager
8539 Rockfish Circle
Fountain Valley, CA 92708
Telephone: (714) 847-2424

David S. Collins, AIA
810 Plum Street, Suite 4
Cincinnati, OH 45202
Telephone: (513) 621-7298

Dennis L. Pitts
508 University Village
Richardson, TX 75081
Telephone: (214) 690-0242

Appendix

Information Sources continued

David P. Tyree
Northwest District Manager
P.O. Box 419
Georgetown, CA. 95634
Telephone: (916) 333-0317

National Wood Flooring Association (NWFA)
11046 Manchester Road
St. Louis, MO 63122
Telephone: (314) 821-8654
Fax: (314) 821-7242

Wood Flooring

National Oak Flooring Manufacturers' Association
P.O. Box 3009
Memphis, TN 38173-0009
Telephone: (901) 526-5016
Fax: (901) 526-7022

Oak Flooring: Quality Standards

National Particleboard Association
18928 Premiera Court
Gaithersburg, MD 20879
Telephone: (301) 670-0604
Fax: (301) 840-1252

Particleboard

North American Wholesale Lumber Association Inc. (NAWLA)
3601 Algonquin Road
Suite 400
Rolling Meadows, IL 60008
Telephone: (708) 870-7470
Fax: (708) 870-0201

Lumber Sales

Northeastern Lumber Manufacturers Association, Inc. (NELMA)
272 Tuttle Road
P.O. Box 87 A
Cumberland Ctr., ME 04021-0687
Telephone: (207) 829-6901

Lumber Products

Pacific Lumber Inspection Bureau (PLIB)
P.O. Box 7235, 3801-150th Street, #202
Bellevue, WA 98008-1235
Telephone: (206) 746-6542
Fax: (206) 746-5522

Lumber Grading

Society of American Wood Preservers Inc. (SAWP)
7297 Lee Highway, Suite 205
Unit P
Falls Church, VA 22042
Telephone: (703) 237-0900

Treated Wood

Society of Fire Protection Engineers (SFPE)
60 Batterymarch Street
Boston, MA 02110
Telephone: (617) 482-0686

Fire Protection Engineering
Fire Research
Fire Modelling

Southeastern Lumber Manufacturers Association (SELMA)
P.O. Box 1788
Forest Park, GA 30051
Telephone: (404) 361-1445
Fax: (404) 361-5963

Wood Products

Southern Forest Products Association (SFPA)
P.O. Box 52468, 2900 Indiana Avenue
New Orleans, LA 70152
Telephone: (504) 443-4464
Fax: (504) 443-6612

Wood Products

Southern Pine Inspection Bureau (SPIB)
4709 Scenic Highway
Pensacola, FL 32504-9094
Telephone: (904) 434-2611
Fax: (904) 433-5011

Lumber Grading

Truss Plate Institute (TPI)
583 D'Onofrio Drive, Suite 200
Madison, WI 53719
Telephone: (608) 833-5900
Fax: (608) 833-4360

Wood Trusses

Underwriters' Laboratories Inc. (UL)
333 Pfingsten Road
Northbrook, IL 60062
Telephone: (708) 272-8800
Fax: (708) 272-8129

Fire Standards

West Coast Lumber Inspection Bureau (WCLIB)
6980 SW Varns Street
P.O. Box 23145
Tigard, OR 97223
Telephone: (503) 639-0651
Fax: (503) 684-8928

Lumber Grading

Appendix

Information Sources continued

Western Wood Products Association (WWPA)
522 S.W. Fifth Ave.
Yeon Building
Portland, OR 97204-2122
Telephone: (503) 224-3930
Fax: (503) 224-3934

Wood Products: Consumer Information

Wood Moulding and Millwork Producers, Inc. (WMMP)
P.O. Box 25278
1730 SW Skyline Boulevard
Portland, OR 97225
Telephone: (503) 292-9288
Fax: (503) 292-3490

Architectural Woodwork

Wood Truss Council of America (WTCA)
401 North Michigan Avenue
Chicago, IL 60611
Telephone: (312) 644-6610
Fax: (312) 321-6869

Wood Trusses

Appendix

Photo Information

Page	Designer	Photographer	Location	Subject
Section 1				
3	N/A	Stone Consolidated	Not known	Nature
4	N/A	Stone Consolidated	Not known	Forest
5	N/A	Stone Consolidated	Not known	Tree nursery
6	Not known	Hellmut Schade	Steinbach, MB	Barn detail
7	Not known	Hellmut Schade	Montebello, QC	Hotel
8	Not known	Hellmut Schade	Bell's Corners, ON	Ornamental detail
9	Chung Hung	Hellmut Schade	Ottawa, ON	Wood sculpture
9	Alex Wyse & Ken Guild	Hellmut Schade	Ottawa, ON	Wood sculpture
10, 11	Scogin, Elam & Bray	Timothy Hursley	Atlanta, GA	Residence
12	Team Four Inc.	Alise O'Brien	Ureka, MO	Visitor centre
13	Towend, Stefura, Baleshta and Nicholls	Dionne Photography	Walden, ON	Visitor centre
14	Charles Henry Robinson	Environment Canada	Coaticook, QC	Residence
14	William Hughes	Environment Canada	Halifax, NS	Church
15	Thomas Hooper	Environment Canada	Victoria, BC	Residence
15	Not known	Environment Canada	Halifax, NS	Residence
16, 17, 18	Faye Jones	Timothy Hursley	Picayune, MS	Interpretation centre
18	Jersey Devil	Steve Badanes	Richmond, VA	Residence
19	Jersey Devil	Kenneth M. Wyner	Richmond, VA	Residence
20, 21	Cardwell/Thomas & Associates	Richard Cardwell	Belfair, WA	Residence
22	Ferdinand S. Johns	Harlan Hambright Assoc.	Taneytown, MD	Residence
23	Gärtl Ag Uetendorf and BCN	Prof. Natterer	Wimmis, Switzerland	Bridge
23	R.J. Dietrich, A. Skrabl	Prof. Natterer	Essing, Germany	Bridge
24, 25	Ihor Stecura	Roman Stecura	Niagara Falls, ON	Church
26, 27	L.M. Lang	Prof. Natterer	Vienna, Austria	Industrial building
28	FSC Groves Hodgson Manasc Architects Ltd.	Richard Isaac	Wabasca, AB	Recreational building
28	Kilborne Engineering	Western Archrib	Saint John, NB	Industrial storage building
29	LeMoyne Lapointe Magne architectes et urbaniste	LeMoyne Lapointe Magne	Montréal, QC	Fair building (Roller coaster)
30, 31	Barton Myers	Timothy Hursley	Waterloo, ON	Museum
32, 33	Geier + Geier	Prof. Natterer	Bad Dürrheim, Germany	Swimming pool complex
34, 35	Cardwell/Thomas & Associates	Richard Cardwell	Belfair, WA	Residence
36	Zweifel and Leins	Prof. Natterer	Schwanden, Switzerland	Civic centre
37	Haisch	Prof. Natterer	Munich, Germany	Church
37	Atelier 4	Prof. Natterer	Bad Wörishofen, Germany	Civic centre

Appendix

Photo Information continued

Page	Designer	Photographer	Location	Subject
38, 39	Architects Hawaii, Ltd.	Robert Kulesh	Pohnpei, HI	Courthouse
40	Unibauamt	Prof. Natterer	Weihenstephan, Germany	Cafeteria
41	Fischer, Glaser, Kretschmer	Prof. Natterer	Regensburg, Germany	Swimming pool complex
42, 43	Unibauamt	Prof. Natterer	Weihenstephan, Germany	School
44	Gubert	Prof. Natterer	Unterhaching, Germany	Church
45	A. Franck, Bauabteilung W. Wicker	Prof. Natterer	Zwesten, Germany	Civic centre
46, 47	Gärtner	Prof. Natterer	Augsburg, Germany	Church
48	Merkle	Prof. Natterer	Rossbach, Germany	Administration building
49	Eberl, Weippert	Prof. Natterer	Schwaiganger, Germany	Equestrian arena
50, 51	Frei Otto Und Planungsgruppe Gesternig	Prof. Natterer	Bad Münder, Germany	Industrial building
52	Atelier Gamme	Prof. Natterer	Lausanne, Switzerland	Model of storage building
52	Atelier Gamme	Prof. Natterer	Lausanne, Switzerland	Storage building
53	Unibauamt	Prof. Natterer	Weihenstephan, Germany	Model
53	Unibauamt	Prof. Natterer	Weihenstephan, Germany	Model
54, 55	TRA Architecture Engineering Planning Interiors	Richard Cooke	Eugene, OR	Airport terminal
56	Midyette/Seieroe Associates	Andrew Kramer	Cedaredge, CO	Church detail
57	David Kellen Architect	Tim Street-Porter	Santa Monica, CA	Restaurant
58	FSC Groves Hodgson Manasc Architects Ltd.	Richard Isaac	Wabasca, AB	Recreational building
59	Not known	Hellmut Schade	Ottawa, ON	Historical residence
60	Wiens Architects Ltd.	John Fulker	Regina, SK	Visitor centre
61	Arthur Dyson	Scot Zimmerman	Sanger, CA	Residence
62, 63	FSC Groves Hodgson Manasc Architects Ltd.	Richard Isaac	Wabasca, AB	Recreational building
63	Not known	Prof. Natterer	Thbingen, Germany	Town hall
64, 65	Paré Fortin architectes	Gilles Fortin	Gaspé, QC	Visitor centre
66	Not known	Hellmut Schade	Pincher Creek, AB	Grain elevator

Section 2

Page	Designer	Photographer	Location	Subject
75	TRA Architecture Engineering Planning Interiors	Richard Cooke	Eugene, OR	Airport terminal
76	McFarland Christianson Architects, A Joint Venture	Peter Turje	Prince Rupert, BC	Community centre

Appendix

Photo Information continued

Page	Designer	Photographer	Location	Subject
77	James Volney Righter Architects Inc.	Wheeler Photographics	MA	Residence
78	Jack Durham Haynes, Architect	Jack D. Haynes	Atlanta, GA	Residence
78	The Hulbert Group BC Ltd.	Rick Etkin Photographs	Vancouver, BC	Research facility
79	Not known	Hellmut Schade	Ottawa, ON	Residence
79	O'Brien/Atkins Associates	Otto Baitz, Allen Weiss	Raleigh, NC	Airport terminal
80	D.E. Schaefer Architect Ltd.	David Schaefer	Edmonton, AB	Church
80	Henry Hawthorn Architect Ltd.	Roger Brooks	Vancouver, BC	PSL and fasteners
80	Design Guild	Claire Brett Smith, Stephanie Bacon	Chestnut Hill, MA	Swimming pool pavilion
81	Ivan G. Dickinson Architect	Rick Masters	Orangeville, ON	Arena
82	Bialosky & Partners Architects	E.B. Meyer, Jack Bialosky Jr.	Chagrin Falls, OH	Swimming pool pavilion
82	N/A	Malak Photographs Ltd.	Salmon Arm, BC	Lumber

Section 3

Page	Designer	Photographer	Location	Subject
101	Jerome Markson Architects	Art James, APA	Rexdale, ON	Recreational building
102	Susan Maxman Architects	Tom Bernard	Lower Oxford Township, PA	Recreational building
102	N/A	CWC	N/A	Dimension lumber
103	Susan Maxman Architects	Tom Bernard	Lower Oxford Township, PA	Recreational building
104	George Robb	William Santillo Architect	King, ON	School
105	The Coal Harbour Architectural Group	Geoffrey Massey	Hernando Island, BC	Residence
106	The Hulbert Group BC Ltd.	Rick Etkin Photographs	Vancouver, BC	Research facility library
107	Cardwell/Thomas & Associates	Richard Cardwell	Belfair, WA	Residence
108	The Hulbert Group BC Ltd.	Rick Etkin Photographs	Vancouver, BC	Research facility
108	N/A	CWC	N/A	Prefabricated wood I-Joists
109	Dalla-Lana/Griffin Architects	Scott Alpen Photogenics	Vancouver, BC	Office building
109	N/A	Dave Rice-Trus Joist	N/A	LVL
110	Ivan G. Dickinson Architects	Rick Masters	Orangeville, ON	Arena
110	N/A	Walter Horvath	N/A	Glulam
111	Ivan G. Dickinson Architects	Rick Masters	Orangeville, ON	Arena
112	Tigerman McCurry	Bruce Van Inwegen	Yorkville, IL	Recreational building

Appendix

Photo Information continued

Page	Designer	Photographer	Location	Subject
113	The Hulbert Group BC Ltd.	Rick Etkin Photographs	Vancouver, BC	Research facility
113	N/A	Derrick Murray, (MacMillan Bloedel)	N/A	PSL
114	Downs-Archambault Architect	Garry Otte	Whistler, BC	Postal station
115	Dennis A. Christianson	Debbie Christianson	Edmonton, AB	Residence
116	Susan Maxman Architects	Tom Bernard	Lower Oxford Township, PA	Recreational building

Section 4

Page	Designer	Photographer	Location	Subject
179	Griffiths, Rankin, Cook Architects	Roy Grogan	Nepean, ON	Sailing club assembly hall
180	N/A	CWC	N/A	Plank decking
180	William Maclay Architects & Planners	Esto Photographics	Killington, VT	Hotel
181	Wicker	Prof. Natterer	Zwoston, Germany	Hospital entrance
182	Allen Kube Associates	Erin Burrows	Kelowna, BC	Hotel
182	N/A	Walter Horvath	N/A	OSB/waferboard
182	Dominique Anthony Costantino Architect	Roy Grogan	Ottawa, ON	Apartment building
183	Lemermeyer Architect Inc.	Wayne Heartwell	St. Paul, AB	Church
184	Jones and Manning Architects	Dr. Ron Gillis	Point Prim, PE	Residence
184	Barry Hobin Architect	Al Patrick	Nepean, ON	Wood foundation
185	Allan Rae Architect	Pedro Ho Lenscape Inc.	Mississauga, ON	Warehouse
185	Scogin, Elam & Bray	Timothy Hursley	Atlanta, GA	Residence
186	N/A	Council of Forest Industries of B.C.	Not known	Plywood

Section 5

Page	Designer	Photographer	Location	Subject
217	Roth Knibb Architects	Brian Thompson	Guelph, ON	Residence
218, 219	Strasman Architects Inc.	J. Rieder	Bramalea, ON	Transit station
220	N/A	CWC	N/A	Connection detail
220	William C. Rutledge	Western Archrib	Westlock, AB	Connection detail
220	Brock Simini Architects	Tedd Benson	Brattleboro, VT	Beam splice
221	D.E. Schaefer Architect Ltd.	David Schaefer	Edmonton, AB	Church
221	Ivan G. Dickinson Architect	Rick Masters	Orangeville, ON	Arena connection detail
221	Harrison Fagg	Western Archrib	Malna Loa, HA	Connection detail
222	N/A	CWC	N/A	Shear plate dapping tool
222	N/A	CWC	N/A	Connection detail
222	N/A	CWC	N/A	Split ring dapping tool
222	N/A	CWC	N/A	Connection detail

Appendix
Photo Information continued

Page	Designer	Photographer	Location	Subject
222	CUH2A	Everett Scott	Harmony Township, NJ	Assembly hall
223	Brock Simini Architects	Tedd Benson	Brattleboro, VT	Retail building
223	N/A	CWC	N/A	Timber joinery
224, 225	Glass Associates, Inc.	Mark Citret/ Jane Lidz	Oakland, CA	School
226	N/A	CWC	N/A	Framing connectors
226	N/A	CWC	N/A	Glulam rivets
226	Ivan G. Dickinson Architect	Rick Masters	Orangeville, ON	Glulam rivet connection
226	N/A	Council of Forest Industries of B.C.	N/A	Plywood nailing
227	Ferdinand S. Johns	F.S. Johns	Annapolis, MD	Mercantile building
228	Kammerer, Belz & Partner	Prof. Natterer	Ötlingen, Germany	Civic centre
228	Haid	Prof. Natterer	Leichieenfels, Germany	Gymnastics hall

Section 6

Page	Designer	Photographer	Location	Subject
295	The Troyer Group, Inc.	Scott Leonard	Montgomery, IN	Restaurant
296	Not known	Malak Photographs Ltd.	Vinton, QC	Manufacturing plant
297	Allan Rae Architect	Pedro Ho Lenscape Inc.	Mississauga, ON	Office and warehouse
297	Not known	Andrew Burrows	Kelowna, BC	Warehouse
298	N/A	Council of Forest Industries of B.C.	United Kingdom	Plywood stressed-skin panels
299	Barry Hobin Architect	Al Patrick	Nepean, ON	Permanent wood foundation
299	Not known	Halliday Homes	Carleton Place, ON	Permanent wood foundation
300	Dalla-Lana/Griffin Architects	Scott Alpen Photogenics	Vancouver, BC	Office building
300	Not known	Council of Forest Industries of B.C.	United Kingdom	Plywood shearwalls
300	D.E. Schaefer Architect Ltd.	David Schaefer	Edmonton, AB	Framing detail
300	Koliger Schmidt Arch. Engineers	Western Archrib	Lac Labiche, AB	School
301	Lemermeyer Architect Inc.	Wayne Heartwell	St. Paul, AB	Church
301	The Hulbert Group BC Ltd.	Rick Etkin Photographs	Vancouver, BC	Research facility
302	K. Schmidhuber	Prof. Natterer	Straubing, Germany	Residence

Section 7

Page	Designer	Photographer	Location	Subject
361	J. Robert Thibodeau Architecte	David Laforge	Lac Homininque, QC	Residence
362	Hartman-Cox Architects	Robert Lautman	McLean, VA	Church

Appendix

Photo Information continued

Page	Designer	Photographer	Location	Subject
362	Not known	Hellmut Schade	Montebello, QC	Hotel
363	Not known	Hellmut Schade	Woodstock, ON	Courthouse
363	Henry Hawthorn Architect Ltd.	Roger Brooks	Vancouver, BC	Office building
363	Allan Rae Architect	Pedro Ho Lenscape Inc.	Mississauga, ON	Warehouse
364	Faye Jones	Timothy Hursley	Picayune, MS	Landscaping
364	J. Robert Thibodeau Architecte	David Laforge	Lac Homininque, QC	Residence
365	Duo Dickinson, Architect	Mike Hales	Madison, CT	Residence
365	Natale Scott Browne Architects	Natale Scott Browne Architects	Parry Sound, ON	Marina building
366	Venturi, Scott Brown and Associates	Tom Bernard	Stoney Creek, CT	Residence
367	Dalla-Lana/Griffin Architects	Scott Alpen Photogenics	Vancouver, BC	Office building
368	Maibec Industries Inc.	AMBSQ	N/A	Eastern white cedar shingles
368	N/A	Cedar Shake & Shingle Bureau	N/A	Western red cedar shingles & shakes

Section 8

Page	Designer	Photographer	Location	Subject
389	McInturff Architects Andrew Lautman	Julia Heine	Washington, DC	Residence
390	Mohr	Prof. Naterrer	Regensburg, Germany	Gymnasium hall
391	Leslie Rebanks Architects	Fraser Day	Toronto, ON	Food retail store
392, 393	Scogin, Elam & Bray	Timothy Hursley	Atlanta, GA	Office building
393	Treffinger, Walz, MacLeod	Karl Riek	San Francisco, CA	Office stair detail
394	Henry Hawthorn Architect Ltd.	Roger Brooks	Vancouver, BC	Office building
395	Chesapeake Associates Architects, Inc.	J. Tyler Campbell	Tolchester Beach, MD	Residence
396, 397	Treffinger, Walz, MacLeod	Karl Riek	San Francisco, CA	Office building
398	McInturff Architects	Julia Heine	Washington, DC	Residence
399	O'Brien/Atkins Associates	Otto Baitz, Allen Weiss	Raleigh, NC	Airport lounge
400	Zimmer Gunsul Frasca Partnership	Strode Eckert Photographic	Portland, OR	Public library
401	Arthur Dyson, AIA	Scot Zimmerman	Sanger, CA	Stair detail
402, 403	N/A	CWC	N/A	Wood samples
404	Design Guild	Claire Brett Smith, Stephanie Bacon	Chestnut Hill, MA	Swimming pool pavilion

Appendix

Photo Information continued

Page	Designer	Photographer	Location	Subject
Section 9				
427	Susan Maxman Architects	Tom Bernard	Lower Oxford Township, PA	Recreational building
428, 429	Bruno Freschi Architects	Garry Otte	Ucuelet, BC	Visitor centre
430	Henry Hawthorne Architects	Garry Otte	Vancouver, BC	Exhibition complex
431	Rudy P. Friesen & Assoc.	Henry Kalen	Steinbach, MB	Museum
432	Bruno Freschi Architects	Garry Otte	Ucuelet, BC	Visitor centre
432	John Robert Carley Architect	John Robert Carley	Belleville, ON	Residence
433	Henry Hawthorne Architects	Garry Otte	Vancouver, BC	Exhibition complex
434	N/A	Walter Horvath	N/A	Solid stains
435	N/A	Walter Horvath	N/A	Semi-transparent stains
436, 437	N/A	Lee Valley Tools	N/A	Interior stains
438	Treffinger, Walz, MacLeod	Karl Riek	San Francisco, CA	Office boardroom
438	Collins Fulker McDonell Maltby Architects	John Fulker	Armstrong, BC	School assembly room